SECOND BOOK

OF

SANSKRIT

SECOND BOOK
OF
SANSKRIT

Being a Treatise on Grammar with Exercises

By

Sir Ramkrishna Gopal Bhandarkar

Enlarged and Revised by
Shridhar R. Bhandarkar

GYAN

Published by

Gyan Publishing House
5, Ansari Road
Daryaganj, New Delhi-110002
Phone: 011-47034999, 9811692060
E-mail: books@gyanbooks.com

Distribution Network
gyanbooks.com
India, USA, Canada, UK, Australia, France

ISBN : 978-81-212-2470-3 (HB)
First Published, 1868

2nd Impression 2021

Printed at: Gyan Press, Delhi.

Second Book of Sanskrit
Author: Sir Ramkrishna Gopal Bhandarkar

इयं

संस्कृतमदिरान्तःप्रवेशिका

नाम पाठावलिः

अनेकपण्डितपरिषद्भिर्धर्मशास्त्राचार्य तत्त्वमीमांसाचार्येति
भारतवर्षराजाधिराजेन च राजपुरुषविशेषे-
त्युपपदैर्भूषितनाम्ना

भाण्डारकरोपाभिधेन गोपालसूनुना रामकृष्णेन

विरचिता।

ततसूनुना मास्तर् आव् आर्तेस्युपपद्धारिणा

श्रीधरेण च

तभिर्दिद्धदिश संस्कृत्य प्रपंञ्चिता।

PREFACE TO THE FIRST EDITION

This Second Book of Sanskrit has been prepared under instructions from Sir A. Grant, Director of Public Instruction. Its plan is nearly the same as that of the First Book, which the student is supposed to have read and mastered. Each lesson consists of four parts : Ist, Grammar, 2nd, Sanskrit sentences for translation into Sanskrit–both intended to exercise the student in the rules of Grammar given at the top of the Lesson; and 4th, a Vocabulary.

This and the First Book together contain as much Grammar as is needed for all practical purposes, perhaps more. I have adopted the terminology of the English Grammarians of Sanskrit, but have strictly followed Pânini, as explained by Bhattojî Dîkshita in his Siddhântakaumudî. Most of the rules are mere translations of the Sûtras. Be sides the terms Guṇa, Vṛiddhi, and a few others, which have been adopted from Native Grammarians by nearly all European writers the subject, I have found it necessary to appropriate two more, *viz.*, *Seṭ* and *Aniṭ*. The prejudice against mere Native terms, in deference to which Professor Benfey seems in his smaller Grammar to have discarded even the words Guṇa and Vṛiddhi, without substituting any others, is, in my humble opinion, very unreasonable, when it is difficult to frame new words to designate the things which they signify. It is very inconvenient to have to describe the same thing again and again whenever one has occasion to speak of it. It will at the same time be somewhat difficult for the learner to make out, when a thing is so described in a variety of cases, that it is the same. Words adapted to express a particular meaning are as necessary here as in other affairs of human life. What an amount of inconvenience would it, for instance, entail, if, whenever we had to speak of the human race, we were, instead of being allowed to use the word "man," made to describe man's physical and rational nature! But I must not elevate an ordinary truism to the rank of a newly-discovered truth.

The general rules of Grammar, and such exceptions as are important, have been given in this book; those of the least importance only being omitted. Such an omission is apt to render a book liable to the charge of inaccuracy. But it is unavoidable in an elementary work, and after all it will produce little or no practical inconvenience.

There is one point in Sanskrit Grammar, in my explanation of which I have departed from ordinary usage, though I think I do agree with Pâṇini and his commentators. It is the sense to be attached to the so-called Aorist. The most laborious student of a dead language is not alive to all the nice shades of meaning, which are plain even to the uninstructed when a language is living. Even to a Mahâ-Paṇdita in these days the sound of भवते is not at all so disagreeable as that of होएल is to the genuine Marâthâ peasant. We know of the distinction between the Âtmanepada and Parasmaipada only *in theory*, but that between the ए and and ई of the Marathi Habitual Past of the एल and ईल of the Future, we *feel*. We must, therefore, to determine this question about the Aorist, appeal to such Sanskrit works as we have reason to suppose, must have been written when Sanskrit was a spoken language. The Kâvyas, the Nâtakas and most of the Purâṇas will not do for our purpose. Such books as the Saṁhitâs of the Vedas, the Brâhmaṇas, or even those portions of the two great Epics which do not bear indications of having been subsequently tampered with must be referred to. To institute such a wide research I have neither had the necessary time nor the necessary means. But the Aitareya Brâmaṇs, which I have read, seems almost to decide the point. In this work, wherever stories are told, the so called Imperfect or the Perfect is always used, and the Aorist never occurs, *On the contrary, when the persons in the story are represented as speaking with one another they use the Aorist, and the only sense that can be attached to it in these cases is that of the English Present Perfect; in other workds, it indicates simply the completion of an action that has just or recently been done. The reason why the Aorist accurs in these cases only is that there is no scope for *recent past time* in mere narration; and things that have just or recently occured can come to be spoken of only when persons are talking with each other. The peice given at the end of this book contains passages remarkably illustrating what I say. The story goes :–"Har iś chandra said to Varuṇa' 'Let a son be born to me and I will then offer him as a sacrifice to you'. 'Well', said Varuṇa, 'You have got a son, sacrifice him to me now'. Then said Hafiśchandra, 'When a victim becomes ten days old, then he is fit to be sacrificed. Let the boy becomes ten days old, I will then sacrifice him to you'. 'Well', said Varuṇa. The boy became ten days old, sacrifice him now to me', and thus it proceeds. Now in this and the remaining portion of the Khaṇḍa the verbs "said" (occuring several times), "was born," "became" and others that are used by the narrator speaking in his own person are always in the Perfect; while "have got", "has become", &c., used by Varuṇa with reference to the boy, are in the Aorist. The latter clearly refer to a time just gone by. In the same manner. in the stroy of Nâbhânedishṭ

*In the passage noticed below, we have स ह संगाहं प्रापत्, where प्रापत् is the Aorist of आप with प्र and is used in the narration of a past event. But in the whole of the Brâhmaṇa there is, so for as I can recollect, not a single instance besides this, where the narrator uses the narrator uses the Aorist in speaking of a past action. The evidence being then so overwhelming, some other explanation must be attempted in the present case and this example ought by no means to be taken to invalidate the position in the text. Perhaps when the reading of Vedic books was fixed, प्रापत् and प्राप्नोत् which occurs immediatly after, were, through mistake, made to exchange places.

ha, related in the fourteenth 'Kbaṇḍa of the Fifth Pañchikâ, the verbs and used by Nâbhânedishṭha and evidently, from the context, denoting events that have just happened, are in the Aorist, as also used by Rudra. While when the author, in narrating the strory, speaks of certain things as having taken place, he invariably uses the Imperfect, the event from his point of view having occurred at a remote past time. Similar instances, in which the Aorist on the one hand, and the Imperfect or the Perfect on the other, are used exactly in the same way, occur in 1-23, 2-19, 3-33, 4-17,* 6-33, 6-34, 7-27, 7-28, 8-7, 8-23†, while narratives, in which the Perfect or the Imperfect only is used, and where there is either no conversation, or when there, is it is only with reference to present or future time, are innumerable. 7-26, and 5-34 may also be consulted.‡

---

*The cows held a sacrificial session with the object of get ting horns; after a year they got horns, and then they say to themselves :– यस्मै कामायादीक्षामह्यापाम तमुत्तिष्ठामः, *i.e.*, 'The object for which we undertook this sacrificial ceremony we *have got.* We now rise or break up" Here आपाम is the Aorist of 'to obtain.' and evidently means 'have got or obtained;' while अदीक्षामहि is the Imperfect of दीक्ष् and certainly does not indicate an event that has just happened.

† Some of these passages have been given in the lesson on the Aorist.

‡ To show how rich the language of this Brâhmaṇa is in verbal form, and especially of the Aorist, I will here give a list of the forms of the Aorist referred to in the text. It will be shown further on that the Brâhmaṇa follows the rules of Pâṇini faithfully in the use of the Aorist, and the following list will show that the forms also of this tense strictly obey the rules laid down by that grammarian, except in a few cases.

अज्ञनि	आदित	मा परिगात	आसिषत	अग्रहीत्
अभूत	अवादीः	अह्यत्	अमंस्त	अचारीत्
अज्ञत	अकृत	अभू	अस्तृत	अहौषित्
अपत्सत	अदीक्षिष्ट	अवधीः	अदात्	अगासीत्
अवोचत्	मा पात्	अवोचः	अवधीत्	अवोचत्
अभाक्त	अक्	अवोचम	अजीजनत्	अशंसीत्
अभाक्षुः	मा दुषत्	अवोचन्	अजैषीः	अयाक्षीत्
मा छथाः	आपाम	आज्ञास्थाः	अदुक्षः	मा गात
अदुः	अदर्शम	आज्ञासम	अवाक्षीः	

of these 44 forms only 5 अज्ञत, अकृत, अकर्, अरभराम् and अभुक्ष do not conform to the rules laid down by Paṇini for the Bhâshâ or Sanskrit current in his time. (1885)

We thus see that the so-called Aorist deuotes recent past time or the mere completion of an action, and thus resembles the English Present Perfect. And this is confirmed by what Pâṇini says on the subject. The Sûtras which give the senses of the three past tenses are लुङ् 3-2-110: अनद्यतने लुङ् 3-2-111; परोक्षे लिट् 3-2-115. They are thus to be interpreted—'लुङ् or the Aorist indicates past time; लुङ् or the Imperfect shows a past action done previous place before this day, and लिट् or the perfect, a past event which took place before this day, and which was not witnessed by the speaker". Now the first sûtra gives a general rule, the second is an exception to it, and the third an exception to this again; the past time, therefore, léft according to pâṇini's system of rules and exceptions fcr लुङ् to indicate, is अद्यतन, that is to say, *this day's* लुङ् can also by these Sûtras indicate *past time generally, i.e.*, express simply the *completion* of an action without reference to any particular past time. For, the category *past time* can admit of three divisions only according to the principle indicated in the sûtras, *viz*,. past time *generally* and not *specifically*, the time *of this day*, and the past time *Previous* to this day. The last is taken up by लुङ् and लिट्; and the first two belong, therefore, toलुङ्. By another Sûtra नानद्यतनवत्क्रियाप्रबन्धसामीप्ययोः, Pânini 3-3-135, लुङ् expresses recent and continuous past action in addition. So that according to pânini लुङ्, indicates (1) Past time generally, (2) the past time of this day and not previous to this day and (3) recent past time. Now all these characteristics we find in the English Present Perfect and not in the indeffinite Past. For, *firstly*, if we want to express simply the completion of an action, i.e., past time generally without reference to any particular past time, we do not use the Indefinite Past in English, but the Present Perfect. 'I read Sir Walter Scott's Ivanhoe' necessarily implies some *particular* time when the action of reading was done; in other words, the sense of the sentence is not complete without the specification of some time. We must add some such expression as 'two years ago' or the particular time must be understood from the context. But when we say 'I have read Sir Walter Scott's Ivanhoe', there in no such necessity. *Secondly*, the English Present Perfect, like the Sanskrit लुङ्, can denote, if it denotes any specific time at all, the past time at all, book *to-day*' is good English; but 'I have read the book *yesterday*' or '*a year ago*' is not. And *thirdly*, the Present Perfect, as is generally admitted, denotes recent time is English.

My object has been to render this as much a Sanskrit Reading Book as a book on Sanskrit Grammar; in other words, not only to teach grammatical forms to the student but to enable him to construc Sanskrit. I have, therefore, in addition to the sentences composed by myself, given in nearly all the lessons a good many extracts containing examples of the particular rules, from original Sanskrit works, such as the Aitareya Brâhmana, Upanishads, the Mahâbhârata, Kâdambarî, the Pañchatantra, and the Raghuvaṁśa. With the same object, three long prose pieces illustrative of three differeent styles, and one poetical have been given at the end. One of the former is from the Aitareya Brâhmaṇa. chosen on account of its richness in verbal forms and the strength, purity, and simplicity of its style. The English sentences have, of couse, all been composed by me.

I hope Teachers and Students will find this book useful. Such improvements as experience may show to be necessary will be made in subsequent editions.

Ratnagiri,
8th April 1868. } R. G. B.

PREFACE TO THE SECOND EDITION.

The observations made in the Perface to the last edition as to the sense of the Aorist have been confirmed by serveral passages I have met with in the Saṁhitâs of the Vedas and in Brâhmaṇas other than the Aitareya. But since this is hardly the place for an elaborate essay on the subject, I forbear to make any addition to what I have already said on the subject. I have only re-cast the remarks containd in the preface on the meaning of the Sûtras of Pâṇini bearing on the question.

Bombay,
19th April 1870. } R. G. B.

PREFACE TO THE THIRD EDITION

Grammar was not an empiric study with Pâṇini and the other ancient grammarians of India. Those great sages observed carefully the facts of their language and endeavoured always to connect them together by a law or rule and to bring these laws again under still more general laws. Sanskrit Grammar has thus become a science at their hands. and its study possesses an aducational value of the same kind as that of Euclid and not much of the student has to go through a certain process of synthesis. He has to mark the mutual connections of the rules he has learṅt, and, in each given case, to find out which of them, for the conditions involved, hold good in that case, and to apply them in regular succession, until he arrives at the form required. A mere unscientific teaching of the forms as such and mixing them up unconnectedly into a list, our grammarians never resorted to, so long as they could trace a resemblance even between two of them, if not more.

Convinced of the utility of this system, I tried in this book to adhere to pânini so for as was convenient or practicable, and to give his general rules instead of splitting them up into the particular cases they comprehend. In this manner I was also able to compress a great deal of matter into a comparatively small space. But the book necessarily became difficult, since instead of placing a readin-made form him to constitute it for himself. Experience, however, both as a learner and a teacher, has taught me that Sanskrit Grammar learnt according to the latter method is more easily and longer remembered than if was, was not at all difficult in the hands of a good teacher. But, to meet the vlews of those who think otherwise, I have, in this edition, increased the number of examples without interfering with the system, and added explanations to show how to derive them and how, generally, to apply the rules in particular cases. All this new matter has been printed in small type. I have thus myself done, in a great measure, what I expected teachers to do and what, I as a teacher, once did. Several other changes and alterations have been made in this adition. Separate vocabularies have been given for the English exercises, the two lessons on the second conjugation have been expanded into four, the number of verses from Bhartṛihari has been reduced and the passage from kâdambarî removed and another, somewhat shorter and much simpler, from the same work, substituted for it. I have also here and there added a few rules, especially in the lessons on compounds, and given a few more exercises.

I was not so sanguine about the success of this book as of the First. But I am very happy to perceive that this also as met with favour, howsoever humble, of facilitating and promoting the study of the language of the ancient Rishis among their modern descendants.

Bombay,
15th April 1870. } R. G. B.

PREFACE TO THE SIXTH EDITION.

The following are the principal changes and additions made in the present edition:—(1) The first lesson in the previous editions treated of the Potential Mood of the first Group of conjugations. But that mood having now been transferred to the First Book, the lesson has been taken out. The first lesson now treats of the Irregularities of the 1st, 4th, 6th, and 10th conjuations, to which are attached Sanskrit and English sentences for exercise, with Sanskrit and English vocabularies. (2) The lesson on the Futures and the Conditional, together with the portion treating of the and put after the Perfect, in accordance with the practice in our High Schools of teaching it immediately after the latter. (3) All the Sanskrit into English vocabularies occurring in the body of the book have been collected together into a general Glossary at the end, as also the English into Sanskrit vocabularies. (4) A few verses which could be easily gathered from the Kîrtikaumudî, Bhattikâvya, and Halâyudha's Kavirahasya have been added to the exercises here and there. It is true that the authors of the last two works are perhaps likely to be considered as having used words not in common use in the extant Sanskrit literature or never used in that all. It should, however, be borne in mind that the first lived probably in the same century as Bâna and before Bhavabhûti, both of whom are recognised as standard authors, and the second about two centuries after; that there must have been a great deal more of Sanskrit literature extant in their timw than thaere is at prsent; and that, there object being the same as that of this and the First Book, viz., to teach the language, they propably did not use words without having met with instances of their use in the literature existing in their time.

Poona,
31st August } S. R. B.

CONTENTS

PAGE.

PREFAOES v

LESSON I. IRREGULARITIES belonging to the 1st, 4th, 6th and 10th Conjugations ... 1

II. FIFTH AND EIGHTH CONJUGATIONS— ... Present Tense 11

III. ———Imperfect Tense 17

IV. ———Imperative and Potential ... 20

V. NINTH CONJUGATION—Present and Imperative 25

VI. ———Imperfect and Potential ... 31

VII. SECOND CONJUGATION—Present and Imperative 34

VIII ———Imperfect and Potential ... 44

IX. SECOND CONJUGATION (*Continued*)— ... Present and Imperative ... 49

X. ———Imperfect and Potential ... 58

XI. THIRD CONJUGATION 62

XII. SEVENTH CONJUGATION 71

XIII. PERFECT 78

XIV. ———(*Continued*) 86

XV. *Part I.*—FIRST AND SECOND FUTURES, AND CONDITIONAL 96

Part II. PASSIVE FORMS 10

XVI. DECLENSIONAL IRREGULARITIES ... 105

LESSONXVII. NUMERALS 119

XVIII. COMPARATIVE AND SUPERLATIVE DEGREES OF Adjective, &c ... 127

XIX. COMPOUNDS—Dvandva and Tatpurusha 134

XX. ———Bahuvrîhi and Avyayîbhâva ... 142

XXI. CAUSALS 149

XXII. AORIST—First, Second and Third Varieties. 154

XXIII. ———Sixth and Seventh. Varieties ... 163

XXIV. *Part I.*—Fourth and Fifth Varieties ... 167

Part II.—BENEDICTIVE MOOD ... 177

XXV. DESIDERATIVES... 179

XXVI. VERBAI, DERIVATIVES—Past, Perfect, Future and Potential Participles, &c... 184

SELEOTIONS FOR EXERCISE :—

Form the Aitareya Brâhmaṇa... ... 191

The Three Rogues 195

The Brâhmaṇa and the Cobra... ... 196

Form Bhartṛihari's Nîtiśataka 197

Form Kâdambarî 202

GLOSSARY—Sanskrit into English 205

———English into Sanskrit 249

SECOND BOOK OF SANSKRIT.

LESSON I.

IRREGULARITIES BELONGING TO THE 1ST, 4TH, 6TH AND 10TH CONJUGATIONS.

1. गुप् 'to protect' *Parasm*, धूप् 'to heat' *Parasm.*, विच्छ् 'to go' or 'approach' *Parasm*, पण् *Parasm.*, when it means 'to praise', Parasm., all of the 1st conjugation (except विच्छ् which belongs to the 6th), have आय् added on the them before the conjugational sign; as पणायति, धूपायति, &c., The उ of गुप् takes its Guṇa substitute before this आय् , as गोपायति. आय् is optionally retained in the non-conjugational tenses.* पण् and पन् take the Âtmanepada terminationa when they do not take this आय्, as पणते.

2. भ्राश् Âtm. भ्लाश् Âtm., and भ्रम्, क्रम् क्लम्, त्रस्, लष्, ष्ठिव् and यस् with सम् or without any preposition, all *Parasm*, belong both to the 1st and to the 4th conjugation and त्रुट् Parasm, to the 4th and the 6th; as भ्राशते or भ्राश्यते, &c.

3. The penultimate अ of क्रम् is lengthened, when it takes Parasmaipada terminations in the conjugational tenses, as क्रामति or क्राम्यति; but Âtm., आक्रमते ;similarly ष्ठिव्, क्लम् and चम् 1st conj. with आ, lengthen their vowels.

4. शम्, तम्, दम्, श्रम् and मद् ll of the 4th conjugation, and भ्रम् and क्षम् when of the 4th conjugation, lengthen their vowel in the conjugational tenses; as शाम्यति, भ्राम्यति, or भ्रमति, &c., भ्रम् has भ्रम्यति also.

5. अक्ष्, and तक्ष् when it means 'to shave or pare,' literally and not metaphorically, belong to the 1st and 5th conjugations; as अक्षति or अक्ष्णोति.

6. ध्मा 'to blow,' घ्रा 'to smell' म्ना 'to think' ऋ 'to go',सृ when it when it means 'to run', 'to run' यम् 'to restrain', and शद् 'to perish,' all of the 1st conjugation, substiture in the conjugational tenses धम्, जिघ्, मन्, ऋच्छ्, धौ, यच्छ्, and शीय्, respective; as धमति, जिघ्रति &c. The last is Âtmanepadi in the conjugational tenses.

*For an explanation of this expression see Lesson II.

7. The penultimate उ of गुह् is lengthened before the conjugational sign and before any. strong or Gunamaking termination with an initial vowel; as गूहति.

8. दंश् and सञ्ज् *Parasm.*, स्वञ्ज् *Âtm.*, and रञ्ज् *Parasm.* and *Âtm.*, all of the 1st conjugation, drop their nasal before the conjugational sign; as दशति, स्वजते, &c.

9. When a radical ॠ (long) does not under go Guṇa or Vṛddhi substitute, it is changed to इर् and to उर् if a labial or व् precedes. The इ or उ of these and of roots ending in व् is lengthened when a consonant follows. Thus 4th conj. forms जीर्यति, कॄ 6th conj. किरति, कॄत् 10th conj. कीर्तयति, दिव् and सिव 4th conj. दीव्यति and सीव्यति, &c.

10. Roots of the 4th conjugation ending in ओ drop it before the conjugation sign. Thus, सो forms स्यति; दोद्यति; शो-श्यति; and छो-छ्यति.

11. The ending इ or, उ short or long, is changed to इय् or उव् respectively before अ, the sign of the 6th conjugation (see Rule II, Lesson VII); as रि-रियति, नू-नुवति, धू-धुवति.

12. व्यध् 4th conj. is modified into विध् before the य of that conjugation; as विध्यति.

13. भ्रस्ज् and व्रश्च्, both of the 6th conjugation, are modified into भृज्ज् and वृश्च् in the conjugational tenses, as भृज्जति, वृश्चति, &c.

14. The स् of मस्ज् and is changed to ज् when not dropped (X, p. 54): as मज्जति, &c.

15. लुप्, लिप्, खिद्, कृत्, and पिश् all of the 6th conj, insert a nasal before the final in the conjugational tenses; as लिम्पति, &c.

16. Some roots of the 10th conjugation are exclusively Âtmanepadi, such as तन्त्र्, चित्, भर्त्स्, मन्त्र्, तर्ज्, विद्, दंश्, &c.; as तन्त्रयते, चेतयते, &c.

17. Many roots belong optionally to the 1st or 10th conjugation, such as युज्, पृच्, सह्, वृज्, ह, जॄ, रिच्, तप्, तृप, दृप्, अर्ह् &c. योजति, योजयति, &c.

वैषम्यमपि प्राप्ता धैर्यधनाः स्वधव आत्मनः सञ्चरणव्रत गोपायन्ति।

स्वजनवियोगेन व्यथितं मे मनो निष्ठाशून्यं भ्रमतीव।

मार्गे वन्यानां कुसुमानामामोदमुपजिघ्रन्तौ तौ दम्पती ऋषेराश्रममगच्छताम्।

अयं शीत आकाशवायुस्तव मुखे घर्मजान्स्वेदलवानाचामति।

नदतः सिंहस्य स्वनं श्रुत्वा यथा सर्वे मृगास्त्रसन्ति तथैव भीमस्य शब्दं श्रुत्वा सर्वे योधा अत्रस्यन्।

गगनमध्यमारूढस्य सवितुः प्रचण्डेन तापेन क्लान्तोयं शिखी तरोरालवाले स्थितं शीतमुदकं पर्याप्तमाचामति।

निदाघेऽल्पैरपि तोयैर्मालाकारेण या तरोः पुष्टिर्विरच्यते सा किमनल्पान्यपि तोयानि विश्वतो पिकिरता वारिदेन जनयितुं शक्या।

श्रोत्रियायाभ्यागताय वत्सतरीं महोक्षं महाजं वा निर्वपन्ति गृहमेधिनः। तं हि धर्मं धर्मसूत्रकाराः समामनन्ति।

प्रत्युत्पन्नमतिः प्राप्तां कियां कर्तुं व्यवस्यति।

एतान्यनीकानि महानुभावं गूहन्ति मेघा इव रश्मिवन्तम्।

यावत् प्रतापनिधिराक्रमते* न भानु .
रह्नाय तावदरुणेन तमो निरस्तम्॥

व्यतिषजति पदार्थानान्तरः कोऽपि हेतुर्न
खलु बहिरुपाधीन्प्रीतयः संश्रयन्ते॥

लिम्पतीव तमोऽङ्गानि वर्षतीवाञ्जनं गता॥

असत्पुरुषसेवेव दृष्टिर्निष्फलतां गता॥

त्वं तेनाभिहितः पथ्यं † किं कोपं न नियच्छसि॥

---

* क्रम् with आ when it means "to rise up" is Âtmanepadi, if used of a heavenly body.

† दुह्याच्पच्दण्ड्रुधिप्रच्छिचिब्रूशासुजिमथ्मुषां। कर्मयुक् स्यादकथितं तथा स्यान्नीहृकृष्वहाम्॥ The roots enumerated here and roots having the same sense as these govern two objects, as a general rule, one direct and the other indirect. In the passive the indirect object of the roots from दुह् to मुष् and their equivalents is put in the nominative and the direct in the assusative; and in the case of the roots नी, हृ, कृष् and वह् and their equivalents, the direct object is put in the nominative and the other in the accusative; बलि याचते वसुधाम् *Act.*, 'he hegs the earth of Bali,' बलिर्याच्यते वसुधाम् Pass.; शतं जयति, देवदत्तम् *Act.*, 'he wins a hundred (coins) from Devadatta,' शतं जीयते देवदत्तः *Pass.*; ग्राममजां नयति *Act.*, ग्राममजा नीयते *Pass.*

In the present verse धा with अभि, of which अभिहित is the past part. pass., has the same sense as ब्रू, which means to 'say or speak to.'

*तद्विद्विषां जरति चेतसि भोगतृष्णा।
तेषां वपर्षि विपिनेषु च जारयन्ति॥
सहते शस्त्रसंपातं सहति श्रममाहवे।
उत्साहयति तत्रत्तमपि जेतुं शचीपतिम्॥
पूजामर्हति सर्वेषामृषीणामाऽप्सरसौ।
अर्हयत्यर्घ्यसत्कारं मधुपर्कं च पावनम्॥
न क्षाम्यति क्षितीशानामपराधलवानपि।
अपराधसहस्त्राधि क्षमते यो द्विजन्मनाम्॥
नाहिर्देशयते कंचित्तद्देशे गरुडाज्ञया।
यदि प्रमादाद्दशाति तस्मिन्न क्रमते † विषम्॥
न तर्जति रुषा कंचिन्नीचमप्युपकारिणम्।
परं तर्जयते दुष्टान् समन्तात्संगतान्मिथः॥
कोटिभिः पणते नित्यं राष्ट्रे तस्य वणिग्जनः।
यक्षाश्चापि पणायन्ति तद्विभूतिं गृहेगृहे ‡॥
सर्वोऽभिलषति श्रीमानिन्द्रियार्थोपसेवनम्।
अभिलष्यत्यसौ योगी तेभ्य एव निवर्तनम्॥
लष्यति प्रतिपक्षाणां स लक्ष्मीं बाणवृष्टिभिः।
न लष्यति मतिस्तस्य सकलेऽप्यर्थसंशये॥
अर्जते धर्ममेवैकमर्थं धर्मार्थमर्जति।
अर्जयत्यूर्जिताल्लोकान् स धर्मेणैवश्वतान्॥
सर्वस्य जायते मानः स्वहिताच्च प्रमाद्यति।
वृद्धौ भजति चापथ्यं नरो येन विनश्यति॥
भजन्ति विपदस्तूर्णमतिक्रामन्ति संपदः।
तान्मदान्नावतिष्ठन्ते§ ये मते न्यायवादिनाम्॥
प्राज्ञास्तेजस्विनः सम्यक्पश्यन्ति च वदन्ति च।
तेऽवज्ञाता महाराज क्राम्यन्ति विरमन्ति §§च॥

---

*This and the following nine stanzas refer to a king of the name of Kṛishṇa.

† When क्रम is used in the sense of 'operating' or 'having effect' it is Âtmanepadi.

‡ The doubling of a crude noun or declensional form has the sense of 'every'; as गृहेगृहे 'in every house,' दिनेदिने 'every day.'

§स्था with सम्, अव, प्र, or वि takes the Âtmanepada terminations.

§§रम् with वि, आ, परि or उप is Parasmaipadi.

जीर्यन्ति जीर्यतः केशा दन्ता जीर्न्ति जीर्यतः।
जीवनाशा धनाशा च जीर्यतोऽयं न जीर्यति॥
अहो खलभुजङ्गस्य विचित्रोऽयं वधक्रमः।
अन्यस्य दशाति श्रोत्रमन्यः प्राणैर्वियुज्यते॥
विधौ विध्यति सकोधे वर्म धर्मः शरीरिणाम्।
स एव केवलं तस्मादस्माकं जायतां गतिः॥
विहितस्याननुष्ठानान्निन्दितस्य च सेवनात्।
अनिग्रहाच्चेन्द्रियाणां नरः पतनमृच्छति॥

It is the power of God, by which this wheel of the world goes round [भ्रम्]

Enraged at his ingratitude Vishṇudatta out him up [तक्ष with सम्] with with harsh words.

In that assembly the necklaces of many of the kings rising up in haste broke [त्रुट्] by their pressing against one another.

Does the unforgiving serpent bite [दंश्] from a desire for blood the person touching him with his foot?

Having first bowed to Vasishṭha, the preceptor of the family of the Ikshvâkus, Râma embraced [स्वञ्ज्] his brothers.

Indrajit being kelled, grief burnt [भ्रस्ज्] Râvaṇa like fire on account of his untimely death.

Taking away that, by which I live, you try [यम्]to take away my life.

Attracted by the flame of the lamp, the moth subdenly fell upon it and died [ऋ*with acc. of.मृत्यु] .

Wishing to make the elephant turn back, Aja pierced [व्यध्] him with an arrow.

In the fight with the Râkshasas Râna mowed [वृश्च्]many hundreds of his enemies with his sharp weapons.

The soul of Râma was plunged [मृत्यु]in grief caused by his separation from sîtâ.

"Stake [पण्] they wife, Pâñchhâlî," said the sons of Dhṛitarâshṭra to Yudhishṭhira, when everything besides her had been won by them from him.†

---

*The augment आ of the Imperfect with the following initial ऋ of a root becomes आर् (cf. rule, p.62, F. B.)

† See note †, page 3.

I took great trouble [यस् with प्र] for the recovery of the jewel snatched away by the bird.

He, who is at enmity* with the great quickly perishes [शद्].

Thousands of faults are committed by me every moment; forgive them all. O God !

Oh the inexpressible power of this maid, that not only things that live serve her, but also those that do not live !

This wind, moist with the spray of the adjoining river, gently shakes [धू] *Atimukta* creeper in the garden.

When Aja blew [ध्मा] his conch, his warriors, who had fled away, returned and saw the armies of his enemies asleep.

VOCABULARY I.

Roots

अर्ज् *1st conj.* Parasm. and *10th conj.* to acquire, to obtain, to earn.

अर्ह् *1st conj. Parasm.* and *10th conj.* to deserve.

ऋज् *1st conj. Âtm.* to acquire, to obtain.

कृत् *6th conj. Parasm.* to cut.

कॄ *6th. conj. Parasm.* to strew; *with* वि, to scatter.

कृत् *10th conj.* to celebrate, to Praise, to glorify.

क्रम् *Parasm*, to walk, to step; to operate, to have effect; *with* आ, to approach, to step or tread upon, to rise, to rise up; *with* अति, to step or go beyond, to part from.

क्लम् Parasm. to be or become fatigued, to be exhausted, to be depressed.

क्षम् *4th conj. Parasm.* to forgive.

गुह् *1st conj. Parasm.* and *Âtm.* to conceal.

घ्रा *1st conj. Parasm. with* उप, to, smell. [to drink;with आ.

चम् *1st conj. Parasm* to lick up,

चित् *10th conj. Âtm.* to have life or motion.

जनय causal of जन्, to cause, to bring about; जनयितुम् *Inf.*

जॄ *1st and 4th conj. Parasm.* and *10th conj.* to grow old, to waste away, to wear out.

तक्ष् *1st conj. Parasm.* to parc, chop; *with* सम्, to cut to pieces, to wound, to hurt by words

तर्ज् *1st conj. Parasm.* and *10th conj. Âth.* to threaten, to menace, to reprove. afraid.

त्रस् *Parasm.* to tremble, to be

त्रुट् *Parasm.* to break, to snap.

---

*Use *Âtm.* here which is a *denominative* from *n.* 'emity', and is to be conjugated like roots of the 1st conjugation, as 3rd pers. sing. pres.

दंश् *1st conj. Parasm.* and *10th conj. Âtm.* to bite. to sting.

धू *6th conj. Parasm.* to shake, to agitate.

नद् *1st conj.* parasm. to sound, to roar, to thunder.

नश् *with* वि, to perish.

पण् *1st conj.* to praise, to bet or stake at play, to gamble.

भ्रम् *Parasm.* to wander, to revolve.

भ्रस्ज् *1st Conj. Parasm.* and *Âtm.* to bake, to scorch.

मस्ज् *6th conj. Parasm.* to sink, to be immersed.

म्ना *1st conj. Parasm.* to repeat over in the mind, to repeat; *with* सम् and आ, to repeat, to repeat by tradition, to prescribe, to rule.

यम् *1st conj. Parasm.* to keep in, to hold back, to restrain; *with* नि.

यस् *4th conj. Parasm.* to Strive, to endeavour; *with* प्र.

युज् *with* वि *in the pass.*, to be separated from. [to perform.

रच् *with* वि, *to arrange. to effect.*

रम् *with* वि, to stop.

लष् *Parasm.* to desire; *with* अभि, to desire, to covet, to crave.

लिप् *6th conj. Parasm.* and *Âtm.* to smear, to anoint.

लप् *4th conj. Parasm.* to be destroyed, to disappear or vanish.

लुप् *6th conj. Parasm.* and *Âtm.* to take away, to rob, to plun to deprive of.

वप् *1st conj. Parasm.* and *Âtm.* to shear, to cut, to sow; *with* , निर् to offer sacrificial food, to present.

वृष् *1st conj. Parasm.* to rain, to shower down, to pour down.

व्यध् *4th conj. Parasm.* to pierce, to wound. mow, to tear.

व्रश्च् *6th conj. Parasm.* to cut, to

शद् *1st conj. Parasm.* to decay.

श्रि *with* सम्, to resort to, to rest on, to depend upon.

सह् *with* उद् to be able, to be adequate, to be up to, to feel equal to.

सञ्ज् *1st conj. Parasm.* to cling, to adhere to; *with* वि and अति, [व्यतिषञ्ज्] to join together.

सो *4th conj. Parasm.* to bring to an end, to finish, to destroy; with वि and अव, to determine, to resolve, to endeavour, to strive.

स्था with अव, to stay, to abide.

अङ्ग *n.* a limb.

अञ्जन *n.* a black pigment, lampblack.

अननुष्ठान n. (अनुष्ठान n. doing, execution) not doing, omission to do.

अन्य *pron. m. n. f.* another.

अनिग्रह *m.* (निग्रह *m.* restraint not restraining, want of restraint.

अनीक *n.* an army.

अपथ्य n. an unwholesome or wrong thing.

अपराधसहस्र *n.* (सहस्र n. a thousand a thousand of faults.

अभिहित *Past part. Pass.* of भा *with* अभि, spoken to.

अभ्यागत *Past Part.* of गम् *with* अभि and आ, come, arrived; *m.*a (male) guest.

अरुण *m.* the charioteer of the sun.

अर्घ्यसत्कार *m.* (सत्कार *m.* hospitality) hospitality done by means of अर्घ्य i.e. the materials for worshipping or honouring a guest.

अर्थसंशय *m.* (संशय *m.* doubt, danger danger to wealth.

अल्प *m.n.f.* little, few; अनल्प *m.n.f.* many, much.

अवज्ञात *past part. pass.* of ज्ञा with अव, despised, disregarded, disobeyed.

असत्पुरुषसेवा *f.* (सत् *m.n.f.* good, सेवा *f.* service) service of a person who is not good, service done to a bad or wicked person.

अहि *m.*a serpent.

अह्नाय *ind. adv.* instantly, soon, speedily. [sky.

अकाशवायु *m.* the wind in the

आन्तर *m.n.f.* internal. [fume.

आमोद *m.*fragrant smell, per-

आरूढ *past part.* of रुह् *with* आ, ascended.

आलवाल *n.* a basin for water round the root of a tree.

आहव m. battle.

इन्द्रियार्थोपसेवन *n.* (इन्द्रिय *n.* a sense; अर्थ *m.* object, उपसेवन *n.* resorting to, enjoyment) enjoyment fo the objects of the senses, sensual enjoyment.

उपकारिन् *m.n.f.* benevolent.

ऊर्जित *m.n.f.* lofty, excellent.

केश m.a hair.

कोटि *f.* a crore.

कोप *m.* anger.

क्लान्त past part. of क्लम्, fatigued, exhausted. languishing.

क्षितीश *m.* (क्षिति *f.* the earth) loard of the earth, a king.

खलभुजङ्ग *m.* (खल *m.* a villain, भुजङ्ग *m.* a serpent) a serpent in the form of a villain.

खलु ind. verily.

गगनमध्य *m.n.* (गगन *n.* the sky, *m.n.* the middle) the middle of the sky.

गति *f.* resource, refuge.

गरुडाज्ञा *f.* order or command of Garuda (the enemy of the serpent-race).

गृहमेधिन् *m.* the householder who performs domestic rites.

घर्मज *m.n.f.* (घर्म *m.* heat) produced or caused by heat.

चेतस् *n.* mind.

जीवनाशा *f.* (जीवन *n.* living, life, आशा *f.* hope, desire) desire for

तद्देश *m.* his country. [living

तद्विद्विष्* *m.* his enemy.

तद्विभूति *f.* his prosperity.

*Final ष् is changed to ट् or ड् in the nominative singular and before the consonantal terminations.

ताप *m.* heat.

तावत् *adv.* during that time, in the meanwhile

तूर्णम् *adv.* quickly.

तेजस्विन् *m. n. f.* brilliant, spleadid, bright, spirited.

तोय n. water.

दम्पती m. du. wife and husband.

दन्त m. a tooth.

दुष्ट *m.n.f.* wicked.

द्विजन्मन् *m.* (द्वि two, जन्मन् *n.* birth) one who has two births, one belonging to any of the first three castes, a Brâhmaṇa.

द्विष् *m.* (जिह्वा *f.* tongue) one who has two tongues, a serpent.

धनाशा *f.* desire for wealth.

धर्मसूत्रकार *m* (धर्म *m.* law, सूत्र *n.* aphorism) one who composes aphorisms on law, a writer on law.

धर्मार्थम् *adv.* (धर्म, अर्थ) for the sake of religious merit.

धैर्यधन *m.n.f.* (धैर्य *n.* courage, fortitude) one whose wealth is fortitude.

निदाघ *m.*the hot season,summer.

निन्दित *past part. pass.* of निन्द्, censured, censurable.

निरस्त *Past part. pass.* of अस् to throw *with* निर् dispersed.

निवर्तन *n.* desisting, adstaining, adstinence.

निष्ठाशून्य *m.n.f.* (निष्ठा *f.* fixity, शून्य *m.n.f.* void) void of fixity, unsteady.

निष्फलता *f.* fruitlessness

नीच *m.n.f.* mean, low, in a low position.

न्यायवादिन् *m.n.f.* (न्याय *m.* what is right) one who speaks what is right.

पतन *n.* falling, falling from virtue, depravation, ruin.

पथ्य *n.* what is wholesome or salutary.

पदार्थ *m.* a thing, an object.

परम् *conjunc.* but.

पर्याप्तम् *adv.* fully, to one's heart's content.

पावन *m.n.f.* purifying, pure, holy.

पुष्टि *f.* nourishment.

प्रचण्ड *m.n.f.* hot, fierce.

प्रतापनिधि *m.* (प्रताप m heat) store of heat.

प्रतिपक्ष m. an enemy.

प्रत्युत्पन्नमति *m.n.f.* (प्रत्युत्पन्न *past. part.* of पद् *with* प्रति and उद्) ready-witted, quick, sharp.

प्रमाद m.a mistake.

प्राण *m.* (plural) life.

बहिरुपाधि *m.* (उपाधि m. an attribute, a peculiarity, environment) outward attributes, peculiarities or environments.

बाणवृष्टि *f.* (वृष्टि *f.* a shower a shower of arrows.

भानु *m.* the sun.

भोगतृष्णा *f.* (भोग *m.* worldly enjoyment, तृष्णा *f.* thirst thirst for wordly enjoyment.

मत *n.* opinion, advice, conunsel.

मधुपर्क *m.* an offering of honey, curdled milk &c., to a guest on his arrival.

महाज *m.*a great goat.

महानुभाव *m.n.f.* of great nobility, noble.

महाराज *m.*a great king. [bull.
महोक्ष *m.*(उक्षन् *m.* a bull) a great
मान *m.* pride, arrogance.
मालाकार m. a gardener.
मिथः *adv.* mutually, together.
यावत् *adv.* for which while, while.
रण *n.* a battlefield.
[sun.
रश्मिवत् *m.* (रश्मि *m.* a ray) the
राष्ट्र *n.* a kingdom, a nation.
रुष् *f.* anger.
लक्ष्मी *f.* the goddess of wealth and beauty; splendour, glory.
वणिग्जन *m.* (वणिज् *m.* a merchant) merchants.
वत्सतरी *f.* a heifer.
वधक्रम *m* the process or manner of killing.
वन्य *m.n.f.* belonging to a forest or woods.
वपुस् *n.* body.
वर्मन् *n.* armour.
वारिद *m.* a cloud. [curious.
विचित्र *m.n.f.* wonderful,
विपिन *n.*a forest.
विश्वतः**adv.* in all directions.
विहित *past part. pass.* of धा *with* वि, prescribed by the scriptures.
वृद्धि f. prosperity.
वैषम्य *n.* difficulty, calamity
व्यथित *past part.* of व्यथ् afflicted.
शक्य *m.n.f.* possible [Indra.
शचीपति *m.* the husband of
शनैस् adv. slowly.
शब्द *m.* voice, a word.

शरीरिन् *m.n.f.* ono having a body; *m.*a human being, a man.
शस्त्रसंपात *m.* (शस्त्र n.a weapon, संपात *m.*falling on) a stroke of a weapon. [ing.
शाश्वत *m.n.f.* eternal, everlast-
शिखिन् m.a peacock.
शीत *m.n.f.* cold.
श्रम m. fatigue.
श्रोत्र n. ear
श्रोत्रिय *m.*a Brâhmaṇa learned in the Vedas.
संगत *Past part.* of गम् with सम् united.
सकल *m.n.f.* whole, all.
सक्रोध *m.n.f.* angry.
सदाचरणव्रत *n.* (व्रत n,a vow the vow of good or virtuous conduct.
सपदि *ind. adv.* at once.
समन्तात् *adv.* round about.
सम्यक *adv.* correctly, well.
सेवन *n.* serving, resorting to, practising.
स्थित *Past part.* of स्था, adiding, being, existing.
स्वजनवियोग *m.* separation from one's own men or relations.
स्वन *m.* noise, roar.
स्वहित *n.* one's own good.
स्वेदलव *m.* (स्वेद *m.*perspiration a particle or drop of perspiration.
हेतु *m.* a cause.

---

* तस् added to substantives gives them the sense of the ablative and sometimes of the locative.

Adjoining संनिहित *Past part. pass.* of धा *with* सम् and नि.
Aja अज *m.* name of a person.
Atimukta creeper अतिमुक्तलता f.
Attracted विलोभित *past part. pass.* of the caus. of लुभ् *with* वि.
Blood शोणित *n.*
Desire काङ्क्षा *f.*
Enraged क्रुद्ध *past part.* of क्रुध्.
First प्रथमम् *adv.*, आदौ *loc. sing.* of आदि.
flame शिखा *f.*
Gently मन्दम् *adv.*
Grief शोक *m.*
Harsh परुष *m.n.*, (words) परुषाक्षर *m.n.f.*
Haste, in, ससंभ्रमम् *adv.*
Ikshvâkus the, इक्ष्वाकु *m.* (*used in the plural*) name of the line of kings to which Râma belonged.
Indrajit इन्द्रजित् *m.* the son of Râvaṇa.
Inexpressible अनिर्वचनीय *m.n.f.* अनिर्वर्णनीय *m.n.f.* किम् *m.n.f. with* अपि added.
Ingratitude कृतघ्नता *f.*
Moist आर्द्र *m.n.f.*
Moth पतङ्ग *m.*
Necklace हार *m.*
Pâñchâli पाञ्चाली *f.* a princess of the country of Pañchâlas.
Power प्रभाव *m.*
Pressing against each other परस्परसंघट्टन *n.*
Recovery प्रत्यागम *m.*
Snatched away आक्षिप्त *past part. pass* of क्षिप् *with* आ.
Spray कण *m.* सीकर *m.*
Suddenly सहसा *adv.*
Turn, wishing to make one, निवर्तयिष्यत् *fut. part. act.* of the *caus.* वृत of *with* नि.
Unforgiving अमर्षण *m.n.f.*
World, wheel of the, जगच्चक्र *n.* ब्रह्माचक्र *n.*

LESSON II.
FIFTH AND EIGHTH CONJUGATION.

The Sanskrit Verb has ten tenses and moods together. In four of these, viz., the Present, the Imperfect, the imperative and the Potential, the verbs undergo peculiar modifications, with reference to which they are divided into nine conjugational classes* These four are called conjugational or special tenses and moods.

1. With respect to these, the ten conjugations of the Sanskrit grammarians may be arranged into two groups, the first comprising. The general characteristic of the first is that the base † ends in अ, and of the second that it does not end in अ.

---

*Sanskrit Grammarians reckon ten, but the augment अय, which the original root undergoes in the tenth conjugation, appears not only in four tenses and moods indicated in the text but in several others also.

† See note †, p. 91, First Book.

General Rules with regard to the Conjugational Tenses of the Second Group.

2. Before certain terminations, the roots together with the conjugational signs undergo peculiar modifications. With reference to these, we will divide the terminations into two classes, calling one set strong and the other *weak*.

Parasmaipada.

3. The singulars are strong.

Exception—The singulars of the Potential and tch second person singular of the Imperative.

4. The duals and plurals are weak.

Exception— The duals and plurals of the Imperative first person.

Therefore, the singulars of all persons of the Present and the Imperfect, and the third person singular and all numbers of the first person of the Imperative are strong and the rest weak.

Âtmanepada.

5. All the terminations are weak.

Exception—Thos of the first person Imperative, which are strong.

6. Before strong terminations the ending vowel and the penultimate short of the base take their Guna substitute.

Present Tense.

7. In the second group of conjugation the parâsmaipada terminations of the Present are the same as those of the first group, but the Âtmanepada differ in the following particulars:-

(1) The vowel इ occurring in some of the Âtmanepada terminations given in the First Book is replaced by आ (2) The first person singular termination is ए (3) The न् in the third person plural is dropped.

Therefore the terminationa are:-

	Sing	*Dual*	*Plur*
1st pers.	ए	वहे	महे
2nd "	से	आथे	ध्वे
3rd "	ते	आते	अते

1. नु in the fifth and उ in the eighth conjugation are added on to the root in the conjugational tenses before the terminations are applied.

5th conjugation.

चि *Parasm.* and *Âtm.* 'to collect.'

	Sing.	*Dual.*	*Plur.*
1st pers	चिनोमि	चिनुवः-चिन्वः	चिनुमः-चिन्मः
2nd "	चिनोषि	चिनुथः	चिनुथ
3rd "	चिनोति	चिनुतः	चिन्वन्ति

Here नु being added on the root चि, the base is चिनु. The ending उ of this becomes ओ i.e., the whole becomes चिनो before the strong मि, सि, and ति; while it remains unchanged before वस्, मस् &c, the weak terminations.

(a) The vowel उ of a termination is dropped optionally before व् and म् provided it is not preceded by a conjunct consonant.

Hence we have चिनुवः-चिन्वः, चिनुमः-चिन्मः in the above and चिनुवहे-चिन्वहे, चिनुमहे-चिन्महे below, but in the forms आप्नुवः and आप्नुमः of the root आप् the उ is never dropped.

1st pers.	चिन्वे	चिनुवहे-चिन्वहे	चिनुमहे-चिन्महे
2nd "	चिनुषे	चिन्वाथे	चिनुध्वे
3rd "	चिनुते	चिन्वाते	चिन्वते

Here all the terminations being weak, नु is not changed to नो anywhere.

आप् *Parasm.* 'to obtain.'

	Sing.	*Dual*	*Plural.*
1st pers.	आप्नोमि	आप्नुवः	आप्नुमः
2nd "	आप्नोषि	आप्नुथः	आप्नुथ
3rd "	आप्नोति	आप्नुतः	आप्नुवन्ति

(b) In this conjugation, after roots ending in a consonant the उ of नु is changed to उव् when follwed by a weak termination beginning with a vowel.

Hence we have आप्नुवन्ति in the above, the root आप् ending in a consonant.

8th Conjugation.

तन् *Parasm.* and *Âtm.* 'to stretch.'

	Sing.	*Dual*	*Plur*
1st pers.	तनोमि	तनुवःतन्वः	तनुमःतन्मः
2nd "	तनोषि	तनुथः	तनुथ
3rd "	तनोति	तनुतः	तन्वन्ति

	Sing.	Dual	Plur.
1st pers.	तन्वे	तनुवहे-तन्वहे	तनुमहे-तन्महे
2nd "	तनुषे	तन्वाथे	तनुध्वे
3rd "	तनुते	तन्वाते	तन्वते

By (a), p.13, we have तनुव or तन्वः, &c.

9. कृ 'to do,' 8th Conj. Parasm. and Âtm. assumes the form कर् before the strong, and कुर् before the weak terminations, in the conjugational tenses.

	Parasm.			*Âtm.*		
	Sing.	*Dual*	*Plur.*	*Sing*	*Dual*	*Plur.*
1st pers.	करोमि	सर्वः	कुर्मः	कुर्वे	कुर्वहे	कुर्महे
2nd "	करोषि	कुरुथः	कुरुथ	कुरुषे	कुर्वाथे	कुरुध्वे
3rd "	करोति	कुरुतः	कुर्वन्ति*	कुरुते	कुर्वाते	कुर्वते

(a) In the case of कृ the उ is necessarily dropped before व् and म्. Hence only कुर्वः, कुर्मः,&c.

यज्ञेषु सोमं सुन्वतेऽध्वर्यवः।
प्रत्यहं प्रातरुत्थायोपवनं च गत्वा पुष्पाण्यवचिनोमि।
महात्मनां यशांसि दिक्षु प्रतन्वन्ति कवयः।
दुःखपीडितामपि माँ हृदयमर्मच्छिद्भिर्वचनैः किं पुनर्दुनोषि।
द्वाःस्थौ पुरुषौ राजकुलस्य द्वारमपावृणवाते।
पुण्यकृतः स्वेषां सुचरितानां फलं स्वर्गलोकेऽश्नुवते।
आर्याः संसारसुखानि त्यक्तवा किमर्थमरण्यवासमङ्गीकुरुध्वे।
श्रुतिमनोहरांश्चित्रालेपाञ्शृणुमः।
आकाशं मेघा वृण्वते।
हे जगन्नायक व वयं चर्मचक्षुषा तव विभूतिमुपवीक्षितुं शक्नुमः।
यत्त्वं कुरुषे तदन्यथा विधातुं कः शक्नोति।
केनापि रक्षसा हृतमस्माकं तुरगं वयं विचिनुमः।
वारंवारमीश्वरस्याराधनां साधवः कुर्वन्ति।
सत्कृतिर्मनुष्यस्य कीर्ति सर्वेषु देशेषु तनोति।
दुरापमपि लोकेऽस्मिन् यद्यद्वस्त्वभिवाञ्छति।
तत्तदाप्नोति मेधावी तस्मात्कार्यः समुद्यमः।

---

*न् is not changed to ण् when it is followed by a consonant of the dental class.

*न दुनोति दयालुत्वाद्वचसा कंचिदप्यसौ।
दुरुक्तैरपि दीनानां मनस्तस्य न दूयते॥
सोमं सुनोति यज्ञेषु सोमवंशविभूषणः
पुरः सुवति संग्रामे स्यन्दनं स्वयमेव सः॥

You connot [शक्] conquer your passions.

We make [कृ] pilgrimages to kâdî every year.

The châtaka begs [यच्] water, but does not obtain [आप्] it.

Dost thou hear [श्रु] what I say?

I do not express [वृ with वि] the thought, because it is sinful.

I shut [वृ with सम्] the gates of the palace.

The two instructors expound [वृ with वि] the principles of Nyâya to their pupils.

You only lay bare [कृ with आविस्] your own littleness by doing † so.

Misers hoard [चि with सम्] money.

Prudent people accomplish [साध्] their own purpose with ease.

I saw an animal. It has a thick tail, which it shakes [धु] constantly.

VOCABULARY II.

Roots of the Fifth Conjugation.

अश् *Âtm.* to get, to enjoy, to pervade.

आप् *Parasm.* to obtain.

चि *Parasm.* and *Âtm.* to collect; *with* वि, to search, to seek, to look for; *with* सम् to hoard.

दु *Parasm.* to give pain to, to tease, to afflict.

धु or धू *Parasm.* and *Âtm.* to shake.

धृष् *Parasm.* to dare, to brave.

वृ *Parasm.* and *Âtm.* to cover; *with* अप and आ, to open; वि, *with* to expound, to express; *with* सम् to shut; *with* आ, to restrain, to curb.

शक् *Parasm.* to be able.

---

*This stanza and the next refer, as similar ones in the last lesson, to a king of the name of Kṛishṇa.

† Use the present participle here qualifying you.

श्रु (शृ) *Parasm.* to hear.

साध् *Parasm.* to accomplish.

सु Parasm. and Âtm. to extract Soma juice.

Roots of the Eighth Conjugation.

कृ *Parasm.* and *Âtm.* to do; *with* वशी, to conquer; with अङ्गी to betake oneself to, to accept; *with* आविस् to lay bare, to open; *with* तिरस् to despise; *with* प्रति, to retaliate, to counteract, to resist.

तन् *Param.* and *Âtm.* to stretch to spread, as a sacrifice, i.e. to perform it; *with* प्र, to spread.

यन् Âtm. to beg.

अध्वर्यु *m.* a sacrificial priest whose duty it is to prepare and throw the oblations into the fire.

अन्यथा *ind.* otherwise.

अरण्यवास *m.*(अरण्य *n. a.* forest and वास *m.* dwelling) residence in a forest.

आराधना *f.* worship. [be done.

कार्य *m.n.f.* deserving or fit to

चर्मचक्षुस् *n.* (चर्मन् *n.* hide, skin, and चक्षुस् *n.* the eye) the physical eye.

चित्रालाप *m.* (चित्र diversified, and आलाप *m.*conversation) conversation on diverse subjects.

जगन्नायक *m.* (जगत् *n* the universe, नायक *m.* lord) the Lord of the universe.

तुरग *m.* a horse,

दयालुत्व *n.* kindness.

दीन *m.n.f.*poor, needy, afflicted.

दुखः पीडित *m.n.f.* afflicted with pain.

दुराप *m.n.f.* difficult to obtain.

दुरुक्त *n.* inproper words, words not well-spoken.

दू *4th conj. Âtm* to be pained

द्वाःस्थ *m.n.f.* door-keeper.

द्वार *n.* door.

पुण्यकृत *m.n.f.* (पुण्य *n.* merit and कृ to do) meritorious.

पुरस् *ind.* in front, to the front.

प्रत्यहम् *ind.* (प्रति every and अहन् *n.* day) every day.

यज्ञ *m.* a sacrifice.

राजकुल *n.* (राजन् *m.* and कुल *n.* a house, a palace) a royal

वारंवारम् *adv.* often. [Palace.

विभूति *f* power or greatness.

श्रुतिमनोहर *m.n.f.* (श्रुति *f.* ear and मनोहर m.n.f. charming charming to the ear.

संग्राम *m.*a battle.

संसारसुख *n.* (संसार *m.* worldly existence, सुख *n.* happiness, enjoyment) enjoyment of a wordly existence.

सत्कृति *f.* a meritoriour deed, a

समुद्यम *m.* exertion. [good action.

सू *6th conj. parasm.* to impel, to push forward

सोमवंशविभूषण *m.n.f.* (सोम *m.* the moon) one who adorns the

*The forms which some roots assume in the conjugational tenses are are enclosed within brackets.

lunar race, an ornament of the luner raće (of kings).
स्यन्दन *m.* a chariot.
स्वयम् *ind.* in person, of himself.
हृदयमर्मच्छिद् m.n.f. (हृदय n. the heart, मर्मन् *n.* the vital parts, and छिद् to cut) piercing the vital parts of the heart.

Because यतः *ind.* हि *ind.*
Constantly अनिशम् *adv.*
Ease सौकर्य *n.*
Every year प्रतिसंवत्सरम् *adv. ind.*
Fight, to, युद्धाय, युद्धे, योद्धुम्.
Gate द्वार *n.*
Instructor अध्यापक *m.n.f.*
Littleness लघुता *f.*
Miser कदर्य *m.*
Own स्वीय *m.n.f.*
Passion मनोधर्म *m.* इन्द्रियवृत्ति *f.* इन्द्रिय *n.*
Pilgrimage यात्रा *f.*
Principle तत्त्व *n.* नय *m.*
Prudent दूरदर्शिन् *m.n.f.* चतुर *m.n.f.*
Purpose कार्य *n*
Sinful पाप *m.n.f.*
Thick स्थूल *m.n.f.* विपुल *m.n.f.*
Thought संकल्प *m.* बुद्धि *f.*

LESSON III

FIFTH AND EIGHTH CONJUGATIONS-*Continued.*

Imperfect.

1. The Parasmaipada terminations are the same as those given for the first group.

The Âtmanepada termination are also the same but the इ of इताम् and इथाम् is replace by आ [see 7. (I), Page 12]; and the third pers, plural is अत.

The terminations are, therefore as follows:—

	Sing.	*Dual*	*Plur*
1st pers.	इ	वहि	महि
2nd "	थास्	आथाम्	ध्वम्
3rd "	त	आताम्	अत

5th conj.

आप *Parasm.* '*to obtain.*'

	Sing.	*Dual*	*Plur*
1st. pers.	आप्नवम्	आप्नुव	आप्नुम
2nd "	आप्नोः	आप्नुतम्	आप्नुत
3rd "	आप्नोत्	आप्नुताम्	आप्नुवन्

अश् *Âtm.* '*to Pervade.*'

	Sing.	*Dual*	*Plur*
1st. pers.	आश्नुवि	आश्नुवहि	आश्नुमहि
2nd "	आश्नुथाः	आश्नुवाथाम्	आश्नुध्वम्
3rd "	आश्नुत	आश्नुवाताम्	आश्नुवत

The singular Parasm. being strong, becomes in the first set of paradigms. The of this is changed to i.e. becomes in &c., by (b), p.13.

चि *Âtm.* 'to collect.'

	Sing.	*Dual*	*Plur*
1st. pers.	अचिन्वि	अचिनुवहि-अचिन्वहि	अचिनुमहि-अचिन्महि
2nd "	अचिनुथाः	अचिन्वाथाम्	अचिनुध्वम्
3rd "	अचिनुत	अचिन्वाताम्	अचिन्वत

8th Conj.—तन् 'to stretch.'

Parasm.

	Sing.	*Dual*	*Plur*
1st. pers.	अतनवम्	अतनुव-अतन्व	अतनुम-अतन्म
2nd "	अतनोः	अतनुतम्	अतनुत
3rd "	अतनोत्	अतनुताम्	अतन्वन्

Âtm.

	Sing.	*Dual*	*Plur*
1st. pers.	अतन्वि	अतनुवहि-अतन्वहि	अतनुमहि-अतन्महि
2nd "	अतनुथाः	अतन्वाथाम्	अतनुध्वम्
3rd "	अतनुत	अतन्वाताम्	अतन्वत

We get अचिन्वहि, अतन्व, अतन्वहि, &c., by (a), p.13. The forms of are:-

1st pers.	अकरवम्	अकुर्व	अकुर्म
	&c.	&c.	&c.

by 9 and (a), p.14.

देवा वै यज्ञमतन्वत तांस्तन्वानान अभ्यगच्छन्।
हे संजय कुरुक्षेत्र मामकाः पाण्डवाश्च किमकुर्वत तत्कथय।
रामादीनानेतुं दूतानयोध्यां प्राहिणोजनकः।
एकस्मिन्निबिडेऽरण्ये वसन्फलमूलादीनामशनेन वृत्तिमकुर्वि।
कथन नो याः कथा वृद्धेभ्यस्त्वमशृणोः।
रामं युद्धेऽघृष्णुवन्राक्षसाः।
उद्यमं कुर्वन्नपि फलं नैवाप्नवं तस्माद्भवितव्यतैवात्रोपालल्या।
ईदृशैः कर्मभिर्महत्पुण्यं त्वं समचिनुथाः।
भो भो अध्वर्यवः सोमं यूयमसुनुध्वं न वेति पृच्छति होता।
रामलक्ष्मणौ सीतामरण्येऽन्विष्यन्तौ महान्तं कालं* समीहितं नैवाश्नुवाताम्।
आपतिता आपदः प्रत्यकुर्म भवतां साहाय्येन।

*A noun expressing duration is put in the accusative case.

The enemies of the king dared [धृष्] to fight with him.

Daśaratha performed [तन्] a sacrifice on the banks of the Sarayû.

The ministers of the king sent [हि with प्र] me to watch the moverments of the enemy.

we flung open [कृ with अप and आ] the gates of the fortress.

What thou didst [कृ] still gives pain to [दु] thy friends.

I could [शक्] not ascend to the top of the mountain.

Where did you look for [चि with वि] the books which were lost?

The (two) girls gathered* [चि with अव] flowers in the garden yesterday for themselves.

They restrained [यम् with आ], with efforts, their desires, anger and greed, and contemplating the Brahman obtained [आप्]eternal felicity.

Babhruvâhaṇa wonnded [क्षण् or क्षिण्] Arjuna in the breast with anarrow.

In the battle the horses of the warriors were killed, but they obtained [आप्] others and fought again.

Thou and Râma committed † [कृ] a sin for which you both deserve punishment.

VOCABULARY III.

क्षण्, क्षिण्, *8th conj. Parasm.* to wound.

हि *5th conj. Parasm.* to go; *with* प्र, to send.

अन्विष्यत् *Pres part* of इष् *4th conj. Parasm.* with अनु searching.

अशन *n.* eating.

ईदृश *m.n.f.* such.

उपालभ्य *m.n.f.* blameable, deserving reproach.

कुरुक्षेत्र *n.* name of a place where the Kurus fought.

गम् *with* अभि, to attack.

निबिड *m.n.f.* without interstices, dense.

फलमूलादि *m.n.f.* (मूल root) furits, roots and others.

---

*The Âtmanapada from fo the root should be used here. When a root is both Âtmaneadi and Parasmaipadi. the forms of the former are used when the result of the action is confined to one's own self, and of the latter when it is directed to another person.

† When there are two or more subjects of different persons connected by "and" the verb is put in the first person, if one of the subjects be of the paerson; otherwise in the second person.

भवितव्यता *f.* fate, destiny.

मामक *m.n.f.* mine.

रामादि *m.* (राम proper name and आदि beginning Râma and others.

वृत्ति *f.* livelihood, maintenace.

वृद्ध *m.n.f.* old.

वै *ind* an expletive.

सञ्जय *m.* proper name.

समीहित *m.n.f.* what is desired; n.a desired object.

साहाय्य *n.* friendship, help.

हे *interj.* a vocative partiole, oh!

होतृ *m.* a sacrificial priest whose duty it is to repeat the mantras.

Babhruvâhana बभ्रुवाहन *m.* son of ARjuna, the Pâṇḍava.

Both उभ *pron.*

Desire काम *m*

Eternal शाश्वत *m.n.f.*

Felicity सुख *m.n.f.*

Fortress दुर्ग *n.*

Greed लोभ m.

Killed हत *past part. pass.*

Lost नष्ट *past part.*

Movement व्यापार *m.*

Other अपर *m.n.f. pro*

Punishment दण्ड *m.*

Still *adv.* अद्यापि *ind.*

Sarayû सरयू *f.* a river near Ayodhyâ.

Watch, to, निरूपयितुम् *inf.* of रूप् *10th conj. with* नि.

VOCABULARY IV.

FIFTH AND EIGHTH CONJUGATIONS-*Continued.*

Parasmaipada.

Imperfect.

1. In the second group of conjugations is the termination of the second person singular of the Imperative. is dropped in the 5th conjugation when the root ends in a vowel and in the 8th in all cases.

Hence the terminations are as follows:-

	Sing.	*Dual*	*Plur*
1st. pers.	आनि	आव	आम
2nd "	हि	तम्	त
3rd "	तु	अतनुताम्	अन्तु

आप् *5th conj.*

	Sing.	*Dual*	*Plur*
1st. pers.	आप्नवानि	आप्नवाव	आप्नवाम
2nd "	आप्नुहि	आप्नतम्	आप्नुत
3rd "	आप्नोतु	आप्नुताम्	आप्नुवन्तु

सु *5th conj.*

	Sing.	*Dual*	*Plur*
1st. pers.	सुनवानि	सुनवाव	सुनवाम
2nd "	सुनु	सुनुतम्	सुनुत
3rd "	सुनोतु	सुनुताम्	सुन्वन्तु

Here the three numbers of the first person being strong. is नु changed to which again, being followed by the initial आ of the terminations, becomes नव् and with आ, नवा. Hence आप्नवानि, आप्नवाव etc.

The 2nd pers. sing. is weak in addition to the duals and plurals of that the 3rd pers.

Potential.

2. या is to be prefixed to the terminations of the Imperfect. The third person plural termination is

They are thus:-

	Sing.	*Dual*	*Plur*
1st. pers.	याम्	याव	याम
2nd "	यास्	यातम्	यात
3rd "	यात्	याताम्	युस्

चि *5th conj.*

	Sing.	*Dual*	*Plur*
1st. pers.	चिनुयाम्	चिनुयाव	चिनुयाम
2nd "	चिनुयाः	चिनुयातम्	चिनुयात
3rd "	चिनुयात्	चिनुयाताम्	चिनुयुः

All the terminations here being weak, there is no Guṇa in any case.

Âtmanepada.

Imperative.

3. As in the Present and the Imperfect, the इ of the Âtmanepada terminations of the Imperative is in the second group of conjugations replaced by, and the न् of the 3rd pers plur. dropped.

The terminations, therefore, are:-

	Sing.	*Dual*	*Plur*
1st. pers.	ऐ	आवहै	आमहै
2nd "	स्व	आथाम्	ध्वम्
3rd "	ताम्	आताम्	अताम्
1st. pers.	चिनवै	चिनवावहै	चिनामहै
2nd "	चिनुष्व	चिन्वाथाम्	चिनुध्वम्
3rd "	चिनुताम्	चिन्वाताम्	चिन्वताम्

	Sing.	*Dual*	*Plur*
1st. pers.	अश्रवै	अश्रवावहै	अश्रवामहै
2nd "	अश्रुष्व	अश्रुवाथाम्	अश्रुध्वम्
3rd "	अश्रुताम्	अश्रुवाताम्	अश्रुवताम्

The three numbers of the 1st pers. of the Imperative being the only ones strong in the Âtmanepada, we have here the change of नु to नो, and then to नव् in these cases only.

Potential

4. The terminations are the same as those of the Âtmanepada Potential of the first group of conjugations.

	Sing.	*Dual*	*Plur*
1st. pers.	चिन्वीय	चिन्वीवहि	चिन्वीमहि
2nd "	चिन्वीथाः	चिन्वीयाथाम्	चिन्वीध्वम्
3rd "	चिन्वीत	चिन्वीयाताम्	चिन्वीरन्
1st. pers.	अश्नुवीय	अश्नुवीवहि	अश्नुवीमहि
2nd "	अश्नुवीथाः	अश्नुवीयाथाम्	अश्नुवीध्वम्
3rd "	अश्नुवीत	अश्नुवीयाताम्	अश्नुवीरन्

As to the change of नु to नुव् in all these forms remember (b).p.13.

5. The forms of roots of the 8th conjugation are similar to those of चि, with उ only added on t them instead of नु. कृ loses its conjugationa उ before the Potential terminations beginning with य्.

Imperative.

Âtm.

	Sing.	*Dual*	*Plur*
1st. pers.	तनवै	तनवावहै	तनवामहै
2nd "	तनुष्व	तन्वाथाम्	&c.

Parasm.

1st. pers.	तनवानि	तनवाव	तनवाम
2nd "	तनु	&c.	&c.

Potential Parasm.

1st. pers.	कुर्याम	कुर्याव	कुर्याम
2nd "	कुर्याः	कुर्याताम्	कुर्यात
3nd "	कुर्यात	कुर्याताम्	कुर्युः

तन्वीय *Pot. Âtm. 1st pers. sing.*
तनुयाम् *" Parasm. "*
कुर्वीय *" Âtm. "*
करवाणि *Impera. Parasm. 1st pers. sing.*
करु *" " 2nd "*
करवै *" Âtm. 1st "*

We have in some of the above forms by 9, p.14.

खादिरं यूपं कुर्वीत स्वर्गकामः खादिरेणैव वै यूपेन देवाः स्वर्गं लोकमजयंस्तथैवैतद्यजमानः खादिरेण यूपेन स्वर्गं लोकं जयति।

दुःखसंतापेन पच्यन्त इव मेऽङ्गान्युत्क्वथ्यत एव हृदयं प्लुष्यत इव दृष्टिर्ज्वलतीव शरीरम्। अत्र यत्प्रातकालं तत्करोतु भवान्।

वत्स प्रसन्नोऽद्य ते कथय किं ते प्रियं करवाणि।

हे ऋत्विजोऽद्य सुत्यादिने सोमं सुनुध्वम्।

कथं नाम प्रभोरादेशमुल्लङ्घयितुं शक्नुयाम्।

एतैरालापैरात्मनः कार्पण्यं मापावृणुध्व।

राजन्यनुरागमाविष्कुर्वतां जना यतस्तेषां संकटानि नश्येयुः

आत्मनः पुत्राणां प्रवृत्त्युपलब्धये दासं श्रीनगरं प्रहिणु।

राजन्प्रीताः स्मः शुश्रूषया तवैतया तस्मात्सर्वैर्गुणैरुपेतं पुत्र मवाप्नुहिः।

श्रृणुत रे पौरः। अयं वसन्तसेनाघातकश्चारुदत्तो वधस्तम्भं नीयते तद्यदीदृशं कर्म केऽपि कुर्वीरन्दण्डमप्येतादृशं प्राप्नुयुः।

मृतं शरीरमुत्सृज्य काष्ठलोष्टसमं क्षितौ।
विमुखा बान्धवा यान्ति*धर्मस्तमनुगच्छति॥
तस्माद्धर्मं सहायार्थं नित्यं संचिनुयाच्छनैः।
धर्मेण हि सहायेन तमस्तरति दुस्तरम्॥
पूर्वे वयसि तत्कुर्याद्येन वृद्धः सुखं वसेत्।
यावज्जीवेन तत्कुर्याद्येनामुत्र सुखं वसेत्॥
श्वःकार्यमद्य कुर्वीत पूर्वाह्णे चापराह्णिकम्।
न हि प्रतीक्षते मृत्युः कृतामस्य न वा कृतम्॥

---

* *Pres. 3rd pers. plur of* या *2nd conj. Parasm. 'to go.'*

Let the servant cover [स्तृ] the floor with carpets.

Let Brâhmaṇas go about the world and seek [चि with वि] with Nala.

I would do [कृ] it, if he should bid me.

Do not despise [कृ with तिरस्] with your enemies, for they are powerful.

Weak men should not if they are wise, brave [धृष्] strong men.

In a soma sacrifice the priests should extract [सु] the juice of the soma plant.

Hear [श्रु] what he says! "Thou art a fool", says he.

I wish you would send [हि with प्र] your sons to England for aducation.

Let us accomplish [साध्] our purpose as long as he is well disposed towards us.

Do not tease [दु] those harmless birds.

VOCABULARY IV.

अनुराग m. Love good will.
अमुत्र *adv.* in the next world.
आपराह्णिक *m.n.f.* belonging to the latter part of the day.
आलाप *m.*a talk.
ईक्ष् *with* प्रति, to see, to care.
उपेत *past puss. part.* of इ with उप, united with, posessing.
ऋत्विज् *m.*a. sacrificial priest.
एतादृश *m.n.f.* of this kind.
कथं नाम *ind.* how indeed? how possible?
कार्पण्य *n.* meanness.
काष्ठलोष्टसम *m.n.f.* (काष्ठ *n.* wood, लोष्ट *m.* and *n.* a lump of earth, and सम् like) like wood and a lump of earth.
क्वथ् *Ist conj. parasm.* उद् with to boil.
क्षिति *f.* the earth.
खादिर *m.n.f.* of a tree named खदिर.
चारुदत्त *m.* name of a person.
ज्वल् *Ist conj. Parasm.* to burn, to blaze.
तद् *adv.* therefore.
दुस्तर *m.n.f.* difficult to surmount, insurmountable.
दुःखसंताप *m.* (दुःख *n.* pain, and संताप *m.* heat) heat of the pain, sorrow, affliction.
पूर्वाह्ण *m.* the first part of the [day.
प्रसन्न *Past part.* of सद् *with* प्र, pleased, propitious.
प्रवृत्त्युपलब्धि *f.* (प्रवृत्ति intelligence, and उपलब्धि getting) getting intelligence.
प्राप्तकाल *m.n.f.* (प्राप्त *past part.* of आप् *with* प्र arrived, and काल *m.* time) that of which the

time has arrived, suited to the occásion. [pleased.

प्रीत *past part. pass.* of प्री,

प्लुष् *1st conj. Parasm.* to burn.

यजमान *m.* a sacrificer.

यावज्जीवेन *adv.* as long as life endures.

यूप *m.* a sacrificial post to which the animal is tied.

लङ्घ् *1st and 10th conj. Parasm.* and Âtm. to go; *with* उद् to violate, to transgress.

वधस्तम्भ *m.* (वध *m.* killing, स्तम्भ and *m.*a. post) gallows

वसन्तसेनाघातक *m.*(वसन्तसेना *f.* name of a woman and घातक *m.* destroyer) murderer of वसन्तसेना. [turned away from.

विमुख *m.n.f.* with the face

शनैः *adv.* gradually, slowly.

शुश्रूषा *f.* service, attendance on.

श्वःकार्य *n.* to-morrow's duty or work.

सहाय *m.*a helper, a companion.

सुत्यादिन *n.* (सुत्या *f.* the extraction of Soma juice is drunk in the Soma sacrifice.

स्तृ *5th conj. Parasm.* and *Âtm.* to cover; with सम्

स्वर्गकाम *m.n.f.* one longing after heaven.

Bid दिश् *with* आ.

Carpet कुथ *m.*

Education अध्ययन *n.* विनयन *n.*

Floor भूमि *f.*

Go about चर्

Harmless अनपकारिन् *m.n.f*

Juice रस *m.*

Nala नल *m.* name of a king.

Soma sacrifice सोमयाग *m.*

Towards प्रति (governing an accusative).

Weak दुर्बल *m.n.f.*

Well-disposed स्निग्ध *past part.* of स्निह्, सस्नेह *m.n.f.*

LESSON V.

NINTH CONJUGATION.

Present and Imperative.

1. In the ninth conjugation ना is inserted between the root and the terminations. The ना assumes the form of नी before the weak terminaitons beginning with consonants, and न् before the weak terminations beginning with vowels.

The terminations belonging to the second group of conjugation have been shown in the last three lessons.

क्री *Parasm. and Âtm. 'to buy'*

Present-Parasm

	Sing.	*Dual*	*Plur*
1st. pers.	क्रीणामि	क्रीणीवः	क्रीणीमः
2nd "	क्रीणासि	क्रीणीथः	क्रीणीथ
3rd "	क्रीणीते	क्रीणीतः	क्रीणन्ति
		Âtm.	
1st. pers.	क्रीणे	क्रीणीवहे	क्रीणीमहे
2nd "	क्रीणीषे	क्रीणाथे	क्रीणीध्वे
3rd "	क्रीणीते	क्रीणाते	क्रीणते
		Imperative-Parasm.	
1st. pers.	क्रीणानि	क्रीणाव	क्रीणाम
2nd "	क्रीणीहि	क्रीणीतम्	क्रीणीत
3rd "	क्रीणातु	क्रीणीताम्	क्रीणन्तु
		Âtm.	
1st. pers.	क्रीणै	क्रीणावहै	क्रीणामहै
2nd "	क्रीणीष्व	क्रीणाथाम्	क्रीणीध्वम्
3rd "	क्रीणीताम्	क्रीणाताम्	क्रीणताम्

Mark the strong and weak terminations here with reference to the clanges of ना .

2. When a root ends in a consonant the Imperative second person singular parasm is made up simply by adding आन to the root; as मुष् 'to steal' मुषाण' steal (thou).'

मुष् *Parasm.-Imperative*

1st. pers.	मुष्णानि	मुष्णाव	मुष्णाम
2nd "	मुषाण	मुष्णीतम्	मुष्णीत
3rd "	मुष्णातु	मुष्णीताम्	मुष्णन्तु

अग्नितप्तं सुवर्णं विलिनाति*
प्रियायै दातुं पुष्पस्त्रजं † ग्रथ्नमि।
दोहनकाले वत्सं स्तम्भे बध्नन्ति।
अस्मिन्नरण्ये मार्गं कर्तुं तरूँल्लनीहि।
अयं तव सदाचारस्ते लक्ष्मीं पुष्णातु।
युद्धेषु वीराः शत्रूणां शिरोभिर्भूमिमास्तृणते।

Vide p. 29, note. † Vide p. 28, note †.

उद्धतं गच्छन्त्यास्तव गलितमुत्तरीयं गृहाणैतत्।
विवाहविधौ कन्यायाः पाणिं वरो गृह्णाति।
सुवर्णशतं दत्त्वा वयमश्वं महाजवं क्रीणीमहे।
अपेक्षितं वृणतां भवन्त इत्यस्मानवदत्कृपालुर्भगवान्।
रुद्रो देवानवददहं वरं वृणै। वृणीष्वेति तेऽभाषन्त।
पावकस्तीर्थोदकं च पापकृतः पुनीत इति ब्राह्मणा वदन्ति।
क्षणध्वांसिनों मनुजा वयमनाद्यनन्तस्य परमेश्वरस्य कथं तत्त्वं जानीमः।
अस्मिन्महति दुर्भिक्षे धान्यं न लभ्यते ततः किमश्नाम कथं च जीवितं धारयाम।

*धूनोति चम्पकवनानि धुनोत्यशोकं
चूतं धुनाति धुवति स्फुटितातिमुक्तम्।
वायुर्विधूनयति चम्पकपुष्परेणूं-
स्तत्कानने ध्वति चन्दनमञ्जरीश्च॥

बाणावलिं किरत्याजौ करोति शरमण्डपम्।
कृणोति करिणः शत्रोः स कृणाति हयान्परान्।
स्तम्भते पुरुषः प्रायो यौवनेन धनेन च।
न स्तभ्नाति क्षितीशोऽपि न स्तभ्नोति युवाप्यसौ॥
कृणात्यसौ द्विषां दर्पं शिरस्तेषां निकृन्तति।
कीर्तयन्ति गुणांस्तस्य विस्मयेन दिवौकसः॥
स्तृणोति बाणजालैः स रणे वीरवरूथिनीम्।
तच्छिरोभि†स्तृणात्युर्वीं तृणराजफलैरिव॥
सवप्रैऽपि नानृतां वाणीं संगृणाति स भूपतिः।
यस्य संगिरते किंचित्तस्मै तत्प्रतिपादयेत् ‡॥
लिनाति धर्म एवासौ नेन्द्रियार्थेषु लीयते॥

---

*This stanza and similar ones in this, as well as subsequent lessons, refer to a king of the name of the name of Krishna, verses referring to whom have already been given in two of the previous lessons.

† When a visarga precedes a श्, ष् or स् which is followed by a hard consonant, it is optionally dropped.

‡ A root in its causal sense is, as a general rule, conjugated as if it were a root of the 10th conjugation.

प्रीणाति यः सुचरितैः पितरं स पुत्रो
यद्भर्तुरेव हितमिच्छति तत्कलत्रम्।
तन्मित्रमापदि सुखे च समक्रियं य-
देतत्त्रयं जगति पुण्यकृतो लभन्ते॥

The wind shakes [धू] the tops of trees.

Do (thou) not steal [मुष्] money; for the officers of the king punish those who do it (steal money).

We eat [अश्] nothing on fasting-days.

The Brâmaṇas now-a-days take [ग्रह्] prize-money (Dakshiṇâ) even from Yavanas.

Purchase [क्री] (thou) large heaps of corn for me at Bombay.

Govinda lops [लू] off the branches of the tree.

Let Nârâyaṇa fill [पृ] his pot with water at the tank.

Thou dost not know [ज्ञा] their fraudulent schemes.

Let them curb [ग्रह with नि] their desires which often carry them astray.

I always please [प्री] everybody coming to my house.

I have stayed here for a long time; permit [ज्ञा with अनु] with me to go.

O Gods! you purify [पू] sinful men when they simply remember you

VOCABULARY V

Roots of the Ninth Conjugation

अश् Parasm. to eat.	ग्रह (गृह) Parasm. and Âtm to take; *with* नि to curd
क्री Parasm. and Âtm to buy.	ज्ञा (जा) Parasm. and Âtm. to know; with अनु to permit.
क्लिश् Parasm. to torture, to give pain to	पुष् Parasm to nourish [please.
*क्षुभ् Parasm. to agitate.	प्री Parasm and Âtm to love to
ग्रन्थ् Parasm to put together.	

---

*In the case of this root the of the न् conjugational sign in not changed to ण्.

† In this conjugation the penultimate nasal of a root is dropped.

प्लुष् *Parasm.* to burn.
बन्ध् *Parasm* to tie, to fasten.
मी *Parasm* and *Âtm* to destroy.
मुष् *Parasm.* to steal.
श्री *Parasm.* and *Âtm* to cook.
स्तम्भ् *Parasm* to stop to become stiff or rigid, to become haughty.
***पू** *Parasm* and *Âtm* to purify.
ली *Parasm.* to melt, to be dissolved, to be absorbed; *with* वि, to melt. [off.
लू *Parasm* and *Âtm* to cut, lop
स्तॄ *Parasm.* and *Âtm* to cover *with* आ to cover, to spread.
कॄ *Parasm.* and *Âtm* to kill to destroy.
जॄ *Parasm.* to become old, to wear out.
गॄ *Parasm. with* सम् to speak.
धू *Parasm.* and *Âtm* to shake.
पॄ *Parasm* to fill
दॄ *Parasm.* to tear.
वॄ *Parasm.* and *Âtm* to choose

अग्नितप्त *m.n.f*(अग्नि, and तप्त heated) heated by fire.
अनाद्यनन्त *m.n.f.* (अनादि with out beginning, and without end अनन्त) having neither beginning nor end.
अपेक्षित *n.* (*past pass. part.* of ईक्ष् *with* अप) what is desired.
अशोक *m.*name of a kind of tree.
आजि *m.f.* a fight, a battle.
उत्तरीय *n.*an upper garment.
उद्धतम् *past. part.* of हन् *with* उद् used as an *adv.* carelessly, tumultuously.
उर्वी *f.* the earth. [turultuously.
करिन् *m.*an elephant.
कलत्र *n.* wife. [to kill.
कृ *5th conj. Parasm.* and *Âtm.*
कृपालु *m.n.f.* kind
क्षणध्वंसिन् *m.n.f.* (क्षण m.a moment, ध्वंसिन् perishing) perishing in a moment.
क्षितीश *m.* (क्षिति *f.* the earth) lord of the earth, a king.
गलित Past part. of गल् dropped.
गॄ *6th conj. Parasm.* to swallow: with सम् *Âtm* to promise.
चन्दनमञ्जरी *f.* (चन्दन m.a sandal tree, मञ्जरी *f.* a blosson, a flower stalk a sprout) a blossom, &c., of the sandal tree.
चम्पकपुष्परेणु *m.* (चम्पक *m.*a kind of tree with fragrant flowers, रेणु *m.* pollen) the pollen in the flowers of *champakas.*
चम्पकवन *n.*a collection or grove of champaka trees. [flower.
चूत *m.*a mango tree; n its
तच्छिरस् *n.* his head.
तत्कानन *n* (कानन *n.*a forest a grove)his grove or forest.
तीर्थोदक *n.* (तीर्थ *n.*a holy thing, such as a river, and उदक *n.* water) holy water.
तृणराजफल *n.* (तृणराज *m.*a palmtree) a fruit of the palm-tree.
त्रय *n.*a collection fo three.
दत्त्वा absol. of दा 'to give', having given.
दर्प *m.* pride.

***पू** and the following ten roots shorten their ending vowel in the conjugation tenses.

दोहनकाल *m.*(दोहन *n.* millking काल *m.* time) time of milking.

धू (धून) *10th conj. with* वि, to shake.

धू *1st conj. Parasm.* and *Âtm* to shake. to set in motion.

पर *pron.m.n.f.* other, belonging to another or the other party.

परमेश्वर *m.* the Supreme Ruler of the Universe; God.

पादय *with* प्रति, causal of पद् *with* प्रति, to make over, to give.

पापकृत् *m.n.f* (पाप n. sin, and one कृत् who has done) one who has committed sin.

पावक *m.*fire.

पुष्पस्रज् *f.*(पुष्प *n.* and स्रज् f. a garland) a garland of flowers.

प्रायस् *ind.* mostly, in most cases.

बाणजाल *n.* (जाल *n.* a collection) a number or multitude of arrows.

मनुज *m.*a man.

महाजव *m.n.f.* (महत् great, and जव *m* speed) very swift.

*युवन् *m.*a Youth, a young man.

यौवन *n.* youth.

रुद्र *m.* the god Śiva.

ली *4th conj. Âtm* to cling or press closely, to be absorbed, to be dissolved.

वर *m.* a boon or gift.

वह्नि *m.* fire

विवाहविधि *m.* (विवाह *m.* marriage and विधि *m.* ceremony) the ceremony of marriage.

विस्मय *m.* admiration, amazement.

वीरवरूथिनी *f.* (वरूथिनी *f.* an army) an army of warriors or heroes.

शरमण्डप *m.n.* a bower or shed made of arrows.

सदाचार *m.* (सत् *m.n.f.* good. and आचार m. conduct) good conduct.

समक्रिय *m.n.f* (सम equal, and क्रिया *f.* doing) doing equally. even-handed.

सुवर्णशत *n.*(सुवर्ण *m.*a golden coin, and शत *n.*a hundred) a hundred coins of gold.

स्तम्भ् *1st conj. Âtm.* and *5th conj. parasm.* to become fixed or rigid, to become haughty.

स्तम्भ *m.* a post.

स्तृ *5th conj. Parasm.* and *Âtm.* to cover, to spread, to strew.

स्फुटितातिमुक्त *n.* an opened *atimukta* flower.

स्वप्न *m.* a dream.

हय *m.* a horse.

Astray उत्पथम् *adv.*

Bombay मुम्बापुरी *f.*

Branch शाखा *f.*

Fasting-day उपवासदिन *n.* (उपवास *m* a fast, and दिन *n.* a day).

Fraudulaent scheme कपटप्रबन्ध *m.*

Now-a-days संप्रति *adv. ind.*

Officer of the king राजपुरुष *m.*

Pot कुम्भ *m.*

Simply केवलम् *adv.*

Stay स्था; stayed स्थित past part.

Yavana यवन *m.* a foreigner, a Mahomedan; a Greek (in ancient times).

---

*The declension of this words is irregular. See Lesson XVI.

† In the 5th conj. this root drops its nasal in the conjugational tenses as it does in the 9th (See note †, p. 28)

LESSON VI.

NINTH CONJUGATION-*Continued.*

Imperfect.

Parasm.

	Sing.	*Dual*	*Plur*
1st. pers.	अक्रीणाम्	अक्रीणीव	अक्रीणीम
2nd "	अक्रीणाः	अक्रीणीतम्	अक्रीणीत
3rd "	अक्रीणीत्	अक्रीणीताम्	अक्रीणन्

Âtm.

1st. pers.	अक्रीणि	अक्रीणीवहि	अक्रीणीमहि
2nd "	अक्रीणीथाः	अक्रीणाथाम्	अक्रीणीध्वम्
3rd "	अक्रीणीत	अक्रीणाताम्	अक्रीणत

Potential.

Parasm.

1st. pers.	क्रीणीयाम्	क्रीणीयाव	क्रीणीयाम
2nd "	क्रीणीयाः	क्रीणीयातम्	क्रीणीयात
3rd "	क्रीणीयात्	क्रीणीयाताम्	क्रीणीयुः

Remember that the terminations of the Parasmaipada potential are weak. They begin with a consonant; therefore, ना become नी by 1, p. 25.

Âtm.

1st. pers.	क्रीणीय	क्रीणीवहि	क्रीणीमहि
2nd "	क्रीणीथाः	क्रीणीयातम्	क्रीणीयात
3rd "	क्रीणीत	क्रीणीयाताम्	क्रीणीयुः

1st pers. Imperf. मन्थ् Parasm. अमथ्नाम्-अमथ्नाम्-अमथ्नीम (vide p. 28, note†); लू Parasm. अलुनाम्-अलुनीव-अलुनीम (vide p.29.note*), Âtm अलुनि-अलुनीवहि-अलुनीमहि, &c., &c.

कार्तिक्येकादश्यां कथयत कान्पदार्थानाश्नीत।

क्व तानि वस्त्राणि यानि त्वमक्रीणीथाः।

रे परिचारक किमर्थमद्य भूमिं कटैर्नास्तृणाः।

यज्ञांस्तन्वाना वयं बहून्पशून्यूपे देवेभ्योऽबध्नीम।

तस्मिमन्देशे मया सार्धं योद्धुं बहवो भटा आगतास्तानहमेकाकी शस्त्रास्त्रैरमृद्नाम्।

न कन्यायाः शुल्कं गृह्णीयादिति शास्त्रप्रतिषेध सत्यपि केचिदुदरंभरयो ब्राह्मण गृह्णन्त्येव।

दमयन्त्याः स्वयंवरकाले बहवो राजानो मामियं वृणीत मामियं वृणीतीति मन्यमानाः कुण्डिनपुरमागता रङ्गं प्राविशन्। कलं वुवूर्षुर्दमयन्ती रङ्गागतान्नृपान्प्रेक्षमाणा नलतुल्याकृतीन्पञ्च पुरुषानपश्यत्। ततः संदेहान्नलं नृपम्। तेषां चत्वारो नलरूपधारिण इन्द्रादयो देवा इति ज्ञात्वाभाषत। कथं देवाञ्जानीयां कथं च नलं नृपं बोधेयम्। यदा सा देवाञ्शरणं गता तदा ते स्वीयानि रूपाण्याविरकुर्वन्। पश्चान्नलं नृपं दमयन्त्यवृणीत। अनन्तरं देवानां कोपं प्रतिकर्तु तावुभौ स्तुतिभिस्तानप्रीणीताम्। ततो देवा नलं वरैरन्वगृह्णन्।

यत्कृतेऽरीन् व्यगृह्णीम समुद्रमतराम च।
सा हतेति वदन् राममुपातिष्ठन्मरुत्सुतः॥

Having made the mountain Mandâra their churning handle, the gods churned the [मन्थ्] ocean.

I sold [क्री with वि] my books and furniture, but did not get much money.

Indra reduced to atoms [मृद्] his enemy Vṛtra, who was a Brâhmaṇa. He thus committed the sin of Brâhmṇa-murder, of which we did not purify [पू] him.

When didst thou put together [ग्रन्थ्] the sayings of the Ṛishis?

If you should please [प्री] the gods by your piety, they would bestow favours on [ग्रह with अनु] you.

Râma and Lakshmaṇa lived in this forest with Sîtâ, and ate [अश्] roots and fruits.

Why did you pluck [लू with वि and प्र] from their stems the flowers in the garden, notwithstanding* I told you not to do so?

If I took [ग्रह्] Govinda's book the master would reprove me.

Did you not know [ज्ञा] that the pâṇḍavas resided for one year † in the country of Virâṭa?

Use the Genitive Absolute here. † See note, p.18.

*क्री *with* वी *Âtm* to sell.

ग्रह् *9th conj. with* अनु to receive in a friendly manner, to favour; *with* वि, to be at war with.

ज्ञा *9th conj. with* अभि, to recognize. [churn

मन्थ् *9th conj. Parasm.* to

मृद् *9th conj. Parasm.* to pound, to reduce to atoms.

इन्द्रादि (इन्द्र and आदि beginning, with Indra at the head) Indra and others.

उदरंभरि *m.n.f* (उदर n. stomach and भृ to fill) one who fills his belly or stomach, selfishly greedy.

एकाकिन् *m.n.f.* alone, solitary.

कट *m.* a mat.

कार्तिक्येकादशी *f.* (कार्तिकी *f.* belonging to the month of Kârtika, and एकादशी f. eleventh) the eleventh day of Kârtika.

कुण्डिनपुर *n.* name of a city, the capital of the Vidarbhas or Berars.

कोप *m.* anger, resentment.

चत्वार *numer.nom. plur.* four.

दमयन्ती *f.* name of a woman, the wife of Nala.

नलतुल्याकृति m.n.f. (नल *m.*,तुल्य *m.n.f.* like, and आकृति *f.* form) having the form of Nala.

नलरूपधारिन् *m.n.f.* (नल, रूप and धारिन् assumed the form of Nala.

पञ्च Numer. nom. and acc. plur. five.

परिचारक *m.* attendant.

भट *m.* a soldier.

मरुत्सुत *m.* the son of the wind, Mâruti, a monkey soldier devoted to Râma.

यत्कृते *ind.* for whose (relative) sake, for whom.

रङ्ग *m.* the place where any great thing is done, stage.

रङ्गागत *m.n.f.* come to the stage.

रूप *n.* form.

वुवूर्षु *m.n.f.* desirous of choosing.

शस्त्रास्त्र *n.* weapons of all kinds.

शास्त्रप्रतिषेध *m.* (शास्त्र *n.* scripture, and शास्त्र *m.* prohibition) scriptural prohibition.

शुल्क *m.n.* the money given to the parents of a bride originally as a purchase price.

संदेह *m* doubt.

सार्धम् *ind.* with (used with the *instrumental.*)

स्था *with* उप, to go to.

स्वयंवरकाल *m.*(स्वयंवर *m.* choice of a husband, and काल *m.* time) time of choosing a husband.

*क्री with परि, वि or अव is Âtmanepadi only.

Brâhmaṇa-murder ब्रह्महत्या f.
Churning-handle मन्थानदण्ड m. (मन्थान n. a handle), मन्थान m.
Furniture गृहोपस्कर m.
Piety भक्ति f. देवनिष्ठा f.
Reprove भर्त्स् 10th conj Âtm. with निद्,दिश् 6th conj. with प्रति and आ.
Root मूल n.
Saying वचन n. उक्ति f.
Stem स्कन्ध n.
Virâta विराट m. name of a king.
Vṛitra वृत्र m an enemy of Indra.

LESSON VII
SECOND CONJUGATION.

Present and Imperative.

In the second conjugation the terminations are directly applied to the roots.

2nd conj. Parasm. 'to go'

Present.

	Sing.	*Dual*	*Plur*
1st. pers.	यामि	यावः	यामः
2nd "	यासि	याथः	याथ
3rd "	याति	यातः	यान्ति

Imperative.

1st. pers.	यानि	याव	याम
2nd "	याहि	यातम्	यात
3rd "	यातु	याताम्	यान्तु

Here the root itself undergoes no charge. The forms are made up simply by adding the terminations. स्ना,रा,ला,पा 'to' Protect ख्या, मा, भा, प्सा, श्रा, and दा 'to cut' are to be thus conjugated.

Nearly all roots of this conjugation not ending in आ are irregular. We will proceed to notice the peculiarities of most of these.

2. The अ of अस् is dropped before the weak terminations; as स्तः 3rd pers. dual, सन्ति 3rd pers. plur.

Parasm. Present

	Sing.	*Dual*	*Plur*
1st. pers.	अस्मि	स्वः	स्मः
2nd "	असि	स्थः	स्थ
3rd "	अस्ति	स्तः	सन्ति

Here the 2nd. pers. sing. which by the rule ought to be असिस, drops one स्.

Present. Imperative.

	Sing.	*Dual*	*Plur*
1st. pers.	असानि	असाव	असाम
2nd "	एधि	स्ताम्	स्त
3rd "	अस्तु	स्ताम्	सन्तु

The three number fo the 1st pers. being strong, the अ is not dropped; एधि, 2nd pers. sing., is irregular.

when in certain cases this root takes Âtm. terminations, the forms of the Present Tense are:-

1st. pers.	हे	स्वहे	स्महे
2nd "	से	साथे	ध्वे
3rd "	स्ते	साते	सते

The अ, is dropped, all the terminations being weak. स् is changed to ह् in the 1st per. sing. and it is dropped before ध्वे by the following rule:-

I. The preceding स् is dropped before a termination beginning with ध्.

3. The ending vowel of शी, 'to lie down', takes its Guṇa substitute before all the personal terminations.

In the case of this root र् is prefixed to the terminations of the third person plural.

Âtm. Present.

	Sing.	*Dual*	*Plur*
1st. pers.	शये	शेवहे	शेमहे
2nd "	शेषे	शयाथे	शेध्वे
3rd "	शेते	शयाते	शेरत

Âtm. Imperative.

1st. pers.	शये	शेवहे	शेमहे
2nd "	शेषे	शयाथे	शेध्वे
3rd "	शेते	शयाते	शेरते

शी becomes शे, which before vowels is changed to शय्. Hence शये, शयाथे, &c.

र् being prefixed to अते and अताम् we have रते and रताम्.

4. The ending उ (short) of roots takes its Vṛddhi substitute, *i.e.*, becomes औ, when followed by a strong termination beginning with a consonant.

II. The ending इ or उ, short or long, of a root is changed to इय् or उव् when followed by a weak termination beginning with a vowel.

नु *Parasm. Present.*

	Sing.	*Dual*	*Plur*
1st. pers.	नौमि	नुवः	नुमः
2nd "	नौषि	नुथः	नुथ
3rd "	नौति	नुतः	नुवन्ति

Parasm. Present.

1st. pers.	नवानि	नवाव	नवाम
2nd "	नुहि	नुतम्	नुत
3rd "	नौतु	नुताम्	नुवन्तु

We have नौमि, नौषि, &c., in the case of the strong terminations मि,सि, &c., They have an initial consonant, while in the 1st person Imperative, though the terminations are strong, they begin with a vowel. Hence the उ of नु is changed to Guṇa by the general rule (6, p. 12), and thus we have नो, which becomes नव् before the vowel. यु to join' is to be thus conjugated.

After स्तु and रु the the augment ई is optionally prefixed to the terminations beginning with a consonant.

Parasm. Present.

	Sing.	*Dual*	*Plur*
1st. pers.	स्तौमि-स्तवीमि	स्तुवः-स्तुवीवः	स्तुमः-स्तुवीमः
2nd "	स्तौषि-स्तवीषि	स्तुथः-स्तुवथिः	स्तुथ-स्तुवीथ
3rd "	स्तौति-स्तवीति	स्तुत-स्तुवीतः	स्तुवन्ति

Before ति and the other strong terminations the उ takes Vṛiddhi by 4, above; but when thee terminations have इ prefixed to them by 5, they cease to have an initial consonant, and hence in that case we have Guṇa and thus by the change of स्तु to स्तो and स्तव् we have स्तवीति, &C. When the weak terminations have ई prefixed, the final उ of the root becomes उव् by II, above. Hence &c.When the weak terminations have इ prefixed, the final of the root becomes by II, above. Hence स्तुवीतः, &c. The 3rd pers. अन्ति has no initial consonant, therefore no ई can be put before it. Hence we have one form only.

The forms of the Imperative should be made up on these principles. स्तौतु—स्तवीतु *3rd pers. sing.*, स्तुहि—स्तुवीहि *2nd pers. sing.*, स्तवानि *1st pers. sing.*, स्तवाव *1st pers. dual &c.*

The Âtmanepada paradigms स्तुते-स्तुवीते *Pres. 3rd pers. sing.* स्तुवाते *3rd pers. dual,* स्तुवते *3rd pers. plur.* should be constructed in the same way.

रु should be similarly conjugated.

6. After ब्रू the strong terminations beginning with a consonant have the augment ई prefixed to them.

Parasm. Present.

	Sing.	*Dual*	*Plur*
1st. pers.	ब्रवीमि	ब्रूवः	ब्रूमः
2nd "	ब्रवीषि	ब्रूथः	ब्रूथ
3rd "	ब्रवीति	ब्रूतः	ब्रुवन्ति

The last by 11., p.36. The Âtm. forms are ब्रूते *3rd pers. sing.*, ब्रुवाते *3rd pers. dual,* ब्रुवते *3rd pers. plur., &c. The Imperative 1st pers.* ब्रवाणि, *&c.*

7. The following are five irregular forms of the Present Tense of a defective root, which means 'to speak'; आह *3rd pers. sing,* आहतुः *3rd pers. dual,* आहुः *3rd pers. plur,* आत्थ *2nd pers. sing,* आहथुः *2nd pers. dual.*

8. The terminations of the first person of the Imperative as appended to सू 'to give birth to' are weak.

Âtm. Present —सूते *3rd pers. sing.,* सुवाते *3rd pers. dual,* सुवते *3rd pers. plur., &c;* Imperative —सूष्व *2nd pers. sing.* सुवै *1st pers. sing.* सुवावहै *1st pers. dual.* सुवामहै *1st pers. plur.*

9. After रुद्, स्वप्, श्वस्, अन् and जक्ष् the augment इ is prefixed to the terminations beginning with any consonant except; य्; रोदिमि, रुदिवः, &c.

Parasm. Present.

	Sing.	*Dual*	*Plur*
1st. pers.	रोदिमि	रुदिवः	रुदिमः
2nd "	रोदिषि	रुदिथः	रुदिथ
3rd "	रोदिति	रुदितः	रुदन्ति

Imperative on the same principles —रुदिहि *2nd pers. sing.,* रोदानि *1st pers. sing.,* &c. The other roots should be similarly conjugated.

The 3rd pers.plur. termination of जक्ष् loses its न्, as will be subsequently noticed.

10. The root इ 'to go' Parasm. is an exception to Rule II., p. 36. It is changed to य् before a weak termination with an initial vowel.

Parasm. Present.

	Sing.	*Dual*	*Plur*
1st. pers.	एमि	इवः	इमः
2nd "	एषि	इथः	इथ
3rd "	एति	इतः	यन्ति

Imperative—1st pers. अयानि, *&c.*

इ with अधि 'to study' Âtm. present.

1st. pers.	अधीये	अधीवहे	अधीमहे
2nd "	अधीषे	अधीयाथे	अधीध्वे
3rd "	अधीते	अधीयाते	अधीयते

Separated from अधि, the last three forms are इते, इयाते, इयते, in which we see इ is changed to इय् before आते and अते, and so on with the rest.

1st pers. Imperat.—अध्ययै-अध्ययावहै-अध्ययामहै इ taking its Guṇa becomes ए, which again is changed to अय् and with the terminations the forms are अयै, &c.

Âtm.

Imperative.

1st. pers.	आसै	आसावहै	आसामहै
2nd "	आस्स्व	आसाथाम्	आध्वम्
3rd "	आस्ताम्	आसाताम्	आसताम्

By I, p. 35, स् is dropped before ध्वम्.

अस्मिञ्जगति ये सन्ति कवयस्तान्नमस्कृत्यैतं ग्रन्थमारभे।

पृच्छ बालकः किं रोदिति।

हे कृपानिधे जगदात्मंस्त्वां ब्रह्मादयः सर्वे देवाः स्तुवन्त्यृ षयश्च सर्वे।

ईदृशं त्वां शरणमुपैमि। प्रसीद। पाहि मां नरकाद्घोरात्।

अस्यां पाठशालायां बालकाः काव्यमधीयते।

तरुषु मधुरं रुवन्ति वायुश्च शीतलो वाति तस्माद्रम्यमिदं स्थानम्। अत्रैव वृक्षमूले शिलामध्यासामहै*।

भो भोः पौराः क्व गतोऽस्माकं महाराजः। किं ब्रूथ। देव्या सह क्रीडाशैलमध्यास्त इति। एवमस्तु। अहं तत्र गच्छामि सर्वं च वृत्तं कथयामि।

अकिंचनो वितृष्णश्च सुखं स्वपिति रात्रौ।

ये प्राणन्ति जीवन्ति च तेषां जडानां चादिहेतुं मे ब्रूहि।

वत्से समाश्वसिहि समाश्वसिहि। अयमागतस्तव पुत्रको यं त्वं मृत मन्यसे।

गोविन्दः स्मितेनात्मनः कोपमह्नुते।

अश्विनौ मदनमपि सौन्दर्येऽतिशयाते।

रात्रावुदयते चन्द्रो दिवोदयति भास्करः।

उदेति स सदैवोग्रं नोदीयन्ते च विद्विषः॥

प्राणिनामुपकाराय प्राणिति प्रियदर्शनः।

प्राण्यते पुण्यपुरुषः श्रेयसे यशसे च सः॥

स स्तौति भास्करं भक्त्या नौति पापहरं हरम्॥

एधि कार्यंकरस्त्वं मे गत्वा प्रवद राघवम्।

दिदृक्षुर्मैथिली राम पश्यतु त्वाऽविलम्बितम्॥

ते जन्मभाजः खलु जीवलोके येषां मनो ध्यायति विश्वनाथम्।

वाणी गुणान्स्तौति कथां शृणोति श्रोत्रद्वयं ते भवमुत्तरन्ति॥

धर्मदूषण नूनं त्वं नाजाना नाशृणोरिदम्।

निराकृत्य यथा बन्धूंल्लघुत्वं यात्यसंशयम्॥

भूमौ शेते दशग्रीवो महार्हशयनोचितः।

नेक्षते विह्वलं मां च न मे वाचं प्रयच्छति॥

समाश्वसिमि केनाहं कथं प्राणिमि दुर्गतः।

लोकत्रयपतिर्भ्राता यस्य मे स्वपिति क्षितौ॥

---

*When शी, स्था and आस् are preceded by the preposition अधि, they govern the accusative of the place where the actions are preformed.

रोदिम्यनाथमात्मानं बन्धुना रहितस्त्वया।
प्रमाणं नोपकाराणामवगच्छामि यस्य ते॥
आस्ते भग आसीनस्योर्ध्वस्तिष्ठति तिष्ठतः।
शेते निपद्यमानस्य चराति* चरतो भगः॥
गाधोदके मत्स्य इव सुखं विन्देत कस्तदा।
अनवाप्तेषु कामेषु मृत्युरभ्येति मानवम्॥
जातमेवान्तकोऽन्ताय जरा चान्वेति देहिनम्।
अनुषक्ता ह्ययेनैते भावाः स्थावरजङ्गमाः॥
निन्दन्तु नीतनिपुणा यदि वा स्तुवन्तु।
अद्यैव वा मरणमस्तु युगान्तरे वा
न्याय्यात्पथः प्रविचलन्ति पदं न धीराः॥

We do not believe (श्वस् with वि) in Govinda's words

You praise those, who deserve censure.

The birds sleep (or lie down) (शी) on the banks of the Gomatî.

Child, do not cry, (रुद्) here comes (इ with अभि and आ) your mother with (having taken) sweetmeat in her hands.

These two cows bring forth (सू) calves every year.

Dost thou not know (इ with अव) that Janaka was Râma's father-in-law?

What subject do thou and thy brother study (इ Âtm. with अधि) at school ?

On the tops of high mountains men respire (श्वस् with नि) with difficulty.

It seems (भा) to me that the people of this place are poor.

Breathes (अन् with प्र) there the man who smites the poor and the helpless?

A lazy man sleeps (स्वप्) for a long time.

Those, who adore (आस् with उप) another than the true God, do not attain eternal felicity.

Tell (ब्रू) us what srot of an animal a horse is.

---

*Irregular for चरति or र lengthened for the sake of the metre.

VOCABULARY VII.

Roots of the Second Conjugation.

अन् Parasm. to breathe; प्र, *with* to breathe, to live.

*अस् Parasm. to be.

आस् Âtm. to sit; *with* अधि, to sit; *with* उप, to adore, to worship.

इ Parasm. to go; *with* शरणम् and उप, to submit, *with* अधि, to go towards; *with* आ, to come; *with* अव to know; *with* उद्, to rise, to flourish.

इ *with* अधि Âtm. to study.

ख्या *Parasm.* to tell.

जक्ष् *Parasm.* to eat.

दा *Parasm.* to cut.

नु *Parasm.* to praise.

पा *Parasm.* to protect.

प्सा *Parasm.* to devour.

*ब्रू Parsam. and Âtm to speak.

भा Parsam. to seem, to appear, to shine.

या *Parasm.* to go.

यु *Parasm.* to join.

रा *Parasm.* to give. [aloud.

रु *Parasm.* to make noise, to cry.

रुद् *Parasm.* to weep, to bewail, to lament for.

ला *parasm.* to give or take.

वस् *Âtm.* to dress.

वा *Parasm.* to blow.

शी *Âtm.* to lie down, to sleeps; *with* अति, to surpass.

श्रा *parasm.* to cook.

श्वस् *parasm.* to breathe; with नि, to respire; *with* वि, to believe, to cofide; *with* सम् and आ, to calm one-self, to take courage.

सू *Âtm.* to give birth to.

स्तु *Parsam.* and *tm.* to praise.

स्ना *Parsam.* to bathe.

स्नु *Parsam.* to drop, to ooze

स्वप् *Parsam.* to sleep.

ह्नु *Âtm.* to conceal: *with* अप or *with* नि.

अकिंचन *m. n. f.* (अ, not and किंचन *n.* something) he who has nothing, poor.

अण् *4th conj. Âtm.* with प्र, to breathe, to live.

अनाथ *m. n. j.* helpless.

अनुषक्त (अनु and सक्त *past pass part.* of सञ्ज्) accompanied.

अन्त *m.* end, destruction.

अन्तक *m.* the god of death.

अय् *1st conj.* Âtm. *with* उद् to rise.

अविलम्बितम् *adv.* without delay.

अश्विन् *m.* (used in the dual) the twin celestial physicians so called.

असंशयम् *adv.* without doubt.

आदिहेतु *m.* the first cause. आसीन *m.n.f.* sitting (pres part. of आस्).

---

*The roots अस् and ब्रू are used in the conjugational tenses only.

आहव m. a battle.

इ 1st conj. Parasm. *with* **उद्** to rise.

ई 4th conj. Âtm. *with* **उद्** to rise, to rise up.

उग्रम् *adv.* mightily, powerfully, formidably.

उपकार *m.* abenevolent action, doing good to another.

ऊर्ध्व *m.n.f.* erect, upper.

कार्यंकर *m.n.f.* one who does some business (for another).

काव्य n.a poem.

कृ *8th conj. with* **नमस्** to bow to; *with* **निस्** and **आ**, to repudiate, to give up, to forsake.

कृपानिधि *m.* (**कृपा** *f.* mercy, and **निधि** *m.* store) store of mercy, one very merciful.

क्रीडाशैल *m.* (**क्रीडा** *f.* amusement, diversion, **शैल** m. a mountian) a pleasure mountain or embankment.

क्षिति *f.* the earth, the ground.

खलु *ind.* verily.

गाधोदक *n.* (**गाध** *m.n.f* shallow and **उदक** n. water shallow water.

गोमती *f.* name of a river.

घोर *m. f.* horrible.

चल् *with* **प्र** and **वि** to remove, to move aside.

जगदात्मन् *m.* (**जगत्** n. the world, and **आत्मन्** *m.* the soul) the Soul of the world.

जड *m.n.f.* inanimate.

जन्मभाज् *m.n.f.* one who is born; *m.* a man.

जीवलोक *m.* the world of living beings, this world.

दरिद्र *m.n.f.* poor.

दिदृक्षु *m.n.f.* desirous of seeing.

दिवा *ind.* adv. by day.

दुर्गत *m.n.f.* distressed, miserable.

देहिन् *m.* he who has a body; a *n.* a collection of two.

दूष *m.n.f.* one that contaminates or violates what is right.

ध्यै *1st conj. Parasm.* to contemplate or meditate upon.

नरक *m.n.* hell.

निपद्यमान *pres part.* of **पद्** *with* **नि**, lying down.

नीतिनिपुण *m.n.f.* (**नीति** *f.* politics or prudence, **निपुण** *m.n.f.* proficient) proficient in politics, or very prudent.

नूनम् *ind.* certainly, verily.

न्याय्य *m.n.f.* just, right, proper.

पथः (*ablative sing.* of **पथिन्** *m.* road) form the way.

पद *n.* a footstep.

पापहर *m.n.f.* one that takes away sin.

पुण्यपुरुष *m.* a holy or virtuous man.

प्रमाण *n.* measure, extent.

प्रियदर्शन *m.n.f.* one with a pleasing look.

ब्रह्मन् *n.* the divine cause and essence of the universe.

ब्रह्मादि *m.* (**ब्रह्मन्** *m.* and **आदि** beginning) the god rahmâ and others.

भग *m.* luck, prosperity.

भव *m.* the world, worldly existence.

भाव *m.* a thing.

भास्कर *m.* the sun.

भिन्न *m.n.f.* different.

मधुरम् *adv.* sweetly.

महाराज *m.* lord, a great king.

महार्हशयनोचित *m.n.f.* (महार्ह *m.n.f.* costly, शयन *n.* a bed, उचित *m.n.f.* to) accustomed or used to costly or rich beds.

मानव *m.* a man.

मैथिली *f.* princess of Mithilâ, Sitâ.

यथेष्टम् *adv.* according to fancy, to one's heart's content, as one chooses.

युगान्तर *n.* (युग *n.* age, period, अन्तर another) another age or period.

रम्य *m.n.f.* pleasant.

रहित *m.n.f.* deprived of, bereft of.

राघव *m.* a descendant of Raghu.

लघुत्व *n.* littleness, dishonour.

लोकत्रयपति *m.* (त्रय n. a collection of three, पति *m.* lord) the lord of the three worlds, *viz.* Heaven, the Earth and the lower regions.

वत्सा *f.* dear, a female child.

वितृष्ण *m.n.f.* (वि devoid of, and तृष्णा *f.* desire) free from any desire.

विश् *with* सम् and आ, to enter in, come in.

विश्वनाथ *m.* Lord of the universe, God.

विह्वल *m.n.f.* overwhelmed, afflicted.

वृक्षमूल *n.* (वृक्ष *m.* a tree and मूल *n.* root) the root of a tree.

वृत्त *n.* what has taken place, an event.

शीतल *m.n.f.* cool.

श्रोत्रद्वय *n.* a pair of ears.

सद् (सीद्) *Ist. conj. Parasm.* to sit; *with* प, to be gracious or pleased.

सायम् *adv.* in the evening.

स्थावरजङ्गम *m.n.f.* (स्थावर *m.n.f.* immoveable and जङ्गम *m.n.f* moveable) immoveable and moveable.

स्मित *n.* smile.

हर *m.* the god Śiva.

Calf वत्स *m.*

Difficulty असौकर्य *n.* कष्ट *n.*

Father-in-law श्वशुर *m.*

Helpless अनाथ *m.n.f.*

High तुच्छ *m.n.f.*

Lazy अलस *m.n.f.* तन्निरत *m.n.f.* place of this अवस्थ *m.n.f.*

Stnite कृ 8th conj with आप or 10th नि; पीड् conj.

Subject विषय *m.*

Taken, having, गृहीत्वा *absolutive* of ग्रह्.

The God; true सत्यस्वरूप *m.n.f.* God परमात्मन् *m.*

What sort of कीदृश *m.n.f.*

Word वचस् *n.* वचन *n.*

LESSON VII

SECOND CONJUGATION—*continued.*

Imperfect and Potential.

1. After roots ending आ in the termination of the Imperfect third person plural is optionally उस्, before which the ending vowel is dropped.

Imperfect.

	Sing.	*Dual*	*Plur*
1st. pers.	अयाम्	अयाव	अयाम
2nd "	अयाः	अयातम्	अयात
3rd "	अयात्	अयाताम्	अयान्-अयुः

Here by dropping the आ of या and appending the temporal. augment we have अय् and with उस्, अयुः

Potential.

	Sing.	*Dual*	*Plur*
1st. pers.	यायाम्	यायाव	यायाम
2nd "	यायाः	यायातम्	यायात
3rd "	यायात्	यायाताम्	यायुः

The terminations are same as those given in 2. p. 21.

2. After the root अस् 'to be', the terminations स् and त् of the Imperfect take the augment ई long.

1st. pers.	आसम्	आस्व	आस्म
2nd "	आसीः	आस्तम्	आस्त
3rd "	आसीत्	आस्ताम्	आसन्
pot.3rd pers.	स्यात्	स्याताम्	स्युः, &c.

3. After रुद्, स्वप्, श्वस्, अन् and, जक्ष् the augment ई or अ is prefixed to the स् and त् of the Imperfect.

1st. pers.	अरोदम्	अरुदिव	अरुदिम
2nd "	{ अरोदीः / अरोदः }	अरुदितम्	अरुदित
3rd "	{ आसीत् / अरोदत् }	आस्ताम्	आसन्

For the insertion of इ in अरुदिताम् &c. see 9, p.37. The third pers. plur. termination in the case of जक्ष् is उस्, which will be noticed hereafter.

	Sing.	Dual	Plur
Potential—3rd pers.	रुद्यात्	रुद्याताम्	रुद्युः *&c.*
शी { *Imperf. 3rd pers.*	अशेत	शयीयाताम्	शयीरन्
Pot. "	शयीत	शयीयाताम्	शयीरन्

See 3, p.35 and for the terminations, 1, p. 17, and 4, p. 22.

स्तु			
Imperf. 3rd pers.	अस्तौत् अस्तवीत् अस्तुत अस्तुवीत	अस्तुताम् अस्तुवीताम् अस्तुवाताम्	अस्तुवन् *Parasm.* अस्तुवत *Âtm.*
Pot. 3rd pers.	स्तुयात् स्तुवीयात् स्तुवीत	स्तुर्याताम् स्तुवीयाताम् स्तुवीयाताम्	स्तुयुः *Parasm.* स्तुवीयः स्तुवरिन् *Âtm.*

For Vṛidhi see 4, p. 36, and for the optional augment ई, 5, p. 36, and explanation.

	Sing.	Dual	Plur
Parasm. Imperf. 3rd pers	अब्रवीत्	अब्रूताम्	अब्रुवन्
Âtm. " "	अब्रूत	अब्रुवाताम्	अब्रुवत
Parasm. Pot. "	ब्रूयात्	ब्रूयाताम्	ब्रूयुः
Âtm. " "	ब्रुवति	ब्रुवीयाताम्	ब्रुवीरन्

See 6, p. 37.

इ *imperf. 3rd pers.*	ऐत्	ऐताम्	आयन्

The temporal augment is आ, which, along with the ए in the sing. and the इ in other places, takes the Vridhi of ए or इ (see First Book, p. 62.). In the third pers. plur. इ with अन् forms यन् (10, p. 38) and with the temporal augment, आयन्.

Âtm. with *Imperf. 3rd pers.*

Before आताम् the इ is changed to इय् (11, p. 36), which with the termination, is इयाताम् ; with the temporal augment it is ऐयाताम् as in the last case, and with अधि, अध्यैयाताम्. It undergoes the same changes before all other vowel terminations. Pot. *3rd pers. sing.* अधीयीत, &c.

2nd pers. Imperf. आस्थाः आसाथाम् आध्वम्.

अहरहः स्नात्वा संध्यामुपासीत।

दशरथस्य भार्या कौसल्या चैत्रे नवम्यां तिथौ मध्याह्ने पुत्रं रामं प्रासूत।

पारिक्षितस्य जनमेजयस्य सत्रं सारमेयोऽभ्यैत्।

तत्र च जनमेजयस्यर्त्विजस्तमताडयन्।

सोऽरोदीद्रुदंश्च मातरमयात्।

मातापृच्छद्वत्स किं रोदिषि।

सोऽब्रवीज्जनमेजयस्य सत्रमायं तत्र केऽपि मां प्राहरन्।

मातावदर्त्कि त्वमकरोः किं तानस्पृशः।

सोऽभाषत नाहं मर्यादामत्यायम्।

सरमा सत्रभूमिं गत्वोच्चैर्वाचाब्रूत।

अयं मे पुत्रको * न युष्मानस्पृशत्तत्किमेनमनपराधिनमताडयत।

तां न कोऽपि प्रत्यभाषत। तेन क्रुद्धा सा देवशुनी सरमा जनमेजयं शप्त्वा गृहमयात्।

द्रोणाच्छस्त्रविद्यामध्यैयत पाण्डवाः कुशलवौ वाल्मीकेरध्यैयातां कर्णश्च परशुरामादध्यैत।

अभिवाद्य गुरुं ब्रूयादधीष्वां भगवन्निति।

अनिषण्णो गुरौ नासीत।

विदेहानुपयन्तो वयमेकरात्रं गङ्गायास्तीरेऽवसाम तत्र च पूर्वरात्रे नाना रम्याः कथाः कृत्वानन्तरमस्वपिम।

ब्रूयात्क्षमी गभीरोऽसीति बत युधिष्ठिर प्रभुं को न।

कथमहं बली स्यां कथं मयि प्रजा विश्वस्युः कथं च प्रकृतयो

मामुपासीरन्नित्येवं चिन्तयतस्तस्य रात्रिरयात्।

ततः प्रामुह्यतां वीरौ राघवावरुतां तथा।

उष्णं च प्राणितां दीर्घमुच्चैर्व्याक्रोशतां तथा॥

यथा काष्ठं च समेयातां महोदधौ।

समेत्य च व्यपेयातां तद्वद्भूतसमागमः॥

The sons of Dhṛitaràshtra gambled with the sons of Pându and deprived them of all their wealth. The Pâṇḍavas then went [इ†] to a forest.

---

*क is a diminutive termination.

† इ with अधि is here used in the sense of teaching.

Thither many Brâmanas follwed [इ with अनु] them.

Then said [ब्रू] Yudhishtthira to them, "You should not follow [इ with अनु] us, we are [अस्] now without wealth and cannot give you food."

The Brâhmanas then said [ब्रू], "We are [अस्] able to earn our own food."

Yudhishthira then did not reject [ख्या with प्रति and आ] them.

But he was* unwilling that the Brâhmanas should work for their own food.

He then asked his spiritual adviser what he should do.

He told him, "Praise [स्तु] the sun."

Yudhishthira then praised [स्तु] the sun, and when the sun was pleased, got from him a cooking utensil, from which they always got as much food as they wanted.

The wives of Sagara gave birth to [स्तु] many sons.

I did not sleep [स्वप्] last night.

When did you bathe [स्ना] in the waters of the Ganges?

The women of Vraja cried [रुद्] aloud when Krishna went to Mathurâ.

I studied [इ with अधि] Nyâya at Benares.

If I were [अस्] in Hastinâpura, I should say [ब्रू] to Dhritarâshtra that it was not proper to deprive the Pândavas of their wealth by dishonest gambling.

None should rely [श्वस् with वि] on the words of the wicked.

VOCABULARY VIII.

अनपराधिन् *m. n. f.* guiltess.
अनिषण्ण *m. n. f.* not sitting.
अहरहः *ind.* every day.
आप् *5th conj. with* अव, to attain.
इ *with* वि and अप, to separate; *with* सम् and आ, to unite, to come together.
उच्चैः *ind* adv. loudly, aloud.
उष्णम् *adv.* hotly.
एकरात्र *n.* one night.
कर्ण *m.a* proper name. [bearin
क्षमिन् *m. m. f.* patient, for-
कुश *m.* and लव *m.* sons of Râma.
क्रुश् *1st conj. parasm. with* वि and आ, to cry out aloud, to lament
गभीर *m. n. f.* deep, grave.

*Use a verb having the sense of *willing* with न.

चैत्र *m.* the first month of the Hindu year.

जनमेजय name of the son of . Parikshit, grandson of Arjuna.

तद्वत् odv. like that, in the same manner.

तिथि *m. f.* a day of th month.

दीर्घम् *adv.* for a long time, long, deeply.

देवशुनी *f.* the bitch of the gods.

श्रोण *m.* a proper name. [night.]

नवमी *f* the ninth day of the fort-

नाना *ind.* different, many.

पारिक्षित *m.* son of Parikshit.

पूर्वरात्र *m.* (**पूर्व** prior, **रात्रि** *f.* the night) the prior or first part of the night.

प्रकृति *f.* subject, people, ministerial officers.

बत *ind. particle* implying surprise, sorrow, &c. [answer.

भाष् *1st conj. Ãtm.* with **प्रति,** to

भूतसमागम *m.* coming together or union of animals or beings.

मध्याह्न *m* (**मध्य** the middle and **अहन्** n. day*)* midday.

मर्यादा *f.* bound, limit. [noon.]

महोदधि *m.* the great ocean

मुह् *with.* **प्र,** to faint.

वाल्मीकि *m.* the name of a sage.

विदेह *m.* the name of a country *(in the plural).*

शप् *1st conj. Parasm* and *Ãtm.* to course; **शप्त्वा** *ind. Past part.*

शस्त्रविद्या *f.* (**शस्त्र** *and* **विद्या**) *art* or knowledge of war.

सत्र *n.* a sacrificial session.

सत्रभूमि *f.* the place of sacrifice.

सरमा *f.* name of the bitch of the gods.

संध्या *f.* twilight [at the moraing and evening twilights and in the noon prayers are offered by Brâhmanas]. [dog.

सारमेय *m.* the son of Sarmamâ, a

Aloud **उच्चैः** *ind.*

Cooking utensil **स्थाली** *f.*

Deprive of **ह** *1st conj.* with **अप.**

Dishonest gambling **कपटद्यूत** *n.* (**कपट** *n.* fraud, and **द्यूत** *n.* gambling).

Food **अन्न** *n.*

Gamble **दिव्** *4th conj.* parasm.

Last night **गता रात्रि** *f.*

Mathurâ **मथुरा** *f.* the name of a place.

Proper **युक्त** *past. psrt.* of **युज्;**

उचित *m. n. f.* [kind.

Sagara **सगर** *m.* the name of a

Spiritual adviser **उपाध्याय** *m.*

पुरोहित *m.* [**अप.**

What **ईक्ष्** *1st conj.* Ãtm. with

Whcked (person) **शठ** *m.* **खल** *m.* **दुरात्मन्** *m.*

Whithout wealth **धनहीन** *m. n. f.*

Women of Vraja. **व्रजाङ्गनाः** *f.* *nom. plur.*

Work **परिश्रम कृ** *8th conj.* Parasm. and Ãtm.

LESSON IX
SECOND CONJUGATION—continued.

In applying the terminations to the remaining roots of this conjugation several phonetic changes take place which we will now notice.

I. The ending ह् of a root is changed to ढ्, when it is followed by any consonant, except a nasal or a semi-vowel, or * by nothing.

Thus, लिह् which, followed by ति, the 3rd pers. sing. termination of the Present] becomes first लेह् + ति by 6, p. 12, is changed to लेह् + ति because the त् of ति is not a nasal or a semi-vowel Now,

II. The initial त् and थ् of a termination following a soft aspirate or the fourth letter of a class are changed to ध्.

The ढ् of लेढ् is a soft aspirate, therefore the ति is changed to धि, and thus we have लेढ् + धि. When linguals and dentals are combined, the dentals substitute the corresponding linguals (see note*, p. 21, First Book). We thus get लेढ् + ढि. Then,

III. ढ् followed by ढ् is dropped, and the preceding vowel (except ऋ), if short, is made long.

Thus, we come to लेढि. When the 3rd pers. dual termination तस् is applied, we have by I. लिढ् + तस् by II. लिढ् + धस् and then लिढ् + ढस्, and by III. लीढः :, the short इ being rendered long. There is no Guṇa here, the termination तस् being weak (uide 4, p. 12). The 3rd pers. plur. is लिहन्ति; the termination अन्ति beginning with a vowel, no phonetic change takes place. In the 2nd pers. sing. We have, सि being strong, लिढ् + सि by I. Here, before can सि be changed to षि by note*, p.21, First Book, we have a special rule, uiz:—

IV. ढ् or ष् followed by स् is changed to क्.

---

*Followed by nothing, i. e., the letter stands at the end of a word or form. It is not meant that is should not be followed by any other word in a sentence. The expression is to be understood in the sense throughout.

By this we get लेक् + सि. Then सि becomes षि by note‡, p. 97, First Book. Thus we arrive at लेक्षि.

Hence the paradigms of the Present Thnse Parasm. are:—

	Sing.	*Dual.*	*Plur.*
1st pers.	लेह्मि	लिह्वः	लिह्मः
2nd "	लेक्षि	लीढः	लीढ
3rd "	लेढि	लीढः	लिहन्ति

लीढः 2nd pers. dual and लीढ 2nd pers. plur. should be made up like लीढः 3rd pers, dual. Before मि, वः and मः no phonetic change takes place, मि and मः beginning with a nasal and वः with a semi-vowel. The Âtm. forms are as follows:—

1st pers.	लिहे	लिह्वहे	लिह्महे
2nd "	लिक्षे	लिहाथे	लिढ्वे
3rd "	लीढे	लीहाते	लिहते

These should be made up in the same way as those snown above.

1. The second person sing. termination of the Parasm. Imperative of the second group of conjugation is धि when the base ends in any consonant except a nasal or a semi-vowel.

Imperative.

Parasm.

1st pers.	लेहानि	लेहाव	लेहाम
2nd "	लीढि	लीढम्	लीढ
3rd "	लेढु	लीढाम्	लिहन्तु

Atm.

Remember that the three nos. of the 1st pers. are strong, and the 2nd pers. sing. Parasm. weak.

V. Roots beginning with द् and ending in ह् change the ह् to घ् under the same circumstances as those mentioned in Rule I.

Thus दुह्, when the termination ति is appended to it, becomes, ति being strong, दोघ् + ति. By II., p.49, it is दोघ् + धि. Then

VI. In the body of a word or grammatical form

the preceding consonant, except a nasal, subsitutes the third or soft unaspirate of its class, when followed by the third or fourth letter (soft unaspirate or aspirate) For ष्, ड् is substituted in these circumstances.

Thus we have दोग् + धि i. e. दोग्धि. The dual should be similarly made up. In the plural दुहन्ति, there is no phonetic change. When the 2nd pers. sing. सि is appended, we have by V. दोघ् + सि. In this condition, before applying the rule in notet† p. 5, First Book, we have.

VII. When a root has or consists of a syllable beginning with ब्, ग्, द्, and ending with a soft aspirate (fourts leeter), the ब् is changed to भ्, ग् to घ्, and द् to ध्, when the syllable is followed by स्, ध्व् or nothing.

By this we have धोघ् + सि; then by note†, p. 5, First Book धोक् + षि, by† p. 97, First Book, धोक् + सि; written धोक्षि. The paradigms, therefore, are :—

Parasm. Present.

	Sing.	*Dual.*	*Plur.*
1st pers.	दोह्मि	दुह्वः	दुह्मः
2nd "	धोक्षि	दुग्धः	दुग्ध
3rd "	दोग्धि	दुग्धः	दुहन्ति

Atm. Pres. 3rd pers. दुग्धे-दुहाते-दुहते; *2nd pers.* धुक्षे-दुहाथे-धुग्ध्वे, *&c.*

Parasm. Imperat. 3rd pers. दोग्धु-दुग्धाम्-दुहन्तु, *&c.*

Atm. Imperat 3rd pers. दुग्धाम्-दुहाताम्-दुहताम्: *2nd pers.* धुक्ष्व-दुहाथाम्-धुग्ध्वम्, *&c.*

2. a. The of is dropped before a weak termination beginning with a consonant except a nasal or a semi-vowel, and the penultimate अ before one beginning with a vowel.

b. जहि is the second person singular of the Imperative.

c. The ह् of this root is vhanged to when immediately followed by न्,

VIII. In the body of a word or grammatical form न् and म्

are changed to the nasal of the class to which the following letter (not nasal itself) belongs, and to an anusuâra when followed by ह्, स्, श् and ष्.

Parasm. Present.

	Sing.	*Dual.*	*Plur.*
1st pers.	हन्मि	हन्वः	हन्मः
2nd "	हंसि	हथः	हथ
3rd "	हन्ति	हतः	घ्नन्ति

Here न् is dropped in the 2nd and 3rd pers. dual and 2nd pers. plur., because the termination are weak and have an initial consonant which is neither a nasalnor a semi-vowel, and is changed to an anusvûra by VIII before सि. अन्ति being a weak termination with an initial vowel, penultimate अ is dropped, and we have ह्न् + अन्ति, which by 2 c. is घ्नन्ति.

when in certain cases this root takes Âtmanepada terminations the forms of the Present Tense are :—

1st pers.	घ्ने	हन्वहे	हन्महे
2nd "	हसे	घ्नाथे	हध्वे
3rd "	हते	घ्नाते	घ्नते

As above, न् is dropped here before the consonants which are neither nasals nor semi-vowels, and अ before the vowels. In the latter case ह् is changed to घ्.

Imperat. Parasm. 3rd pers. हन्तु-हताम्-घ्नन्तु. *2nd pers. sing.* जहि. *1st pers. sing.* हनानि. *Âtm. 3rd pers.* हताम्-घ्नाताम्, *&c.*

3. The roots ईश् and ईड् have the augment इ attached to them before terminations beginning with स् and ध्व्, except that of the Imperfect second person plural.

IX. Roots ending in or and the rcots व्रश्च्, भ्रस्ज्, सृज् भृज्, यज्, राज्, भ्राज् change their final to ष्, when followed by any consonant except a nasal or a semi-vowel, or by nothing

ईश् *Âtm. Present.*

	Sing.	*Dual.*	*Plur.*
1st pers.	ईशे	ईश्वहे	ईश्महे
2nd "	ईशिषे	ईशाथे	ईशिध्वे
3rd "	ईष्टे	ईशाते	ईशते

Before ते, the श् of this is changed to ष्. Then the dental त् becoming ट्, ते becomes टे; hence we have ईष्टे. To से and ध्वे the augment इ being prefixed, we have ईशिषे and ईशिध्वे.

Imperat. 3rd pers. ईष्टाम्-ईशाताम्-ईशताम्, &c.; ईशै *1st pers. sing.*

4. The penultimate ऋ of मृज् takes its Vriddhi substitute before the strong termination, and optionally before the weak ones with an initial vowel.

मृज् *Present.*

1st pers.	मार्ज्मि	मृज्वः	मृज्मः
2nd "	मार्क्षि	मृष्ठः	मृष्ठ
3rd "	मार्ष्टि	मृष्टः	मृजन्ति-मार्जन्ति

The final ज् of this being changed to ष् before ति, तस् &c, by IX., we have मार्ष्टि मृष्टः, &c. In the first case and in the sing. of the other persons, the ऋ is changed to आर् by the above rule and optionally so in the 3rd pers. plur. Before सि, ज् is changed to ष् by IX. and ष् to क् by IV., p. 49, and the सि itself becoming षि, we have मार्क्षि.

Imperat. 3rd pers. मार्ष्टु-मृष्टाम्-मृजन्तु or मार्जन्तु. *2nd pers sing* मृड्ढि.

In the last, termination is धि by 1, p. 50; the ज् of मृज् is chaged to ष् by IX., and this ष् becomes ड् by VI. pp. 50-51.

5. The व of वश् is changed to उ before the weak terminations.

1st pers.	वश्मि	उश्वः	उश्मः
2nd "	वक्षि	उष्ठः	उष्ठ
3rd "	वष्टि	उष्टः	उशन्ति

वश्+ति-वष्+ति by IX., p. 52.—वष्+टि (note*. p.21, F.B.)-वष्टि; वश्+सि-वष्+सि by IX., p. 52.—वक्+सि by IV., p. 49.—वक्+षि-वक्षि. उष्टः, &c.by above.

वश्+धि by 1, p. 50-उश्+धि-उष्+धि-उष्+ढि (note*, p.21, F.B.)-उड्ढि. by VI., pp. 50-51.

6. The vowel of *Parasm.* is changed to before the consonantal weak terminations.

7. The termination of the third person plural, as appended to the roots शास्, जक्ष् चकास्, दरिद्रा and जागृ, loses its न्.

The Imperative second person singular of शास् is शाधि and of चकास्, चकाद्धि or चकाधि.

	Sing.	*Dual.*	*Plur.*
1st pers.	शास्मि	शिष्वः	शिष्मः
2nd "	शास्सि	शिष्ठः	शिष्ठ
3rd "	शास्ति	शिष्टः	शासति

शास्+तस्—शिस्+तस् by 6–शिष्+तस् (स् being changed to ष्)—शिष्+टस् (note*, p. 21, F.B.)–शिष्टः, शास्+अति by 7 (not अन्ति)—शासति.

जागृ—*Parasm. Present 3rd pers.* जागर्ति—जागृतः—जाग्रति. *Imperat. 2nd pers sing.* जागृहि. *1st pers. sing.* जागराणि.

8. The final आ of दरिद्रा is dropped before the weak terminations beginning with a vowel and changed to इ before those with an initial consonant.

3rd pers. दारिद्राति-दरिद्रितः-दरिद्रति, *&c.*

9. The Imperative forms of विद् are optionally made up by adding the corresponding forms of कृ to विदाम्.

Imperative 3rd pers. वेत्तु or विदांकरोतु-वित्ताम् or विदांकुरुताम्-विदन्तु or विदांकुर्वन्तु, *&c.*

Present 3rd pers. वेत्ति, वित्तः; विदन्ति, *&c.*

X. When a conjunct consonant, the first member of which is स् or क्, is at the end of a word, or is followed by any consonant, except a nasal or a semi-vowel, the स् or क् is dropped.

Thus in चक्ष्+ते, the first member of क्ष् is and it is followed ते, by the त् of which is not a semi-vowel nor a nasal; hence क् is dropped, and we have चष्+ते and by note*, p. 21, F.B., चष्टे. In the case of the 2nd pers. sing. we have चक्ष्+से; the क् is dropped as above and we have चष्+से; then by IV., p. 49, चक्+से, and से becoming षे (note‡, p. 97, F. B.), the form is चक्षे. The paradigms, therefore, are:—

चक्ष् *Ātm. Present.*

	Sing.	*Dual.*	*Plur.*
1st pers.	चक्षे	चक्ष्वहे	चक्ष्महे
2nd "	चक्षे	चक्षाथे	चड्ढ्वे
3rd "	चष्टे	चक्षाते	चक्षते

चक्ष्+ध्वे–by X, चष्+ध्वे–by note*, p. 21., F.B. चष्+ढ्–and by VI., pp. 50-51, चड्ढ्वे.

Imperative 3rd pers. चष्टाम्-चक्षाताम्, &c., &c.

द्विष्-द्वेष्टि *3rd pers. sing. pres.* &c. दिह्-देग्धि *3rd pers. sing. pres. Parasm.*, &c.

सविता वै प्रसवानामीष्टे*।

गोपः सायं धेनूर्दोग्धि † पयः।

अधुनाखिलं भरतवर्षं महाप्रतापा आङ्ग्लभौमाः प्रशासति।

तस्मिन्पुष्पे भ्रमरौ मधु लीढः।

अग्निमीळे पुरोहितं यज्ञस्य देवमृत्विजम्।

योऽस्मान्द्वेष्टि यं च वयं द्विष्मस्तं घ्नन्त्विमान्यस्माभिः पठ्यमानानि मन्त्राक्षराणि।

हे जगन्नाथाखिलस्यैतस्य वस्तुजातस्य त्वमीशिषे।

हे दीनबन्धो यद्यन्मे नम्रस्य पापं भवेत्तत्तत्प्रतिजहि।

शत्रुं हन्तुं शरान्विषेण देग्धि।

आचक्ष्व क्व मामेकाकिनीमत्र विहायाकरुण यासि।

यं मां धर्ममाचड्ढ्वे † तमेव प्रत्यहमाचरामि।

वत्से न युक्तं ते मङ्गलकाले रोदितुं प्रमृड्ढ्यश्रूणि। अथवा सख्यौ प्रमृष्टाम्।

भाष्यकृत्पतञ्जलिः कात्यायनस्य वचनानि विस्तरतो व्याचष्टे।

शिष्यस्तेऽहं शाधि मां त्वां प्रपन्नम्।

शास्त्यरीन् धर्ममाशास्ते कीर्तिमाशंसते पराम्।

स शंसति सतां वृत्तं विशसत्युत्पथास्थितान्॥

ईट्टे त्रिविष्टपास्थाने तत्कीर्तिं वासवः स्वयम्।

ईडयन्ति नरेन्द्राश्च भूमावुद्भूतविस्मयाः॥

या निशा सर्वभूतानां तस्यां जागर्ति संयमी।

---

*The root ईश् governs the genitive of the object.

† See note †, p. 3.

यस्यां जाग्रति भूतानि सा निशा पश्यतो मुनेः ॥
य एनं* वेत्ति हन्तारं यश्चैनं मन्यते हतम्।
उभौ तौ न विजानीतो नायं हन्ति न हन्यते ॥
करोति पापं योऽज्ञानान्नात्मनो वेत्ति च क्षयम्।
प्रद्वेष्टि साधुवृत्तांश्च स लोकस्यैति वाच्यताम् ॥
प्राप्य चाप्युत्तमं जन्म लब्ध्वा चेन्द्रियसौष्ठवम्।
न वेत्त्यात्महितं यस्तु स भवेदात्मघातकः ॥

How many times in the day dost thou milk [दुह्] cows?

Do not drive the bee from the flower, let is lick [लिह्] honey.

Those, who thoughtlessly kill [हन्] animals. never enjoy happiness.

The people of eities sweep [मृज् with सम्] the streets clean. whenever their kings enter them.

In the last quarter of the night, the pupils of the Rishi get up [जागृ] and learn the Vedas.

We do not know [विद्] whether Ràjagriha or Pàtaliputra was the capital of Magadha.

Do not hate [द्विष्] good men.

May the Queen and her descendants rule [शास्] us long.

Let your reverence explain [चक्ष् with वि and आ] this aphorism.

VOCABULARY IX.

Roots of the Second Conjugation.

ईड् *Âtm.* to praise.

ईश् *Âtm.* to be master of, to rule.

चकास् Parasm. to shine.

†चक्ष् *Âtm.* to speak; with आ, to tell; with वि and आ, to explain.

जागृ *Parasm.* to be awake.

---

* The soul is referred to here.

† Used in the Conjugational Tenses and the Perfect. It substitutes ख्या Parasm. and Âtm. in the non-conjugational Tenses and optioally in the Perfect.

दरिद्रा *Parasm.* to be poor.

दिह् *Parasm.* and *Âtm.* to besmear.

दुह् *Parasm.* and *Âtm.* to milk.

द्विष् *Parasm.* and *Âtm.* to hate.

मृज् *Parasm.* to wipe, to clear; with प्र to wipe off; with सम्, to sweep.

अकरुण *m. n. f.* (अ not, and करुणा *f.*) ruthless, one who has no compassion.

आत्मघातक *m. n.* (आत्मन् self, and घातक destroyer) self-destroyer, one who ruins himself.

आत्महित *n.* (आत्मन् and हित good) one's own good.

इन्द्रियसौष्ठव *n.* (इन्द्रिय *n.* limb or sense, and सौष्ठव *n.* beauty, goodness) handsome make, healthy or sound frame.

ईड् *10th conj.* to praise.

उत्पथास्थित *m. n. f.* (उत्पथ *n.* a wrong path, आस्थित *past part.* of स्था *with* आ, one who has taken to) one who has taken to a wrong path.

उद्भूतविस्मय *m. n. f.* (उद्भूत *past part.* of भू *with* उद् to rise, to be produced) one in whom wonder or amazement has been born

कात्यायन *m.* name of a great Grammarian.

क्षय *m.* destruction, ruin.

जगन्नाथ *m.* (जगत् *n.* the universe and नाथ *m.* lord) the Lord of the universe.]

लिह् Parasm. and *Âtm.* to lick.

वश् *Parasm.* wish, to shine.

*विद् *Parasm.* to know.

शास् *Parasm.* to govern, to regulate, to discipline.

शास् *Âtm.* *with* आ, to wish, to desire.

हन् *Parasm.* to kill.

तत्कीर्ति f. his fame.

त्रिविष्टपास्थान n. (त्रिविष्टप *n.* heaven,आस्थान n. assembly) the heavenly assembly, the assembly of the gods.

दीनबन्धु *n.* (दीन *m. n. f.* poor, बन्धु *m.* brother) brother of those that are poor.

देव *m. n. f.* shining.

नम्र *m. n. f.* humble.

नरेन्द्र *m.* a king.

पठ्यमान (*pres. pass. part.* of पठ् *1st conj.* to recite or read) what is being recited.

पतञ्जलि *m.* name of the author of a great grammatical work called the Mahâbhâshya.

पुरोहित *m.* the family priest; chaplain.

प्रपन्न *m. n. f* (*past part.* of पद् with प्र) one who has submitted or surrendered himself.

प्रसव *m.* anything that is producde, produce.

भाष्यकृत् *m.* the writer of a Bhâshya or explanatory discourse, a commentator.

मङ्गलकाल *m* (मङ्गल *n* anything

* The forms of the Present Tense of this root are also made up by adding to it the terminations of the Perfect as वेद, विदतुः, &c. (See Lesson XIII.)

fortunatedor auspicious, and काल time) an auspicious occasion.

मन्त्राक्षर *n.* a syllable of a holy or Vedic verse.

वस्तुजात *n.* (वस्तु *n.* जात *n.* a collection) a collection of things.

वाच्यता *f.* censurableness, liability to censure.

वासव *m.* the god Indra.

विस्तरत: *adv.* in detail.

विहाय (*abso.* fo हा to abandon *with* वि) having abandened.

शस् *1st conj. Parasm. with* वि, to kill, to destroy.

संयमिन् *m.* a sage who has curbed his passions, an ascetic.

सर्वभूतानि *n. Nom. Acc. plur.* all existing things.

सवितृ *m.* the sun.

साधुवृत्त *m. n. f.* (साधु *m. n. f.* good, and वृत्त *n* conduct) well-conducted.

सायम् *ind.* in the evening.

हन्तृ *m. n. f.* a killer.

Aphorism सूत्र *n.*

Bee भ्रमर *m.*

Capital राजधानी *f.*

Desndant वैश्य *m. n. f.* कुलज *m. n. f.*

Drive चुद् *10th conj. with* प्र.

How many times कतिकृत्व : *ind.*

Last चरम *m. n. f.*

Magadha मगधा: *m. used in the plur.*, name of a country or its people.

Never न कदा.

Pâtaliputra पाटलिपुत्र *n.* name of a city om Magadha.

Quarter (तुरीयो भाग:) याम *m.*

Râjagriha *n.* राजगृह name of city in Magadha.

Read पठ् *1st conj. Parasm.*

Street रथ्या *f.*

Thoughtlessly *adv.* रभसात्, मोहात्.

Whenever यदा यदा-तदा तदा.

Your reverence भगवान् or भवान् *Nom. sing.*

LESSON X

SECOND CONJUGATION—*continued.*

Imperfect.

I. The स् and त् of the 2nd and 3rd pers. sing. of the Imperfect are dropped after a cosonant.

II. Any consonant except a nasal at the end of a word or form is.changed to the first or third of its class. ष् is changed to ट् or ड्

a. Thus, in the Imperfect 3rd pers. sing. We have first अलिह् + त् and then अलेह् + त् by, 6, p. 12 त् is dropped by I. and there remains अलेह् Now by I., p. 49, ह् is changed to ढ्; whence we have अलेढ् and by this rule, अलेट्. Similarly, the स् of the 2nd pers sing. is dropped and by the same rules we have the same form, *vix.* अलेट् or अलेड्. The paradigms, therefore, are:—

	Sing.	*Dual.*	*Plur.*
1st pers.	अलेहम्	अलिह्व	अलिह्म
2nd "	अलेट्-ड्	अलीढम्	अलीढ
3rd "	अलेट्-ड्	अलीढाम्	अलिहन्

अलीढाम् &c. like लीढ *3rd pers. dual. pres., &c.*, (for which see the last Lesson).

Atm.

1st pers.	अलिहि	अलिह्वहि	अलिह्महि
2nd "	अलीढा:	अलिहाथाम्	अलीढ्वम्
3rd "	अलीढ	अलिहाताम्	अलिहत

b. अदुह् + त्-अदोह् + त् by. 6, 12–अदोह् by, I, p. 58–अदोघ् by V., p. 50–अधोघ् by II., p. 58 above. Similarly when स् is applied we have अधोक्-ग्.

1st pers.	अदोहम्	अदुह्व	अदुह्म
2nd "	अधोक्-ग्	अदुग्धम्	अदुग्ध
3rd "	अधोक्-ग्	अदुग्धाम्	अदुहन्

Âtm. 3rd pers. अदुहाताम् अदुहत; *2nd pers. sing* अदुग्धा:ए थ by II p. 49.

c. अहन् + त् by I., p.58; अहन् + ताम् (dual)–अहताम् , न् being dropped by 2 a., p 51; अहन् + अन् (plur.)–अह्न् + अन् by 2. a. (latter part), p. 51–– अघ्नन् by 2 c., p. 51.

1st pers.	अहनम्	अहन्व	अहन्म
2nd "	अहन्	अहतम्	अहत
3rd "	अहत	अघ्नाताम्	अघ्नत
Âtm 3rd pers.	अहत	अघ्नाताम्	अघ्नत

1. अमृज् + त्-अमार्ज् + त् by. 4, p. 53–अमार्ज् by 1.,58–

अमार्ष् by IX, p. 52–* अमार्ट्-ड् by II, p. 58. Similarly, we have अमार्ड्-ड् *2nd pers. sing.*

	Sing.	*Dual.*	*Plur.*
1st pers.	अमार्जम्	अमृज्व	अमृज्म
2nd "	अमार्ट्-ड्	अमृष्टम्	अमृष्ट
3rd "	अमार्ट्-ड्	अमृष्टाम्	अमृजन्-अमार्जन्

1. The termination of the Imperfect third person plural is उस् in the case of विद् , शास् , जक्ष् , चकास् , दरिद्रा and जागृ.

द्विष् takes this termination optionally.

III. The ending of a root is optionally changed to or visarga in the Imperfect second person singular.

Thus अवेद् + स्-अवेत्-द् or अवेः

	Sing.	*Dual.*	*Plur.*
1st pers.	अवेदम्	अविद्व	अविद्म
2nd "	अवेः-अवेत-द्	अवित्तम्	अवित्त
3rd "	अवेत्-द्	अवित्ताम्	अविदुः

2. The ending vowel takes its Guṇa before उस्.

जागृ—*Parasm. Im f. 3rd pers.* अजागः-अजागृताम्-अजागरुः, &c अजागृ+त्—अजागात्+त् and by I., p. 58, अजागर्-अजागः.

IV. The ending स् of a root is changed to त् or द् before the termination त् , and optionally before स्.

शास् *Parasm.*

1st pers.	अशासम्	अशिष्व	अशिष्म
2nd "	अशाः-अशात्-द्	अशिष्टम्	अशिष्टः
3rd "	अशात्-द्	अशिष्टाम्	अशासुः

अशास् + त् : त् drpped we have अशास् , and by the above अशात्-द्.

ईश् *Imperf. Âtm. 3rd pers.* ऐष्ट-ऐशाताम्-ऐशत: *2nd pers. plur.* ऐड्ढ्म्. श् is changed to ष् by IX., p 52, and ष् to ड् by VI, pp. 50-51 and ध्व to ढ्.

ईश् *Imperf. Âtm. 3rd pers.* अवद्-ड्-औष्टाम्-औशन्. Before ताम् , &c, the व being changed to उ, the temporal augment आ with the उ forms Vṛiddhi, i e. औ.

---

* A conjunet consonant with र् as its first member is allowed at the end of a word, but not when स् is the secona member.

Petential.

दुह्

	Parasm.			*Âtm.*		
	Sing.	*Dual.*	*Plur.*	*Sing.*	*Dual.*	*Plur.*
1st pers.	दुह्याम्	दुह्याव	दुह्याम	दुहीय	दुहीवहि	दुहीमहि
2nd "	दुह्याः	दुह्यातम्	दुह्यात	दुहीथाः	दुहीयाथाम्	दुहीध्वम्
3rd "	दुह्यात्	दुह्याताम्	दुह्युः	दुहीत	दुहीयाताम्	दुहीरन्

हन् Parasm. 3rd pers. हन्यात्-हन्याताम्-हन्युः Âtm. 3rd pers. घ्नीत-घ्नीयाताम्-घ्नीरन्.

सायं प्रातर्धेनुमग्निहोत्रायाधोगृषिः।

दण्डकायां बसन्तौ रामलक्ष्मणौ रक्षसां सहस्त्राण्यहताम्।

चाणक्योऽकिंचनों ब्राह्मणो नन्दानद्वेबुद्धि प्रभावाञ्च तानहन्।

तेषां च राज्यं चन्द्रगुप्तो नाम नृपतिश्चाणक्यस्य शिष्योऽशात्।

देवानां संदेशं हरन्नलो दमयन्त्या अन्तःपुरं प्राविशत्। प्रविशन्तं च तं देवानां वराद्रक्षितारो नाविदुः।

केचिद्बटवस्तडागस्य तटमुपगता लोष्टैर्भेकानभ्यघ्नन्।

स राजा दिग्विजयादारभ्यात्मनः सर्वं वृत्तान्तं गन्धर्वकन्याया * आचष्ट।

यथा पाण्डवा रणे नास्मान्हन्युस्तथा क्रियताम्।

कश्चित्कुक्कुरो यज्ञमण्डपं गतो हवींष्यवालेट्। तवर्त्विजस्तमाघ्नन्सर्वं च समुपाहृतं यज्ञियं द्रव्यं त्यक्त्वा मण्डपं सममार्जन्।

राजानो धर्मेध वसुधां शिष्युः।

The Mauryas ruled [शास्] the earth after the Nandas.]

The warriors of the Kalingas told [चक्ष्] us thus:—

"The angas, who hated [द्विष्] us for a long time invaded our territory. We fought a battle with them and killed [हन्] their commanders. Their king did not know [विद्] this; wherefore he came in person to the feld of battle. But seeing his men killed, he returned to his kingdom."

---

* See note†, page 109, F. B.

Did you milk [दुह्] the cows yesterday?
Hari was awake [जागृ] the whole night pereating the Vedas.
A man should clean [मृज् with प्र] his face every morning.

VOCABULARY X.

अग्निहोत्र *n.* sacrifice to Fire.
कुक्कुर *m.* a dog.
गन्धर्वकन्या *f.* the daughter of a Gandharva.
चन्द्रगुप्त *m.* name fo a king.
चाणक्य *m.* name of a person.
तट *m.n.f.* bank, margin.
दिग्विजय *m.* (दिश् *f.* quarter. विजय *m.* conquest) conquest of the quarters, or of all regions.
द्रव्य *n.* a thing.
नन्द *m.* name of a royal race, an individual of it.
बटु *m.* a boy.
भेक *m.* a frog.
मण्डप *m.* a shed, an enclosure.
यज्ञमण्डप *m.* an enclosure prepared for a sacrifice.
यज्ञिय *m. n. f.* pertaining to sacrifices.
रण *n.* a battle.
वसुधा *f.* the earth.
वृत्तान्त *m.* account, occurrence.
समुपाहृत (*past pass. part.* of हृ *with* सम्, उप and आ) collected.
सहस्र *n.* a thousand.
हन् *with* अभि or आ to strike.

Angas अङ्गाः *plur.* name of a people or of their country.
Commander चमूपति *m.* सेनापति *m.*
Field of battle. रणभूमि *f.*
In person. स्वयम् *ind.*
Invade हृ *1st conj.* Parasm. with अभि.
Kalingas कलिङ्गाः *plur.* name of a people or of their country.
Maurya मौर्य *m.* name of a dynasty, an individual of it.
Repeat पठ् *1st* conj. Parasm.
Territory विषय *m.*

Lesson XI.

THIRD CONJUGATION.

1. In this conjugation the roots undergo reduplication before the terminations are applied.

2. *General Rules of Reduplication.—a.* The vowel, and if there are more than one the first, is reduplicated, together with the initial consonant, if any.

b. A radical hard aspirate (2nd letter) is changed to the hard unaspirate (1st letter) of its class in the reduplicative syllable; and a radical soft aspirate (4th letter), to the soft unaspirate (3rd letter).

Thus the reduplication of फल् by 2 *a.* is फफल्, and by the first part of the above, पफल्; धा-धाधा-दधा by the second part of the above and 2 *f.*; भी-भीभी-बिभी.

c. A radical guttural is changed to the corresponding palatal (subject to the above rule) and ह् to ज्.

खन्-खखन् by 2 *a*;—छखन् by 2 *c.* and by 2 *b.*; हा-हाहा by 2 *a.*;—हहा by 2*f.*; and जहा by the above.

d. If a conjunct consonant begins a root, the first member of it only with the vowel is reduplicated.

ह्री by the above ह्रीह्री—by 2 *c.* and 2 *f.* जिह्री.

e. Exception :— If the first member be a sibilant and the second a hard letter, the hard letter is reduplicated, as स्पर्ध्-पस्पर्ध्.

f. A radical long vowel becomes short, and a radical be ऋ comes अ; as ह्री—जिह्री; दा—ददा; कृ—चकृ.

3. *Irregularities applicable to the third conjugation* :—

The vowel of the reduplicative syllable of मा, हा 'to go', भृ and पृ or पृ and ऋ is changed to इ and that of the reduplicative syllable of निज्, विज् and विष् takes its Guṇa substitute.

4. The reduplicative इ of ऋ is changed to इय्. (See 8, p. 80.).

5. The termination of the third person plural Parasm. loses its nasal, as well as that of the Âtm.

6. The termination of the third person plural of the Imperfect Parasmaipada is उस्, before which the final आ of all roots is dropped, and the final इ, उ, and ऋ, short or long, take their Guṇa substitute. (Comp. I and 2, p, 60).

भृ *Parasm.*

Present.

	Sing.	*Dual.*	*Plur.*
1st pers.	बिभर्मि	बिभृवः	बिभृमः
2nd "	बिभर्षि	बिभृथः	बिभृथ
3rd "	बिभर्ति	बिभृतः	बिभ्रति

Imperfect.

	Sing.	*Dual.*	*Plur.*
1st pers.	अबिभरम्	अबिभृव	अबिभृम
2nd "	अबिभः	अबिभृतम्	अबिभृत
3rd "	अबिभः	अबिभृताम्	अबिभरुः

Imperative.

1st pers.	बिभराणि	बिभराव	बिभराम
2nd "	बिभृहि	बिभृतम्	बिभृत
3rd "	बिभर्तु	बिभृताम्	बिभ्रतु

Potential.

1st pers.	बिभृयाम्	बिभृयाव	बिभृयाम
2nd "	बिभृयाः	बिभृयातम्	बिभृयात
3rd "	बिभृयात्	बिभृयाताम्	बिभृयुः

बिभृ by 2 a., 2 *b.* and 3. Remember the rule aout Guṇa before the strong terminations (6. p. 12). बिभ्रति by 5.

Imperf. 3rd pers. sing. ; अबिभृ+त्; by 6, p. अबिभर्त्, 12 and by 1, p. 58 अबिभर्-अबिभः (Note‡, p. 6, F. B.); *3rd pers. plur.* अबिभरुः by 6.

Âtm. Pres. 3rd pers.	बिभृते	बिभ्राते	बिभ्रते
" *Imperf.* "	अबिभृत	अबिभ्राताम्	अबिभ्रत
ह्री *Parasm. Pres. 3rd pers.*	जिह्रेति	जिह्रीतः	जिह्रियति (II. 36.)
" " *Imperf. 3rd pers.*	अजिह्रेत्	अजिह्रीताम्	अजिह्रयुः (6).

7. The ending vowel of मा and हा 'to go' is changed to ई when followed by a weak termination beginning with a consonant, and dropped before one beginning with a vowel.

मा *Âtm. Pres. 3rd pers.*	मिमीते	मिमाते	मिमते
Similarly हा *Âtm.* 'to go'	जिहीते	जिहाते	जिहते
Imperf. 3rd pers.	अमिमीत	अमिमाताम्	अमिमत
	अजिहीत	अजिहाताम्	अजिहत

मिमा by 3. ते having an initial consonant, the. आ of मा is changed to ई and thus we have मिमीते. Before आते, अते, &c. the आ is dropped, the terminations beginning with a vowel.

8. The आ of हा 'to abandon' undergoes the same changes as above, but the ई is optionally shortened. Before Potential terminations beginning with य the आ of this root is dropped and in the Imperative second person singular it is

optionally retained, so that in the in the latter there are three forms. *uiz.*, जहाहि, जहिहि, जहीहि.

हा 'to abandon' *Parasm.*

	Sing.	*Dual.*	*Plur.*
1st pers.	जहामि	जहिवः-जहीवः	जहिमः-जहीमः
2nd "	जहासि	जहिथः-जहीथः	जहिथ-जहीथ
3rd "	जहाति	जहितः-जहीतः	जहित
Imper f. 3rd pers.	अजहात्	अजहिताम्-अजहीताम्	अजहुः
Imperat "	जहातु	जहिताम्-जहीताम्	जहतु
Pot. "	जह्यात्	जह्याताम्	जह्युः

8. The ई of भी is optionally shortened before the weak terminations with an initial consonant.

I. The ending ई of a root, short or long not preceded by a conjunct consonant, is changed to य् before weak termination with an initial vowel, when the base consists of more than one syllable.

बिभी+ अति= बिभ्यति the base बिभी consisting of two syllables; but जिह्री+ अति= जिह्रियति, for the ई of ह्री is preceded by ह्, which is a conjunct consonant.

Pres. 3rd pers.	बिभेति	बिभितः-बिभीतः	बिभ्यति	*Parasm.*
Imperf. "	अबिभेत्	अबिभिताम्-अबिभीताम्ः	अबिभयुः	"
Imperat. 1st pers.	बिभयाति	बिभयाव	बिभयाम	"

10. दा and धा lose the ending vowel before the weak terminations, and then धा assumes the form धत् before स्, ध्व, त् and थ्. The Imperative second person singalar form of the Parasm. are देहि and धेहि.

धा 'to put or hold'

	Parasm.			*Âtm.*		
	Sing.	*Dual.*	*Plur.*	*Sing.*	*Dual.*	*Plur.*
Present.	दधामि	दध्वः	दध्मः	दधे	दध्वहे	दध्महे
	दधासि	धत्थः	धत्थ	धत्से	दधाथे	धद्ध्वे
	दधाति	धत्तः	दधति	धत्ते	दधाते	दधते

	Parasm. Sing.	Parasm. Dual.	Parasm. Plur.	Âtm. Sing.	Âtm. Dual.	Âtm. Plur.
Imperfect...	अदधाम्	अदध्व	अदध्म	अदधि	अदध्वहि	अदध्महि
	अदधाः	अधत्तम्	अधत्त	अधत्थाः	अदधाथाम्	अधद्ध्वम्
	अदधात्	अधत्ताम्	अदधुः	अधत्त	अदधाताम्	अदधत
Imperative...	दधानि	दधाव	दधाम	दधै	दधावहै	दधामहै
	धेहि	धत्तम्	धत्त	धत्स्व	दधाथाम्	धद्ध्वम्
	दधातु	धत्ताम्	दधतु	धत्ताम्	दधाताम्	दधताम्
Potential...	दध्याम्	दध्याव	दध्याम	दधीय	दधीवहि	दधीमहि
	दध्याः	दध्यातम्	दध्यात	दधीथाः	दधीयाथाम्	दधीध्वम्
	दध्यात्	दध्याताम्	दध्युः	दधीत	दधीयाताम्	दधीरन्

In धद्ध्वम्, &c. the त् is changed to द्, being followed by a soft consonant which is not a nasal. In अदधुः, आ is dropped by 6, p. 63. Remember that the terminations of the first pers. of the Imperative, except ऐ, begin with आ.

दा should be similarly conjugated.

11. The penultimate short vowel does not take its Guna substitute before the wowel storng termingations in this conjugation; नेनिजानि *1st pers. imperat.*

Present parasm. 3rd pers. नेनेक्ति-नेनिक्तः *Âtm.* नेनिक्ते-नेनिजाते-नेनिजते.

Before ति, ज् is changed to क् by note †, p.97, F. B.

Parasm. Imperf. 1st pers.	अनेनिजम्	अनेनिज्व	अनेनिज्म
Âtm. " "	अनेनिजि	अनेनिज्वहि	अनेनिज्महि
Parasm Imperat. "	नेनिजानि	नेनिजाव	नेनिजाम
Âtm. " "	नेनिजै	नेनिजावहै	नेनिजामहै

	Parasm.	*Âtm.*
हु *Parasm. 3 pers.*	जुहोति जुहुतः जुह्वति।	अजुहोत् अजुहुताम् अजुहवुः.

Imperat. 2nd pers. sing. जुहुधि. The termination here is धि, instead of हि, as a special case.

The उ of हु before a vowel weak termination is, in the conjugational tenses and moods, changed not to उव् by II., p. 36, but to व्.

मा *Âtm. 3rd pers.* मिमीते मिमाते मिमते। अमिमीत अमिमाताम् अमिमत

See 7, p. 64.

हा	" "	जिहीते	जिहाते	जिहते।	अजिहीत	अजिहाताम्	अजिहत
पृ	*Par.* "	पिपर्ति	पिपृतः	पिप्रति।	अपिपः	अपिपृताम्	अपिपरुः
पॄ	" "	पिपर्ति	पिपूर्तः	पिपुरति।	अपिपः	अपिपूर्ताम्	अपिपरुः
ऋ	" "	इयर्ति	इयृतः	इय्रति।	ऐयः	ऐयृताम्	ऐयरुः

ऋ in the case of पॄ is changed to उर् by 9., p. 2. ऋ-ऋऋ by 2 a, p. 62—इऋ by 3, p. 63—इयृ by 4, p. 63. आ+इयृ=ऐयृ.

विज् *Par. 3rd pers.* वेवेक्ति वेविक्तः वेविजति। अवेविजम् अवेविज्व अवेविज्म (*1st pers.*)

विज्	*Âtm. 3rd pers.*	वेविक्ते	वेविजाते	वेविजते	*Prcsemt.*
विष्	*Parasm.* " "	वेवोष्टि	वेविष्टः	वेविषति	
	Âtm. " "	वेविष्टे	वेविषाते	वेविषत	

धान्यं मिमीते कुडवेन।

अग्नौ समिधो जुहोत्यध्वर्युः।

यथा मे पिता धर्मं न प्रजहातु तथा मे वरं देहि।

*येभ्य सर्वे लोका अबिभयुस्तान्राक्षसानरणये रामोऽहन्

भर्त्रा सह पितुः समीपं गच्छन्ती जिह्रेमीत्यवदच्छकुन्तला।

कृष्णश्चक्रमबिभरार्जुनो गाण्डीवं दर्योधनभीमसेनौ गदामबिभृतामन्ये सर्वे योधाः साधारणं धनुरबिभरुः।

ब्राह्मणोऽब्राह्मणो वा यः कोऽपि निर्धनोऽशक्तश्च भवेत्तस्म-धनं दत्त।

रामभार्यां जहाहि जहिहि जहीहीति त्रिर्बिभीषणो रावणमुपा-दिशत्

यस्मिन्कन्यामलंकृत्य वरमाहूय तस्मै तां ददति स ब्राह्मो विवाह उत्तमफलकः।

हरि चरणयोः प्रक्षिप्तोऽयं पुष्पाणामञ्जलिर्नः कल्याणं विधत्ताम्

---

* Verbs implying fear and protection from danger govern the ablative of the object from which the fear or danger proceeds.

† The student should remember that the original form is अबिभर्.

पुरोहितास्तेषां गृहं गत्वा प्रथमं पादानवानेनिजुः पश्चात्स-मन्त्रकं कर्म व्यदधुः।

ददाति द्रविणं भूरि दाति दारिद्र्यमर्थिनाम्।
सोऽवदायति कीर्तिं च शिरोऽवद्यति विद्विषाम्॥
संदधाति धनुर्ज्यायां यदैवेषून् रुषान्वितः।
तदैव तं भयाक्रान्ताः संधियन्ति धराधिपाः॥
न जहाति सदाचारं स सदा चारणस्तुतः।
उज्जिहीते जगज्जित्वा तस्य कीर्तिः सुरालयम्॥
न क्लाम्यति दिनं कृत्स्नं ददानोऽपि धनं बहु।
न च क्लाम्यति संग्रामे निघ्नन् गज घटाशतम्॥
न्यायप्रवृत्तो नृपतिरात्मानमपि च प्रजाः।
त्रिवर्गेणोपसंधत्ते निहन्ति ध्रुवमन्यथा॥
अधर्मान्नात्रसः पाप लोकवादान्न चाबिभेः।
दैवाद्बिभीहि काकुत्स्थ जिह्रीहि त्वं तथा जनात्॥
मिथ्या *मामभिसंक्रुध्यन्नवशां शत्रुणा हृताम्।
आनन्दं ब्रह्मणो विद्वान्न बिभेति कदाचन॥
यद्ददासि विशिष्टेभ्यो यच्चाश्नासि दिनेदिने।
तत्ते वित्तमहं मन्ये शेषं कस्यापि रक्षसि॥
न बिभेति यदा चायं यदा चास्यमान्न बिभ्यति।
यदा नेच्छति न द्वेष्टि ब्रह्म संपद्यते तदा॥

The sons of Dhritràshtra abandoned [हा] the cows and fled from the feld of battle.

Janaka gave [दा] his daughter Sitâ to Râma, he having bent the bow of Siva.

Brave men do not fear [भी] their enemies.

I kept [धा with आ] my money in that house that the king's man might not take it.

---

* क्रुध् and द्रुह् when preceded by a preposition govern the accusative of the person or thing against whom or which the feeling is directed and not the dative.

Make peace [धा with सम्] with your powerful enemies, that your whole country may not be destroyed.

Art thou no ashamed [ह्री] to go about naked ?

The Smṛitis command [धा with वि] the remarriage of widows.

Why didst thou shut [धा with पि or अपि] the ears, when Govinda was telling a story ?

Women wear [धा with परि] ornaments on their persons.

One should distinguish [विज् with वि] self-respect from rudeness.

Whsh [निज् with अव] thy hands and feet, and then begin thy Saṃdhyâ-adoration.

The officer of the king measured [मा] the length of the land.

The hermits fill [पृ or पॄ] their gourds with water at the lake.

VOCABULARY XI.

Roots of the Third Conjugation.

दा *Parasm.* and *Âtm.* to give.

धा *Parasm.* and *Âtm.* to hold, to put, with वि, to execute, to do, to command (as in religious works); *with* परि, to wear; *with* सम्, to make peace with, to put or lay on, to fix on: *with* उप and सम्, to join, to cause to attain; *with* अपि or पि, to shut; *with* नि, to place, to keep; *with* अव, to attend.

निज् *Parasm.* and *Âtm.* to purify; *with* अव, to wash.

पृ or पॄ or *Parasm.* to fill.

भी *Parasm.* to fear.

भृ *Parasm.* and *Âtm.* to to support, to bear.

मा *Âtm.* to measure.

विज् *Parasm.* and *Âtm.* to separate, to distinguish; *with* वि.

विष् *Parasm.* and *Âtm.* to surround.

हा *Âtm.* to go; *with* उद् to go upwards, to ascend.

हा *Parasm.* to abandon.

हु *Parasm.* to sacrifice.

ह्री *Parasm.* to blush, to be ashamed.

अञ्जलि *m.* the cavity formed by joining the hands.

अन्यथा *adv.* otherwise.

अन्वित *past part. pass.* of इ *with.*

अनु, followed, accompanied with, full of.

अर्थिन् *m.n f.* a beggar.

अवश *m.n f.* helpless.

अशक्त *m.n f.* weak, unable.

उत्तमफलक *m n.f.* (उत्तम *m.n.f.* good, excellent, फल *n.* fruit, and क *suf.*) of good fruit or result.

काकुत्स्थ *m* a male descendant of Kakutstha, Râma.

कुडव *m.* measure of corn.

कृ *with* अलम्, to adorn.

कृत्स्न *m n.f.* [with.

क्रुध् *with* (अभि and सम्, to be angry.

गजघटाशत *n.* (घटा *f.* an array, a host, शत *n.* a hundred) a hundred arrays or hosus of elephants.

गदा *f.* a mace. [bow.

गाण्डीव *n.* the name of Arjuna's.

चारणस्तुत *m.n.f.* (चारण *m.* a bard) praised by bards.

त्रिः *adv.* thrice.

त्रिवर्ग *m.* collection of three, *viz.*, *Dharma* or religious merit, *Artha* or wealth, and Kâma or desires or fulfilment of desires.

दिनेदिने *adv.* every day, day by day

दुर्योधनभीमसेनौ *m.* dual दुर्योधन and भीमसेन (comp.)

मसेनौ *m n.f.* (दुर्योधन *m.n.f.* good, भीमसेन excellent,

दै *1st conj.* Parasm. *with* अव, to purify, to cleanse.

दो *4th conj.* Parasm. *with* अव, to cut, to cut off.

द्रविण *n.* wealth, money.

धनुर्ज्या *f.* (ज्या *f.* the string [of a bow]) the string of a bow.

धराधिप *n.* (धरा *f.* the earth, अधिप *m.* a lord) lord of the earth, a king.

धि *6th conj.* Parasm. *with* सम्, to make peace with.

ध्रुवम् *adv.* certainly.

निर्धन *m. n. 'f.* without wealth, poor.

न्यायप्रवृत्त *m. n. f.* (न्याय *m.* justice, uprightness, प्रवृत्त *past part.* of वृत् *with* प्र to proceed) one whose conduct is just or upright.

पद् *4th conj. Âtm. with* (सम्, to become.

प्रादुस् *adv.* or *prep.* (used with *uerbs*) visible, manifest.

विभीषण *m.* a particnlar form of marriage in use among Brâhmaṇas.

भयाक्रान्त *m. n. f.* (आक्रान्त *past. part. pass.* of क्रम *with.* आ overtaken, overcome) overcome by fear.

प्रादुस् *ind. adv.* falsely.

रामभार्या *f.* the wife of Râna.

रुष् *f.* anger.

लोकवाद *m.* the censure of people.

विद्वस् *perf. part.* of विद् (to know) knowing.

विशिष्ट *m. n. f.* respectable (person).

व्यास *m.* the great author of the Mahâbhârata, an epic poem.

शकुन्तला *m.* name of a lady, wife of a king named Dushyanta.

शेष *m. n.* remainder, all others.

समन्त्रकम् *adv.* by mantras, *i.e.*, by repeating mantras.

समिध् *f.* small sticks of a sacred tree, such as *udumbara,* to be thrown into the sacrifical fire.

साधारण *m. n. f.* ordinary.

सुरालय *m.* (सुर *m.* a god, आलय *m.* a place of abode) the abode of the gods, heaven.

हन् *with* नि, to kill, to destroy, to ruin.

Battle field रणभूमि *f.*

Bent नामित *past part. pass. of the causal of* नम्; रामेण धनुषि नामिते, 'Rama having bent the bow.'

Destroyed ध्वस्त *past part.* of ध्वंस्, उच्छिन्न, *past part. pass.* of छिद् *with* उद्.

Flee अय् *1st conj.* Âtm. with परा of पला. changed to उद्.

Gourd कमण्डलु *m.*

Hermit वानप्रस्थ *m.* यति *m.*

Length आयाम *m.*

Naked नग्न *m. n. f.*

Person शरीर *n.* देह *m.*

Remarriage पुनरुद्वाह *m.*

Rudeness अविनय *m.*

Samdhyâ-adoration संध्यावन्दन *n.*

Self-respect स्वाभिमान *m.*

Lesson XII.

Seventh Conjugation.

1. In this conjugation, न is inserted between the radical vowel and the final consonant before the strong, and न् before the weak terminations. The rules about the changes of letters given in Lessons IX and X ought to be observed in appending the terminations.

2. The original nasal of the root is dropped.

3. ने is inserted before the final of तृह् instead of न when it is followed by the consonantal strong terminstions.

Parasmaipada.

Present—रुध् 'to obstruct.'

	Sing.	*Dual.*	*Plur.*
1st pers.	रुणध्मि	रुन्ध्वः	रुन्ध्मः
2nd "	रुणत्सि	रुन्द्धः	रुन्द्ध
3rd "	रुणद्धि	रुन्द्धः	रुन्धन्ति

रुन्द्ध+ ति = रुणध्+ ति by 1, above—रुणध्+ धि by II., p. 49 रुणद्+ धि or रुणद्धि by VI, pp. 50–51; रुन्द्धः &c. similarly. In रुणत्सि the ध् is changed to त् by note †, p. 5., F. B.

Imperfect.

	Sing.	*Dual.*	*Plur.*
1st pers.	उरुणधन्	अरुन्ध्व	अरुन्ध्म
2nd "	अरुणाः-त्-द्	अरुन्द्धम्	अरुन्द्ध
3rd "	अरुणत्-द्	अरुन्द्धाम्	अरुन्धन्

3rd pers. sing. अरुणध्, the termination त् being dropped by I., p. 58—अरुणत्-द् by II., p. 58. In the 2nd pers. sing. the द् is optionally changed to Visarga by III., p. 60. अरुन्द्धाम्, &c. like रुणद्धि.

Imperative.

1st pers.	रुणधानि	रुणधाव	रुणधाम
2nd "	रुन्द्धि	रुन्द्धम्	रुन्द्ध
3rd "	रुणद्धु	रुन्द्धाम्	रुन्धन्तु

See 4, p. 12, and 1, p. 50.

Potential.

1st pers.	रुन्ध्याम्	रुन्ध्याव	रुन्ध्याम
2nd "	रुन्ध्याः	रुन्ध्यातम्	रुन्ध्यात
3rd "	रुन्ध्यात्	रुन्ध्याताम्	रुन्ध्युः

Âtmanepada.

Present.

1st pers.	रुन्धे	रुन्ध्वहे	रुन्ध्महे
2nd "	रुन्त्से	रुन्धाथे	रुन्द्ध्वे
3rd "	रुन्द्धे	रुन्धाते	रुन्धते

Imperfect.

1st pers.	अरुन्धि	अरुन्ध्वहि	अरुन्ध्महि
2nd "	अरुन्द्धाः	अरुन्धाथाम्	अरुन्द्ध्वम्
3rd "	अरुन्द्ध	अरुन्धाताम्	अरुन्धत

Imperative.

1st pers.	रुणधै	रुणधावहै	रुणधामहै
2nd "	रुन्त्स्व	रुन्धाथाम्	रुन्द्ध्वम्
3rd "	रुन्द्धाम्	रुन्धाताम्	रुन्धताम्

Potential.

1st pers.	रुन्धीय	रुन्धीवहि	रुन्धीमहि
2nd "	रुन्धीथाः	रुन्धीयाथाम्	रुन्धीध्वम्
3rd "	रुन्धीत	रुन्धीयाताम्	रुन्धीरन्

अञ्ज् *Pres. 3rd pers. sing.* अनक्ति, the nasal being dropped by 2] p. 71, and ज् changed to क् by note †, p. 97. F. B.

Imperf. 3rd pers sing. आनक्-ग्. *Imperat. 2nd pers. sing.* by अङ्ग्धि

पिष्- *Pres. 3rd pers. sing.* पिनष्टि, the ति being changed to टि by note*, p. 21, F. B.

Imperf 3rd pers. sing. पिष् + धि by 1, p. 50-पिन्ष् + धि by I, p. 71—पिन्ष् + ढि by note,*, p. 21, F. B.-पिन्ड् + ढि by VI, pp. 50-51. पिण्ड्ढि by VIII, p. 51-52.

Imperf 3rd pers. sing. अपिनष् by I, p. 71 and 1, p. 58—अपिनट्-ड् by II, p. 58.

रिच् *Parasm. Pres. 3rd pers. sing.* रिणच् + ति-रिणक् + ति by note†, p. 97, F. B.—रिणक्ति. *Imperat. 2nd pers. sing.* रिङ्ग्धि

Imperf. 3rd pers. sing. अरिणक्-ग्.

भिद्- *Paras. Pres. 3rd pers. sing.* भिनत्ति *Imperat. 2nd pers. sing.* भिन्द्धि. *Imperf. 2nd pers. sing.* अभिनः-त्-द्.

हिंस्—*Imperat. 2nd pers. sing.* हिन्धि, स् being dropped by I. p. 35. *Imperf. 3rd pers. sing.* अहिनत्-द् ; *2nd pers. sing.* अहिनः-त्-द्, by IV, p. 60.

तृह्- *Pres. 3rd pers. sing.* तृणेह् + ति by 3, p. 71 तृणेद् + ति-तृणेढ् + धि-तृणेढ् + ढि-तृणेढि just like लेढि p. 49; तृण्ढः *dual;* तृ + न् + ह् + अन्ति-तृंहन्ति by VIII, pp. 51-52. Similarly, अतृणेट् like अलेट्.

दीनाय याचमानाय धनं ददतं मां मा रुन्द्धि पापमेव तस्मात्त्वाश्रयेत्।

किर्मीरस्य शरीरं चूर्णवदपिनड्भीमसेनः।

रिपोः करिणां गण्डस्थलान्यभिन्दत वीराः

अद्यप्रभृति त्वां कोशागारे नियुनज्मि तदात्मनोऽधिकारेऽप्रमत्तो भव।

तस्यां तवानुरागमस्माकं पुरो व्यर्थं किं व्यनक्षि किं तेन लभेथाः। तामेव गच्छ।

अरण्ये केचित्पशवोऽन्यान्हिंसन्त्यतस्तान्हिंस्रान्बुवन्ति।

रे रे पान्था जाले निपतितोऽहम्। अत्रागत्य मे पाशांश्छिन्त।

यत्किंचिल्लभसे तद्भुङ्क्षीथाः। अन्यस्य कस्यचिद्धनं मा गृध्य।

न हिंस्यात्सर्वाणि भूतानीत्येतं विधिमक्षरशो जैना अनुसरन्ति।

स्वगृहमार्गतमर्थिनं रघुः कियद्बुस्विष्यते त्वयेत्यन्वयुङ्क्त।

रात्रौ नाभुङ्क्षि मह्यं किंचिद्भक्षयितुं देहि।
वेत्ति सर्वाणि शास्त्राणि गर्वस्तस्य न विद्यते।
विन्ते धर्मे सदा सद्भिस्तेषु पूजां च विन्दति॥
वृणक्ति वृजिनैः सङ्गं वृक्ते च वृषलैः सह।
वर्जत्यनार्जवोपेतैः स वर्जयति दुर्जनैः॥
न संपृणक्ति कृपणैः संपृक्ते न पृथग्जनैः।
संपर्चति सदाचारैः संपर्चयति पण्डितैः॥
नियुङ्क्ते गुल्मपालान् स नियोजति नियोगिनः।
नियोजयत्यनीकस्थान् स्वयं चात्मनि युज्यते॥
न हिनस्ति वृथा जन्तूंस्तृणान्यपि न हिंसति।
तमेव हिंसयत्येकं यस्तदाज्ञां विलङ्घते॥
खिद्यतेऽसौ न भृत्येषु याचकेषु न खिन्दति।
खिन्ते तेष्वेव ये द्रव्यं दीयमानं न गृह्णते॥
प्रणिङ्क्ते दक्षिणीयानां विप्राणां चरणौ च सः।
यत्पादौ मुकुटज्योत्स्नाजलैर्नेनेक्ति राजकम्॥
भिनत्ति संशयं शास्त्रे विदुषां सूक्तिभिस्सदा।
छेदयत्यसिधाराभिर्विद्विषां मस्तकं च सः॥
यत्पादौ मुकुटज्योत्स्नाजलैर्नेनेक्ति राजकम्॥
भिनत्ति संशयं शास्त्रे विदुषां सूक्तिभिस्सदा
छेदयत्यसिधाराभिर्विद्विषां मस्तकं च सः॥
मनो नोद्विजते तस्य ददतोर्थमहर्निशम्।
उद्विनक्ति तु संसारादसारात्तत्त्ववेदिनः॥
केचिद्द्युम्नाय धावन्ति प्रद्युम्नाय च केचन।
नोद्युङ्क्ते कोऽपि धर्माय सर्वाभिप्रेतहेतवे॥
पीडाकरममित्राणां कर्तव्यमिति शक्रजित्।
अब्रवीत् खड्गकृष्टश्च तस्या मूर्धानमच्छिनत्॥
तृणेह्मि देहमात्मीयं त्वं वाचं न ददासि चेत्॥
कामान्दुग्धे विप्रकर्षत्यलक्ष्मीं कीर्तिं सूते दुष्कृतं या हिनस्ति॥
तां चाप्येतां मातरं मङ्गलानां धेनुं धीराः सूनृतां वाचमाहुः॥

would cut down [छिद्] the branch of the tree if Hari should not pervent [रुध्] me.

He pounded [क्षुद्] those medicinal drugs to give them to his brother, who is ill.

Many Brâhmaṇas dined [भुज्] every day in the Visrâma-palace with the last Brâhmaṇa-king.

A whirlwind destroys [भञ्ज्] trees and houses.

I laid open [अञ्ज् with वि] my griefs to (before) him and his heart was melted* with pity.

Let the honour appoint [युज् with नि] him to the post of the commander of the forces; he is a brave and skilful man.

Why do you prevent [रुध्] me from† going to Kãsi?

When and where dost thou dine [भुज्] usually?

We grind [पिष्] our corn with our hands in India; in England they grind by means of machines.

Whom shall I appoint [युज् with नि] to the office of the counsellor?

I now particularise [शिष् with वि] the different kinds of brutes.

Do not destroy [भञ्ज्] all his hopes of prosperity.

The Yavana besieged [रुध्] Sâketa.

VOCABULARY XII.

Root of the Seventh Conjugation.

अञ्ज् *Parasm.* to anoint; *with* वि, to make manifest, or lay open.

इन्ध् *Âtm.* to kindle.

क्षुद् *Parasm.* and *Âtm.* to pound, to reduce to powder or dust.

खिद् *Âtm.* to be distressed, to be displeased or offended.

छिद् *Parasm.* and *Âtm.* to cut.

तृह् *Parasm.* to kill, to destroy.

पिष् *Parasm.* to grind.

पृच् *Parasm.* *with* सम्, to come in contact, to associate.

भञ्ज् *Parasm.* to destroy, to break.

भिद् *Parasm.* and *Âtm.* to split.

भुज् *Parasm.* to enjoy; *Âtm.* to dine, to eat.

युज् *Parasm.* and *Âtm.* to join;

* Sanskrit idiom: *Was wet with pity.*

† See construction of the first of the Sanskrit sentences in this lesson.

with अनु, to put a question to; *with* नि, to appoint; *with* उद्, to endeavour, to exert.

रिच् *Parasm.* and *Âtm.* to evacuate.

रुध् *parasm.* and *Âtm.* to obstruct, to prevent, to besiege.

विज् *Parasm. with* उद्, to tremble, to fear, to be disgusted. [cuss.

विद् *Âtm.* to reason upon, to dis-

वृज् *Parasm.* to avoid, to shun.

शिष् *Parasm.* to distinguish; *with* वि, to particularise.

हिंस् *Parasm.* to kill, to destroy.

अक्षरशः *adv.* literally.

अगार *n.* house.

अद्यप्रभृति *adv.* (अद्य to-day, and प्रभृति from) from to-day, or henceforward.

अधिकार *m.* post, power, office.

अनार्जवोपेत *m. n. f.* (अन् not, आर्जव *n.* strainghtness, strainghtforwardness, उपेत *Past part. pass.* of इ, with उप accom-panied) not possessed of strainghtforwardness, one who is without strainghtfor-wardness.

अनीकस्थ *m. n. f.* (अनीक *n.* an army, स्था to stand) one in the army, a soldier.

अन्य *pron.* another.

अप्रमत्त *m. n. f.* (अ and प्रमत्त careless) not careless, careful.

अर्थिन् *m.* a suppliant.

अलक्ष्मी *f.* bad luck] poverty.

असार *m. n. f.* (सार *m.* essence) unsubstantial, unprofitable, useless.

असिधारा *f.* (धारा *f.* edge) the edge of a sword.

अहर्निशम् *adv.* day and night.

आत्मीय *m. n. f.* one's own.

काम *m.* desire.

कियत् *m. n. f.* how much.

किर्मीर *m.* name of a giant.

कृपण *m. n. f.* mean, miserly, little-minded.

कृष् *1st conj. Parasm.* to draw; *with* वि and प्र, to make worse, to reduce.

कोशागार *n.* a store-house, a treasure-house.

खड्गकृष्ट *m. n. f.* (खड्ग *m.* a sword) one who has drawn out his sword.

खिद् *4th conj. Âtm.* and *6th conj. Parasm.* to be distressed, to be displeased or offended.

गण्डस्थल *n.* temples of an elephant.

गुल्मपाल *m.* (गुल्म *m.* a rort) protector or keeper of a fort.

गृध् *4th conj. Parasm.* to be greedy for, to covet.

चूर्ण *m. n.* dust, powder; चूर्णवत् like dust, to dust.

चेत् *ind.* if. [divide.

छिद् *10th conj.* to cut off, to

जैन *m.* a follower of Jaina, a person belonging to the Jain sect.

तत्त्ववेदिन् *m. n. f.* one who knows the truth or real philosophy.

दक्षिणीय *m. n. f.* deserving of *dakshinâ* [give.*

ददत् *pres. part.* of दा *3rd conj.*, to

दीन *m. n. f.* poor.

दुष्कृत *n.* a wicked deed, wickedness, sin.

* See Art. 23, Lesson XVI.

द्युम्न *n.* wealth.

निज् *2nd conj. Âtm.* with प्र, to wash.

नियोगिन् *m.* a minister, an officer.

पान्थ *m.* a traveller.

पाश *m.* a net, a snare.

पीडाकर *m. n. f.* that which gives pain.

पृच् *1st conj. Parasm. 2nd conj. Âtm.* and *10th conj. with* सम्, to come in contact, to associate

पृथग्जन *m.* a low person, a mean fellow.

प्रद्युम्न *m.* the god of love.

मङ्गल *n.* welfare, prosperity, what is holy.

मस्तक *m. n.* the head.

मुकुटज्योत्स्नाजल *n,* (मुकुट *n.* a crown) the water [in the form] of the light or lustre of crowns.

मूर्धन् *m.* the head.

यत्पाद् *m.* whose foot.

युज् *4th conj. Âtm.* to curb one's mind.

युज् *1st conj. Parasm.* and *10th conj.* to unite; *with* नि, to appoint.

विज् *n.* multitude of kings, all the kings.

विज् *6th conj. Âtm. with* उद्, to tremble, to fear, to be disgusted.

विप्र *m.* a Brâhmaṇn

वृज् *1st conj. Parasm. 2nd conj. Âtm.* and *10th conj.* to avoid, to shun.

वृजिन *m.* a wicked person.

वृथा *adv.* in vain, uselessly.

वृजिन *m.* Śûdra, a sinner, a reprobate.

शक्रजित् *m.* The conqueror of Śakra or Indra, the son of Râvana.

श्रि *1st conj. Parasm.* and *Âtm. with* आ, to cling to, to go to, to resort to.

सदाचार *m. n. f.* (सत् *m. n. f.* good, आचार *m.* conduct) one whose conduct is good.

सर्वाभिप्रेतहेतु *m.* (अभिप्रेत *past part. pass.* of इ *with.* अभि and प्र, desired, aimed at) yhe cause of [the attainment of] all desired objects.

सदाचार *m. n. f.* (सत् *m. n. f.* good, आचार *m.* conduct) one whose conduct is good.

सर्वाभिप्रेतहेतु *m.* (अभिप्रेत *past part. pass.* of इ *with.* अभि and प्र, desired, aimed at) the cause of [the attainment of] all desired objects.

सुनृत *m. n. f.* agreeable, pleasant.

हिंस् *1st conj. Parasm.* and *10th conj.* to kill, to destroy.

हिंस्र *m. n. f.* murderous, carnivorous.

Brâhmaṇa-ing ब्राह्मणराज *m.*

Branch शाखा *f.*

Brute पशु *m.*

Counsellor मन्त्रिन् *m.* धीसचिव *m.*

Different विविध *m. n. f.*

Ill रुग्ण *m. n. f.*

Medicinal drug मन्त्रिन् *f.*

Office अधिकार *m.*

Pity ब्राह्मणराज *f.*; दयार्द्र *m. n. f.* melted with pity.

Post पद *n*

Sâketa साकेत *n.* name of a town.

Skilful चतुर *m. n. f.* कुशल *n. f.*

Usially प्रायेण *ind. adv.* प्रायः *ind adv.*

Viśrâma-palace विश्रामप्रासाद *m.*

Whirlwind चक्रवात *m.* झञ्झावात

Lesson XIII.

NON-CONJUGATIONAL TENSES.

Perfect.

1. *General* :— The augment इ is prefixed to those non-conjugational termination which begin with any consonant except य्, before they are applied to certain primitive* roots. Such roots we will call *Seṭ* and the others *Aniṭ*. The number of the former is far greater than that of the latter; but the latter are more important and are more generally to be met with in Sanskrit literature.†

2. The following are the terminations of the Perfect :—

---

* *I.e.* such roots as consist of one syllable only. There are derived roots such as those of the 10th conjugation (*eg.* चोरय कथय), causals, &c., which are always *Seṭ*.

† The following verses separating the *Seṭ* from the *Aniṭ* roots may be learned by heart by the pupil, as easier to remember than long lists :—

ऊदृदन्तैर्यौतिरुक्ष्णुशीङ्स्नुनुक्षुश्विडीङ्श्रिभिः । वृङ्वृञ्भ्यां च विनैकाचोऽजन्तेषु निहताः स्मृताः ॥ *I. e.*, amongst roots ending in a vowel, all consisting of one syllable, with the exception of those that end in ऊत् and ॠत् (*i.e* long ऊ and long ॠ), of यु and the others that follow, are अनुदात्त or *Aniṭ* ; i.e.. again, of roots of one syllable ending in a vowel those that end in ऊ and ॠ and the others enumerated are *Seṭ*, and all the rest *Aniṭ*, डीङ् *i. e.* डी 'to fly' Âtm., वृङ् *i. e.* वृ Âtm., वृञ् *i. e.* वृ Âtm. and Parasm.

शक्लृ पच् मुचि रिच् वच् विच् सिच प्रच्छि त्यज् निजिर् भजः । भञ्ज् भुज् भ्रस्ज् मस्जि यज् युज् रुज् रञ्ज् विजर् स्वञ्जि सञ्ज् सृजः ॥ अद् क्षुद् खिद् छिद् तुदि नुदः पद्य भिद् विद्यातिर् विनद् । शद् सदी स्विद्यतिः स्कन्दि हदी क्रुध् क्षुधि बुध्यति ॥ बन्धिर् युधि रुधी राधि व्यध् शुधः साधि सिध्यती । मन्य हन् आप् क्षिप् छुपि तप् तिपस्तृप्यति दृप्यति ॥ लिप् लुप् वप् शप् स्वप् सृपि यभ् रभ् लभ् गम् नम् यमो रमिः । क्रुशिर् दंशि दिशी दृश् मृश् रिश् रुश् लिश् विश् स्पृशः कृषिः ॥ त्विष् तुष् द्विष् दुष् पुष्य पिष् विष् शिष् शुष् श्लिष्यतयो घसिः । वसतिर् दह् दिहि दुहो नह् मिह् रुह् लिह् वहिस्तथा ॥ अनुदात्ता हलन्तेषु धातवो द्व्यधिकं शतम् ॥ In these verses the-*Aniṭ* roots are enumerated. For the exigencies of the metre, soine roots have an इ attached to them, and some others have their conjugational sign and ति added on. The word अनुदात्त in the last line is equivalent to *aniṭ*.

The statements made in these veses are true generally in non-conjugational tenses; but in *special cases* they require modincations. The modifications necessary in the case of the Perfect are noticed above in the text.

Parasmaipada.

	Sing.	*Dual.*	*Plur.*
1st pers.	अ	व	म
2nd "	थ	अथुस्	अ
3rd "	अ	अतुस्	उस्

3. Here there are only three terminations, *viz.*, थ, व. and म्, capable of taking the augment इ. *(a)* In the case of कृ, सृ, भृ, *वृ, स्तु, द्रु, स्रु, and श्रु, they do not take it; while, *(b)* as applied to all other roots व, म, and थ do take इ, but *(c)* थ in the case of *Aniṭ* roots ending in short ऋ does not admit it, while *(d)* after. *Aniṭ* roots with a final vowel or having an. अ in them, it takes it optionally.

Âtmanepada.

	Sing.	*Dual.*	*Plur.*
1st pers.	ए	वहे	महे
2nd "	से	आथे	ध्वे
3rd "	ए	आते	इरे

4. The learner will see that these terminations, with the exception of the singular and plural of the third person, are the same as those of the Present of the 2nd group of conjugations. Unaugmented ध्वे, becomes ढ्वे when in a form it is perceded by any vowel except अ or आ. When it takes इ, it undergoes the change optionally when that इ is preceded by य्, र्, ल्, व्, or ह्.

5. The terminations capable of taking इ do admit it after all roots except the eight enumerated above.

6. A few roots such as गुप् *(1st conj. Par)*, त्रप्, सिध् *1st conj.* 'to turn out auspiciously' or 'to regulate,' क्षम्†, मृज, क्लिद्, अञ्ज्, स्यन्द्, कृप्, गुह्, गाह्, रध्, नश्, तृप्, दृप्, गृह्, द्रुह्, मुह्, स्नुह्, स्निह्, अश् 'to pervade,' &c,, which are optionally *Seṭ*. in all non-conjugational tenses, are so in the Perfect also. स्वृ‡, सू *2nd & 4th conj.*, धू *5th & 9th conj.*, are also optionally *Seṭ*, but in the Perfect they admit इ necessarily necessarily before all except थ.

---

* The 2nd pers. sing., however, of this root is ववरिथ.

† In the case in which this root does not admit of इ the forms of the 1st pers. dual and plural are चक्षण्वहे and चक्षण्महे *i.e.* the म् is changed to ण्. The rule is that the final म् of a root is changed to न् when followed by व् or म्.

‡ स्वृ is necessarily *Seṭ* in the Second Future and the Conditional.

7. *Base.* The initial consonant with the following vowel is reduplicated according to the rules given in Lesson XI. An initial vowel is reduplicated without the following consonant.

8. The reduplicative इ is changed to इय्, and उ to उव्, when followed by a dissimilar vowel, and, when it is not, the two vowels combine and form (long) ई, and (long) ऊ. The reduplicative इ of the root इ 'to go' is lengthened before the weak terminations of the Perfect.

Thus उख्-उउख् by above-by 9 below उओख् and by this उवोख्. So इष्-इइष्-इएष्-इयेष्. When no Guṇa takes place, we have उख्-उउख्-ऊख् and इष्-इइष्-ईष्; also इ-इइ-ईइ, and the last इ being changed to य् by 10, p. 38, we have ईयतुः-ईयुः.

9. The dual and the plural terminations of the Parasmaipada and all Âtmanepada ones are weak and the singulars of the former strong. (*a*) The penultimate short vowel takes its Guṇa substitute before the latter, and (*b*) the final vowel and the penultimate अ take Vṛiddhi iptionally in the first and necessarily in the third person singular. (*c*) In the 2nd person singular, the ending vowel takes Guṇa and the penultimate अ remains unchanged.

बुध् *Parasm.*

	Sing.	*Dual.*	*Plur.*
1st pers.	बुबोध	बुबुधिव	बुबुधिम
2nd "	बुबोधिथ	बुबुधथुः	बुबुध
3rd "	बुबोध	बुबुधतुः	बुबुधुः

बुध्-बुबुध् by 7—बुबोध्, by 9 (*a*) बुबोध, बुबुधिव-See 3 (*b*) p. 79.

Âtm.

1st pers.	बुबुधे	बुबुधिवहे	बुबुधिमहे
2nd "	बुबुधिषे	बुबुधाथे	बुबुधिध्वे
3rd "	बुबुधे	बुबुधाते	बुबुधिरे

कृ *Parasm.*

1st pers.	चकार-चकर	चकृव	चकृम
2nd "	चकर्थ	चक्रथुः	चक्र
3rd "	चकार	चक्रतुः	चक्रुः

कृ-कृकृ-चकृ by 2 *c.* and 2 f., p. 63—चकार् by 9 (*b*) above-चकार-चकर, चकृव, चकर्थ &c. by 3 (*a*), p. 79

Atm.

	Sing.	*Dual.*	*Plur.*
1st pers.	चक्रे	चकृवहे	चकृमहे
2nd "	चकृषे	चक्राथे	चकृढ्वे
3rd "	चक्रे	चक्राते	चक्रिरे

For ह्वे see 4, p. 79.

नी *Parasm.*

1st pers.	निनाय-निनय	निन्यिव	निन्यिम
2nd "	निनयिथ-निनेथ	निन्यथुः	निन्य
3rd "	निनाय	निन्यतुः	निन्युः

नी-नीनी by 7, p. 80-निनी by 2 *f.*, p. 63-निनै by 9 (*b*), p. 80—निनाय *3rd pers. sing;* निनी-निन्यतुः by I., p. 65. See also 3 (*d*) p. 79 and 9 (*c*), p. 80, for निनयिथ-निनेथ.

Âtm. 1st pers. निन्ये-निन्यिवहे-निन्यिमहे, &c.

गद् *3rd pers.* जगाद-जगदतुः-जगदुः &c., &c.

10. Roots ending in ऋ preceded by a conjunct consonant, and in (long) ॠ, and the roots जागृ and ऋ change the final vowel to its Guna, i.e., अर् before even the weak terminations of this tense. शृ, दृ and पृ do it optionally, and shorten the vowel when they do not. ऋच्छ् also changes its initial to its Guna.

स्मृ

1st pers.	सस्मार-सस्मर	सस्मरिव	सस्मरिम
2nd "	सस्मर्थ	सस्मरथुः	सस्मर
3rd "	सस्मार	यस्मातुः	सस्मरुः

See 2 (*d*), p. 63 and 3 (*b*) and (*c*), p. 79. शशार, शशरतुः-शश्रतुः, शशरुः-शश्रुः, &c.

11. A few roots of the 6th conjugation, such as कुद्, स्फुद्, बुद्, स्फुर् नू, and धू, do not take Guṇa or Vṛiddhi veen before striong terminations except those of the 1st and 3rd pers. sing. of the Perfect, the अय of the causal, and the इ of the third pers. sing. of the Passive Aorist; तुत्रोट (3rd sing.), तुत्रुटिथ. In the Perfect first pers. sing., however, such of them, as are capable of taking Vṛiddhi, optionally, take Vṛiddhi alone and not Guṇa. and the others optionally take Guṇa; नुनाव or नुनुव, चुकोट or चुकुट.

12. Some roots, such as अस् and ब्रू, are defective and have no forms for the non-conjugational tenses.

13. In the case of roots ending in आ, (*a*) the termination अ of the singulars of the 1st and 3rd person Parasmaipada is replaced by औ. (*b*) The final आ is dropped before the weak terminations beginning with a vowel, and before such as take the augment इ.

Parasm.

	Sing.	*Dual.*	*Plur.*
1st pers.	जज्ञौ	जज्ञिव	जज्ञिम
2nd "	जज्ञिथ-जज्ञाथ	जज्ञथुः	जज्ञ
3rd "	जज्ञौ	जज्ञतुः	जज्ञुः

ज्ञा-जज्ञा, and अ being changed to औ, we have जज्ञौ. आ being dropped before इथ [see 3 (*d*), p. 79] and the vowel terminatons, we have जज्ञ+इथ=जज्ञिथ, जज्ञथुः and &c.

14. The final ए, ऐ, and ओ of roots is replaced by आ before all terminations whatever, except those of the conjuational. tenses and the present participle.

ग्लै *3rd pers.* जग्लौ-जग्लतुः-जग्लुः. *2nd pers,* जग्लिथ-जग्लाथ, &c.

15. (*a*) भू, as reduplicated, assumes the form बभूव्. (*b*) The ज् of जि is changed to ग्. the ह् of हि to घ् and the च् of चि to क् optionally, in the Perfect.

बभूव, बभूविथः जिगाय-जिगय, जिग्यव, जिगेथ-जिगयिथ, *3* (*d*), P. 79; जिघाय, चिकाय or चिचाय.

16. The penultimate अ of गम्, हन्, जन्, खन्, and घस् is dropped before the weak terminations beginning with a vowel. ह् becomes घ् throughout, and जन् and घस्, after dropping अ, become ज्ञ् and क्ष् respectively.

हन्

1st pers.	जघान-जघन	जघ्निव	जघ्निम
2nd "	जघनिथ-जघन्थ	जघ्नथुः	जघ्न
3rd "	जघान	जघ्नतुः	जघ्नुः

17. The base of इ with अधि 'to study' is अधिजगा in the Perfect, अधिजगे, अधिजगाते, अधिजगिरे &c.

18. (*a*) सृ and दृश् substitute र for ऋ, *i.e.* become स्रज् and द्रश्, when followed by a consonantal strong termination.

(*b*) These roots admit of इ optionally in the case of थ.

सृज्—सृजृज् ससृज्+ थ by above—सस्रष्+ थ by IX, p. 52—सस्रष्+ ठ by note*, p. 21. F.B—सस्रष्ठ.

Similary दद्रष्ठ. Also ससर्जिथ and ददर्शिथ. प्रच्छ्-पप्रच्छिथपप्रष्ट by 3 (*d*), p. 79.

19. *Âniṭ* roots having ऋ for their penultimate change it to र optionally, when followed by a strong* termination beginning with a hard consonant; as दद्रप्थ or ददर्प्थ, तत्रप्थ or ततर्प्थ. ददर्पिथ Also. ततर्पिथ.

* *I.e.* any termination which occasions a Guṇa or Vṛiddhi change in the preceding.

20. अद् substitutes घस् optionally in the Perfect. When so substituted, घस् takes इ necessarily before थ. For the weak forms see 16 above.

21. The Perfect shows that the action took place at a very remote time, or that that it was not witnessed by the speaker. It is generally used to narrate events of the remote past; and in the first person it is used to show something done by the speaker of which he was unconscious, or when the speaker wants to deny emphatically an action by denying another, which includes it or on which it depends. (See 1. 2 of the Sanskrit sentences below).

बहु जगद पुरस्तात्तस्य मत्ता किलाहम्।
भुक्तं त्वया कलिङ्गेषु। नाहं कलिङ्गाञ्जगाम।
पुरा किल दुष्यन्तो नाम राजा बभूव। स एकदा मृगयां कर्तुं वनमियाय। तं तस्य सैनिका अमात्याश्चानुजग्मुः। तस्मिन्कानने दुष्यन्तो बहून्मृगाञ्जघान। एकं मृगं पलायमानमनुसरन्मार्गे दिव्याश्रमपदं ददर्श। तस्य सैनिकाः पूर्वस्मिन्नेव स्थाने तस्थुः। कण्वस्यायमृषेराश्रम इति ज्ञात्वा तं प्रविवेश। प्रविश्य च को नु भो अत्रेति पप्रच्छ। कण्वस्य कृतिका दुहिता शकुन्तलाश्रमाद्बहिरागत्य दुष्यन्तं स्वागतं व्याजहार। शकुन्तलां चारुसर्वाङ्गीं दृष्ट्वा दुष्यन्तस्तां चकमे। तस्याः पाणिं गान्धर्वेण विधिना राजा जग्राह। अनन्तरं कंचित्कालं तावुभौ तस्मन्नाश्रमे चिक्रीडतुः। रममाणं राजानं प्रेक्ष्य सैनिकाः पुरं निववृतिरे। राजापि पश्चात्स्वं नगरमुपययौ।
कियद्वसु ब्राह्मणेभ्यो यूयं दद। न वयं तेभ्यः किंचिद्ददिम।
उन्मादं वीक्ष्य पद्मानां कुमुदानां च मन्दताम्।
क्षणिकत्वं विभूतीनां चेतसा निश्चिकाय सः।
शुश्राव रामस्तत्सर्वं प्रतस्थे च ससैनिकः॥
तस्तनुर्जज्वलुर्मम्लुर्जग्लुर्लुलुठिरे क्षताः।
मुमूर्च्छुर्ववमू रक्तं ततृषुश्चोभये भटाः॥
जम्बुमाली जहौ प्राणाम् ग्राव्णा मारुतिना हतः॥
बभागण स न मे मायां जिगायेन्द्रोऽपि किं नृभिः॥

A king named Gâdhi gave [दा] his daughter to Richîka, the son of Bhṛigu.

She gave birth [सू] to a son named Jamadagni.

Jamadagni married [नी* with परि] Reṇukâ.

He once got very angry (कुप्) with her for her indiscretion, and commanded [दिश्] her sons to kill her.

None did [कृ] it except his youngest son Paraśuràma.

He cut off [छिद्] her head woth his axe.

Jamadagni was pleased [तुष्] with the act, and said [धा with अभि], "O son, choose a gift."

Paraśuràma begged [वृ] that his mother might be resorted to life again (revive), and be free from her sin.

Then said [ह Âtm. with वि and आ] Jamadagni, "So let it be." and Renukà rose up [स्था with उद्] alive.

Some time after, king Kàrtavîrya came [गम् with आ] to the hermitage.

And he and his soldiers destroyed [भञ्ज्] all the trees, laid waste [उत्सन्नं कृ] the ground, and carried off [ह with अप] the Rishi's cows. Paras uramá was [भू] not at home. When he came he came, he fought [उध्] with Kártavîrya and killed [हन्] him.

when the sons of Kártavîrya heard [श्रु] of this, they were very angry [क्रुध्] and went [गम्] to the hermitage.

Observin Jamadagni alone, they discharged [क्षिप्, or मुच्] arrows at him and killed him.

When Paraśuráma returned [वृत् with नि] home, he was enraged, and resolved [चि with निस्] to exterminate the Kshatriyas.

He asked [प्रच्छ् or युज् with अनु] the sons of Kàrtavîrya, "Did you kill my father?" "No; we never killed him," said [गद्] they.

But Paraśuràma knew [ज्ञा] that that they ewre guilty, and killed them and all other Kshatriyas.

---

* All roots beginning with न्, except नर्द् 10th conj, नाथ्, नाध्, नन्द्, नक्ष्, नृ and नृत्, change the न् to ण्, when preceded by a prepostiton containing र्. Between the र् and the न्, those letters only which are given in note ||, p. 15, F. B. may intervene and not others. According to some नाथ्, नृ and नन्द् are not exceptions.

VOCABULARY XIII.

उख् *1st conj.* Parasm. to go.
उन्माद *m.* joy, bloom.
उपरि *adv.* above. [both sides.
उभय *pron m. n. f.* belonging to.
एकदा *adv.* once.
कण्व *m.* name of a Ṛishi.
कम् *10.th* conj. Âtm.* to love.
कलिङ्ग *m.* name of a country (in
कानन *n.* a forest [*the plur.*)
कुमुद *n.* a night lotus.
कृतिका *f.* adopted (daughter).
क्रुध् *4th. conj.* Parasm. to be enraged.
क्षणिकत्व *n.* momentariness.
क्षत *past part. pass.* of क्षण्, wounded.
गद् *1st conj.* Parasm. to speak.
गान्धर्व *m.* a particular form of marriage in which the only thing essentialis the mutual consent of the bridegroom and the bride.
गुप् † *1st conj.* ti protect.
ग्रावन् *m.* a stone.
घस् *1st conj. Parasm.* to eat.
चारुसर्वाङ्गी *f.* (चारु beautiful, सर्वाङ्ग all limbs beautiful. [conclude.
चि *with.* (निस् , to determine, to
जम्बुमालिन् *m.* name of a Râkshass.
[ardent to glow.
ज्वल् *1st conj. Parasm.* to be
तृष् *4th conj. Parasm.* to feel thirsty.
दिव्याश्रमपद *n.* (दिव्य celestial, आश्रमपद *n.* hermitage) beautiful hermitagem.
दृप् *4th conj. Parasm.* to be proud.
द्रु *1st conj. Parasm.* to run.
नु *ind.* a particle showing doubt or guess.
पद्म *n.* a lotus that blooms by day.
पलायमान (*pres. part.* of अय *1st conj. Âtm.* to go *with* परा, the र being changed to. ल) running.
पुरस्तात् *adv.* before, in front.
पूर्व *pron.* previous (person or
बहिस् *adv.* out. [thing).
भण् *1st conj. Parasm.* to speak.
मत्त *past. part* of मद्, intoxicated.
मन्दता *f.* dullness, withered condition.
माया *f.* jugglery, deceitful tricks.
मूर्छ् *1st conj. Parasm.* to faint.
म्लै *1st conj. Parasm.* to grow weary, to become faint or
रक्त *n.* blood. [languid.
रध् † *4th conj. Parasm.* to hurt.
लुठ् *1st conj. Âtm.* to roll on the ground.
वम् *1st conj. Paras.* to vomit.

---

*The termination अय of the 10th conj. is optinally dropped in the non-conjugational tenses in the case of this root. All other roots of this conjugation preserve the अय, with the final अ dropped, in all non-conjugational tenses and moods, except the Benedictive Parasm. and Aorist.

† आय् it optionally added to this and the other roots given in Art. 1., in the non-conjugational tenses and moods.

† रध् and जभ् insert a न् after their अ before terminations beginning with a vowel; Vṛiddhi becaus it ceases to be the penultimate when न् is inserted.

रध्, however. however, does not insert the न् in the Aorist or when it takes इ, except in the Perfect.

विभूति *f.* wealth, prospertity.
ससैनिक *m. n. f.* accompanied by soldiers.
सिध् *1st conj. Parasm.* to regulate, to turn out well or auspiciously.
स्तन् *1st conj. Parasm.* to cry, to thunder. [affection to.
स्निह् *4th conj. Parasm.* to bear
स्नु *2nd conj. Parasm.* to flow.
स्वृ *1st conj. Parasm.* to sound.
हत *past part. pass.* of हन्, struck.

Alive जीवन्ती *f. pres. part. act.* of w जीव्, सजीवा *f.* (जीव *m.* life and स for सह *ind.* with).
Axe परशु *m.* [Rishi.
Bhṛigu भृगु *m.* the name of a
Except ऋते *ind.**
Exterminate मूल *10th conj.* with. उद्; उन्मूलयितुम् *inf.*
Free मुक्त *past pass. part.* of मुच्; मुक्ता *f.*; to be free मुच् *pass.*
Gadhi गाधि *m.* the name of a king.
Indiscretion व्यभिचार *m.* [Ṛishi.
Jamdagni जमदग्नि *m.* name of a
Kârtavîrya कार्तवीर्य *m.* the name of a king killed by Paraśurâma.
Named नाम *ind.* नाम्ना *instr. sing* of नामन्.
Never नैव *ind.* न कर्हिचित् *ind.*
Reṇukâ रेणुका *f.* wife of Jamadagni and mother of Paraśu- râma.
Revive जीव् *with.* पुनर्.
Richîka ऋचीक *m.* name of a Ṛishi.
Very भृशम् *adv.*
Youngest कनिष्ठ *m. n. f.*

LESSON XIV.

NERFECT—Continued.

When a root has an अ between two simple consonants and the radical consonant is not changed in reduplication, the अ is replaced by ए and the reduplicative syllable dropped before the weak terminations, and before the थ of the 2nd person singular of the Parasmipada when it takes इ.

तन् *Parasm.*

	Sing.	*Dual.*	*Plur.*
1st pers.	ततान-ततन	तेनिव	तेनिम
2nd "	तेनिथ	तेनथुः	तेन
3rd "	ततान	तेनतुः	तेनुः

तन् incets all the conditions in the rule; नन्द् does not, because it has a conjunct consonant; and गद् and भण्, because in the reduplicative syllable their initial consonants become ज् and ब respectively.

---

* ऋते governs the Ablative.

Therefore we have :

	Sing.	*Dual.*	*Plur.*
3rd pers.	ननन्द	ननन्दतुः	ननन्दुः
2nd "	जगाद	जगदतुः	जगदुः
3rd "	बभाण	बभणतुः	बभणुः

and not नेन्दतुः, गेदतुः, भेणतुः, &c.

2nd pers. sing. of पच्, पेचिथ-पपक्थ, of शक्, शेकिथ-शशक्थ. थ takes इ optionally by 3 *(d)*, p. 79. When it does take it, the above change takes place, and not when it does not. च् is changed to क् by note †, p. 97, F. B.

2. The roots तॄ, फल्, भज्, त्रप्, and राध् *(5th conj.)* when it means 'to offend', change their अ or आ to ए similarly, and जॄ भ्रम, त्रस्, फण्, राज्, भ्राज्, भ्राश्, भ्लाश्, स्यम् and स्वन् do it optionally.

The roots here enumerated do not come under the general rule in 1.

तॄ-ततॄ by 2 *f.*, p. 63 ततर्+ अतुः by 10, p. 81, and by the above तेरतुः. So त्रेपे, त्रेपाते, &c. बभ्राम-बभ्रमतुः or भ्रेमतुः-बभ्रमुः or भ्रेमुः, &c.

3. Roots beginnig with व and the roots शस् and दद् do not undergo this change.

वम् *3rd pers.* ववाम-ववमतुः-ववमुः.

4. The following roots and some others change their य्, व् and र् to इ, उ and ऋ respectively before weak terminations generally:—*वच्, यज्, वप्, वह्, वस्, *1st conj.*, वे, व्ये, ह्वे, श्वि, वद्, स्वप्, जय, वश्, व्यच्, प्रच्छ्, व्रश्च्, भ्रस्ज्, ग्रह्, and व्यध्. From this list प्रच्छ्, व्रश्च्, adn भ्रस्ज् are to be removed in the case of the Perfect. This change or the vowel so substituted is called *Saṁpreasâraṇa.*

5. Before the strong terminations of the Perfect. Saṁpreasâraṇa takes place in the reduplicative syllableonly. The reduplicative syllable of व्यध् is वि throughout.

6. The vowel following a Saṁpreasâraṇ is dropped.

7. When the two members of a conjunct are capable of taking Saṁpreasâraṇa the latter only takes it.

---

* This change does not take place, when the first eleven of the roots in the text are followed by the weak terminations of the conjugational tenses, where possible.

यज्

	Parasm.			*Âtm.*		
	Sing.	*Dual.*	*Plur.*	*Sing.*	*Dual.*	*Plur.*
1st pers.	इयाज-इयज	ईजिव	ईजिम	ईजे	ईजिवहे	ईजिमहे
2nd "	इयजिथ-इयष्ठ	ईजथुः	ईज	ईजिषे	इजाथे	ईजिध्वे
3rd "	इयाज	ईजतुः	ईजुः	ईजे	ईजाते	ईजिरे

यज्-ययज्-इअयज् by 5 —इयज् by 6—इयज. यज्-इज् by 4 and 6—इयज्-ईज्+ अतुःईजतुः. यज्.इयजिथ or इयज्+ थ by 3 (d), p.79—इयष्+ थ by IX., p. 52-इयष्+ ठ = इयष्ठ by note* p. 21, F. B. व्यध्-व्यव्यध्*-विअव्यध् by 5 and 7-विव्यध् by 6-विव्याध. स्वप्—स्वस्वप्-सुस्वप्—† सुष्वप्+ अ-सुष्वाप. व्यध्-विध्-विविध्+ अतुः-विविधतुः. स्वप्-सुप्-सुषुप्+ अतुः-सुषुपतुः. वच् by *3rd pers. Parasm.* उवाच, ऊचतुः, ऊचुः—*2nd pers. sing.* उवचिथ or उवक्थ—*Âtm.* ऊचे, ऊचाते, &c.

I. (*a*) The ह् of the roots द्रुह्, मुह्, स्नुह् and स्निह् is optionally changed to घ् *i.e.*, to घ् or ढ् when it is followed by any consonant except a nasal or a semi-vowel or by nothing.

मुमोहिथ, मुमोह्+ थ (by 6, p. 79) = मुमोढ्+ थ or मुमोघ्+ थ = मुमाढ or मुमोग्ध.

(*b*) The final ह् of नह् is changed to ध् under the same circumstances; नेहिथ, and ननह्+ थ = ननध्+ थ-ननद्ध.

II. When the ढ् of वह् is dropped by III., p. 49, the preceding अ or आ is changed to ओ.

वह्--ववह्-उवह्+ थ-उवद्+ थ by I, p. 49—उवढ्+ ध by II., p. 49-उवढ्+ ढ by note*, p. 21, F. B.—उवढ by III. p. 49, but by this उवोढ instead of उवाढ.

II. When the ढ् of वह् is dropped by III., p. 49, the preceding अ or आ is changed to उवाढ.

8. (*a*) The modified base of वे *Parasm* and *Âtm.* 'to weave', before the strong terminations of the Perfect is उवय; and ऊय्, or ऊव् before the weak; and that of व्ये *Parasm.*, and *Âtm.*, 'to cover', is विव्यय् before the former and विवी before the latter. उवय् admits इ before थ.

---

* Note this divergence from rule 7, p. 80, in the strong terminations, when a root capable of taking saṁprasâraṇa begins with a conjunt consonant.

† Roots beginning with a स्, that is followed by a vowel or a dental, and the roots स्वद्, स्विद्, स्वञ्ज्, स्वप् and स्मि change their स् to ष्, when preceded generally in the same word or grammatical form by any vowel except अ or आ or by a guttural. सेक्, सृप्, सृज्, सृ, स्तृ, सृ and स्त्यै are exceptions.

Otherwise, 14, p. 82 would be applicable. व्ये-व्येव्ये-वुइएव्ये by7—विव्ये by 6—विव्यै+अ=विव्याय So also वे in the strong forms.

(b). The base of ह्वे *Parasm.* and *Âtm,* 'to call or challenge', is हु throughout; and of श्वि, शु.

I. e., They take Saṃprasàraṇa before also the strong terminations of the Perfect. ह्वे-हुउए-हु by 6 above.

(*c*) वे So also श्वि are also conjugated from the unmodified oase. वे-वा by 14, p. 82-वा-ववौ, ववतुःए ववुः, by 13 (*a*) & (*b*), p. 81.

9. अद्, ऋ and व्ये admit of इ necessarily before थ.

2nd pers. sing. आरिथ *3rd pers.* आर-आरतुः-आरुः.

10. मस्ज् and नश् insert a न् after their अ before strong terminations beginning with a consonant; as ननंष्ठ when थ does not take इ.

11. (*a*) If the reduplicative syllable consists of अ only, the अ is lengthened.

(*b*) Roots beginning with अ and ending with a double consonant, and those with an initial ऋ and the root अश् 'to pervade', insert न् after the reduplicative syllable.

	Sing.	*Dual.*	*Plur.*
उर्द् *3rd pers.*	आनर्द	आनर्दतुः	आनर्दुः
अन्त् "	आनन्त	आनन्ततुः	आनन्तुः
ऋज् "	आनृजे	आनृजाते	आनृजिरे

12. (*a*) The Perfect of roots beginning with any vowel (except अ or आ) which is itself long, or being short, is followed by a conjunct consonant, is formed by adding आम् to the root and then appending the forms of the reduplicate Perfect of कृ, भू, or अस्. ऋच्छ् is an exception. (*b*) The Perfect of roots of the 10th conjugation, Causals, Desideratives, and other derived roots, or, generally, of roots of more than one syllable, is also formed in this way.

This is called the Periphrastic Perfect.

(*c*) When a root is Âtmanepadi, it takes the Âtmanepada forms of कृ, and a Parasmaipadi root takes the Parasmaipada forms.

a. ईश् *Âtm.*

	Sing.	*Dual.*	*Plur.*
1st pers.	ईशांचक्रे	ईशांचकृवहे	ईशांचकृमहे
2nd "	ईशांचकृषे	ईशांचक्राथे	ईशांचकृढ्वे
3rd "	ईशांचक्रे	ईशांचक्राते	ईशांचक्रिरे

Also ईशामास, ईशांबभूव, &c.

b. कथ् *10th conj. Parasm.*

1st pers.	कथयांचकार-चकर	कथयांचकृव	कथयांचकृम
2nd "	कथयांचकर्थ	कथयांचक्रथुः	चथयांचक्र
3rd "	कथयांचकार	कथयांचक्रतुः	कथयांचक्रुः

Also *Âtm.* कथयांचक्रे, &c.

अय is retained in most of the non-conjugational tenses. (See note*, p. 85.)

13. (*a*) दय्, अय्, कास् and आस् take the Periphrastic Perfect necessarily, and उष्, विद् (*2nd conj.*), and जागृ optionally.

(*b*) भी, ह्री, भृ (*3rd conj.*), and हु also take it optionally, but the base of these is reduplicated as in the 3rd conjugation and then आम् and the helping verb appended.

14. आम् is a strong termination, wherefore the final vowel and the penultimate short, except that of विद्, take their Guṇa before it.

आसांचक्रे, विदांचकार or विवेद, बिभयांचकार, जिह्रयांचकार, बिभरांचकार, &c.

15. मृ takes the Parasmaipada terminations in all non-conjugational tenses, except the Aorist and the Benedictive; ममर्थ.

16. The passive of the Perfect is formed by making up the forms according to the rules given in these two lessons and appending the Âtmanepada terminations, whether the root is Parasmaipadi or Âtmanepadi in the active.

गतायां रात्रौ सुप्ता वयं किल बहु विलेपिम।

युधिष्ठिरेण पृष्टो लोमशोऽगस्त्यस्य प्रभावं कथयामास।

कृतयुगे कालेया इति विश्रुता दानवा वृत्रं समाश्रित्य महीं स्वर्ग लोकं च भृशं पीडयांचक्रुः। नैतत्कर्तुमानर्हुस्ते।

तान्हन्तुं सेन्द्रा विबुधा न शेकुः।

ते ब्रह्माणमुपसंगम्योचुर्भगवन्नखिलं त्रैलोक्यं दानवैरर्द्यते किमत्र करवाम है

परमेष्ठ्युवाच भो देवा दधीचमृषिं गत्वा तस्यास्थीनि याचध्वम्। तेषां वज्रं कृत्वा वृत्रं हत।

तथेति प्रतिज्ञाय ते सर्वे दधीचस्याश्रममुपययुः।

तमृषिं देवाः प्रणेमुस्तस्यास्थीनि च ययाचिरे।

ततः स महात्मा त्रैलोक्यस्य हितायात्मनः प्राणानुत्ससर्ज।

तस्य परासोरस्थीनि देवा जगृहुस्त्वष्टारं च गत्वा तं * तेषामुग्रं वज्रं कारयामासुः।

ततस्त्वष्टा शक्रमुवाचैतद्गृहीत्वा वृत्रं जहि।

इन्द्रेण सहिता देवा रोदसी आवृत्य तिष्ठन्तं कालेयैरभिरक्षितं च वृत्रमासेदुः। तांश्च युद्धायाजुहुविरे।

तैः सह देवानां तुमुलं युद्धं समापेदे। रजोभिः सर्वा दिशो व्यानशिरे। दानवेभ्यश्च देवा भृशं त्रेसुः।

इतस्ततः प्रधावतां तेषां वेगं देवा दौर्बल्यान्न सेहिरे भीताश्च पलायामासुः।

तादृशांस्तान्दृष्ट्वेन्द्रो विष्णुं शरणं वव्राज।

ततो विष्णुरात्मनस्तेज इन्द्रे निदधे देवाश्च महर्षयश्चापि तथा विदधिरे।

ततो रणधुरामेकोऽपीन्द्र उवाह।

स वृत्रस्य वधाय महद्वज्रं मुमोच। तेन हतो वृत्रो भूमौ सुष्वाप।

कोट्याकोट्या पुरद्वारमेकैकं रुरुधे द्विषाम्॥

तत्कर्म वालिपुत्रस्य दृष्ट्वा विश्वं विसिष्मिये।

संत्रेसू राक्षसाः सर्वे बहु मेने च राघवः॥

सुग्रीवो मुमुदे देवाः साध्वित्यूचुः सविस्मयाः।

बिभीषणोऽभितुष्टाव प्रशशंसुः प्लवंगमाः॥

राघवो न दयांचक्रे दधुर्धैर्ये न केचन।

मम्रे नतज्ञवद्धीर्हाहेति च विचुक्रुशे॥

---

* See 12, Lesson XXI.

*प्राणा दध्वंसिरे गात्रं तस्तम्भे च प्रिये हते।
उच्छश्वास चिराद्दीना रुरोदासौ ररास च॥
लोहबन्धैर्बबन्धे नु वज्रेण किं विनिर्ममे।
मनो मे न विना रामाद्यत्पुस्फोट सहस्रधा॥
उत्तेरिथ समुद्रं त्वं मदर्थेऽरीञ् जिहिंसिथ।
ममर्थ चातिघोरां मां† धिग्जीवितलघूकृताम्॥
मालिन्यं मार्जयामास चन्द्रमास्तिमिरैः कृतम्।
खलैर्दत्तं मृषा दोषमिव सत्पुरुषः सताम्।

‡ऐन्द्रेण ह वै महाभिषेकेण संवर्त आङ्गिरसो मरुत्तमाविक्षितमभिषिषेच। तस्माद् मरुत्त आविक्षितः समन्तं सर्वतः पृथिवीं जयन्परीयायाश्वेन च मेध्येनेजे। §तदप्येष श्लोकोऽभिगीतः।

मरुतः परिवेष्टारो मरुत्तस्यावसन्गृहे।
आविक्षितस्य कामप्रेर्विश्वेदेवाः सभासद इति॥

When the leader of the Kâleyas was killed [हन्- *pass.*], they fought [युध्] desperately, but the gods subdued [जि] them at last.

They then held a consultation [मन्त्र or मन्त्रं कृ] and resolved [चि with निस्] to destroy the universe.

They thought [मन्] the death or destruction of all Rishis and Brâhmaṇas to be the best means to that end, for the universe depended [श्रि with आ or लम्ब् with अव] on the religious austerities they went through [तप् or चर्] and the sacrifices they performed [तन् or हृ with आ].

---

* This stanza refers to the state of Sîtâ, when she saw her husband, Râma, lying on the ground, as if dead, under the influence of Indrajit's missile. The next two stanzas are her words of lamentation on the occasion.

† The indeclinable धिक् governs the accusative.

‡ ऐन्द्रो महाभिषेक was a particular form of coronation according to which Indra was crowned king by the gods. That same form, when used in the case of mortal kings, rendered them invulnerable, and enabled them to conquer the whole earth.

§ तद् is here equivalent to तस्मात्.

They therefore, concealed [छद् with प्र] themselves during the day in the sea; and at night stalked [चर्] abroad, killed [हन्] a great many Brâhmanas, and tormented [पीड् or] all people.

The hermitages of Vasishṭha Bhârgava. and other Rishis were laid waste [साद् *caus.* with अव्] and rendered [कृ] tenantless; afterwards they burnt [दह्] them.

No men sacrificed [यज्] and the gods were afraid [भी or त्रस्].

They did not know [ज्ञा] who did all this, and so went [गम् with उप] to Vishṇu and begged [याच्] his assistance.

Vishṇu told [कथ् or चक्ष्] them that the Kâleyas did this at night and lay concealed in the sea during the day.

He commanded [दिश् with आ] them to go to Agastya and request his to drink off the sea.

The gods went [गम् with उप] to the sage, bowed [गम् with उप] to him, and praised [गम् with उप] his might.

He asked [प्रच्छ्] them the purpose of their visit.

This they told [कथ्] him; whereupon Agastya went [या] to the sea, and the gods followed [ई or या with अनु] him. He drank [पा] the sea, and the Kâleyas were drawn [कृष् with आ] out from their place of refuge.

Then a battle took place [पद् with सम् and आ] and the gods killed [हन्] them.

VOCABULARY XIV.

अगस्त्य *m.* the name of a sage.

अतिघोर *m. n. f.* very horrible or wicked.

अन्ततः *adv.* at last.

उभय *past part pass.* of गै *1st conj. Parasm. with* अभि, sung.

अर्थ *with.* प्र *10th conj. Âtm.* to request.

अर्द् *1st* and *10th conj.* to afflict, to torment.

अश् *5th conj. Âtm.* with वि, to pervade.

*अस्थि *n.* a bone.

आङ्गिरस *m.* a descendant of अङ्गिरस्.

आविक्षित *m.* the son of अविक्षित्.

* See Lesson XVI. Art. 11.

इ *2nd conj. Parasm with* परि, to circumambulate.

इतस्ततः *adv.* to and fro.

उ a particle.

उग्र *m. n. f.* austere, keen, severe.

उष् *1st conj. Parasm.* to burn.

एकैक *pron. m. n. f.* one by one, each one.

ऐन्द्र *m. n. f.* belonging to Indra.

कामर्धि *m.* one whose desires are fulfilled.

कारय *caus.* of कृ, to cause anything to be done.

कालेय *m.* name of certain giants.

कृतयुग *n.* the first of the four ages according to Hindu mythology.

क्रुश् *1st conj Parasm. with* वि, to cry out.

चर् *1st conj. Parasm.* to go, to stalk abroad.

चिराद् *adv.* after a long time.

छद् *10th conj. with* प्र, to conceal anything.

जीवितलघूकृत *m. n. f.* disgraced or degradd by life or by continuing to live.

तप् *1st conj. Parasm.* to perform religious austerities.

तादृश *m. n. f.* like that.

तिमिर *m. n.* darkness, dark.

तुमुल *m. n. f.* violent, tumultuous.

त्रस् *with* सम् to be afraid.

त्रैलोक्य *n.* the three worlds.

दद् *1st conj. Âtm.* to give.

दधीच *m* the name of a Ṛishi.

दय् *1st conj. Âtm.* to have compassion.

दानव *m.* a demon.

*दिश् *f.* direction.

दीन *m. n.f.* helpless, poor.

दोष *m.* censure or calumny.

दौर्बल्य *n.* weakness.

धिक् *ind.* fie upon!

पतङ्गवत् *adv.* like moths.

परमेष्ठिन् *m.* the god Brahmâ.

परासु *m. n. f.* dead.

परिवेष्टृ *m.* one who distributes food at the table.

पुरद्वार *m.* the gate of a city.

प्रभाव *m.* prowess, greatness.

प्लवंगम *m.* a monkey.

फण *1st conj. Parasm.* to go.

फल् *1st conj. Parasm.* to bear fruit.

बहु *adv.* highly, much.

बिभीषण *m.* name of a brother of Râvaṇa and ally of Râma.

† भ्रस्ज् *6th conj. Parasm. & Âtm.* to bake.

भ्राज् *1st conj. Âtm.* to shine.

भाश् *1st conj. Âtm.* to shine.

भ्लाश् *1st conj. Âtm.* to shine.

मदर्थे *adv.* for me.

मन्त्र् *10th conj. Âtm.* to hold a consultation, to consult.

मरुत् *m.* a god.

---

* See Lesson XVI, art. 22.

† This root has two bases, भ्रस्ज् and भर्ज्, in all non-conjugational tenses, except the Benedict. Parasm. The. स् of भ्रस्ज् is changed to ज् when not dropped (X, p. 54.)

मरुत्त *m.* name of a king.

महाभिषेक *m.* (महत् *m. n. f.* great and अभिषेक *m.* sprinkling water as on the head of a king when he is crowned great coronation.

मालिन्य *n.* darkness, dirtiness.

मृज् *10th conj.* to wipe off.

मृषा *ind.* falsely.

मेध्य *m. n. f.* fit or destined to be sacrifced.

रणधुरा (रण *m. n.* and धुर् *f.* yoke) the brunt of battle.

रस् *1st conj. Parasm.* to sceam.

रोदसी *n. dual.* heaven and sarth.

लप् *1st conj. Parasm. with* वि, to lament.

लम्ब् *1st conj. Âtm. with* अव, to depend upon.

लोमश *m.* the name of a Ṛishi.

लोहबन्ध *m.* (लोह *m. n.* iron, बन्ध *m.* a bond, a fetter) a fetter of iron.

वज्र *m. n.* adamant.

वालिपुत्र *m.* the son of Vâli, a monkey chief.

विबुध *m.* a god.

विश्रुत *m. n. f. past pass. part.* of (श्रु *with.* वि, famous, famed as.

विश्वेदेवाः *m. plur.* all the gods.

वेग *m.* speed, velocity.

शक्र *m.* a name of Indra.

श्रि *with.* आ, to depend on.

संवर्त *m.* the name of a priest

सत्पुरुष *m.* a good man.

सभासद् *m.* a member of an assembly or court.

समन्तात् *adv.* round about.

सर्वतः *adv.* in every direction.

सविस्मय *m. n. f.* with wonder, wondering. [parts.

सहस्रधा *adv.* into a thousand.

साधु *adv.* well.

सुग्रीव *m.* name of a monkey chief and ally of Râma.

सृज् *with.* उद्, to abandon.

सेन्द्र *m. n. f.* with India.

स्तु *with.* अभि, to praise.

स्फुट् *6th conj. Parasm.* to break, to split asunder.

Death वध *m.*

Desperately प्रसह्य *ind. adv.* आत्मनिरपेक्षम् *adv.* साहसेन *instr.* used as an *adv.*

Destroy छिद् *7th conj. with* उद्, सूद् *10th conj. with* नि; उच्छेत्तुम *inf.* निषूदयितुम् *inf.* [साद *m.*

Destruction ध्वंस *m.* नाश *m.* अवसाद *m.*

End कार्य *n.* फल *n.*; फलावाप्तये *dat.* for attainment of the fruit or end.

Means उपाय *m.* अभ्युपाय *m.*

Might प्रभाव *m.*

Place of refuge आश्रमस्थान *n.*

Purpose प्रयोजन *n.*

Religious austerities तपांसि *plur.*

Tenantless निर्जन *m. n. f.*

Visit आगमन *n.* आगम *m.*

LESSON XV.
Part I.

First and Second Fytyres abd Cibdutuibak

1. First Future.

1. To the root should be added the affix तृ, before which the final vowel or the penultimate short takes Guṇa. Nominative forms of the nouns thus made up are to be considered as the forms of the third person; and in the first and second persons, the corresponding forms of the Parasmaipada present tense of अस् should be appended to the nominative singular. When a root is Âtmanepadi, the Âtmanepada forms of अस् should be added.

2. To the affix तृ, इ is to be prefixed after *Seṭ* roots and optionally after those that are optionally *Seṭ Aniṭ* roots, of course, do not admit it. The roots इष्, सह्, लुभ्, रुष्, and रिष्, admit इ optionally before तृ.

3. The augment in the case of the root ग्रह् is long in all non-conjugational tenses except the Perfect. वृ and roots ending in ॠ (long) optionally lengthen it in all non-conjugational tenses except the Perfect, Benedictive Âtm., and Aorist Parasm.

4. When the ह of सह् is dropped by III. P. 49, the preceding अ or आ is changed to ओ, as that of वह् in the same circumstances. (See II., p. 88.)

Parasm.

भू

	Sing.	*Dual.*	*Plur.*
1st pers.	भवितास्मि	भवितास्वः	भवितास्मः
2nd "	भवितासि	भवितास्थः	भवितास्थ
3rd "	भविता	भवितारौ	भवितारः

सह्-सह + ता-सढ् + ता—सढ् + धा-सढ् + ढा-साढा-सोढा-by 4, p. 96. वह् similarly, वोढा; लभ् + ता-लभ् + धा-लब्धा; दह् + ता-दध् + ता-दध् + धा-दग्धा; नह + ता by I (*b*), p. 88—नध् + धा-नद्धा; सृज + ता-स्रज् + ता-स्रज् + ता by 18, p. 82 -स्रष् + ता-स्रष् + टा-स्रष्टा; स्रष्टा; सृज्-सर्प्ता or स्रप्ता by 19, p. 82. तृप्-तर्पिता, तर्प्ता or त्रप्ता.

Âtm.

मुद्

	Sing.	*Dual.*	*Plur.*
1st pers.	मोदिताहे	मोदितास्वहे	मोदितास्महे
2nd "	मोदितासे	मोदितासाथे	मोदिताध्वे
3rd "	मोदिता	मोदितारौ	मोदितारः

See 2, pp. 34-35.

II.—Second Future.

1. The terminations of this tense are made up by perfixing स्य to those of the Present. The augment इ is to be prefixed to स्य, or not, or optionally, according to the nature of the root. Before the terminations, the final vowel and the penultimate short take Guṇa.

I. The final स् of a root is changed to त्, when followed by a *non-personal termination with an initial स्.

2. After गम् *Parasm.*, हन् and roots ending in ऋ (short), इ is to be prefixed to स्य in this tense, though these roots are *Aniṭ* and optionally after कृत् and नृत्, though they are *Seṭ*.

3. क्लृप्, वृत् वृध्, श्रृध् and स्यन्द्, are optionally Parasmaipadi in the Second Future, and when so, the स्य does not take इ as appended to them. This holds good in the case of क्लृप् in the First Future also.

लभ् Atm.

	Sing.	*Dual.*	*Plur.*
1st pers.	लप्स्ये	लप्स्यावहे	लप्स्यामहे
2nd "	लप्स्यसे	लप्स्येथे	लप्स्यध्वे
3rd "	लप्स्यते	लप्स्येते	लप्स्यन्ते

* By this expression are meant all terminations with the exception of those which express number and person as मि, सि, ति, &c, and one or two others.

भू *Parasm.*

	Sing.	*Dual.*	*Plur.*
1st pers.	भविष्यामि	भविष्याव:	भविष्याम:
2nd "	भविष्यसि	भविष्यथ:	भविष्यथ
3rd "	भविष्यति	भविष्यत:	भविष्यन्ति

लभ् + स्य-लप् + स्य + ते-लप्स्यते; दिश + स्य-देश्-देष्-देक् + ष्यति-दक्ष्याति; दुह+ स्य-दोह-दोध्-धोध्-धोक् + ष्यति-धोक्ष्यति; दृश् + स्य- द्रश् by 18, p. 82-द्रष्-द्रक् + ष्यति-द्रक्ष्यति; सृप्+ स्यति-सर्प् or स्रप् by 19, o. 82-सर्प्स्यति or स्रप्स्यति: तृप्-तर्पिप्यति, तर्प्स्यति or त्रप्स्यति; वृध् + स्य-वर्ध्-वर्त्-वर्त्स्यति or वर्धिष्यते by 3, p. 97; स्यन्त्स्यति, स्येन्दिष्यते स्यन्त्स्यते.

III.—CONDITIONAL.

I. In the Conditional, the terininations of the Imperfect are appended to स्य instead of those of the Present. The temporal augment अ is to be prefixed to the root; in other respects the forms are exactly like those of the Second Future.

लभ् *Âtm*

	Sing.	*Dual.*	*Plur.*
1st pers.	अलप्स्ये	अलप्स्यावहि	अलप्स्यामहि
2nd "	अलप्स्यथा:	अलप्स्येथाम्	अलप्स्यध्वम्
3rd "	अलप्स्यत	अलप्स्येताम्	अलप्स्यन्त

भू *Parasm.*

	Sing.	*Dual.*	*Plur.*
1st pers.	अभविष्यम्	अभविष्स्याव	अभविष्याम
2nd "	अभविष्य:	अभविष्यतम्	अभविष्यत
3rd "	अभविष्यत्	अभविष्यताम्	अभविष्यन्

2. इ with अधि optionally substitutes गा for इ in the Aorist and the Conditional. It is then changed to गी before consonants; as अध्यैष्यत or अध्यगीष्यत 3rd pers. sing.

3. The passive forms of non-conjugational tenses and moods are made up simply by appending the Âtmanepada terminations to the base.

4. The Second Future expresses futurity generally, and specifically the *futurity of this day.* The First Future expresses specifically the *futurity ont of this day.* The Conditional is used in those conditional sentences, in which the non-performance of the action is implied. It expresses both future and past times. In the latter particular, it resembles the English Pluperfect Conditional.

हरिद्वारं गमिष्यामि तत्र च गङ्गया उद्भमं हिमाचलं च द्रक्ष्यामि सर्वासां देवतानां पूजां च विधाय स्वकीयं ग्रामं प्रतिनिवर्त्स्यामि।

यद्यत्ते हितकरं तत्सर्वं कर्तुं यतिष्ये।

स्वामिनादिष्टोऽपि पुष्पाणि नानयसि यदानीतानि न वेति स प्रक्ष्यति तदा किं प्रतिवक्ष्यसि।

अस्माकं मित्रं हिरण्यको नाम मूषकराजो गण्डकीतीरे चित्रवने विसति सोऽस्माकं पाशांश्छेत्स्यति।

यदि मे बाणपथमायास्यस्यसंशयं मरिष्यसि।

सुवृष्टिश्चेदभविष्यत्तदा सुभिक्षमभविष्यत्।

यदि स धर्ममत्यक्ष्यद्दुःखभाक्समवर्तिष्यत।

कुसुमपुर एकस्मिन्गृहे शत्रुणा पातितमग्निं यदि कृष्णवर्मा न निरवापयिष्यत्तदा सर्वमेव नगरमग्निरधक्ष्यत्।

कुम्भकर्णस्य गात्राणि रामो रणे कर्त्स्यतीति केन संभावितम्।

पुष्करेण भ्रात्रा द्यूते जितो नलो राज्यात्परिभ्रष्टो दमयन्त्या सह वनमियाय। तत्रापि कलिना बहुविधैश्छलैः पीडितः सुप्त दमयन्तीमुत्सृज्यैकस्मिन्स्थले जगाम। गच्छंश्च महान्तं दाव ददर्श। तन्मध्ये कर्कोटको नाम नाग आसीत्। तं स राजाग्नेर्मध्यादुद्धृत्य कानिचित्पदानि निनाय। दशमे पदे कर्कोटको नलमदशत्। तेन नैषधस्य स्वीयं रूपमन्तरधीयत। आत्मानं विकृतं दृष्ट्वा स राजा विस्मितस्तस्थौ।

ततः कर्कोटको नागः सान्त्वयन्नलमब्रवीत्।
मया तेऽन्तर्हितं रूपं नं त्वां विद्युर्जना इति॥
यत्कृते चासि निकृतो दुःखेन महता नल।
विषेण संवृतैर्गात्रैर्यावत्त्वां न विमोक्ष्यति।
तावत्त्वयि महाराज दुखं वै स निवत्स्यति॥
अनागा येन निकृतस्त्वमनर्हो जनाधिप।
क्रोधादसूययित्वा तं रक्षा मे भवतः कृता॥

न ते भयं महावीर दंष्ट्रिभ्यः शत्रुतोऽपि वा।
ब्रह्मर्षिभ्यश्च भविता मत्प्रसादान्नराधिप॥
राजन्विषनिमित्ता च न ते पीडा भविष्यति।
संग्रामेषु च राजेन्द्र शश्वज्जयमवाप्स्यसि॥
गच्छ राजन्नितः सूतो बाहुकोऽहमिति ब्रुवन्।
समीपमृतुपर्णस्य स हि चैवाक्षनैपुणः॥
अयोध्यां नगरीं रम्यामद्य वै निषधेश्वर।
स तेऽक्षहृदयं दाता राजाश्वहृदयेन वै॥
इक्ष्वाकुकुलजः श्रीमान्मित्रं चैव भविष्यति।
भविष्यसि यदाक्षज्ञः श्रेयसा योक्ष्यसे तदा॥
समेष्यसि च दारैस्त्वं मा स्म शोके मनः कृथाः*।
राज्येन तनयाभ्यां च सत्यमेतद्ब्रवीमि ते॥
स्वं रूपं च यदा द्रष्टुमिच्छेथास्त्वं† नराधिप।
संस्मर्तव्यस्तदा तेऽहं वासश्चेदं निवासये।
अनेन वाससा च्छन्नः स्वं रूपं प्रतिपत्स्यसे।
इत्युक्त्वा प्रददौ तस्मै दिव्यं वासोयुगं तदा॥
एवं नलं च संदिश्य वासे दत्त्वा च कौरव‡।
नागराजस्ततो‡ राजंस्तत्रैवान्तरधीयत॥

मरिष्यामि विजेष्ये वा हताश्चेत्तनया मम।
हनिष्यामि रिपूंस्तूर्णं न जीविष्यामि दुःखितः॥
स्मेष्यन्ते मुनयो देवाः कथयिष्यन्ति चानिशम्।
दशग्रीवस्य दुर्नीतैर्विनष्टं रक्षसां कुलम्॥
मधुकर मदिराक्ष्याः शंस तस्याः प्रवृत्तिं
वरतनुरथवासौ नैव दृष्टा त्वया मे।
यदि सुरभिमवाप्स्यस्तन्मुखोच्छ्वासगन्धं
तव रतिरभविष्यत्पुण्डरीके किमस्मिन्॥

---

* This is the form of the 2nd pers. sing. of the Âtm. Aorist of कृ with the temperal augment dropped (See 2, Lesson XXII).

† The Âtmanepada is here an irregularity.

‡ This refers to the king to whom the story of Nala is narrated.

अकरिष्यदसौ* पापमतिनिष्करुणैव सा।
नाभविष्यमहं तत्र यदि तत्परिपन्थिनी॥

If I do not see [दृश्] Nala to-day. I will throw [त्यज् with परि] myself into a fire, and perish [सृ].

The king does not tell me the object of his visit. Wel, I shall know [ज्ञा] it in the end.

Sudeva, go to Ṛituparṇa, and tell him, "Damayantî is going to [will] institute [स्था with आ] a new Swayaṁvara; many princes and kings go there, and it will come off [वृत् with प्र] to-morrow."

"If you wish, go to Kuṇḍinapura in a single day; for as soon as the sun rises [इ with उद्], she will choose [वृ] a second husband."

Damayantî gave much wealth to Parnâda and said, "I will give [दा]. you more when Nala comes [गम् with आ]. Thou hast done much for me, none else will do [कृ] so much; for now, as a consequence of your effort†, I shall soon be united [युज् pass., इ or गम् with सम्] to my husband."

Oh Bâhuka! thou shouldst not deceive me; how will these weak horses bear [वह् with नी] me to Kuṇḍinapura in a single day?

We will now mount [रुह् with आ] our horses and run swiftly.

Bâhuka said to the king, "Thou hast told me the number of leaves and fruits on this tree. Well, I will fell [caus. of ‡शद् or छिद्] it in your presence, and count the leaves."

I will not touch [स्पृश्] you, because you eat with Châanâlas.

I do not know when he will begin [रभ with आ] to construct a house to live in.

---

* Said of a wicked woman who wanted to kill a young maid out of spite for her husband, but was prevented by a holy dame, who is the speaker.

† यत्सामर्थ्यात् or some such expression should be used.

† The द् of this root is changed to त् in the causal.

Had Yajñadatta made a bow [नम् with प्र] to him when he entered the house, he would not have considered [मन्] him a conceited fellow.

Had he gone [रभ with आ] into the presence of his enemy unguarded, the enemy would have killed [रभ with आ] him.

Had the cobra bitten [दंश्] him at the time, and had there been [भू] nobody to get medicine, Devadatta would certainly have died [मृ or रम् with उप].

Thou wilt, by my blessing, enjoy [भुज्] supreme power in this world, and get [आप् with लभ्] a son possessing all thy virtues; keep all thy subjects contented.

PART II.

PASSIVE.

In addition to the rules given in the First Book and in some lessons of this, the student should commit to memory the following :—

1. य added to roots in the conjugational tenses is weak.
2. The following changes take place before the य of the passive.

a. Roots ending in ऋ change it to रि; as क्रियते from कृ.

b. ऋ preceded by a conjunct consonant and of the roots जागृ and ऋ is is changed to Guṇa; as स्मर्यते from स्मृ.

c. Art. 4, Lesson XIV., holds good in this case; as उच्यते from वच्.

d. दा and धा and other roots assuming these forms*, मा, स्था, गै, पा 'to drink,' सो and हा 'to abandon,' change their final vowel to ई before य; as दीयते, धीयते, &c.

e. A final इ or उ is lengthened; as जीयते from जि, स्तूयते from स्तु.

f. Art. 9, p. 2, is also applicable here.

g. Some roots such as मन्थ्, अञ्च् 'to go,' शंस्, दंश्, सञ्ज्, रञ्ज्, अञ्ज्, भञ्ज्, स्कन्द्, ग्रन्थ्, स्तम्भ्, बन्ध्, भ्रंश्, &c. drop their nasals.

---

* Whenever this expression is used, always understand दा *2nd conj.* 'to cut,' and दै *1st conj.* 'to purify,' to be excepted.

3. The passive forms of the First and Second Future, the Conditional, the Aorist and the Benedictive are, in the case of roots ending in a vowel and of ग्रह् and दृश्, optionally made up by changing the vowel to its Vṛiddhi*, and appending the Âtmanepada terminations of those tenses and moods, with इ prefixed to them, even when the root is Aniṭ. य् is added to roots ending in आ in these optional forms.

a. Explain the following :—

स्तर्यते, स्तीर्यते, तीर्ये, पूर्ये, ऊह्यते, अवसीयते, भाविष्यते, धानिष्यते, भविष्यते, दर्शिष्यते, द्रक्ष्यते, हारिष्यते, नायिष्यते, नेष्यते, स्थास्यते, हरिष्यते, स्थायिष्यते.

b. Write down the passive forms of the Second Futnre of :—

ह, हृ, वप्, यज्, सह्, नह्, रुह्, लिह्, बन्ध्, ग्लै, हा, भिद्, वृत्, रुच्, दु, लू, सो, स्तु, रु, शास्;

and of the Present and Imperfect of the following :—

भृ, वप्, यज्, दृ, वृ, कृ, सृ, स्मृ, व्यच्.

VOCABULARY XV.

अक्ष *m.* dice used in gambling.

अक्षज्ञ *m. n. f.* one who knows (the secret of playing at) dice.

अक्षनैपुण *m. n. f.* one who is possessed of skill in playing at dice. [ing dice.

अक्षहृदय *n.* the secret of manag.

अतिनिष्करुण *m. n. f.* (अति very, very much) very pitiless or cruel.

अनर्ह *m. n. f.* not deserving.

अनागस् *m. n. f.* innocent, not guilty. [stantly, continnously.

अनिशम् *adv.* frequently, con-

अश्वहृदय *n.* the secret ofmanaging horses.

असंशयम् *adv.* codonbtedly.

असूययति† to wish ill to, to bear malice to.

इक्ष्वाकु *m.* the progenitor of the solar race of kings.

ईश्वर *m.* ruler.

उद्गम *m.* source, springing up.

कर्कोटक *m.* name of a serpent.

कलि *m.* the principle of evil.

कुण्डिनपुर *n.* name of a town.

कुम्भकर्ण *m.* name of a brother of Râvaṇa.

कुलज *m. n. f.* (कुल *n.* family, and ज from जन्, to be produced) born in a family, of the race of.

* This does not apply to जागृ which takes Guṇa only, while it does apply to नू and धू of the 6th conjugation, which generally do not take either Guṇa or Vṛidhi. (See 11, p. 81.)

†This is a nominal verb, formed from असूया by dropping the final vowel and adding अय as in the 10th conjugation.

कृ *with* नि, to injure, to wrong.
कृते *ind.* for, on account of.
कौरव *m.* a descendant of the Kurus.
गण्डकी *f.* name of a river; गण्डकीतिर n. a bank of the Gaṇḍakî.
गात्र *n.* limb, body.
चित्रवन *n.* name of a forest.
छल *m.n.* fraud.
तनय *m.* a son.
तन्मध्ये (तद् and मध्ये) in the midst of it.
तन्मुखोच्छ्वासगन्ध *m.*(उच्छ्वसि *m.* breathing, गन्ध *m.* perfume, smell) the fragrance of the breath of her mouth.
दंष्ट्रिन् *m.* an animal having sharp teeth, a snake.
दशम *m.n.f* tenth.
दाव *m.* a forest conflagration, a [forest.
दुःखभाज् m.n.f one who suffers pain, unhappy.
दुःखित *m.n.f* afflicted.
दुर्नीत *n.* an evilor imprudent act.
धा *with* अन्तर् to hide or conceal.
निषधेश्वर *m.* lord or king of a country named Nishadha.
नैपुण्य *n.* skill.
नैषध *m.* king of a country named Nishadha, Nala.
पद् *with* प्रति, to attain.
परिपन्थिन् *m.n.f.* one who stands in the way or obstruts; तत्परिपन्थिनी *f.* standing in its way.
परिभ्रष्ट *past part. of* भ्रंश् *with* परि deprived of, fallen, depraved.
पातित (past part. pass. of the causal of पत्) thrown.
पुष्कर *m.* a proper name.
बहुविध *m.n.f.* of various sorts.
बाणपथ *m.* (पथिन् *m.* a way)the way or range of an arrow.
बाहुक *m.* the name of Nala disguised as a charioteer.
मूषक *m.* a mouse; मूषकराज *m.* king of mice.
युग *n.* a pair, a couple; वासोयुग *n.* a pair of clothes.
रति *f.* love.
वच् *with* प्रति, to answer.
वस् *caus. with* नि, to put on a garment, to dress.
वापय *caus.* of वा, *with* निर्, to extinguish.
विनष्ट *past part.* of नश् *with* वि, [destroed.
विस्मित past part. of स्मि with वि, surprised.
शत्रुतस् adv. from an enemy.
शश्वत् adv. prepetually.
संभावित *past pass. part. of caus.* of भू *with* सम्, thought of, thought possible.
संस्मर्तव्य *m.n.f.* to be remem [bered.
सुभिक्ष *n.* abundance of food.
सूत *m.* a charioteer.
स्वकीय *m.n.f* one's own.
हरिद्वार *n.* name of a holy place at the foot of the Himâlayas.
हिमाचल *m.* the Himâlayas.
हिरण्यक *m.* name of a mouse.

Blessing आशिस् *f.**
Conceited अवलिप्त *past part.*
Construct मा *with* निर्.
Deceive धा *with* अति and सम्,लभ् *with* वि and प्र, वञ्च् *10th conj.* Âtm.
End उदर्क *m.* अवसान *n.* परिणाम *m.*; उदर्के &c. in the end.

* See Art, 26, next Lesson.

Fellow का पुरुष *m.* [अनु
Keep contended रञ्ज् *caus,* with
Number संख्या *f.*
Object प्रयोजन n. उद्देश्य *m.*
Parṇâda पर्णाद *m.* a proper name.
Presence, in one's, समक्षम् *adv.* प्रत्यक्षम् *adv.*

Sudeva सुदेव m. a proper name
Supreme power साम्राज्य *n.,* पारमेष्ठ्य *n.*
Unguarded अरक्षित *past part. pass.*
Visit आगमन n.

Lesson XVI.
Declensional Irregularities.

The student should remember the terminations given at the head of Lesson XXV, First Book.

1. We will here notice only the anomalous case forms of several nouns; the rest are to be made up by simply adding the case terminations and observing the general Saṁdhi rules. The vocative singular, except when specidied, is to be considered to be like the corresponding nominative.

2. विश्वपा, शङ्खध्मा, and other nouns whose latter members, or which, in thermselves, are roots ending in आ, drop the ending आ when followed by vowel terminations beginning with the acc. plural.

	Sing.	*Dual.*	*Plur.*
Nom.	विश्वपाः	विश्वपौ	विश्वपाः
Acc. "	विश्वपाम्	विश्वपौ	विश्वपः

3. The voc. sing., the gen. plur., and the first six forms of पति are like those of हरि, and the abl., gen., and loc. sings. are पत्युः-त्युः-त्यौ।

4. The first five forms of सखि are सखा, सखायौ-यः-यम्-यौ; the acc. plur. is सखीन्, and the abl., gen, and loc. sings. and the gen., plur. are सख्युः-ख्युः-ख्यौ-खीनाम् The Voc. sing. is सखे

5. श्री, धी, भू, and other nouns which are derived from roots without the addition of any termination, and the nouns भ्रू and स्त्री change their final इ or उ short or long, to इय or उव् respectively before the vowel terminations. स्त्री take the terminations of नदी, while श्री, धी भ्रू and other feminine nouns of this description take them optionally, in the dat., abl., gen. and loc. sings. and loc. sings. and gen. plur. The

acc. sing. of श्री is स्त्रीम् or स्त्रियम् and the plural स्त्रीः or स्त्रियः The voc. sing. is स्त्रि.

6 Feminine root-nouns in ई, such as धी and श्री, and तरी तन्त्री and लक्ष्मी do not drop the स् of the nom. sing.

स्त्री

	Sing.	*Dual.*	*Plur.*
Nom.	स्त्री	स्त्रियौ	स्त्रियः
Acc.	स्त्रियम्-स्त्रीम्	स्त्रियौ	स्त्रियः-स्त्रीः; &c.
Dat.	स्त्रियै	स्त्रीभ्याम्	स्त्रीभ्यः
Abl	स्त्रियाः	स्त्रीभ्याम्	स्त्रीभ्यः
Gen.	स्त्रियाः	स्त्रियोः	स्त्रीभ्यः
Acc.	स्त्रियाम् &c.		
Voc.	स्त्रि		

श्री

Nom.	श्री	श्रियौ	श्रियः
Acc.	श्रियम्	श्रियौ	श्रियः
Dat.	श्रिये-श्रियै	श्रीभ्याम्	श्रीभ्यः
Abl.	श्रियः-श्रियाः	श्रीभ्याम्	श्रीभ्यः
Gen.	श्रियः-श्रियाः	श्रियोः	श्रियाम्-श्रीणाम्
Loc	श्रियि-श्रियाम् &c.		
Voc.	श्रीः		

भू

Nom.	भूः	भुवौ	भुवः, &c.
Gen.	भुवः-भुवाः	भुवोः	भुवाज-भूणाम, &c.
Voc.	भूः		

7. The ई, or उ, short or long of root-noun, in changed to ण्, or व् when it is not preceded by radical conjuct consonant, and at the same time the noun is preceded by a preposition as applied to the root and not the noun, or by a substantive which in the dissolution of the compound takes an oblique case; as *ग्रामणीः-ण्यौ-ण्यः-ण्यम्ः-प्रधीः-ध्यौ-ध्यःच The loc. sing. of ग्रामणी and other nouns ending in नी is formed by adding the termination आम्ः as ग्रामण्याम् Nouns like ग्रामणी and सेनानी, which primarily signify a male occupation, are decloned like the masculine even when used as adjectives to qualify feminine substantives. Other root-nouns in long ई or ऊ the change these vowels to य् or व् as

* Dissolntion :— ग्रामं नयतीति ग्रामणीः।

obove are, when feminine, declineSd like नदी or वधू For the nom. sing. of the former, sec 6p.ro6.

प्रधी *f.*

	Sing.	*Dual.*	*Plur.*
Dat.	प्रध्यै	प्रधीभ्याम्	प्रधीभ्यः
Abl	प्रध्याः	प्रधीभ्याम्	प्रधीभ्यः
Gen	प्रध्याः	प्रध्योः	प्रधीनाम्

पुनर्भू, also feminine, is similarly declined.

(b) Exceptions- सुधी and nouns ending in भू; as सुधीः-धियौ-धियः, स्वर्भूः-भुवौ-भुवः, &c. These nouns and others that change the ई or ऊ to इय् or उव् When feminine are declined like श्री, see 5p. lo5.

(c) Counter-exceptions, वर्षाभू and पुनर्भू, as वर्षाभ्वा, &c.

8. गो and द्यो change their final ओ to औ in the first tive inflections, as गौः, गावौ-वः, &c. The abl.and gen. sings. are गोः and द्योः All nouns ending in ओ are thus declined.

9. नौ and ग्लौ have no peculiarities.

10. रै before the consonantal terminations becomes रा; as राः, रायौ, &c.; Instr. राया-राभ्याम्-राभिः

11. अस्थि, दधि, सक्थि and अक्षि are to be considered as अस्थन्, दधन्, सक्थन् and अक्षन् when followed by the vowel terminations beginning with the instr. sing. and are declined like nouns ending in अन्. They are declined like वारि in the first two cases.

Nom. Acc.	अस्थि	अस्थिनी	अस्थीनि
Instr.	अस्थ्ना	अस्थिभ्याम्	अस्थिभिः, &c.

A great many roots become nouns without the addition of any termination.

12. The changes of the final ह् of a root when followed by particular consonants have been explained in Lessons IX. and XIV.

Thus in the case of लिह् a root-nouns, the terminations स् being dropped, the ह् is changed to ढ् by I.,p.49 and that to ट् or ड् by II. p. 58. Before भ्याम् and other such terminations itis changed to ड् by VI. pp.50-51. So we have:-

Nom.	लिट्.ड्	लिहौ	अस्थीनि
Instr.	लिहा	लिड्भ्याम्	लिड्भिः

दुह्-स् being dropped, we have, by V. p. 50, दुघ्; by VII p. 51 धुघ् and by II, p. 58, धुक् or धुग्. Before भ्याम् and such other terminations we have दुघ्+भ्याम् by V. p. 50. Then,

13. The change mentioned in VII. Lesson IX, takes place before the consonantal terminations.

By this and VI. pp. 50-51 we have धुग्भ्याम् &c. Loc. plur. धुक्षु.

14. The first five inflected forms of अनडुह् are अनड्वान्—ड्वाहौ-हः-हम्-हौ. The voc. sing, is अनड्वन्. The final ह् is changed to द् when followed by the consonantal terminations; as अनडुद्भ्याम्-अनडुद्भिः, &c.

15. The nom. sing. of दिव् is द्यौः. It becomes द्यु before the consonantal terminations, as द्युभ्याम्.

16. Nouns ending in the syllable हन् such as वृत्रहन्, and the nouns अर्यमन् and पूषन् differ from other nouns ending in अन् in lengthening the penultimate अ in the nom. sing. only. The न् of वृत्रहन् is chenged to ण् when अ is not dropped; as nom. वृत्रहा—हभ्याम्-हभिः instr, &c.

About the change of ह् to घ् when-the अ is dropped see Rule 2 c., p. 51.

17. and change their to when followed by the vowel terminations beginning with the acc. plur., as शुनः, यूनः, मघोनः, cc. plur., &c. In other respects they follow the general declension of nouns ending in अन्.

18. The first five forms of पथिन् are पन्थाः—न्थानौ-नः-नम्-नौ. The final इन् is dropped before the vowel terminations. In other respects it follows the general declension of nouns ending in इन् as पथः acc. plur. पथा-थिभ्याम्-थिभिः instr. &c. The voc. sing. is पन्थाः like the nom sing.

19. मथिन् is declined similarly. ऋभुक्षिन् differs from these only in the non-insertion of the nasal in the first five inflections. ऋभुक्षाः-क्षाणौ-क्षाणः nom.; ऋभुक्षः acc. plur.; ऋभुक्षा instr. ing.

20. The ज् of परिव्राज् obeys rule IX, Lesson IX.

Nom. Sing. परिव्राज्-परिव्राष्, स् being dropped, —परिव्राद्-ड् by II P; 58. Instr. dual परिव्राज्+भ्याम्—परिव्राष्+भ्याम् by the above —परिव्राड्भ्याम् by VI pp. 50-51.

So also Nom. sing. of विश्; विश्-विष् by IX, p. 52, स् being dropped —विद्-ड् II, p. 58. Instr. dual विश्-विष्-विड्भ्याम्.

Decline similarly देवेज्, (देव+यज्), निश्, विश्वसृज्, राज्, &c.

21. प्राच्, प्रत्यच्, उदच्, अवाच्, सम्यच्, and तिर्यच् have a nasal inserted before the final consonant in the first five inflections of the masc. The nom. sings. are प्राङ्, प्रत्यङ्, उदङ् &c. Before the vowel terminations beginning with the acc. plur. and before the neuter nom. and acc. dual ई, प्रत्य, उद्, सम्य and तिर्य, become प्रती, उदी, सभी and तिरश्; as प्रतीचः, उदीचः, समीचः and तिरश्चः acc. plur. masc The feminine forms of these are made up by adding ई to the crude thus modified, as प्राची, प्रतीची, &c.

Masc.

	Sing.	*Dual*	*Plur*
Nom.	तिर्यङ्	तिर्यञ्चौ:	तिर्यञ्चः
Acc.	तिर्यञ्चम्	तिर्यञ्चौ	तिरश्चः
Instr.	तिरश्चा	तिर्यग्भ्याम्	तिर्यग्भिः, *&c.*
		Neut.	
Nom.& Acc.	तिर्यक्-ग्	तिरश्ची	तिर्यञ्चि

22. स्रज्, तादृश्, दिश् and दृश् change the final to क् or ग् when followed by hard or soft consonants, and to either when followed by nothing; nom. sing स्रक् or स्रग् instr. du. स्रग्भ्याम् loc. plur. स्रक्षु.

23. Present participles of the roots enumerated in 7, p. 53, and of those of the third conjugation do not insert before the final in the first five inflections of the masc. In the nom. and acc. plurs.of the neuter, they insert optionally. The nom. and acc. duals of the neuter, and the feminine base are formed by simply adding ई.

बिभ्रत् *Pres. part. of* भृ.

Masc.

	Sing.	*Dual*	*Plur*
Nom.	बिभ्रत्	बिभ्रतौ	बिभ्रतः
Acc.	बिभ्रतम्	बिभ्रतौ	बिभ्रतः, *&c.*

		Neut.	
Nom. & Acc.	बिभ्रत्	बिभ्रती	बिभ्रति-बिभ्रन्ति, *&c.*
Fem.	बिभ्रती		

24. The Present participles of roots ending in आ of the second conjugation, like those of roots of the 6th conjugation, insert न् optionally before the ई, of the feminine and of the neuter nom. and acc. dual; यात्—याती or यान्ती *n. nom. and acc. du. and fem.*

25. The first five forms of पुंस् are पुमान्-मांसौ-मांसः-मांसम्-मांसौ. The voc. sing. is पुमन्. The ending स् is dropped before the consonantal terminations.

26. गिर् and other nouns ending in र् such as पुर्, धुर्, &c., and आशिस् lengthen the penultimate when followed by a consonantal termination, or by notheing. The स् of the last becomes ष् under the usual circumstances. In the case of the loc. plur. we have the following rule:-

I. The change of स् to ष् mentioned in note‡, p.97, F.B. takes place enven if an anusvâra, a visarga, or श्, ष् or स् intervene between the previous vowel and स्; आशीःषु or आशीष्षु.

	Sing.	*Dual*	*Plur*
Nom.	गीः	गिरौ	गिरः
Acc.	गिरम्	गिरौ	गिरः
Instr.	गिरा	गीर्भ्याम्	गीर्भिः, *&c.*

27. अप् is declined in the plural only. The nom. is आपः Its प् is changed to द् before the terminations with an initial भ्; अद्भिः instr.

28. The final न् of अहन् is changed to र् before the nom. and acc. sing. and to visarga before the other consonantal terminations.

Nom.&.Acc.	अहः	अह्नी-अहनी	अहानि
Instr	अह्ना	अहोभ्याम्	अहोभिः

अर्हभीति where अहर् is nom. sing.

29. पूर्व, पर, अवर, दक्षिण, उत्तर, अपर, अधर, and स्व, when they indicate mere relation (in space time, or person). and अन्तर when it means 'under-garment' are declined like pronouns. They are optionally so declinec in the nom. plur. and abl. and loc. sings as पूर्वे or पूर्वाः, पूर्वात् or पूर्वस्मात्, पूर्वे or पूर्वस्मिन्.

30. The following ten words, which are pronouns and are declined as such, form the sing. of the nom. and acc. neuter by adding त् or द्:— अन्य, अन्यतर, कतर, यतर, यतम, ततर, ततम, एकतम, इतर; as अन्यत्-द्, कतरत्-द्.

31. The nom. plural masc. of चरम, अल्प, अर्ध, कतिपय, and नेम is optionally formed like that of pronouns. नेम is a pronoun.

32. पपी, ययी and other masc. nouns ending in ई form their acc. sing. and plur. by adding म् and न् repectively.

33. The word क्रोष्टु is declined as if it were क्रोष्टृ, necessarily in the first five inflections, and optionally before the vowel terminations beginning with the instr. sing. The voc. sing., except that of the gen. plur., the form of which is क्रोष्टूनाम् alone. The voc. sing. is क्रोष्टो, In other respects it is declined like masculine nouns in उ.

34. The words जरा and निर्जर optionally assume the forms जरस् and निर्जरस् before the vowel terminations; in other respects the first is declined like feminine nouns in आ and the other like nouns in अ; जरा, जरसौ or जरे &c.

35 अर्वन् is declined like nouns ending in वत् except in the nom. and voc. sing. When the negative particle अन् is prefixed it s declined like आत्मन्.

36. उशनस् differs from other nouns ending in अस् (as चन्द्रमस्) in the nom. sing. which is उशना, and the con. sing which is optionally उशनन्, उशनन्, उशन, or उशनः.

37. Before the vowel terminations beginning with the acc. plur. the ending syllable वाह् of certain nouns is changed to ऊह्. the ऊ of which with the preceding अ or आ becomes औ. as विश्वौहः acc. plur. of विश्ववाह् ह् is changed to ढ् &c. as in the case of लिह्, and we have विश्ववाट्-ड् nom. sing. विश्ववाड्भ्याम् instr. dual, &c.

38. The म् of तुरासाह् is changed to ष before the consonantal terminations.

39. दोषन् *m.n.f.* असन् *n.* दत *m.* नस् *f.* मास् *m.* हृद *n.* मांस् (मान्स्) *n.* पृत् *f.* स्नु *m.n.* शकन *n.* उदन् *n.* आसन् *n.* निश् *f.* have no forms for the nom and the sing. and dual of the acc. In other causes they are declined according to the general rules. The स् of मास् and मांस् is dropped before the consouantal terminations मास्, however does not drop its स् before स्.

यदा महान्वैयाकरणः पाणिनिः समजायत तदा व्याकरणविषये प्रारब्धां कानिचिन्मतानि प्रतीचां मतेभ्यों भिन्नानयासन्।

पूर्वेषां संप्रदायमनुसृत्य ग्रन्थारम्भे देवतां स्तौमि।

विधवायाः पुनरुद्वाहः सशास्त्र इत्येके * शास्त्रविरुद्ध इत्यन्ये कलौ प्रतिषिद्ध इत्यपरे वदन्ति।

विवाहविधावर्यमणं पूषणं चाधिकृत्य मन्त्रान्पठन्ति।

अपराधं विना पत्युर्नारी तस्मै प्रकुप्यति।

प्रजापीडनजो वह्नी राज्ञः श्रियं कुलं प्राणांश्च दहति।

यस्मिञ्शकटे सोमो †राजानीयते तस्य धुर्यन्यतरोऽनड्वान्युक्त स्यादन्यतरो विमुक्तोऽथ राजानमुपावहरेयुः।

यूनां बुद्धिः शास्त्रैः संस्क्रियते।

पत्या परित्यक्ता विधवा वा यान्यं पतिं विन्दते सा पुनर्भूर्भवति।

दिवि यथा संख्यातीतास्तारकास्तथैव दाशरथौ रामे गुणाः।

तस्याश्चार्वङ्ग्याः स्त्रिया लावण्यं पश्यन्तो जना लक्ष्णां फलं प्रापुः।

इन्द्रियं वा एतदस्मिँनल्लोके यद्दधि। यद्दध्नाभिषिञ्चतीन्द्रियमेवा-‡ स्मिस्तद § द्धाति।

मधुराभिर्गीर्भिः साधुं सान्त्वयामास गोविन्दः। स साधुश्च तमाशीर्भिरनुगृह्योष्टं प्रदेशं जगाम।

**अस्ना। रक्षः संसृजतात्।

एकः शब्दः सभ्यग्ज्ञातः सम्यक्प्रयुक्तश्च स्वर्गे लोके कामधुग्भवतीति वैयाकरणानां मतम्।

पुण्येऽहनि पुरोधास्तं राज्येऽभिषिषेच मन्त्रं चेमं पपाठ।

---

* See Art. 4, Lesson XVII.

†The sacred plant Soma is often spoken of as राजा or king. The subject of उपावहरेयुः is ऋत्विजः understood.

††This refers to the person who is sprinkled over with water or curdled milk.

§ तद् is here equivalent to 'therefore'.

**When the victim is killed at a sacrifice, its blood is given away to evil spirits. तात् is a termination optionally used to form the 2nd and 3rd pers. sing. of the Imperative, whenm the sense is that of an expression of wish or desire. It is a weak termination.

याभिरिन्द्रमभ्यषिञ्चत्प्रजापतिः सोमं राजानं वरुणं यमं मनुं ताभिरद्भिरभिषिञ्चामि त्वामहं राज्ञां त्वमधिराजो भवेह।

देवासुरा वा एषु लोकेषु संयेतिरे। त एतस्यां प्राच्यां दिशि येतिरे तांस्ततोऽसुरा अजयन्। ते दक्षिणस्यां दिशि येतिरे तांस्ततोऽसुरा अजयन्। ते प्रतीच्यां दिशि तांस्ततोऽसुरा अजयन्। त उदीच्यां दिशि तांस्ततोऽसुरा अजयन्।

आदित्यचन्द्रावनिलोऽनलश्च
द्यौर्भूमिरापो हृदयं यमश्च।
धर्मोऽपि जानाति नरस्य वृत्तम्॥
अवश्य नश्वरे उभे च संध्ये
हास्यं नास्याद्विनिर्याति यत्पुंसामिदमद्भुतम्॥
सत्यं संसृतिगर्तेयं दुःखैः पूर्णा निरन्तरम्।
यतस्तद्व्यतिरेकेण नान्यत्किंचिदिहाप्यते॥
अनित्ये प्रियसंवासे संसारे चक्रवद्गतौ।
पथि संगतमेवैतद्भ्राता माता पिता सखा॥
हृदि विद्ध इवात्यर्थं यया संतप्यते जनः।
पीडितोऽपि हि मेधावी न तां वाचमुदीरयेत्॥
तस्य पृथ्वी प्रसूतेऽर्थं धर्ममर्थः प्रसूयते।
प्रसौति विजयं धर्मः स च प्रसवति श्रियम्।
गर्हते न तथा श्वानं चाण्डालं च न गर्हति।
गर्हयत्याहवे भग्नं यथासौ क्षत्रियं नरम्॥
हते भर्तरि वैक्लव्यात्क्रिन्दन्दि तदरिस्त्रियः।
अजस्रैरश्रुभिस्तासां क्लिद्यन्ति नयनानि च॥
ददात्यसौ धनं भूरि ब्राह्मणेभ्यो दिनेदिने।
ददते ब्राह्मणास्तस्मै संतुष्टा नित्यमाशिषः॥
असौ स्वप्नायमानोऽपि कत्थते नात्मनो गुणान्।
कथयन्ति जना एव तस्य तानद्भुतान् भुवि।

वृश्चिकानां भुजङ्गानां दुर्जनानां च वेधसा।
विभज्य नियतं न्यस्तं विषं पुच्छे मुखे हृदि॥

चन्दनैश्चर्चितेव द्यौर्दिशः काशैरिव श्रिताः।
क्षीरेण क्षालितेवोर्वी शर्वरीशे विराजति॥

यथामिषं जले मत्स्यैर्भक्ष्यते श्वपदैर्भुवि।
आकाशे पक्षिभिश्चैव तथा सर्वत्र वित्तवान्॥

नक्रः स्वस्थानमासाद्य गजेन्द्रमपि कर्षति।
स एव प्रच्युतः स्थानाच्छुनापि परिभूयते॥

बुद्धिमान्पुरुषो जह्याद्भिन्नां नावमिवाम्भसि।
अप्रवक्तारमाचार्यमनधीयानमृत्विजम्॥

जाड्यं धियो हरति सिञ्चति वाचि सत्यं।
मानोन्नतिं दिशति पापमपाकरोति॥

चेतः प्रसादयति दिक्षु तनोति कीर्तिं
सत्संगतिः कथय किं न करोति पुंसाम्॥

मानुषाणा* प्रमाणं स्याद्भुक्तिर्वै दशवार्षिकी।
विहंगानां तिरश्चां च यावदेव समाश्रयः॥

कृष्णसारे ददच्चक्षुस्त्वयि चाधिज्यकार्मुके।
मृगानुसारिणं साक्षात्पश्यामीव पिनाकिनम् †॥

नाधर्मश्चरितो लोके सद्यः फलति गौरिव।
शनैरावर्तमानस्तु कर्तुर्मूलानि कृन्तति॥

When Bharata was crowned. He gave cows to Brâhmaṇas by hundreds. Dirghatamas saw him giving [ददत्] them.

---

* This sets forth the period of possession or enjoyment necessary to constitute ownership in the case of men and lower animals.

†Said to King Dushyanta by his charioten when he was pursning an antelope.

The Northern [उदच्] people regarded slavery as inhuman and fought with the Southern [अवाच्] to root it out.

Uśanas [उशनस्] was the preceptor of the Asuras and Bṛhaspati of the Devas. There exist works on politics of which they are the reputed authors.

They begen to excavate the hill, and effected it after many days [अहन् instr.] .

The headman of the village [ग्रामणी] was asked by the commander whether he would give grain to his army.

The hut near Chitrakûṭa was built by the recluses [परिव्राज्] that dwelt in the vicinity.

Women [स्त्री] shall bring up (take care of) children and men [पुंस्] shall acquire money by hard labour.

Dilîpa's horse was once taken away by Indra [वृत्रहन् or मघवन्].

In the beginning there were waters [अप्] only. On these waters appeared the self-existent [स्वयंभू] Brahma, and by that self-existent being all these things were created.

He is blind of one eye [अक्षि].

The honey in the flowers of the Kunda creeper has been drunk by bees [मधुलिह्].

Idols are made of the bones [अस्थि] of elephants.

He who walks by the path [पथिन्] of truth attains prosperity.

In Greece there were two bills which were called "dogs' [श्वन्] heads"

Thou art commanded by thy husband [पति] to give money to the poor.

His companion [सखि] having gone to Kâśi, he lives here alone.

The name of Aryaman occurs in Zend religious books.

Give me any one [एकतम] of those books.

Brâhmaṇas repeating the Vedas are like frogs [वर्षाभू] croaking in the rains.

VOCABULARY XVI.

अक्षि n. the eye.
अजस्र m.n.f. continuous, frequent.
अत्यर्थम् adv. exceedingly, greatly, every much.
अद्भुत m.n.f. wonderful.
अधर m.n.f. pron. lower, low.
अधर्म m. a wicked action.
अनडुह् m. fire.
अनल m. wind.
अनिल m. wind.
अप् f. water. (*used in the plur.*)
अपर m.n.f. pron. other another.
अप्रवक्तृ m. one who does not speak or teach.
अर्यमन् m. name of a deity, one of the dead forefathers.
अर्वन् m. a horse.
अवर m.n.f. pron. hinder, posterior, inferior.
अवश्यम् adv. certainly, inevitably.
अवाच् m.n.f. southern.
असन् n. blood.
असृज् n. blood.
अहन् n. a day.
आमिष m.n. flesh, bait.
आशिस् f. a blessing.
आसन् n. the mouth.
आस्य n. the mouth.
आहव m. a battle.
इन्द्रिय n. vigor (of limbs).
ईर् *1st conj. Parasm.* and *10th conj. with* उद्, to utter, to speak.
उत्तर m.n.f. pron. upper, subsequent.
उदच् m.n.f. northern.
उदन् n. water.
उन्नति f. loftiness, magnanimity.
उर्वी f. the earth.
उशनस् m. a name of the preceptor of the Asuras.
ऋभुक्षिन् m. a name of Indra.
कपाल m.n. head, skull. [wish.
कामदुह् m.n.f. one fulfilling any
कार्मुक n. a bow; *with* अधिज्य m.n.f. one who has his bow strung.
काश m.n. a kind of white flower.
कुल n. a family.
कृ *with* अप and आ, to remove; *with* अधि, to aim at; *i.e.*, referring to *with* सम्*, to adorn, to refine, to educate.
कृष्णसार m. an antelope.
क्लिद् *4th conj. Parasm.* to be or become wet or damp.
क्लिन्द् *1st conj. Parasm.* to lament.
क्षीर n. milk.
गर्ह् *1st conj. Parasm.* and *10th conj.* to think meanly of, to spurn.
गिर् f. speech.
गृह् *1st conj. Âtm.* to think meanly of, to spurn.
गो m. a bull; f. a cow, speech, the earth. [of a village.
ग्रामणी m. the leader of headman
ग्लौ m. the moon.
चक्रवद्गति m.n.f. (चक्रवत् like a wheel) oen whose movement is like that of a wheel, ever-revolving.
चन्दन n. sandalwood.
चरित *past. part. pass.* of चर्, Practised or done.

* स् is prefixed to कृ when it is preceded by सम् and means "to adorn," or "to collect."

चर्चित *past. part. pass.* of चर्च् besmeared.

चाण्डाल *m.* a pariah, an outcasts.

चार्वङ्गी *f.* a beautiful woman, a *belle.*

चेतस् *n.* the heart, intellect.

जन् *with* सम् to be born, to flourish.

जाड्य *n.* dullness.

तदरिस्त्री *f.* a wife of his enemy.

तद्व्यतिरेक *m.* (व्यतिरेक *m.* exclusion) its exclusion or absenee.

तन्त्री *f.* a musical instrument, lute.

तप् *4th conj. Âtm. with* सम्, to be pained or afflicted.

तरी *f.* a boat.

तादृश् *m.n.f.* like that; *adv.* in that manner.

तिर्यच् *m.* a lower animal; *m.n.f.* horizontal, sideways.

तुरासाह् *m.* a name of Indra.

त्विष् *f.* light, splendour, brightness.

दत् *m.* a tooth.

ददत् *pres. part.* of दा to give.

दक्षिण *m.n.f. pron.* southern.

दधि *n.* curdled milk.

दाशरथि *m.* son of Dasaratha.

दिव् *f.* day, heaven.

दिश् *f.* direction, quarter.

दुर्दम *m.n.f.* diffenlt to be controlled or put down.

दृश् *f.* sight, an eye.

देवेज् *m.n.f.* worshipper of gods.

दोषन् *m.n.* an arm.

द्यो *f.* heaven.

धी *f.* intellect.

धुर् *f.* a yoke.

नक्र *m.* a crocodile.

नश्वर *m.n.f.* perishable.

नस् *f.* the nose.

नियतम् *adv.* verily.

निरन्तरम् *adv.* without interval, closely.

निर्जर *m.* a god.

निर्दय *m.n.f.* wicked.

निश् *f.* night.

पठ् *1st conj. Parasm.* to respeat, to read.

पति *m.* a master, a husband.

पथिन् *m.* a path, a way.

पद् *m.* the foot.

पपी *m.* the sun, a protector.

पर *m.n.f. pron.* another.

परित्यक्त *past. part. pass.* of त्यज् *with* परि, abandoned.

परिव्राज् *m.* a recluse.

पिनाकिन् *m.* a name of Śiva

पुंस् *m.* a town.

पुनर्भू *f.* a widow remarrid.

पुर् *m.* a man.

पुरोधस् *m.* a family priest.

पूर्ण *past. part. pass.* of पृ, filled. full.

पूर्व *m.n.f. porn.* former, eastern.

पृत् *f.* an army.

प्रच्युत *past part.* of च्यु to fall [*with* प्र.

प्रजापीडनज *m.n.f.* (प्रजा *f.*) subjects, पीडन *n.* oppression, and ज, from जन् arising)

arising from the oppression of the subjects.

प्रतिषिद्ध *past. part. pass.* of सिध् *with* प्रति, forbidden, prohibited.

प्रत्यच् *m.n.f.* western.

प्रधी *m.n.* keen, acute, talented.

प्रयुक्त *past part. pass.* of युज् *with* प्र, used.

प्राच् *m.n.f.* eastern.

प्रियसंवास *m.* (संवास *m.* dwelling together) dwelling together of beloved persons, the company of beloved persons.

फल् *1st conj. Parasm.* to bear fruit.

भग्न *past. part. pass.* of भञ्ज् broken down, run away (from the field)

भज् *with* वि, to divide.

भुजङ्ग *m.* a serpent.

भुक्ति *f.* possession, enjoyment.

भू *f.* the earth.

भू *with* परि, to despise, to treat contempthously.

भू *with* परि, to despise, to treat contempthously.

मघवन् *m.* a name of Indra.

मथिन् *m.* a churning handle.

मधुलिह् *m.* a black bee.

मांस् (मान्स्) }
मांस n. } *n.* flesh.

मानोन्नति *f.* (मान *m.* respect) loftiness of respect, great self-respect.

मास् *m.* a month.

मृगानुसारिन् *m.n.f.* following or pursuing an antelope.

यत् *with* सम्, to struggle.

यम *m.* the god of death, the deity presiding over death.

ययी *m.* a way.

या *with* वि and निस्, to go away, to pass away.

राज् *1st conj Parasm.* and *Âtm. with* वि, to shine.

राज् *m.* a king; *m.n.f.* shining.

रै *m.* wealth.

लावण्य *n.* beauty, loveliness.

वर्षाभू *m.* a frog.

वह्नि *m.* fire.

वित्तवत् *m.n.f.* wealthy.

विद्ध *past. part. pass.* of व्यध् pierced, struck, wounded.

विश् *m.* a man of the mercantile caste; *f.* subjects, people.

विश्वपा *m.* the protector of all, God.

विश्ववाह् *m.* the protector or supporter of the universe.

विश्वसृज् *m.* the creator, Brahmâ.

वृत् *with* आ, to turn round, to turn back.

वृत्रहन् *m.* killer of वृत्र, Indra.

वृश्चिक *m.* a scorpion.

वैक्लव्य *n.* agony, affliction.

वैयाकरण *m.* a grammarian.

व्याकरण *n.* grammar.

व्याकरणविषय *m.* the subject of grammar.

शकट *m.* a cart.

शकन् *n.* animal dung.

शङ्खध्मा *m.* a conch-blower.

शनैस् *adv.* slowly.

शर्वरीश *m.* (शर्वरी *f.* the night) the lord of the night; moon.

श्री *f.* wealth, goddess of wealth

श्वन् *m.* a dog.

श्वापद *m.* beast of prey, a beast.

सखि *m.* a friend, a companion.

संख्यातीत *m.n.f.* (संख्या *f.* number, अतीत *m.n.f.* gone beyond) innumerable.

संतुष्ट *past. part.* of तुष् *with* सम्, pleased, satisfied, gratified.

संप्रदाय *m.* a custom, a traditional observance.

संसृतिगर्ता *f.* (संसृति *f.* this world, wordly existence, गर्ता *f.* a pit) the pit of this world or wordly existence.

सत्संगति *f.* company of the [virtuous.

सद् *with* आ *1st conj. Parasm.* to approach, to come to.

सद् *with* प्र (in the causal) to please, to propitiate.

सद्यस् *adv.* at once, immediately.

सध्र्यञ्च् *m.n.f.* good.

सम्राज् *m.* a great king, an em- [peror.

साक्षात् *adv.* in the presence of, in sight of.

सु *1st* and *2nd conj. Parasm. with* प्र, to produce.

सृज *with* सम् to bring in contact with, to unite with.

स्त्री *f.* woman, wife.

स्नु *m.n.* summit.

स्वप्नाय *denom. Âtm.* to be in a dream, to speak in a dream.

स्वयंभू *m.n.f.* self-existent.

हास्य *n.* smile, laughter.

हृ *with* उप and अव, to take down.

Acquire अर्ज् *1st* and *10th conj. with* उप.

Beginning अग्र *n.* आदि *m.*

Blind अन्ध *m.n.f.*

Bring up, *causal* of वृध् वर्धय, *with* सम्, पोषण or भरणं कृ.

Build मा *3rd conj. with* निर्.

By hundreds शतशः *ind.*

Call धा *with* अभि; अभिहित called.

Croak रद् *1st conj. Parasm. with* आ.

Dîrghatamas दीर्घतमस् *m.* name of a Rishi.

Excavate खन् *with* उद्; उत्खनितुम् *inf.*

Grain धान्य *n.*

Inhuman मानवानर्ह *m.n.f.* निर- [नुक्रोशं कर्म.

Politics नीतिशास्त्र *n.*

Rains वर्षा *plur.*

Religious book धर्मग्रन्थ *m.*

Reputed अभिमत *past. part. pass.* प्रसिद्ध *past. part.* कर्तृत्व नाभिमतौ reputed as authors (two).

Slavery दास्य *n.*

Truth ऋत *n.*

Lesson XVII.

Numerals

1. The following is a list of the Sanskrit Cardinal numerals, up to twenty:—

१	एक	One	११.	एकादशन्	Eleven
२.	द्वि	Two	१२.	द्वादशन्	Twelve
३.	त्रि	Three	१३.	त्रयोदशन्	Thirteen
४.	चतुर्	Four	१४.	चतुर्दशन्	Fourteen
५.	पञ्चन्	Five	१५.	पञ्चदशन्	Fifteen
६.	षष्	Six	१६.	षोडशन्	Sixteen
७.	सप्तन्	Seven	१७.	सप्तदशन्	Seventeen
८.	अष्टन्	Eight	१८.	अष्टादशन्	Eighteen
९.	नवन्	Nine	१९.	नवदशन् / एकोनविंशति	Nineteen
२.	दशन्	Ten	२०.	विंशति	Twenty

Up to नवदशन्, These numerals may be considered as adjectives, *i.e.* they take the number and case of the noun to which they are appled, and the first four, the gender also.

2.	विंशति	Twenty	षष्टि	Sixty
	त्रिंशत्	Thirty	सप्तति	Seventy
	चत्वारिंशत्	Forty	अशीति	Eighty
	पञ्चाशत्	Fifty	नवति	Ninety

These may be considered as substantives. They are all feminine; the noun to which they are applied may be of any gender. With a plural noun they are used in the singular, as विंशतिर्ब्राह्मणाः '*twenty*' Brâhmanas. They have duals and plurals like other nouns, but, when these are used, the construction is different: ब्राह्मणानां विंशति *two twenties* of Bràhmanas. They have duals and plurals like other nouns, but, when these are used, the construction is different: ब्राह्मणानां विंशति '*two twenties* of Bràhman', ब्राह्मणानां विंशतयः '*many twenties* of Bràhmaṇas.' The singular may be used similarly; as ब्राह्मणानां विंशतिः *one twenty* of Bràhmaṇas.

3. The numbers intermediate between any two of these are formed by prefixing एक, द्वि, &c, up to नवन् to the lower; but the ninth intermediate number is generally made up by prefixing एकोन* to the higher. In making these compounds the final न् is invariably dropped; द्वि becomes द्वाः त्रि, त्रयः and अष्टन्, अष्टा. But the three latter changes are optional in the case of चत्वारिंशत्, पञ्चशत् षष्टि सप्तति, नवतिः and do not take place at all in the case of अशीति. These numerals also follow the also

* एक+ऊन - less by one.

follow the constructions explained in the preceding paragraph. शत 'a hundred' is a neuter noun,

३१ एकत्रिंशत्	Thirty-one	४२	द्विचत्वारिंशत्	Forty-two
३२ द्वात्रिंशत्	Thirty-two		द्वाचत्वारिंशत्	
३३ त्रयस्त्रिंशत्	Thirty-three	४३	त्रिचत्वारिंशत्	Forty-three
३४ चतुस्त्रिंशत्	Thirty-four		त्रयश्चत्वारिंशत्	
३५ पञ्चत्रिंशत्	Thirty-five	४८	अष्टचत्वारिंशत्	Forty-eight
३६ *षद्त्रिंशत्	Thirty-six		अष्टाचत्वारिंशत्	
३७ सप्तत्रिंशत्	Thirty-seven		&c.	&c.
३८ अष्टात्रिंशत्	Thirty-eight	८२	शीति	Eighty-two
३९ नवत्रिंशत्-एकोनचत्वारिंशत्	Thirty-nine	८३	त्र्यशीति	Eight-three

DECLENSION.

Masculine.

4. एक is declined like a pronoun; as an indefinite pronoun in the sense of the English *one* in "the great ones of this country," it has the dual and the plural. द्वि has the dual only, and in declining is to be considered as द्व, *i. e.*, as a noun ending in अ; द्वौ nom. and acc., द्वाभ्याम् instr., dat, and abl., द्वयो, gen. and loc. त्रि and the other adjectival numerals are declined in the plural only. त्रि follows the general declension of masculine nouns ending in इ. The genitive only is peculiar; it is त्रयाणाम्.

The nom. of चतुर् is चत्वारः and the gen. and the loc. चतुर्णाम् and चतुर्षु. The rest are regular.

After the other adjectival numerals the nom and acc. terminations are dropped, the final न् is eliminated here as before the consonantal terminations, and the अ of अन् is lengthened in the genitive; as पञ्च nom. and acc, पञ्चभिः instr. पञ्चभ्यः dat. and abl.. पञ्चनाम् gen., पञ्चसु loc; षट् or षड् nom. and acc., षड्भिः instr. षड्भ्यः dat. and able , षण्णाम् gen., षट्सु loc.. कति "how many ?" is similarly declined.

अष्टन् gen., षट्सु loc.. कति "how many" is similarly declined.

---

* Here the initial त् of त्रिंशत् is not changed to the corresponding lingual. For. the rule is that dentals are not changed to linguals when they follow a consonant of the lingual class which is at the end of a word or grammatical form as, षट् ते, षट् सन्तः.

अष्टाभिः instr., अष्टाभ्यः dat. and abl., अष्टासु loc. There is no difference in the genitive.

Feminine.

5. एका and द्वा are declined like सर्वा. The feminine forms of त्रि and चतुर् are तिसृ and चतसृ, which are thus declined:—तिस्रः and चतस्रः nom. and acc., तिसृभिः and चतसृभिः instr., तिसृभ्य and चतसृभ्यः dat. and able., तिसृणाम् and चतसृणाम् gen. and तिसृषु and चतसृषु loc.

The feminine forms of other adjectival numerals are not different from the masculine.

Neuter.

6.	एक	एकम्	*Nom. and Acc.*
	द्वि	द्वे	———
	त्रि	त्रीणि	———
	चतुर्	चत्वारि	———

The nuter forms of other adjectival numerals are similar to the masculine.

7. The ordinals corresponding to एक, द्वि, त्रि, चतुर् and षष् are प्रथम, द्वितीय, तृतीय, चतुर्थ and षष्ठ. Instead of प्रथम, अग्रिम and आदिम and of चतुर्थ, तुर्य and तुरीय are also used. From the other cardinal numerals up to दशन् inclusive, they are formed by dropping the final न्, and adding म as पञ्चमः, &c. and after दशन् up to नवदशन्, by simply dropping न्, एकादशः, &c.

8. The ordinals form विंशति and the other substantival numerals, and form their compunds, are formed by adding तम; as विंशतितमः, एकविंशतितमः, त्रिंशत्तमः, एकत्रिंशत्तमः, &c. Another way is by dropping the ति of विंशति, and the final consonant of the rest. Where there is a final, that vowel is changed to अ, but only in compound numerals, the simple ones forming their ordinals in the first way, as विंशः, एकविंशः, त्रिंशः, एकत्रिंशः, षष्टितमः, एकषष्टः—एकषष्टितमः, &c. शत a hundred has शततम.

9. The feminines of प्रथम, अग्रिम, आदिम, द्वितीय, तृतीय, तुर्य and तुरीय are formed by adding आ, and of the rest by changign the final अ to ई, as प्रथमा, द्वितीया, &c., and चतुर्थी, पञ्चमी, एकविंशी, एकविंशतितमी, &c.

10. The nom. plu. of प्रथम *m.* is प्रथमे or प्रथमाः; and the dat., abl., gen. and loc. sings. of द्वितीय and तृतीय or द्वितीया and तृतीया are optionally like those of pronouns ending in अ or आ, as द्वितीयस्मै or द्वितीयाय, &c.

11. Averbs of definite frequency are formed from numerals by the addition of स् to द्वि, त्रि and चतुर् and कृत्वस् to the rest, before which the final न् is dropped. For एक we have सकृत् once. Ex द्विः 'twice,' त्रि 'throco', चतुः 'fourtimes,' पञ्चकृत्वः, षट्कृत्वः, &c.

12. The termination वत् is applied to यद्, तद् and एतद्, and यत् to इदम् and किम्. in the sense of 'as much as.' The three former become या, ता and कि; as तावत् 'that much,' तावान् masc. nom. sing.

पञ्चाशते ब्राह्मणेभ्यः प्रत्यहं कृष्णवर्माऽन्नं ददाति।

गुरोः परिचर्यों कुर्वतस्तस्य द्विचत्वारिंशदहानि व्यतीयुः।

चतस्रो विद्याश्चतुष्षष्टिं कलाश्च चन्द्रापीडोऽशिक्षत।

चत्वारि शृङ्गा* त्रयोऽस्य पादा द्वे शीर्षे संप्त हस्तासो†ऽस्य‡।

श्रावणस्य कृष्णपक्षेऽष्टम्यां तिथौ देवकी कृष्णं सुषुवे।

त्रिः सप्तकृत्वः परशुरामः पृथिवीमक्षत्रियामकरोत्।

सप्तदश सामिधेनीरनुब्रूयात्।

ता एताः सप्तर्चोऽन्वाह § तासां त्रिः प्रथमामन्वाह त्रिरुत्तमां ता एकादश संपद्यन्ते।

त्रयस्त्रिंशद्वै देवा अष्टौ वसव एकादश रुद्रा द्वादशादित्याः प्रजापतिश्च वषट्कारश्च।

॥ शतमनूक्ष्यमायुष्कामस्य। शतायुर्वै पुरुष आयुष्येवैनं**

---

* Nom. plur. of शृङ्ग *n. Vedic.*

† Nom. plur. of हस्त *m. Vedic*

‡ This is repeated when the sacred fire is kindled. It contains a description of the imaginary shape of the fire-god.

§The nominative of this is होता, understood. This refers to the repeating of the verses by the Hotâ at a certain ceremony.

॥ At the ceremony called प्रातरनुवाक, which forms a part of the Agnishṭoma sacrifice, a great many verses are repeated by the priests. The number of these is determined in this passage. For instance, first he says, 'If the sacrificer desires a long life. one hundred verses should be repeated .' Then follows a reason for this; and so on.

This qualifies यजमान or sacrificer. understood.

**This refers to the यजमान.

*तद्यथाति † त्रीणि च शतानि न षष्टिश्चनूच्यानि याकामस्य। त्रीणि च वै शतानि षष्टिश्च संवत्सरस्याहानि। तावान्संवत्सरः संवस्सरः प्रजापतिः प्रजापितर्यज्ञः। ‡ उपैनं यज्ञो नमति यस्यैवं विद्वांस्त्रीणि च शतानि च षष्टिं चान्वाह। सप्त च शतानि विंशतिश्चानूच्यानि प्रजापशुकामस्य। सप्त च वै शतानि विंशातिश्च संवत्सरस्याहोरात्राः।

संविभाजयति श्रीमान् स वित्तेन द्विजोत्तमान्।
धर्मषष्ठांशभागेन तेऽपि संविभजन्ति तम्॥
गर्भादेकादशे कुर्वीत ब्राह्मणस्योपनायनम्।
गर्भादेकादशे राज्ञो गर्भात्तु द्वादशे विशः।
त्रिराचामेदपः पर्वं द्विः प्रमृज्यात्ततो मुखम्॥
खानि चैव स्पृशेदद्भिरात्मानं शिर एव च।
जीवन्तोऽपि मृताः पञ्च व्यासेन परिकीर्तिताः।
दरिद्रो व्याधितो मूर्खः प्रवासी नित्यसेवकः॥
अनारम्भो हि कार्याणां प्रथमं बुद्धिलक्षणम्।
प्रारब्धस्यान्तगमनं द्वितीयं बुद्धिलक्षणम्॥
नष्टे मृते प्रव्रजिते क्लीबे च पतिते पतौ §।
पञ्चस्वापत्सु नारीणां पतिरन्यो विधीयते॥
तिस्रः कोट्योऽर्धकोटी च यानि लोमानि मानवे।
तावतत्कालं वसेत्स्वर्गे भर्तारं यानुगच्छति॥

On the 27 th day of the month a conclave of Paṇḍitas was held.

At that time ninety-nine men were examined, of whom fifty-four were found to be good grammarians.

Teh Paṇḍitas say that there are eighteen Purâṇas and twenty-four Smritis.

Originally there were three Vedas--Rigveda, Yajurveda and Sâmaveda; afterwards there came to be four.

---

* तद् is here equivalent to तस्माद्.

† The subject of this ist he priest होता, understood.

‡ In the Vedic diatect, a preposition need not be immediately prefixed to a verb; several words may intervene.

§This is a deviation from Pâṇini. See last Lesson. Art. 3.

There are now two principal branches or Śâkhâs or Yajurveda.

The Smṛiti of Manu is in twelve chapters, and in the seventh the duties of kings are enumerated.

On the tenth fo the bright half of Âsvina, people in the Deccan give to each other leaves of the Śamî tree, calling them gold.

All enemies were killed by the five Pâṇḍavas.

Râma cut off the ten heads of Râvana.

He gained proficiency in the four learnings (lores), six Śâstras, and sixty-four arts.

Thrice I told him to depart, and when he did not do so, I gave him a kick.

The Hindus believe that there are eight guardians of the eight different quarters.

Of the eighteen *Parvans* of the Mahâbhârata, the third is the best, because it contains many pleasant stories.

The doctor has directed me to take this medicine for* forty-two days.

I have studied seventeen cantos of the Raghuvaṁbhava, nine dramatic plays, and eighty-six pages of Patañjali's Mahâbhâshya.

VOCABULARY XVII.

अक्षत्रिय *m. n. f.* destitute of क्षत्रिय.

अनारम्भ *m.* not beginning.

अनूच्य *pot. pass. part.* of वच् *with* अनु, to be recited.

अन्तगमन *n.* going to the end.

अन्वाह (आह with अनु) (he) recites, repeats.

अब्द *m.* a year.

अर्धकोटी *f.* (अर्ध *n.* half, कोटी *f.* ten millions) five millions.

अहोरात्र *m.* day and night.

आयुष्काम *m.* one wishing to live a long life.

इ *with* व्यति, to pass away.

उत्तम *m. n. f.* last.

उपनायन । *n.* the ceremony of
उपनयन the investiture with the secred thread.

कला *f.* an art.

कार्य *n.* business, work.

* See note*, p. 18.

कृष्ण *m.* the eighth incarnation of Vishṇu.

कृष्णपक्ष *m.* the half of the lunar mouth.

कृष्णवर्मन् *m.* a proper name.

क्लीब *m. n.* neuter, impotent.

ख *n.* the cavities of the human body, as month, nose, &c.

गर्भाष्टम *m. n. f.* (गर्भ. *m.* conception, and अष्टम eighth) eighth from conception.

चन्द्रापीड *m.* name of a prince.

चम् *1st conj. Parasm.* with आ, to take in a little water into the mouth and drink it as a religious ceremony.

तावत्कालम् *adv.* for so along a time.

देवकी *f.* mother of Kṛishna

द्विजोत्तम *m.* one who is best among Brâhamaṇas.

धर्मषष्ठांशभाग *m.* one-sixth part of religious merit as a share.

पतित *m. n. f.* sinful, apostate.

पद् *4th conj. Âtm. with* सम्, to amount to.

परिकीर्तित *past part. pass.* of कृत् with परि, enumerated.

परिचर्या *f.* service, attendance on.

प्रजापति *m.* te god Brahmâ.

प्रजापशुकाम (प्रजा *f.* progeny, पशु *m.* cattle, and काम *m.* wish) one wishing for progeny and cattle.

प्रवासिन् *m.* a traveller.

प्रव्रजित *past part.* of व्रज with प्र, exiled or turned a recluse.

बुद्धिलक्षण *n.* (बुद्धि, *f.* telent, लक्षण *n.* a sign) a sign of talent.

भज् *with* सम् and वि, to admit to a share, to bestow upon.

भाज् . *10th conj.* with सम् and वि, to admit to a share, to bestow upon.

मृज् *with* प्र, to wash.

लोमन् *n.* a hair.

वषट्कार *m.* the cry वौषट् at the time of throwing an oblation into the fire; this is considered a deity.

विद्या *f.* learning, lore.

विद्वस् (*perf. part.* of विद् to know) knowing.

वैश्य *m.* the third order or caste among the Hindus.

व्याधित *m. n. f.* sick.

व्यास *m.* the reputed author of the Mahâbhârata, a Ṛishi.

शतायुस् *m. n. f.* living for a hundred years.

शृङ्ग *n.* a horn. [Hindu year.

अलाभ m. the fifth month of the

संवत्सर *m.* a year.

सामिधेनी *f.* a verse repeated at the time of kindling the sacred fire.

Âśvina आश्विन *m.* name of a month.

Bright half (of the lunar month) शुक्लपक्ष *m.*

Calling अभिदधान *pres. part.* of धा with अभि.

Canto सर्ग *m.*

Conclave समाज *m.* परिषद् *f.* सभा *f.*

Doctor भिषज् *m.* वैद्य *m.*

Dramatic play नाटक *n.*

Duty धर्म *m.*

Enumerated परिकीर्तित *past part. pass.* परिगणित *past. part. pass.*

Found उपलब्ध *past part. pass.* समधिगत *past part. pass.*

Good समीचीन *m. n. f.* निपुण *m.n.f.*

Guardian of a quarter दिक्पाल *m.*

Held (as a meeting) मिलित *past part.*

Kick लत्ता *f.* लत्तया प्रहरति gives [a kick.

Kumârasaṁbhava कुमारसंभव *m.* name of a poem by Kâlidâsa.

Lore विद्या *f.*

Mahâbhârate महाभारत *n.* name of anepic poem celebrating the quarrels and wars between the sons of Pâṇḍu and Dhṛitarâshṭra.

Originally अग्रे *loc. sing.* of अग्र, आदौ *loc. sing.* of आदि.

Parvan पर्वन् *n.* a section, a canto.

Purâṇa पुराण *n.* name of a class of works containing legendary accounts of many things and of a religious and ritualistic character.

Raghuvaṁśa रघुवंश *m.* name of a poem by Kâlidâsa.

Ṛigveda ऋग्वेद *m.* name fo a Veda.

Sâmaveda सामवेद *m.* name fo a Veda.

Śamî शमी *f.* a kind of tree.

Yajurveda यजुर्वेद *m.* the name of a Veda.

LESSON XVIII.

COMPARATIVE AND SUPERLATIVE DEGREES OF ADJECTIVES, &C.

1. ईयस् is a termination of the comparative degree and इष्ठ of the superlavtive. Before these the ending vowel of a word, or the ending consonant, if any, with the preceding vowel, is dropped; as लघु *positive,* लघीयस् *comparative,* लघिष्ठ *superlative;* महत् *pos.,* महीयस् *comp.,* बलिन् *pos.,* बलीयस् *comp.,* &c.

These terminations are applied to adjectives of qulity and not to partioiples and other verbal derviatives, as तर and तम (mentioned below) are.

2. The ऋ occurring in the words पृथु, मृदु, भृश, कृश, दृढ and परिदृढ is changed to र; as पृथु *pos.,* प्रथीयस् *comp.,* and प्रथिष्ठ *sup.*

3. The final syllable (*i. e.* the last vowel with the preced-

and the portion वन् of युवन् are dropped, and the preceding vowel takes Guṇa; as स्थूल, *pos.*, स्थवीयस् *comp.*, and स्थविष्ठ *sup.*

4. The possessive terminations मत्, वत् and विन्, to be presently mentioned, are dropped; as बलवत् *pos.*, बलीयस् *comp.*, and बलिष्ठ *sup.*

5. The following is a list of the irregularities :—

Positive		*Comparative*	*Superlative.*
प्रशस्य	praiseworthy	ज्यायस् श्रेयस्	ज्येष्ठ श्रेष्ठ
वृद्ध	old	ज्यायस वर्षीयस्	ज्येष्ठ वर्षिष्ठ
अन्तिक	near	नेदीयस्	नेदिष्ठ
बाढ़	firm, well	साधीयस्	साधिष्ठ
प्रिय	dear	प्रेयस्	प्रेष्ठ
स्थिर	firm	स्थेयस्	स्थेष्ठ
स्फिर	thick, much	स्फेयस्	स्फेष्ठ
गुरु	heavy	गरीयस्	गरिष्ठ
उरु	wide	वरीयस्	वरिष्ठ
बहुल	many, much	बंहीयस्	बंहिष्ठ
दीर्घ	long	द्राघीयस्	द्राघिष्ठ
बहु	many, much	भूयस्	भूयिष्ठ
युवन्	young	यवीयस् कनीयस्	यविष्ठ कनिष्ठ
अल्प	small	कनीयस् अल्पीयस्	कनिष्ठ अलिपष्ठ

6. The comparative ending in स् should be declined in the manner shown in Lesson XXVII, First Book. Its feminine is formed by the addition of ई and of the superlative by affixing आ; as कनीयसी, कनिष्ठा.

7. तर is another comparative termination, the superlative termination corresponding to which is तम. These are applied not only to adjectives but to nouns, particles and other indeclinables and verbs. In the last case they takes forms तराम् and तमाम् and also when added to indeclinables, except in those instances in which, with the terminations, the indeclinables form adjectives. The words to which these suffixes are added undergo no change.

Ex.—लघु pos.; लघुः, लघुतमः; पाचकतरः, पाचकतमः; पचतितराम्, पचतितमाम्; उच्चैस्तराम्, उच्चैस्तमाम्; उच्चैस्तरः *adj.* उच्चैस्तमः *adj.*

8. The feminie of adjectives ending in तर and तम is formed by affixing आ.

9. Derivatives signifying the 'possessor' of the thing expressed by the base are formed by affixing मत् to substantives; as धीमत् 'talented' from धी 'talent'

10. The म of this termination is changed to व when the base ends in म् or अ (short or long), or has either for its penultimate; as धनवत् 'wealthy' from धन 'wealth': विद्यावत्, यशस्वत्, भास्वत्, किंवत्, लक्ष्मीवत्.

There are a few exceptions, as यवमत्, भूमिमत्, &c.

11. To substantives ending in अ the suffix इन् is also added in this sense, before which the preceding अ is dropped; as दण्डिन्, धनिन् &c. विन् is another termination having this sense. It is applied to some nouns; as यशस्विन्.

12. दृश् *m. n. f.* and दृश *m. n.* (दृशी *f.*) are appended to pronouns in the sense of 'like'. The final letter of the base is dropped and आ added to it; as तादृश 'like that' त्वादृश 'like thee.' इदम् and किम् become इ and की; as ईदृश.

13. The verbal or other forms of कृ, भू, or sometimes अस् are added to a noun or an indeclinable to express the 'doing or being like' the thing denoted by the base.

14. *a.* The ending अ or आ is changed to ई, except in the case of an indeclinable. *b.* The preceding इ or उ is rendered long; and *c.* ऋ (short) is changed to री. *d.* Final न् and the स of मनस्, अरुस्, चक्षुस्, चेतस्, रहस्, and राजस् are dropped.

Ex.— घनीकरोति, घनीभवति, गडीभवति, प्रत्यक्षीकरोति, स्वीकृतम् *n.* शुचीभूतम् *n.* पट्भवनम् *n.*, मात्रीकरोति, दिवाभूता *f.*

ऋग्वेदात्सामवेदस्य महिमा भूयान्।
यज्ञवर्मायोध्यां गच्छन्नध्वनोऽधर्माद्भूयोऽतिकम्याश्राम्यः
कृष्णस्य सुभद्रा यवीयसी स्वसा।
सर्वेषु कुसुमेषु शिरीषकुसुमं भ्रदिष्ठम्।

निःश्रेयसाय कर्मपथाज्ज्ञानमार्गः साधीयान्। श्रेष्ठस्तु सर्वेषां भक्तिमार्गः।

परमात्माणोरप्यणीयान्महतोऽपि महीयान्वर्तते।

धार्तराष्ट्रेभ्यः पाण्डवाः कृष्णसाहाय्याद्बलीयांसः किं तु तेषां योधसमाजो गरीयान्।

दुःखितस्य वृत्तान्तश्रवणेनार्द्रीभवन्ति हृदयान्यनुकम्पिनां महात्मनाम्।

यो यज्ञकर्माणि यथाविधि करोति स प्रजावान्पशुमांस्तेजस्वी ब्रह्मवर्चसी यशस्वांश्च भवति।

विष्णुशर्मण एकपञ्चाशत्पुत्रा आसन्। तेषां ये मध्यमाद्देवदत्ताज्ज्यायांसः पञ्चविंशतिस्ते कनीयोभिः पञ्चविंशत्या कलहं चक्रुः।

सर्वासु नदीषु भागीरथी द्राघिष्ठा विस्तारे वरिष्ठा च। तस्याः सलिलं यमुनायाः शुचितरम्। पर्वतेषु हिमालयः प्रथिष्ठः।

अहो दीप्तिमतोऽपि विश्वसनीयतास्य राज्ञो वपुषः।

ईदृशी मे मन्दभाग्यता यत्र केवलं भर्तुर्विरहो दारकयोरपि।

हा सौम्य हनूमन्क पुनस्त्वादृशस्य साधोर्महोपकारिणः संभवोऽस्मिञ्जगति।

नैतद्विद्मः कतरन्नो गरीयो यद्वा जयेम यदि वा नो जयेयुः।

नेयं मे जटा किं तु वेणीकृतः कचानां कलाप इत्यब्रवीत्काः चित्स्त्री।

दासीभूतां सर्पाणां जनन्याः सेवां कुर्वतीं स्वमातरं बन्धनान्मुमोच गरुडः।

तपश्चरन्रावणः स्वीयानि नव शिरांसि शिवायोपायनीचकारेति शृणुमः।

प्रियतमस्य पुण्डरीकस्य मरणेन सशोकया महाश्वेतया तिरस्कृता विषया दूरीकृतो बान्धवजनोऽङ्गीकृतमरण्येऽवस्थानम्।

एकः पुरुषः प्रियतमायाः प्रासादस्योपरितनीं भूमिं प्रवेष्टुमिच्छुर्वातायनादधोऽवलम्बमानमहिं रज्जूकृत्यारुरोह।

उपरते भर्तरि यत्प्राणाः परित्यज्यन्ते तन्मौर्ख्यम्। उत्तरा विराटदुहिता बालिका विनयवति धीमति विक्रान्ते च पञ्चत्वमभिन्यावुपगतेऽपि प्राणान्न जहौ। अन्या अपि अहस्त्रशः कन्यका अभर्तृमत्यो जाताः सत्यो जीवितानि न तत्यजुरिति भूयते।

जीवनाय मनुजन्मामिह भ्राम्यतामथ कदापि स प्रभुः।
त्वादृशो भवति भाग्ययोगतो वेत्ति यः सदसतां यदन्तरम्॥

Kausalyâ was the eldest [वृद्ध] of the three wives of Dasaratha, and Kaikeyî the yonngest [युवन्].

Sita's bodily form was more slender [तनु] than Draupadi's.

That the greater [बहु] is equal to the less [लघु] is absurd.

In running, the horse is the swiftest [आशु] of all animals.

The virtuous [सद्गुण, पुण्य] are happy [सुख] and deserve respect.

Rukmini was dearer [प्रिय] to Krishna than Satyabhàmâ

When one's luck is bad, even his relations become (as if they were) his enemies [विपक्ष].

What is he called who has wealth [वसु], or fortitude [धैर्य] or fame [यशस्, कीर्त्ति], or land [भूमि]?*

All should become as of one mind [एकचित्त] and having taken this net should fly off.

Indra was the mightiest [ओजस्विन्] and most powerful [बलिन्] of all the gods, and therefore they crowned him king.

The sense of the original passage is rendered (as if) clear [विशद] by a commentator, and sometimes mystified [गूढ].

Damayanti was the most beautiful [सुंदर, चारु] of all the women of the time, and the most devoted [भक्त, अनुरक्त] to her husband.†

Thy heart has at this moment melted (become, as if a liquid [द्रव]) through affection.

The bullocks that are fastened to the yokes of carriages are fatter [पीवर] than common ones.

---

* The student should answer this question.

† Loc. or Gen.

O Sitâ, there is not another woman like thee [त्वद्] so pure, so simple, and so loving [अनुराग, प्रणय], and not another man like me [मद्], so ruthless and so cruel.

VOCABULARY XVIII.

अणु *m. n. f.* little; *m.* an atom, a small particle.
अधस् *ind.* below, down.
अनुकम्पिन् *m. n. f.* compassionate.
अन्तर *n.* difference.
अभिमन्यु *m.* son of Arjuna.
अरुस् *m.* a sore of wound.
अवलम्बमान *press. part. act.* of **लम्ब्** *with* **अव**, hanging.
अवस्थान *n.* residence.
अहि *m.* a snake.
आर्द्र *m. n. f.* wet.
इच्छु *m. n. f.* wishing, wisher.
उत्तरा *f.* daughter of a king named Virâta.
उपरितन *m. n. f.* what is above.
उपायन *n.* a persent.
एकमनस् *m. n. f.* of one mind.
कच *m.* the hair.
कर्मपथ *m.* (**कर्मन्** action, and **पथिन्** a way) way of action, *i. e.*, the performance of religious ceremonies, &c., as a way to eternal bliss.
कलह *m.* a quarrel.
कलाप *m.* bundle, a collection.
कृश *m. n. f.* weak, thin.
कृष्णसाहाय्य *n.* help of Krishna.
क्रम् *1st conj. parasm. with* **अति** to cross, to go over, to transgress.
क्षुद्र *m. n. f.* small, mean.
गरुड *m.* an eagle, the bird of that species used by Vishnu as his car.
जटा *f.* matted hair.
जीवन *n.* livelihood.
जीवित *n.* life.
ज्ञानमार्ग *m.* (**ज्ञान** *n.* knowledge **मार्ग** *m.* a way) the knowledge of God as a way to eternal bliss.
दारक *m.* a male child, a son.
दीप्ति *f.* splendour.
दृढ *m. n. f.* firm, strong.
निःश्रेयस *n.* final beatitude.
परिवृढ *m.* a master, owner.
पुण्डरीक *m.* a proper name; *n* a (white) lotus flower.
पृथु *m. n. f.* large, great.
बन्धन *n.* restraint, imprisoment.
बालिका *f.* a girl.
ब्रह्मवर्चसिन् *m. n. f.* illumined by the Vedas; possessing the splendour coferred by the practice of the Vedic rites.
भक्तिमार्ग *m.* (**भक्ति** *f.* love, devotion, and **मार्ग** *m.* a way) devotion to or love of God as a way to eternal bliss.
भाग्ययोग *m.* (**भाग्य** *n.* luck, good fortune, **योग** *m.* accession) the accession of good luck or fortune.

भृश *m. n. f.* much, mighty.

मध्यम *m. n. f.* middle; *n.* waist.

मनुजन्मन् *m.* (मनु *m.* one of the progenitors of men) one born of Manu, a human being, a man.

मन्दभाग्यता *f.* (मन्द dull, भाग्य fortune, मन्दभाग्य one who is unfortunate) misfortune.

महाश्वेता *f.* name of th daughter of a certain Gandharva.

महोपकारिन् *m. n. f.* very benevolent.

मौर्ख्य *n.* folly.

यज्ञवर्मन् *m.* a proper name.

यथाविधि *adv.* according to the rules laid down in ceremonial works.

यमुना *f.* name of a river.

युग *m. n.* a yoke.

योधसमाज *m.* (योध *m.* a warrior, समाज *m* a multitude) a multitude of warriors, an army.

रज्जु *f.* a rope.

रम् *with* उप *1st conj. parasm.* to die.

रहस् *n.* secrecy, solitariness, a secret; *adv.* secretly, solitarily.

लघु *m. n. f.* small.

वपुस् *n.* the body.

विक्रांत *m. n. f.* courageous, possessing prowess.

विश्वसनीयता *f.* capacity to inspire cofidence.

विषय *m.* an object giving sensual pleasure.

विष्णुशर्मन् *m.* a proper name.

विस्तार *m.* extent.

वृत्तान्तश्रवण *n.* (वृत्तान्त *m.* history, account, श्रवण *n.* hearing) hearing of history or account.

वेणि-वेणी *f.* braided hair.

शिरीष *n.* a kind of flowre.

शुचि *m. n. f.* pure.

संभव *m.* possibility, probability.

सदसत् *m. n. f.* (स with, शोक *m.* sorrow) afflicated with sorrow.

सहस्रश *adv.* by thousands.

सुभद्रा *f.* wife of Arjuna.

सेवा *f.* service.

सौम्य *m. n. f.* gentle.

हनूमत् *m.* name of a monkeydevotee of Rams.

ह्रस्व *m. n. f.* short.

Absurd अयुक्त *past part.* अनुपपन्न *past par.*

Bad प्रतिकूल *m. n. f.* [ति *f.*

Bodily form तनु *f.* वपुस *n* आकृ-

Commentator टीकाकार *m.* टीकाकृत् *m.* [*m. n. f.*]

Common साधारण *m. n. f.* सामान्य

Cruel नृशंस *m. n. f.*

Fastened नियुक्त *past pass. part.;* धुरि नियुक्तः.

Kaikeyî कैकेयी *f.* name of one of the wives of Daśaratha.

Kausalyâ कौसल्या *f.* name of one of the wives of Daśaratha.

Moment क्षण *m.*

Net जाल *n.*

Passage, original, मूलग्रन्थ *m.*

Pure विशुद्धशील *m. n. f.*

Relation बन्धु *m.* बन्धुजन *m.* ज्ञाति *m.* [Krishna.]

Rukmiṇî रुक्मिणी *f.* wife of

Running विद्रवण *n.*
Ruthless निर्घृण *m. n. f.*
Satyabhâmâ सत्यभामा *f.* name of one of the wives of Krishna.
Sense अर्थ *m.*
Simple ऋजु *m. n. f.* आर्जवयुक्त *m. n. f.* सरल *m. n. f.*

LESSON XIX.

Compounds

Dvandva (Copulative) and Tatpurusha (Determinative).

I. 1. In Sanskrit one simple noun* may be compounded with another, and this compound with a third or another compound; or several nouns may be compounded together simultaneously. In this manner we may have a compound consisting of any number of simple words According to the sense or manner in which nouns are thus put together, compounds are divided into several classes.† A compound of the class called Dvandva consists of nouns, which, if not compounded, would be joined by the copulative particle ‡; as

रामश्च कृष्णश्च=रामकृष्णौ; रामश्च लक्ष्मणश्च भरतश्च शत्रुघ्नश्च=रामलक्ष्मण-भरतशत्रुघ्नाः

2. (a) When the compound consists of two nouns, each being understood to be singular, it takes the dual; and the plural, when it contains more than two nouns.

b. The gender of the final noun is the gender of the whole; as कुक्कुटमयूर्याविमे मयूरीकुक्कुटाविमौ. c. A Dvandva compound is singular and neuter when it implies an aggregate or when the things enumerated constitute one complex idea, as आहारनिद्राभयम्. This may be called 'the collective species' of Dvandva (Samâhâra Dvandva). When a compound consists of words

---

* *I. e.* a substantive, an adjective or an indeclinable word

† It should by no means be supposed that any noun may be compounded with any other in any sense. The Sanskrit idiom allows of certain compounds only and not others. Ignorant persons, not knowing this, put forth as Sanskrit what is by no means so. Many minute rules have been given by the grammarians, some of which are reproduced in the text. Pratically the usuage of the best authors is the sefest guide.

‡ There are certain rules as regards the order of precedence of the nouns forming compounds of this class, which are not noticed here.

signifying insects, limbs of the body of an animals parts of an army, objects between which there is natural antipathy, or of common names not denoting an animal, it is always of this रथिकाश्वारोहम्, अहिनकुलम्, धानाशष्कुलि. In other cases this construction depends on the will of the speaker.

3. A word ending in ऋ and implying blood-relationship or some kind of learning changes this vowel to आ when followed by another word ending in ऋ or by पुत्र; as होतापोतारौ, मातापितरौ, पितापुत्रौ.

4. When a collective Dvandva compound ends in a letter of the palatal class, or द, ष, or ह, the vowel added on to it; as वाक्त्वचम्, त्वक्स्रजम्, शमीदृषदम्, वाक्त्विषम्, छत्रोपानहम्. When it is not collective, the अ is not added as in प्रावृट्शरदौ.

II. 1. A compound of the Tatpurusha class consists of two members, the first of which determines the sense of the other,* or is attributive to it. The attributive member may have the meaning of a case, or may be used in apposition to the other, and consist, in this latter case, of an adjective or a substantive. The former we will call an inflectional compound, and the latter an appositional (named Karmadhâraya in Sanskrit Grammars); as राज्ञः पुरुषः=राजपुरुषः (inflectional), गम्भीरो नादः गम्भीरनादः (app.); पुरुषो व्याघ्र इव=पुरुषव्याघ्रः (app.).

2. There are six varieties of the first species corresponding to the six oblique cases :—

a. (1) A noun in the accusative case is compounded with as

(2) When the accusative expresses the duration of a continuous actions or state, it is compounded with another indicative of that action or state; मुहूर्तं सुखम्=मुहूर्तसुखम्.

b. A noun in the instrumental is compounded (1) with another expressive of the effect, and (2) with the words पूर्व, सदृश, सम, ऊन, or words having the sense of ऊन, and with कलह, निपुण, मिश्र, and श्लक्ष्ण.

(3) It si also sometimes compounded with verbal deriva-

---

*In a few cases the attributive member is placed after the order.

tives when the instrumental has the sense of the agent or instrument of the action.

(4) When it signifies an article used to season food, it is compounded with the following word, if that word signifies a kind of food.

Examples.—(1) शङ्कुलया खण्डः=शङ्कुलाखण्डः—(2)मासेन पूर्वः=मासपूर्वः, मात्रा सदृशः=मातृसदृशः, वाचा कलहः=वाक्कलहः, &c.(3) हरिणा त्रातः=हरित्रातः नखैर्भिन्नः=नखभिन्नः, &c.—(4) दध्नौदनः=दध्योदनः, &c.

c. A noun in the dative is compounded with another (1) expressive of the material of which the thing expressed by the first noun is made; as यूपाय दारु यूपदारु (2) It is also compounded with अर्थ, बलि, हित, सुख, and रक्षित. The compound with अर्थ is an adjective and takes the number and gender of the noun it qualifies; as द्विजायायम्=द्विजार्थ ओदनः, द्विजायेयम्=द्विजार्था यवागूः, द्विजायेदम् =द्विजार्थं पयः, भूतेभ्यो बलिः=भूतबलिः, गवे हितम्=गोहितम्, गवे सुखम्=गोसुखम्, गवे रक्षितम्=गोरक्षितम्.

d. A noun in the ablative may be compounded with भय, भीत भीति and भी, and sometimes with अपेत, अपोढ, मुक्त, पतित, and अपत्रस्त. Ex.–चोराद्भयम्=चोरभयम्, सुखादपेतः=सुखापेतः चक्रान्मुक्तः=चक्रमुक्तः स्वर्गात्पतितः=स्वर्गपतितः

e. (1) A noun in the genitive may be compounded with any other noun; as राज्ञः पुरुषः=राजपुरुषः

But there are many exceptions.

It is not compounded iwth verbal derivatives ending in अक and denoting the agent; अपां स्रष्टा, ओदनस्य पाचकः, घटस्य कर्ता, not अप्स्रष्टा, ओदनपाचकः or घटकर्ता.

There are a few counter-exceptions as देवपूजकः, ब्राह्मणयाजकः, &c.

Such genitives again as the following are not compounded:–नृणां द्विजः श्रेष्ठः, सतां षष्ठः, आश्चर्यो गवां दोहोऽगोपेन, &c.

(2) पूर्व, अपर, अधर and उत्तर are compounded with nouns in the genitive, and are placed first. Similarly a word expressive of a part is compounded with a noun in the genitive case expressive of time and is placed first. In both cases the noun in the genitive should signify the whole, of which a part is expressed by the compound; पूर्वं कायस्य=पूर्वकायः, चरमं रात्रेः=चरमरात्रः, . मध्यमह्नः=मध्याह्नः &c.

(3) A noun expressive of the time that has elapsed since a certain occurrence is compounded with the noun expressive of the occurrence. संवत्सरो मृतस्य यस्य (one since whose death it is a year)=संवत्सरमृतः, मासजातः, &c.

f. A noun in the locative is compounded with the following words:-शौण्ड, धूर्त, प्रवीण, निपुण, पण्डित, पटु, कुशल, सिद्ध, शुष्क, पक्व, बन्ध, &c. Ex-वाचि पटुः—वाक्पटुः, सभायां पण्डितः—सभा-पण्डितः, आतपे शुष्कः=आतपशुष्कः, &c.

3. An appositional or Karmadhâraya compound is possible in the following cases :—

a. A noun expressive of the standard of comparison may be compounded with another indicating the common quality or ground of comparison; as घन इव श्यामः=घनश्यामः.

b. A noun expressive of the object of comparison with another such as व्याघ्र, चन्द्र, कमल, पद्म, &c. indicating the standard of comparisons; as पुरुषो व्याघ्र इव=पुरुषव्याघ्रः मुखं चन्द्र इव=मुखचन्द्रः नेत्रं कमलमिव=नेत्रकमलम्, पादः पद्ममिव=पादपद्मम्. Or these may be dissolved thus:-मुखमेव चन्द्रः=मुखचन्द्रः, नेत्रमेव कमलम्=नेत्रकमलम्.

c. A qualifying noun with the qualified noun in most cases; as नीलं च तदुत्पलं च=नीलोत्पलम्, गम्भीरश्चासौ नादश्च गम्भीरनादः.

d. Two declinable participles, the first expressing previous and the second subsequent action; as आदौ स्नातः पश्चादनुलिप्तः= स्नातानुलिप्तः

4. The compound of अ and अन् implying negation, with a noun belongs to the Tatpurusha class.

5. When the first member of an appositional or Karmadhâraya compound is a numeral, it is called, in Sanskrit, Dvigu. A Dvigu implies an aggregate; as त्रयाणां भुवनानां समाहारः= त्रिभुवनम्. A Karmadhâraya with a numeral as the firs term must always be a Dvigu.

6. The following words drop the final vowel or the final consonant with the preceding vowel and add अ under the circumstances mentioned:—

(a) पथिन् at the end of any compound as स्वर्गपथः

(b) सखि and राजन् at the end of a Tatpurusha, as मद्रराजः, कृष्णसखः.

(c) रात्रि at the end of a Tatpurusha when preceded by a

numeral, an indeclinable or a word expressive of a part, such as पूर्व, अपर, &c. or by सर्व, संख्यात or पुण्य, and in a Dvandva when preceded by अहः; as द्विरात्रम्, अतिरात्रः, पूर्वरात्रः, अहोरात्रः.

(d) अहन् at the end of a Tatpurusha, when it is not changed to अह्न by rule 7; as पुण्याहम्, द्व्यहः, उत्तमाहः.

7. अहन् is changed to अह्न at the end of a Tatpurusha when preceded by an indeclinable or a word expressive of a part, such as पर्व, अपर, &c., or by सर्व or संख्यात: सर्वाह्नः, पर्वाह्नः.

8. a. ऋच्, पुर्, धुर् (when it does not mean the yoke of a carriage) at the end of any compound, and (b) गो when it ends a Tatpurusha have अ added to them; as अर्धर्चः—र्चम्, विष्णुपुरम्, रणधुरा, परमगवः

9. a. A Tatpurusha follows the gender of the final noun. *b.* The collective Dvigu is neuter, and that ending in is often times feminine and takes the suffix ईः—as राजपुरुषः, नखभिन्नः-न्ना-न्नम्, पञ्चगवम् (from पञ्चन् and गो) पञ्चपात्रम्, त्रिलोकी.

c. A Tatpurusha (in all its species) ending in रात्र, अह्न and अह is masculine, but when रात्र is preceded by a numeral, and अह by पुण्य, it is neuter, as पूर्वरात्रः, मध्याह्नः, सप्ताहः, द्विरात्रम्, पुण्याहम्.

10. When a neuter Dvigu or Dvandva ends in a long vowel, the vowel is shortened. The short vowel corresponding to ओ and औ is उ and to ए and ऐ is इ; द्विखारि (from द्वि and खारी 'a measure of grain').

प्रयागे चतुरहमुषित्वा काशीपथमुपययावुद्दालकः।

रविवारस्य चरमरात्रे संसाराङ्गारतप्तः कश्चित्पुरुषश्चिच्छेदात्मनः शिरः।

आश्विनस्याद्ये नवरात्रे दुर्गाया महोत्सवः क्रियते।

ननु प्रभाता रजनी। तच्छीघ्रं शयनं परित्यजामि। अथवा लघुलघुत्थितापि किं करोमि। न मे दुःखादुचितेषु प्रभातकरणीयेषु हस्तपादं प्रसरति।

अस्मिन्कलौ खलोत्सृष्टदुष्टवाग्बाणदारुणे।
कथं जीवेज्जगन्न स्युः संनाहाः सज्जना यदि॥
इज्याध्ययनदानानि तपः सत्यं धृतिः क्षमा।
अलोभ इति मार्गोऽयं धर्मस्याष्टविधः स्मृतः॥
रोगशोकपरीतापबन्धनव्यसनानि च।
*आत्मापराधवृक्षाणां फलान्येतानि देहिमाम्॥
†सुखदुःखे समे कृत्वा लाभालाभौ जयाजयौ।
ततो युद्धाय युज्यस्व नैवं पापमवाप्स्यसि।
धर्मार्थकाममोक्षाणां यस्यैकोऽपि न विद्यते।
अजागलस्तनस्येव तस्य जन्म निरर्थकम्॥

यदेतदनुमरणं नाम तदतिनिष्फलम्। अविद्वज्जनाचरित एष मार्गो मोहविलसितमेतदज्ञानपद्धतिरियं रभसाचरितमिदं क्षुद्रदृष्टिरेषातिप्रमादोऽयं मौर्ख्यस्खलितमिदं यदुपरते पितरि भ्रातरि सुहृदि भर्तरि वा प्राणाः परित्यज्यन्ते। स्वयं चेन्न जहति न परित्याज्याः। अत्र हि विचार्यमाणे स्वार्थ एव प्राणपरित्यागेऽयमसह्यशोकवेदनाप्रतिकारत्वादात्मनः। उपरतस्य तु न कमपि गुणभावहति। न तावत्तस्यायं प्रत्युज्जीवनोपायो न धर्मोपचयकारणं न शुभलोकोपार्जनहेतुर्न निरयपातप्रतीकारो न दर्शनोपायो न परस्परसमागमनिमित्तम्। अन्यामेव स्वकर्मफलपरिपाकोपचितामसाववशो नीयते भूमिमसावप्यात्मघातिनः केवलमेनसा संयुज्यते।

The master teaches us eight times in a *fortnight.* ‡

The priests perform an Agnishtoma sacrifice in *six days.*

---

* In a compound, a word ending in consonant, when not the last member of the compound, is treated as before the consonantal case-terminations; आत्मन्+अपराध=आत्म+अपराध=आत्मापराध, विद्वस्+रत्न=विद्वद्रत्न.

† Spoken by Krishna to Arjuna who had expressed his unwillingness to fight.

‡ The student should use Sanskrit compounds for the words printed in italics.

The glory of Râma's exploits was sung in the *seven svargas* and *seven pâtâlas*

The duties of *Brâhmanas, Kshartriyas, Vaiśyas, and sûdras* are mentioned in the Smṛitis of *Manu, Yâjnavalkya, and Asita.*

Râma and Sugrîva made an alliance of mutual assistance.

Raghu, who took with him his great army going towards the eastern sea, appeared like Bhagîratha, who led the Gangâ *fallen from the matted hair of Śiva.*

Traversing the eastern countries in this manner, the conqueror reached the coast of *the great* ocean* (which appeared) *dark on account of the forest of Tâli trees.*

Having rooted out the Vaṅgas (who were) haughty on account of their fleet of ships, he erected triumphal (of triumph) columns in the region between the branches (streams) of the Gaṅgâ.

The king of the Kaliṅgas received him with missiles. as the mountains received Indra, prepared to cut (their) wings, with stones.

The conqueror took away the wealth and not the land of teh lord of mahendra (who was) first captured and then released.

The sea though pushed afar by the arrow of Parasurâma, appeared as if touching the mountain Sahya on account of his extensive army (which joined the two).

VOCABULARY XIX.

अग्निष्टोम *m.* a kind of sacrifice
अङ्गार *m. n.* buring charcoal.
अजा *f.* a she-goat.
अतिनिष्फल *m. n. f.* very fruitless.
अतिप्रमाद *m.* a great error, great carelessness.
अनुमरण *n.* following in death or dying after. as in the case of widows burning themselves with the dead bodies
अलाभ *m.* loss.

‡ becomes when it forms the first member of an applsitional Tatpurusha or Bahuvrîhi.

अलोभ *m.* contentment, absence of greed.

अवश *m. n. f.* being in the power of another, dependent, helpless.

असह्य *m. n. f.* (*pot. part.* of **सह्** *with* **अ**) insufferable.

आचरित *m. n. f.* followed, practised; *n.* practice, act.

आत्मघातिन *m. n. f.* one who commits suicide.

उत्सृष्ट *past part. pass.* of **सृज्** *with.* **उद्,** let go discharged.

उद्दालक *m.* name of a person.

उपचय *m.* store, storing, gathering.

उपचित *past. part. pass.* of **चि** *with* **उप,** collected.

उपरत *m. n. f.* (*p.p.* of **रम्** *with* **उप**) dead, deceased, ceased.

एनस् *n.* sin.

करणीय *n.* what is to be done, a work to be got through, duty.

कलि *m.* the kali age, *i. e.*, the age in which the world at presents is, being the last and most sinful of the four ages.

गल *m.* the throat.

गुण *m.* efficacy, advantage.

चरम *m. n. f.* last.

जय *m.* victory, triumph.

देहिन् *m. n. f.* embodied having a body; *m.* a man, the soul.

निरय *m.* hell.

निरर्थक *m. n. f.* useless, vain.

पद्धति *f.* a away, a mode.

परित्याज्य *m. n. f.* (pot. part. of **त्यज्** with **परि**) deserving to be abandoned.

परिपाक *m.* becoming mature, maturity.

परीताप *m.* pain, affliction.

पात *m.* falling, fall.

प्रतिकार *m.* help against an
प्रतीकार evil, a remedy.

प्रत्युज्जीवन *n* restoring of life, revival.

प्रभात *m. n. f.* (*past part.* of **भा** *with* **प्र**) disappeared (as darkness) and appeared (as light); *n.* daybreak.

मूल *n.* a root, basis.

मोह *m.* follishness, infatuation.

रभस *m.* hastiness, rashness.

रोग *m.* disease, sickness.

लघुलघु *adv* early.

लाभ *m.* acquisition, gain.

वङ्गाः *m. plural* the name of a people or their country.

वह् *1st conj. Parasm.* and *tm. with* **आ,** to bring.

वासर *m. n.* a day.

विचार्यमाण (*pres. part. of the pass. of the caus.* of **चर्** to go with **वि**) being thought or considered.

विलसित *m.* a wanton pastime.

वेदना *f.* agony.

संनाह *m* an armour.

संसार *m.* the world.

स्खलित *n.* a slip, a mistake.

स्तन *m.* the female breast, the nipple.

स्तम्भ *m.* a column.

स्वकर्तव्य *n.* one's duty.

Alliance संधि *m.* सख्य *n.*
Assistance साहाय्य *n.*
Captured गृहीत *past. part. pass.* of ग्रह्
Conqueror विजिगीषु *m.*
Cutting छेद *m.*
Dark श्याम *m. n. f.* [*m. n. f.*
Eastern पूर्व *m. n. f. pron.* प्राच्य
Exploit पराक्रम *m.* अद्भुतचरित *n.*
Fleet of ships नौसाधन *n.*
Haughty उन्नत् *past part.*
Lord नाथ *m.*
Mahendra महेन्द्र *m.* name of a mountain and the adjacent country.
Ocean अर्णव *m.*
Pâtâla पाताल *n.* the nether region.
Prepared उद्यत *past part.* of यम् *with* उद्
Pushed afar दूरोत्सारित; उत्सारित, *past part. pass. of the caus of* सृ *with* उद्
Region between अन्तर *n.* अन्तराल *n.*
Released मुक्त *past. part. pass. of* मुच्
Stream स्रोतस् *n.*
Tâlî ताली *f.* a kind of palm tree.
Touching लग्न *m. n. f.*
Touching स्पृश् *1st and 4th conj. with* आ *Parasm.z*
Wing पक्ष *m.*

LESSON XX.

COMPOUND—*continued.*

Bahurîhi and Avyayîbhâva.

I. 1. Two or more nouns in apposition to each other, with the attributive member placed first, may be compounded and used as an adjective to qualify a substantive. The substantive must not be in apposition to the separate members of the compound. A compound of this nature is called Bahurvîhi; as महाबाहु:, पीताम्बर: As a Karmadhâraya, महाबाहु: is equivalent to महान्बाहु 'great arm;' but as a Bahurîhi, it stands for महान्बाहुर्यस्य 'he whose arm is great;, *i. e.*' 'great armed;' so also पीताम्बर: 'he whose garment is yellow.'

महान्बाहुर्यस्य स:=महाबाहुर्नल:. Here बाहु or महत् does not stand in apposition to नल, but the compound महाबाहु: does, as it qualifies नल. In घनश्यामो नल:, श्याम: is in apposition to नल, wherefore the compound is not a Bahvrîhi. That, therefore, is a Bahuvrîhi in the dissolution of which the यत् is in an oblique case; प्राप्तमुदकं यम् प्राप्तोदको ग्राम:, बह्व्यो नद्यो यस्मिन् बहुनदीको देश:

2. Sometimes the first member of a Bahuvrîhi is not in apposition to the second; as चक्रपाणि: चक्रं पाणौ यस्य he in whose hands there is a wheel.

3. When comparison in involved, the first member may have teh sense of the genitive; as equivalent to चन्द्रस्येव कान्तिर्यस्य. As a Tatpurusha it means simply चन्द्रस्य कान्ति:

4. The negative particle अ or अन् or a preposition sometimes forms a Bahuvrîhi compound with a substantive; as अविद्यमान: पुत्रो यस्य सः=अपुत्रः, निर्गता घृणा यस्य सः=निर्घृण: (see 10 below). विगतं जीवितं यस्य स:=विजीवित:, उद्गता कन्धरा यस्य स:=उत्कन्धर: &c. अविद्यमानपुत्रः, निर्गतघृण: &c. are also admissible by the general rule.

5. A compound of words denoting the cardinal points belongs of tbis class, and signifies the point or direction between those points: as उत्तरपूर्वा 'north-east'. A noun signifying a direction, which when uncompounded is declined like a pronoun is optionally so declined when thus compounded.

6. A compound of स or सह with a substantive when used as an adjective is a Bahuvrîhi; as देवदत्त: सहपुत्रो ग्रामं गत:.

7. An adjectival compound of a numeral, or an indeclinable, or of आसन्न, अदूर or अधिक with a numeral, is a Bahuvrîhi. In this case the final vowel or the final consonant with the preceding vowel, of the latter numeral, and अति of विंशति are dropped and the termination अ is added. Ex: द्वित्रा: 'two or three,' द्विदशा: 'twice ten' उपदशा: 'about ten,' *i. e.*, 'nine or eleven', आसन्नविंशा 'nearly twenty' अदूरत्रिंशा: not far from thirty, अधिकचत्वारिंशा: 'more than forty.' But चतुर् when preceded by उप and त्रि does not drop any letter, but अ is simply added to it; as उपचतुरो: 'about four,' त्रिचतुरा: 'three or four.'

The compounds formed by rules 5-7 are ordinarily dissolved as follows :—

उत्तरस्या: पूर्वास्याश्च दिशोऽन्तरालम्=उत्तरपूर्वा। पुत्रेण सह=सहपुत्र:। द्वौ वा त्रयो वा=द्वित्रा:। द्विरावृत्ता दश=द्विदशा:। दशानां समीपे ये सन्ति ते=उपदशा:। विंशतेरासन्ना:=आसन्नविंशा:।

8. When the last word of a Bahuvrîhi ends in ऋ, or is a feminine noun ending in ई or ऊ, the termination क is added on to it; as ईश्वर: कर्ता यस्य तत् ईश्वरकर्तृकं जगत्, बहुयो

नद्यो यस्मिन्सः=बहुनदीको देशः, रूपवद्वधूकः. The rule is not applicable when the feminine noun is such as is capable of taking इय् or उव् for its final before the vowel case-terminations. स्त्री is a counter-exception.

9. *a* If a Bahuvrîhi ends in अक्षि or धनुस्, these words assume the form of अक्ष and धन्वन्: as कमलाक्षः lotus-eyed, अधिज्यधन्वा 'one whose bow is strung.' *b.* It it ends in गन्ध, this word become गन्धि when उद्, पूति, सु or सुरभि precedes, or when the compound involves comparison; as उद्गन्धि, सुगन्धि पद्मगन्धि &c. *c.* Similary धर्म becomes धर्मन् when preceded by a single word. *d.* When the ending word does not undergo such changes and additions, क is optionally affixed to all compounds of this class except those formed by rules 5-7: as अध्ययननिमित्तको मे वासोऽस्मिन्ग्रामे.

10. The final vowel of a Bahuvrîhi compound, if its last member is गो or a feminine noun ending in आ, is shortened, when no क is added; as चित्रा गावो यस्य सः=चित्रगुः, लक्ष्मीर्भार्या यस्य सः=लक्ष्मीभार्यः. The आ is optionally shortened when is affixed: as लक्ष्मीभार्याकः or लक्ष्मीभार्यकः

II. 1. Adverbial compounds (अव्ययीभाव) are formed by putting together an indeclinable (a preposition or an adverb) and a noun. *a.* Adverbs are to be considered as neuter accusative singulars. *b.* Adverbial compounds ending in take sometimes the termination of the instrumental or locative singular. *c.* A final long vowel becomes short (see 10, p 138). *d.* The ending is dropped, but optionally when the final substantive of the compound is neuter.

Ex. अधिहरि 'in Hari,' अनुविष्णु 'after Vishnu,' *i. e.* 'following Vishnu,' उपगङ्गम् 'near the Gangâ,' अनुगङ्गम् 'along with or by the side of the Gangâ,' यथाशक्ति 'according to one's abilities,' अध्यात्मम् 'on or in the soul,' प्रत्यहम् or प्रत्यह 'every day,' सतृणम् 'together with straw.' These are thus ordinarily dissolved:—

हराविति=अधिहरि। विष्णोः पश्चावत्=अनुविष्णु। गङ्गायाः समीपम्=उपगङ्गम्। गङ्गमन्वायतन्=अनुगङ्गम्। शक्तिमनतिक्रम्य=यथाशक्तिः। आत्मनीति=अध्यात्मम्। अहन्यहनीति=प्रत्यहम् or प्रत्यह। तृणमप्यपरित्यज्य=सतृणम्।

स्नेहरूपस्तन्तुर्मनुजानां हृदयमर्माणि सीव्यति।

भार्यया यद्यदिष्टं तत्तदधिज्यधन्वनस्तस्य भूपतेर्नानासाद्यं किंचिदासीत्।

प्रतिदिनं त्र्यम्बकं यथाविधि पूजयामि यावदवकाशं ग्रन्थानवलोकयाम्यामध्याह्नसमयमक्षमालां गृहीत्वा जपामि।

त्रिचतुराण्यहान्यस्मिन्मे गृहे वस्तुं त्वमर्हसि यावत्तवार्थसिद्धिं करोमि।

आसन्नपञ्चाशा गा ब्राह्मणेभ्योऽददाद्यज्ञवर्मा श्रावणस्य प्रथमे सोमवासरे।

चिरप्रवृत्त एष मृतस्य पुनर्जीवप्रदाने पन्थाः। तथाहि। विश्वावसुना गन्धर्वराजेन मेनकायामुत्पन्नां प्रमद्वरां नाम कन्यामाशीविषविलुप्तजीवितां स्थूलकेशाश्रमे भार्गवस्य नप्ता प्रमतितनयो मुनिकुमार को रुरुर्नाम स्वायुषोऽर्धेन योजितवान्।

अर्जुनं चाश्वमेधतुरगानुसारिणमात्मजेन बभ्रुवाहननाम्ना समरशिरसि शरापहृतप्राणमुलूपी नाम नागकन्यका सोच्छ्वासमकरोत्।

अभिमन्युतनयं च परिक्षितमश्वत्थामास्त्रपावकपरिप्लुष्टमुदरादुपरतमेव निर्गतमुत्तराप्रलापोपजनितकृपो भगवान्वासुदेवो दुर्लभानसूनप्रापितवान्।

*यान्येव सुरभिकुसुमधूपानुलेपनादीनि चन्द्रापीडसमागमसुखोपभोगायानितानि तैरेव मृते तस्मिन्देवतोचितामपचितिं संपाद्य चन्द्रापीडमूर्तौ मूर्तिमतीव शोकवृत्तिरार्तरूपा रूपान्तरमिव तत्क्षणेनैवोपगता गतजीवितेव शून्यमुखी मुखावलोकिनी चन्द्रापीडस्य पीडोत्पीडितहृदयापि रक्षन्ती बाष्पमोक्षमुद्दामवृत्तेः शोकादपि मरणादपि च कष्टतमामवस्थामनुभवन्ती तथैवाङ्के समारोपितचन्द्रापीडचरणद्वया दूरागमनखिन्नेनापि बुभुक्षितेना-

---

* This refers to Kâdambarî, a damsel who goes to a certain appointed place to meet her lover, Chandrâpîda, but finds him dead. Hopes have been held out to her by some supernatural power of her lord's revival, and she has been directed to preserve his body.

प्यप्रतिपन्नस्नानपानभोजनेन मुक्तात्मना राजपुत्रलोकेन स्वपरिजनेन च सह निराहारा कादम्बरी तं दिवसमनयत्।

सज्जन्ति कुञ्जरघटाः खलु तत्प्रयाणे
तं संततं युधि परिष्वजते जयश्रीः।
चेतः समासजति तस्य गुणानुरागा-
द्विद्याविशुद्धहृदये विदुषां समूहे॥
यं न स्पृशन्त्येनमचिन्त्यतत्त्वं दुरन्तधामानमनन्तरूपम्।
मनोवचोवृत्तय आत्मभाजां स एव पूज्यः परमः शिवो नः॥
अयं निजः परो वेति गणना लघुचेतसाम्।
उदारचरितानां तु वसुधैव कुटुम्बकम्।
दंष्ट्राभङ्गं मृगाणामधिपतय इव व्यक्तमानावलेपाः।
नाज्ञाभङ्गं सहन्ते नृवर नृपतयस्त्वादृशाः सार्वभौमाः॥

I saw *five or six* men, *more than fifty-five* cows, and *nearly sixty* dogs on the road.

This is the king of the Aṅgas, *whose love has been sought by celestial damsels.*

In him the goddesses Śrî and Sarasvatî, *whose abodes by nature are different,* live together.

The king, *who heard the account of Mahâśvetâ,* was not able to say a word, *overcome with grief.*

This is a king *of the name of Paraṁtapa, whose spirit is unfathomable* and *who has obtained great fame by keeping his subjects contented.*

I now explain the principles of Nyâya *according to my abilities.*

Locusts fly *towards the fire.*

Raghu erected a trophy or triumphal column *on every mountain.*

Janasthâna is situated on the banks of (along-side of the Godâvarî).

Having sent the girl to her husband's house, and being as if I had paid back a deposit, I am now at ease.

This is the lord of Avanti, who is long-armed, broad-chested, and slender-waisted.

The lotus-eyed maid, whose limbs were delicate, did not fix her affections on him.

Sunandâ spoke to the moon-faced damsel (whose face was like the moon) when she reached the place where was sitting Hemâṅgada, the lord of the Kaliṅgas, whose arm was adorned with Aṅgadas, whose power was equal to that of the mountain Mahendra, and who by his prowess had destroyed his enemies.

VOCABULARY XX.

अक्षमाला *f.* (**अक्ष** *m.* name of a plant, or its seed, and **माला** *f.* wreath or a string) a rosary.

अङ्क *m.* the lap. [of **अक्ष**.

अचिन्त्य *m. n. f.* inconceivable, unimaginable.

अधिज्यधन्वन् *m.* one whose bow is strung.

अनुराग *m.* love, liking

अनुलेपन *n.* an ointment.

अपचिति *f.* worship.

अर्थ *m.* object of desire.

अवलेप *m.* pride.

अश्वमेध *m.* the sacrifice of a horse.

असु *m.* vital breath; life (in this sense it is used in the plural, the vital breaths being five in number).

आ a particle showing up to.

आत्मभाज् *m.* one possessed of a soul, a man.

आनीत *past part. pass.* of **नी** *with* **आ**, brought.

आयुस् *n.* life.

आर्त *m. n. f.* troubled, distressed.

आशीविष *m.* a snake.

आसाद्य *m. n. f.* obtainable.

उत्पन्न *m. n. f.* born.

उदार *m. n. f.* noble, generous.

उद्दामवृत्ति *m. n. f.* of a wild disposition, inordinate, excessive.

उद्धत *m. n. f.* haughty.

उपजनित *past part. pass* of the *causal* of **जन्** *with* **उप**, produced.

उपभोग *m.* enjoyment.

उलूपी *f.* name of a serpent damsel for some time a wife of Arjuna.

कन्यका *f.* daughter, a girl.

कादम्बरी *f.* name of a damsel.

कुञ्जर *m.* an elephant.

कुटुम्बक *n.* family.

कुमारक *m.* a yong boy.

कृतिन् *m. n. f.* one who has ac complished his purposes, good, virtuous.

गतजीवित *m. n. f.* dead.

घटा *f.* a collection, a troop (of elephants).

चिरप्रवृत्त *m. n. f.* having long been in practice.

जप् *1st. conj. Parasm.* to pronounce in a low voice, to mutter (as prayers).

तनय *m.* son. [Śiva.

त्र्यम्बक *m.* an epithet of Rudra,

दंष्ट्रा *f.* a jaw, a fang.

दुरन्त *m. n. f.* whose end is difficult to be reached, infinite.

देवता *f.* deity.

धामन् *m.* lustre, glory.

धूप *m.* incense.

निराहार *m. n. f.* not having eaten, fasting.

निसर्ग *m.* nature.

परिक्षित् *m.* son of अभिमन्यु and grandson of अर्जुन. [vant.

परिजन *m.* an attendant, a ser-

परिप्लुष्ट *past part* of प्लुष् *with* परि, scorched, burnt.

प्रचार *m.* progress, prevalence.

प्रमति *m.* name of a man.

प्रमद्वरा *f.* name of a woman.

प्रयाण *n.* starting, march.

प्रापितवत् *past part. act.* of the *caus.* of आप् *with* प्र, having made to get, having given.

बाष्प *m. n.* a tear.

बुभुक्षित *m. n. f.* hungry.

भार्गव *m.* name of a Rishi.

मान *m.* respect, self-respect.

मेनका *f.* name of a celestial damsel.

यथाविधि *adv.* according to the sacred precepts.

यावत् *adv.* as long as.

युध् *f.* a battle.

योजितवत् *past part. act.* of the *caus.* of युज्, having joined.

रुरु *m.* name of a man.

लोक् *with* अव *1st conj. Âtm.* and *10th conj.* to look at, to see.

विलुप्त *past part.* of लुप् *with* वि, destroyed.

[dharva.

विश्वावसु *m.* the name of a Gan-

व्यक्त *past part. pass.* of अञ्ज् *with* वि, plain, manifest.

शून्यमुखी *f.* having no liveliness of the face, pale-faced, of a dejected countenance.

समागम *m.* company, association.

समारोपित *past. part. pass.* of the *caus.* of रुह् *with* सम् and आ, placed.

सज्ज् *with* सम् and आ, to become attached.

सस्ज् *6th conj. Parasm.* to be or become ready.

सार *m.* power, pith. [reign).

सार्वभौम *m. n. f.* universal (sove-

सिव् *4th conj. Parasm.* to sew together.

सुरभि *m. n. f.* fragrant.

सोच्छ्वास *m. n. f.* having. breath.

स्थूलकेश *m.* name of a sage.

Abode आस्पद *n.* आवास *m.*
Agñada अङ्गद *m.* a kind of ornament.
Broad विशाल *m. n. f.*
Celestial damsel अप्सरस् *f.* सुराङ्गना *f.*
Chest वक्षस् *n.*
Deposit न्यास *m.* निक्षेप *m.*
Different भिन्न *past part. pass* of भिद्.
Every प्रति *prep.*
Fix बन्ध् *9th conj. Pârasm.*
Hemâñgada हेमाङ्गद *m.* the name of a king.
Keeping contented अनुरञ्जन *n.* (as applied to the subjects of a king).
Locust शलभ *m.*
Love अनुराग *m.*
Nature निसर्ग *m.*
Overcome अभिभूत *past part. pass.* of भू *with* अभि, पर्याकुल *m. n. f.* आकुल *m. n. f.*
Paid back प्रत्यर्पित *past part. pass.* of the *caus.* of ऋ *with* प्रति.
Paraṁtapa परंतप *m.* name of a king.
Prowess प्रताप *m.* पराक्रम *m.*
Sought प्रार्थित *past. part. pass* of अर्थ् *with* प्र.
Spirit सत्त्व *n.*
Towards अभि *prep.*
unfathomable अगाध *m. n. f.*
Waist मध्य *n.*

LESSON XXI.

CAUSALS.

1. The causal of a root is formed by the addition of अय, and making the same vowel changes as before the अय of the tenth conjugation; करोति 'he makes,' कारयति 'h causes to make.'

2. The causal form takes either pada.

3. Roots ending in अम् (except कम्, अम् and चम्), and the roots जन्, जॄ (4th conj.), दल्, वल्, त्रप्, वन्, ज्वल् and several others, not very important, do not change their vowel to its Vriddhi. Of these, वम्, नम्, वन्, and ज्वल् change their अ optionally, when not preceded by a reposition; as जनयति, वलयति, नमयति-नामयति, उन्नमयति.

4. Roots ending in आ and the roots ह्री and ऋ add on the augment प् before अय; as दा-दापयति, ह्रेपयति, अर्पयति.

5. Roots ending in ए, ऐ, or ओ substitute आ for their vowels; as धे-धा-धापयति, दो-दा-दापयति. (see 14, p. 8z.)

6. shortens its आ necessarily; ग्लै and स्ना optionally, when not preceded by a preposition; as क्षपयति, ग्लपयति or ग्लापयति, प्रग्लापयति.

7. रुह् substitutes प for ह् optionally; as रोपयति-रोहयति. हन् becomes घात्.

8. रभ् and लभ् insert a nasal before the final; as रम्भयति, लम्भयति.

9. शो, छो, सो, ह्वे, व्ये, वे, and पा, 'to drink' add य् instead of प् before अय; and पा 'to protect' adds ल्; as शाययति, साययति, &c. The roots जि, क्री and इ with अधि substitute आ for their vowels; as जापयति, क्रापयति and अध्यापयति.

10.* The ending अ of अय is dropped when followed by the augment इ. अय itself is dropped, the vowel changes being retained. before *(a)* the past participial termination, *(b)* such as begin with य् and *(c)* those of verbal derivatives which begin with a vowel; as विद् 'to know,' विदित 'known,' and वेदित 'made known'; संहृत्य *prim.*, संहार्य *cause.* The अय with its last अ dropped is retained after a root having a short penultimate before the य of the indeclinable past part; as प्रणमय्य.

11. The causal forms of roots of the 10th conjugation are the same as the primitive.

12. When the causal forms of intransitive roots, of transitive ones having a literary work for their object, and of such as imply motion, knowledge or information, and eating, and of दृश् are used, the agent of the verb in its primitive sense is put in the accusative case. This rule is not applicable to नी and वह् and is optional in the case of ह and कृ. In other cases the primitive agent is in the instrumental case

---

यजमानो यज्ञकर्मर्त्विग्भिरारम्भयति।
इन्द्रः स्वयशः किंनरमिथुनानि गापयामास।
पुष्यमित्रो यजते याजकास्तं याजयन्ति।
कृष्णवर्मा पुत्रेण ब्राह्मणेभ्यः प्रत्यहं शतं गा दापयति।
जानकीं रथमारोप्य जाह्नवीतीरमासाद्य रामाज्ञापितो लक्ष्मणस्तां विजहौ।
प्रभुप्रसादलवोऽप्यधीरप्रकृतेर्दासजनस्य प्रागल्भ्यं जनयति।

---

* The rules in this Article apply to the अय of the 10th conjugation also.

असुरस्य तिग्मतपसा प्रीतात्मा भगवाञ्शंकरः स्वीयं रूपं तं दर्शयामास।

नगेन्द्रसक्तां दृष्टिं कस्यापि क्रन्दितमाकर्ण्य राजा निवर्तयामास।

अस्मिँऽनुष्ठितो धर्मस्तस्य कर्तारं स्वर्गलोकं प्रापयति।

ग्रीष्मकाले धर्मोऽङ्गानि ग्लपयति स्वेदं प्रवर्तयति तृष्णां परिवर्धयति च।

बहिर्द्वारि प्रवृत्तमृषिकुमारकं प्रवेशयितुं प्रतिहारीमाज्ञापयामास राजा।

चिरनष्टमात्मनो बालकं दृष्ट्वा सा सुन्दरी भृशं रुरोद तं च दृढं परिष्वज्याश्रुभिः स्नपयामास।

शत्रूनगमयत्स्वर्गं वेदार्थं स्वानवेदयत्।
आशयच्चामृतं देवान्वेदमध्यापयद्विधिम्।
आसयत्सलिले पृथ्वीं यः स मे श्रीहरिर्गतिः॥

रमयन्ति मनस्तावद्भावाः संसारसंभवाः।
यावन्न श्रूयते साश्रुलोकफूत्कारकाहलः॥

स्वीयं यशः पौरुषं च गुप्तये कथितं च यत्
कृतं यदुपराकाय धर्मज्ञो न प्रकाशयेत्।

वेदाविनाशिनं नित्यं य एनमजमव्ययम्।
कथं सं पुरुषः पार्थ कं घातयति हन्ति कम्॥

नैनं छिन्दन्ति शस्त्राणि नैनं दहति पावकः।
न चैनं क्लेदयन्त्यापो न शोषयति मारुतः॥

संयोजयति विद्यैव नीचगापि नरं सरित्।
समुद्रमिव दुर्धर्षं नृपं भाग्यमतः परम्॥

यदि सत्याभिसंधस्त्वं राजन्ग्रामं प्रवासय।
नव पञ्च च वर्षाणि निर्जने गहने वने॥

युधिष्ठिरस्तु कौन्तेयो मयमाहूय सत्वरम्।
कारयामास वै तेन सभामद्भुतदर्शनाम्॥

---

* This refers to the soul whether of man or a universe.

दृष्टिस्तृणीकृतजगत्त्रयसत्त्वसारा
धीरोद्धता नमयतीव गतिर्धरित्रीम्।
कौमारकेऽपि गिरिवद्गुरुतां दधानो
वीरो रसः किमयमेत्युत दर्प एव॥

The king makes the Brâhmanas accept [*ग्रह् with प्रति] with the money.

Vasishtha caused Daaratha to perform [यज्] a sacrifice.

The wicked deeds of Bâjirâja make us blush [ह्री].

Indra caused Mâtali to bring [नी with आ] Arjuna to heaven in his own car.

He first makes men confide [श्वस् with वि] in him, and then destroys [नश्, सद् with अव or ध्वंस्] them.

Being commanded [ज्ञा with आ] by his Guru, he every day fed [चर्] his cows and made them drink [पा] water.

He finished [आप् with सम्] his morning devotions, after which he fed [भुज्] sixteen Brâhmanas, and then took his own meal.

Râma's going to a forest to live there for fourteen years occasioned [सञ्ज् with प्र] Daśaratha's death.

Sañjaya made Dhitarâshtra hear [श्रु] (told him) what happened on the field of battle, where teh Pândavas and the sons of Dhritarâshtra were fighting.

It is fate that sometimes makes brothers and friends firght [युध्] with each other, and occasionally causes a man even to cut off [छिद्] his own head.

A father should marry [नी with परि, वह् with वि or उद्] his daughter to a well-behaved young man, of a respectable family and of good education.

The verses that this boy has repeated reming [स्मृ] me of the times in which I lived on the top of mount Prasravana with my beloved and my brother Lakshmana

The Śyâparnas went to the sacrifice of Saushadmana, and took their seats within the Vedi, whereupon the king ordered his men to unseat [स्था with उद् †] them; they accordingly unseated them. While being unseated, they cried aloud.

* The causal of the roots is to be used.

* The स् of स्था and स्तम्भ् is dropped after the preposition उद्.

VOCABULARY XXI.

अज *m. n. f.* unborn.

अधीर *m. n. f.* not of a sound or grave mind, little-minded, impatient.

अभिसंधा *f.* promise, determination.

अम् *1st conj. Parasm.* to move.

अमृत *n.* the beverage of gods, nectar.

अर्थ *m.* meaning, true sense

अविनाशिन् *m. n. f.* immutable, undergiong no transformation.

अव्यय *m. n. f.* immutable.

काहल *m.* sound.

किंनर *m.* a certain class of demigods.

कृष्णवर्मन् *m.* the name of a person.

कौमारक *n.* boyhood.

क्रन्दित *past part. (used as a substantive) n.* a cry.

क्लिद् *4th conj. Parasm.* to be wet.

क्षै *1st conj. Parasm.* to pine or waste away.

गति *f.* walk, gaiy.

गहन *m. n. f.* impassable, impregnable.

गुप्ति *f.* secrecy, protection.

गुरुता *f.* greatness grandeur, majesty.

ग्लै *1st conj. Parasm.* to become exhausted.

घर्म *m.* heat.

जाह्नवी *f.* the Ganges.

ज्वल् *1st conj. Parasm.* to blaze, burn.

तिग्म *m. n. f.* austere, severe.

तृष्णा *f.* thirst.

दल् *1st conj. Parasm.* to burst. to tear.

दुर्धर्ष *m. n. f.* inaccessible, unapproachable.

धरित्री *f.* the earth.

नगेन्द्र *m.* the lord of mountains, the mountain Himâlaya.

नित्य *m. n f.* eternal, constant.

निर्जन *m. n. f.* tenantless. lonesome.

नीचग *m. n. f.* resorting to a low man, possessed by a humble man; flowing down a sloping ground.

पार्थ *m.* son of पृथा, name of the Pâdavas.

पुष्यमित्र *m.* name of a king.

पौरुष *n.* manliness, prowess.

प्रकृति *f.* disposition.

प्रतिहारी *f.* female door-keeper.

प्रागल्भ्य *n.* boldness.

फूत्कार *m.* sobbing.

मय *m.* name of an architect.

मारुत *m.* wind.

मिथुन *n.* a couple, a pair.

वम् *1st conj. Parasm.* to vomit.

वल्‌ *1st conj. Âtm.* to go, to cover.

वीररस *m.* warlike feeling, one of the nine poetic sentiments.

श्री हरि *m.* a name of the god Vishnu.

संभव *m.* source.

सत्त्व *n.* power, greatness.

सलिल *n.* water.

स्वेद *m.* sweat, prespiration.

According तथा च, तथा, इत्थम्.
Ory रु 2nd. conj. parasm. क्रन्द् 1st conj. Parasm.
Education विद्या; of good education कृतविद्य m. n. f. संस्कृतचित्त m. n. f. सुविनीत m. n. f.
Family कुल n.
Occasionally कालेकाले, प्रसङ्गवशात्.
Prasravaṅa प्रस्रवण m. name of a mountain.
Repeat पठ् *1st conj. Parasm.*
Respectable विशिष्ट; of a respectable family अभिजनवत् m. n. f. कुलीन m. n. f.
Saushadmana सौषद्मन् m. name of a king.
Sometimes कदाचित्.
Śyâparna श्यापर्ण m. an individual of the श्यापर्ण family, which was a family of priests.
Well-behaved सुचरित m. n. f.

LESSON XXII.
AORIST.

1. The so-called Aorist expresses simply the completion of an action without refernce to any particular time, or a recent or this day's action. It is similar to the English Present Perfect, which, the student will remember. "defines an action as having happened in a portion of time which is not yet expired; it brings a past action into connection with the present time." The Aorist should never be used in narratives*. अजनि ते वै पुत्रः (Ait Brâhmana) 'A son has been born to thee; तदहं तुभ्यमेव ददामि य एव सत्यवादीः (Ait. Brâhmana) 'I give that to thee who hast told only the truth;' उदु श्रिय उषसो रोचमाना अस्थुः (Rigveda Saṁhitâ). The bright splendours of the dawn have arisen (begun to appear).

2. The Aorist is used with the prohibitive particle and has then the sense of teh imperative. The temporal augment is in the case dropped; as 'Do not go'; मानो हिंसीज्जनिता यः पृथिव्याः 'May he, who is the creator of the earth, not hurt (kill) us!'

3. There are seven varieties of the Aorist. The

* In the later Sanskrit literature the three past tenses are promiscuously used, on distinction being observed among them.

temporal augment अ or आ is prefixed to the roots in this tense as in the Imperfect.

I.—*First Variety.*

1. The terminations of the Imperfect are applied to roots with the exception of that of the third person plural, which in this case is उस्. Before उस् the preceding if any, is dropped.

	Sing.	Dual	Plur.
1st pers	अम्	व	म
2nd,,	स्	तम्	त
3rd,,	त्	ताम्	उस्

2. पा 'to drink,' स्था, दा, धा, and other roots assuming the forms of दा and धा in virtue of rule 14, p. 82, गा which is substituted for इ 'to go' in the Aorist, and भू 'to be' belong to this variety.

3. The third person plural termination in the case of भू is अन्; and before the terminations beginning with a vowel is added on to भू

4. घ्रा, धे, शो सो and छो are conjugated in this way optionally (remember rule 14, p. 82). Their other forms are made up according to the sixth variety. धे takes the third Aorist also.

This variety is Parasmaipadi exclusively. Such of the roots belonging to it, as are tmanepadi also, take the fouth or fifth variety in that Pada.

दा—to give.'

	Sing.	*Dual*	*Plur.*
1st pers.	अदाम्	अदाव	अदाम
2nd "	अदाः	अदातम्	अदात
3rd "	अदात्*	अदाताम्	अदुः

आ being dropped before उस् by 1 above, we have अद् + उस्=अदुः Similarly अस्थुः, अगुः, &c.

II—*Second Variety.*

1. अ is added on to the root, and then the termnations of the Imperfect of the first group of conjugations are appended.

* Rule II., p. 58 is applicable in this as in all such acses.

Parasm.

	Sing.	*Dual*	*Plur.*
1st pers.	अम्	व	म
2nd "	स्	तम्	त
3rd "	त्	ताम्	अन्

The is elided before and and lengthened before and (Seep p. 6 note* and p. 5 F. B.).

Âtm.

1st pers.	इ	वहि	महि
2nd "	थास्	इथाम्	ध्वम्
3rd "	त	इताम्	अन्त

The is elided before and lengthened before and as above.

The redical vowels do not take their Guna or Vriddhi substitute.

3. This variety is Parasmaipadi with but a few exceptions.

4. Some roots are conjugated in this way optionally and some necessarily. The most important of these are given in the following lists:—*a.*

Necessarily.

लिप् to anoint.

सिच् to sprinkle.

*ह्वे (ह्व) to call.

These three roots when tmanepadi take this variety optionaly.

अस् (अस्थ्) to throw.

आप् to obtain.

क्रुध् to be angry.

क्लम् to be fatigued.

क्षम् *4th conj.* to forgive.

ख्या (ख्य्) in *Parasm.* and Âtm. to tell.

गम् to go

गृध् to be greedy.

घस् to devour.

तम् to be distressed in body or mind.

तुष् to be satisfied.

तृष् to be thirsty.

दम् to be tamed.

दुष् to be depraved.

द्रुह् to hurt, to act the traitor.

नश् to perish.

पत् (पप्त्) to fall.

पिष् to pulverize, to grind.

पुष् *4th conj.* to nourish.

भ्रम् *4th conj.* to wander, to err.

* The forms which some roots assume before अ are enclosed within bracketss; as आस्थ् + अम् = आस्थम्; अह्व् + अम् = अह्वम्.

मद् to be mad.
मुच् to leave, to release.
मुह् to be silly.
लुप् to cut.
लुभ् *4th conj.* to covet. [to speak.
वच् (वोच्) in *Parasm.* and *Âtm.*
शक् to be able.
शद् to perish, to wither away.
शम् to be calm. [to reulate.
शास् (शिष्) to govern , to reule,
शिष् to distinguish.
शुध् to be purified.
श्रम् to exert one's self.
श्लिष् *4th conj.* to adhere.
सद् to be dejected, to sit.
सिध् *4th conj.* to be ready.
सृप् to move, to creep.
स्निह् to bear affection to.
स्विद् *4th conj.* to perspire
हृष् *4th conj.* to be glad.

b. Optionally

क्षुद् to reduce to powder.
घुष् to proclaim.
च्युत् to drop.
छिद् to cut off.
जृ (जर्) to become old.
तृप् to be satisfied.
दृप् to be proud.
दृश् (दर्श्) to see.
निज् to wash off.
बुध् to know.
भिद् to penetrate.
युज् to join.
रिच् to make empty.
रुद् to cry.
रुध् to obstruct.
विच् to separate.
शुष् *4th conj.* to be pure.
श्वि (श्व) to swell.
स्कन्द् (स्कद्) to jump upwards.
स्तम्भ् (स्तभ्) to obstruct.
स्फुट *1st conj.* to break off,
The following roots of the first conjugation are generally Âtmanepadi, but when they take this variety of the Aorist they become Parasmaipadi:— [wards.
क्लृप् to make for, to tend to-
क्षुभ् to become agitated
द्युत् to shine.
ध्वंस् (ध्वस्) to perish.
भ्रंश् (भ्रश्) to fall.
रुच् to shine.
वृत् to be.
वृध् to increase.
शुभ् to shine, to look decent.
स्यन्द् (स्यद्) to drop. [down.
स्रंस् (स्रस्) to fall down, to drop
स्विद् to perspire.

5. Of these श्वि takes the third and fifth varieties besides this, and the rest, the fouth or the fifth according as they are Anit or Set.

6. श्लिष् takes the seventh variety when it means 'to embrace.'

7. Such of the roots in the two lists as are conjugated in the Âtmanepada, with the exception of those mentioned above, take the fourth or fifth variety in that Pada.

वचपुष्.
पुष्.

	Sing.	Dual	Plur.
1st pers.	अपुषम्	अपुषाव	अपुषाम
2nd "	अपुषः	अपुषतम्	अपुषत
3rd "	अपुषत्	अपुषताम्	अपुषन्

वच् Âtm.

	Sing.	Dual	Plur.
1st pers.	अवोचे	अवोचावहि	अवोचामहि
2nd "	अवोचथाः	अवोचेथाम्	अवोचध्वम्
3rd "	अवोचत	अवोचेताम्	अवोचन्त

III—*Third Variety.*

1. The Aorist forms of roots of the tenth conjugatior and of causals are made up in this way.

2. *a.* The अय is dropped, but the vowel changes and others effectdd in the primitive root before it are retained. *b.* The penultimate vowel is shortened. *c.* Then the root is to be reduplicated according to the general rules. It the syllable following the reduplicative one be short and not prosodially* long, *d.* the अ of the reduplicative syllable is changed to इ; and *e.* its vowel generally, when short and not prosodially long, is lengthened. *f.* To the base so prepared are to be appended अ, and the terminations of the Imperfect as in the second variety.

Thus from भावय (the causal of भू), by droping अय, we have भाव्; by shrotening the penultimate, भव्: by reduplication, बभव्: by changing the reduplicative अ to इ, बिभव्; by lengthening the इ, बीभव्; and by applying अ, the terminations त् and the temporal augment, अबीभवत्. So from स्पन्दयति (caus. of स्पन्द्) we have by *a.* स्पन्द्; पस्पन्द by *c.* 2 *e.* p. 63; अपस्पन्दत् by *f.* For *b.* there is no occasion, since the penultimate is not a vowel, and none also for *d.* and *e.* since स्प, the syllable following the reduplicative प, is prosodially long, being followed by a conjunct consonant स्खलयति (caus. of स्खल्); स्खल् by a.; चस्खल् by *c.* and 2. *e.*, *c.* and *b.*, pp. 62–3; चिस्खल् by d.; अचिस्खलत् by *f.* For *b.* there is no occasion, and also for *e.*, since the vowel इ of the reduplicative syllable चि is prosodially long.

3. *a.* if a root begins with a vowel, the following consonant is reduplicated and इ added to it in the reduplicative syllable.

---

* A syllable is prosodially long when, being short itself, it is followed by a conjunct consonant.

b. When a conjunct consonant with न्, द्, or र् as its first member, follows the initial vowel, the second member is reduplicated.

Thus अद्-आटय-आद् by 2. *a;* अद् 2. *b;* अटिद् 3 *a;* आटिद्, by adding the temporal augment आ (F. B. p. 62); and आटिटत् by 2. *f.* So उन्द्-उन्दय-उन्द्-इन्दिद् by 3b: औन्दिद् by the rule in p. 62 F. B. and औन्दिदत् Similarly अर्ह् has आर्जिहत्. In the two latter cases उन् and अर् are set aside and द् and ह् are reduplicated and इ added to them.

4. *a.* If a root ends in उ, short or long, that vowel is to be substituted for इ in the reduplicative syllable, when the following syllable does not consist of a letter of the labial class or of or य्, र्, ल्, व्, or ज्, followed by अ.

Thus कु causal कावय्-काव्-काव्-चकव् and चिकव् ;but as the root ends in उ, we have चुकव्-चूकव्-अचूकवत् ;but in the case of भू or पू we have अबीभवत् or अपीपवत्, and not अबूभवत् or अपूपवत्.

b. The इ is optionally retained in the case of स्रु, श्रु, द्रु, प्रु, प्लु and च्यु. Ex. अशिश्रवत् or अशुश्रवत् Aor. caus of श्रु.

5. The following roots shorten their penultimate optionally :—

भ्राज्, भाष्, भास्, दीप्, जीव्, मील्, पीड्, and also ह्वे, लुट्, लुप् and a few others; as अपीपिडत् or अपिपीडत्.

पीडय-पीड्-पिपीड्-अपिपीडत् 2. *c.* has no place here When the penultimate is shortenned, we have पीड्-पीड्-पिपिड्-अपीपिडत्.

6. The vowel changes mentioned in Aticle 2, *i. e..* the shortening of the penultimate (c). the substitution of इ for अ (d) and the lengthening of the reduplicative syllable (e) do not take place in the case of the following roots:-

कथ्, वर्, शठ्, रह्, स्पृह्, सूच्, मृग्, ध्वन्, पार् ; कथ्-अचकथत्, वर्-अववरत्.

7. The अ of the reduplicative syllable of स्मृ, दृ, त्वर्, प्रथ्, म्रद्, स्तॄ and स्पश् is preserved, and the इ of those of वेष्ट् and चेष्ट् optionally changed to अ; as असस्मरत्, अददरत् &c., and अववेष्टत् or अविवेष्टत्.

8. गण् has two forms, अजगणत् or अजीगणत्.

2. The roots श्रि, द्रु and स्रु take the third variety in the primitive form. श्वि takes it optionally. धे (see p 155 Art. 4) drops its after reduplication.

In these cases reduplication alone is necessary. श्रि-शिश्रि अत्-अशिश्रियत् by II, p. 36, the being weak; धे-अदधत्.

10. स्थापयति has अतिष्ठिपत्; पाययति, अपीप्यत्; and घ्रापयति, अजिघ्रपत् or अजिघ्रिपत्.

11. The penultimate short of a root is optionally retained, the long ऋ optionally shortened.

वर्तय caus. of वृत्; by dropping the अय we have वर्त्, or वृत् by the above; वृत्-ववर्त्-अववर्तत्. 2. *d.* and *e.* are not applicable. वृत्-विवृत् by 2 *d.*—वीवृत् 2 *e.*—अवीवृतत् कीर्तय prim. or caus. of कृत्; after the dropping of the अय, कीर्त् and कृत् by the above, which give two forms अचिकीर्तत् or अचीकृतत्.

12. Some roots, the most important of which are लोक्, लोच्, शाम्, श्लाघ्, बाध्, सेव्, वेप्, एज्, लाघ्, राध्, ताय्, दाश्, याच्, and राज्, do not shorten the penultimate; as अलुलोकत् and अततायत्

13. ह्वे and स्वप् are, in the Aorist of the causal, to be taken as हु and सुप्, and श्वि optionally as शु. अजूहवत् or अजुहावत् by Art 5., असूषुपत्, अशूशवत्, or अशिश्वयत्.

14. This variety is both Âtmanepadi and Parasmipadi.

हृ 'to carry' caus.

Parasm.

	Sing.	*Dual*	*Plur.*
1st pers.	अजीहरम्	अजीहराव	अजीहराम
2nd "	अजीहरः	अजीहरतम्	अजीहरत
3rd "	अजीहरत्	अजीहरताम्	अजीहरन्

Âtm.

1st pers.	अजीहरे	अजीहरावहि	अजीहरामहि
2nd "	अजीहरथाः	अजीहरेथाम्	अजीहरध्वम्
3rd "	अजीहरत	अजीहरेताम्	अजीहरन्त

काशीं गन्तुकामः श्रीनगरान्निरगात्पण्डितः सह परिवारेण।

भगो अर्यमा सविता पुरंधिर्मह्यं त्वादुर्गार्हपत्याय देवाः।

तस्मिन्गुर्वनुचरे गृहं प्रविष्टे यूयं किमथुनोदस्थात। गुरुरतमिति मत्वा।

अस्मिन्निर्जने वने नष्टमश्वमियन्तं कालमन्विष्यन्नपि न समासदम्।

इदमाम्रफलं वृक्षादपप्तत्। यदि रोचते गृहीत्वा स्वादस्व।

हे गङ्गे यदीदृशेभ्यः पापेभ्यो मामुददीधरस्ततः सत्यमनाथ-शरणमसि विष्णुपदपङ्कजोद्भवासि।

प्रातरारभ्य पञ्चसप्ततिं वृक्षानसिचाम।

वत्सस्य मरणेन तद्विषयकाः सर्वे मनोरथा मेऽध्वसन्।

क्रीडार्थमुपवनमगमतां दंपती तयोर्निवृत्तयोरात्मनः करुणवार्तां कथय।

इयं बालिका दुःखवार्तां श्रुत्वामुहत्। आश्वासयैनामुदकेन च सिञ्च।

इमं ग्राममागगच्छन्तौ भवन्निर्दिष्टे गहने वने नानापक्षिगणसमाकुलं महावटवृक्षं तमदर्शाव।

उपाध्यायो देवानपूपुजदधुनातिथयो यथेष्टं भुञ्जताम्।

अस्मिन्मण्डपे समाहूतान्ब्राह्मणनहमजगणम्। पञ्च शतानि तेषां वर्तन्ते। एतेभ्योऽधुना दक्षिणां दातुमारभस्व।

मञ्चैन्तिता सरणिर्वरीयसेऽधिकारिणे नारुचदतः स तां निरास्थन्नवीनां च स्वयं कल्पितां प्रावीवृतत्।

किं यूयमवोचत। पुनरपि कथयत नाहमवहितोऽभूवम्।

प्रातिष्ठिपत्स बोधार्थं कुम्भकर्णस्य राक्षसान्॥

राघवस्यामुषः कान्तामाप्तैरुक्तो न चार्पिपः॥

मुष्टिनाददरत्तस्य मूर्धानं मारुतात्मजः॥

मुक्त्वा निःश्रीकमप्यब्जं मराली न गातान्यतः।

भ्रमराली त्वगाद्वेगादिदं सदसदन्तरम्॥

We have drunk [पा] Some and have become [भू] immortal.

Devadatta has weighed [तुल्] this gold, make ornaments of it.

The king of the Kalingas has besieged [रुध्] Pâtaliputra, but many of his soldiers have fallen out [भ्रंश्] of the line and are looking for plunder.

Ashtâvakra, coming from a place twelve coss off, is now tired [श्रम्]. Give him food and drink.

He has not been able [शक्] to convince me that my belief in the existence of ghosts is unfounded.

The minister has governed [शास्] the country justly. He is loved by all the people.

Govinda looked for the lost book one whole day, but has not found [गम् with अधि, सद् with सम् and आ] it.

We have cut off [छिद्] a branch of teh Palâśa tree for making a sacrificial post.

Have you not washed [क्षल्] your hands yet?

I have given a hot bath* [स्ना caus.] to my children.

Hast thou not heated [तप् caus]. the water yet, as I told [वच्] you to do?

The owner being dead, they have caused the house to be pulled down [सद् caus. with उद् or नश् caus.] and his clothes to be burned [दह् caus.]

VOCABULARY XXII.

अनाथ *m. n. f.* helpless.

अनुचर *m.* an attendant, a servant.

अब्ज *n.* a lotus.

अवहित (*past part.* of धा *with* अव) attentive.

अष्टावक्र *m.* name of a person.

अस् 4th conj. with to repeal, to abolish.

आप्त *m.* a friend, a well-wisher.

आली *f.* a line or row.

इ *with* निर्, to set out.

करुण *m. n. f.* doleful, lamentable.

कल्पित *past part. pass.* of the causal of क्लृप्, planned, invented.

गन्तुकाम *m. n. f.* desirous to go.

गार्हपत्य *m.* a sacred fire kept perpetually by a house-holder, household duties.

तद्विषयक *m. n. f.* concerning him.

तायृ *Ist conj. Âtm.* to spread.

दीप् *4th conj. Âtm.* to shine.

धृ *with* उद्, to draw out, to save.

धे *Ist conj. Parasm.* to suck, to drink.

ध्वन् *Ist conj. Parasm.* to sound.

नवीन *m. n. f.* new.

परिवार *m.* retinue.

पलाश *m.* a kind of tree.

पुरंधि *m.* name of a deity.

बोध *m.* awakening.

भग *m.* name of a deity.

* Use उष्णोदकेन with the caus. of स्ना.

भ्रंश् *1st conj. Âtm.* and *4th conj. Parasm.* to fall.
मण्डप *m.* temporary hall erected on festive occasions.
मनोरथ *m.* wish, desire.
मराली *f.* a female swan.
मारुतात्मज *m.* the son of the god of wind, Mâruti.
मुष्टि *m. f.* a fist.
मृग् *10th conj. Âtm.* to look for, to search.
रह् *10th conj.* to quit.
वटवृक्ष *m.* a banian tree.
वर् *10th conj.* to choose.
वृत् *with* प्र *(in the causal)* to introduce, to bring into practice.
शठ् *10th conj.* to deceive, to defraud.
श्री *f.* beauty.
सद् *with* सम् and आ, to obtain, to meet with, to find.
समाकुल *m. n. f.* occupied with, full of.
समाहृत *past part. pass.* of हृ *with* सम् and आ, collected.
सरणि-णी *f.* path, disposition or arrangement of things.
सवितृ *m.* the sun.
सूच् *10th conj.* to indicate.
स्वामिन् *m.* owner.

Belief श्रद्धा *f.* विश्वास *m.*
Convince हृ with प्रति *caus.*, प्रतीतिं कृ.
Existence भाव *m.* अस्तित्व *n.*
Ghost प्रेत *m.* वेताल *m.* पिशाच *m.*
Immortal अमृत *past part.* of मृ *with* अ, अमर *m. n. f.*
Justly धर्मेण, न्यायेन.
Line व्यूह *m.* column of an army.
Love स्निह् *4th conj.*; he is loved तस्मिन्स्निह्यति.
Plunder लोप्त्र *n.* लुण्ठन *n.*
Unfounded निर्मूल *m. n. f.*
Yet अद्यापि *ind.*

LESSON XXIII.

AORIST—*contd.*

1, Sixth Variety.

1, The sixth variety of the Aorist is formed by adding to the root the forms of the third Aorist of with some changes, the of being dropped. These forms may be considered as the terminations. They are as follows:—

	Sing.	*Dual*	*Plur.*
1st pers.	सिषम्	सिष्व	सिष्म
2nd "	सीः	सिष्टम्	सिष्ट
3rd "	सीत्	सिष्टाम्	सिषुः

To be able to commit them easily to memory, the learner may regard them as made up of the Imperfect forms of अस्, with the आ dropped and सि prefixed, this latter necessitating the change of the following स् to ष्. Instead of सन्, सुस् should be taken to be the third person plural form, and सि is not to be prefixed to the second and third person singular.

2. Roots ending in आ* , यम्, रम्, and नम्, take this wariety.

3. This variety is Parasmaipadi only.

II—Seventh Variety.

1. This consists in adding to the root the forms of the second Aorist of 'to be' the of being dropped. In other words, add to and append the terminations of the Imperfect with the modifications shown below, These forms, considered as terminations shown below. These forms, considered as terminations, add on to the root.

	Parasm.			*Âtm.*	
1st pers. सम्	साव	साम	सि	सावहि	सामहि
2nd " सः	सतम्	सत	सथाः	साथाम्	सध्वम्
3rd " सत्	सताम्	सन्	सत	साताम्	सन्त

2. This Variety is both Âtm. and Parasm.

3. Anit. † roots ending in श्, ष्, स् and ह्, and having इ, उ, ऋ, or लृ for their penultimate, have their Aorist formed in this way.

4. The root दृश् is an excption.

5. The roots स्पृश्, मृश्, and कृष् optionally take this variety.

6. The third person singular, second person singular and plural, and first person dual of the Âtmanepada of the roots दुह्, दिह्, लिह्, and गुह् are optionally formed by dropping the स or सा and appending the remaining portions of the terminations.

ग्लै *Parasm.*

	Sing.	*Dual*	*Plur.*
1st pers.	अग्लासिषम्	अग्लासिष्व	अग्लासिष्म
2nd "	अग्लासीः	अग्लासिष्टम्	अग्लासिष्ट
3rd "	अग्लासीत्	अग्लासिष्टाम्	अग्लासिषुः

* Roots endig in ए, ऐ and ओ are to be considered asa roots ending in आ, as observed in Art. 14, Lesson XIII.

† Seep p. 78, Note †. Also those roots which are optionally *Set* when they do not take इ.

लि *Parasm.*

	Sing.	*Dual*	*Plur.*
1st pers.	अलिक्षम्	अलिक्षाव	अलिक्षाम
2nd "	अलिक्षः	अलिक्षतम्	अलिक्षत
3rd "	अलिक्षत्	अलिक्षताम्	अलिक्षन्

Âtm.

1st pers.	अलिक्षि	अलिक्षावहि-अलिह्वहि	अलिक्षामहि
2nd "	अलिक्षथाः-अलीढाः	अलिक्षाथाम्	अलिक्षध्वम्-अलीढ्वम्
3rd "	अलिक्षत-अलीढ	अलिक्षाताम्	अलिक्षन्त

अ+लिह्+सत्; लिह्-लिढ् by 1., p. 49-लिक् by IV., p. 49-लिक्+श्त्-लिक्षत् by note† p. 97 F. B.—अलिक्षत्. अ+दिह्+सत्; दिह्-दिध् by V, p-50-धिध् by VII. p 51.—धिक् by note† p. 5 F. B-धिक्+षत् as above-अधिक्षत्. अ+दिश्+सत्; दिश्-दिष् by IX. p. 52-दिक् by IV., p. 49-दिक् +षत् as above—अदिक्षत्. अ+कृष्+सत्; कृष्-कृक् &c. as above ——अकृक्षत्. अ+लिह्+सत; लिह्-लिढ्, &c. as above-अलिक्षत; also लिह्+त-लिढ्+त by 1., p. 49—लिढ्+ध by II., p. 49—लिढ्+ढ by note* p. 21. F. B.—लीढ byIII., p. 49—and with the temporal augment,अलीढ.

नित्यकर्मानुष्ठानायास्नासीस्तच्छूद्रादीन्मा स्पृक्षः।

वेणुधमन्याग्निमध्मासिषम्। तदस्मिन्प्रदीप्ते यह्नावाहुतीः प्रास्य।

भोः पुरोहित भवदाज्ञामनुसृत्य बटवेऽहं सावित्रीमुपादिक्षम्। तदधुनान्यत्करणीयं दर्शय।

विवाहविधेरितिकर्तव्यतामज्ञत्या ब्राह्मणा नाज्ञासिषुस्ततो मां तत्संपादनायाह्वन्।

अस्तमयासीद्रविरिस्त मेरेणावृतं नभः। तत्किमद्यापि गां नाधुक्षत पयः।

कृषीवला भूमिमकृक्षन्परं त्वाद्रासु स्थितेऽपि सूर्ये पर्जन्यो न वर्षति।

मा वयं भ्रातरः परस्परं द्विक्षामेत्यस्माकं पितासन्नमरणो रिक्थस्य समानांश्चतुरो भागानकरोत्।

महाकार्यारम्भे देवो गुरुजनश्च वन्दितव्य इति वचनमनुरुध्य गृहदेवतां मातरं पितरन्यांश्च वृद्धान्प्राणंसिष्म।

कूपतडागादिनिर्माणाय महान्तो यत्ना युष्माभिः कृतास्ते कस्मिन्पर्यवासासिषुः। इदं मधु किं नालिक्षः। रुचिकरमेतत्।

He embraced [श्लिष्] his child and wept [रुद्] bitterly.

We have mounted [रुह् with आ] our horses and are now marching against the enemy.

The flowers, brought yesterday, have now faded [म्लै]; throw them out and bring new ones.

Having told us how chandraketu and Lava fouiht with each other, and how Râma commanded them to be quiet,* he has ceased [रम् with वि Parasm.].

I have not yet thought [मृश् with वि] which would be better for me, the study fo law or of medicine.

Have you smelt [घ्रा] the flower? It is very fragrant.

The king has sat [विश् with उप] upon the throne and is consulting with his ministers.

We have protected [पा] you so long from evil or injury and you now act the traitor towards us; what could be more mournful?

Why hast thou abandoned [हा] an affectionate wife who never did anything you did not like?

VOCABULARY XXIII.

अनुष्ठान *n.* doing, executing.

अस्त *m.* sunset.

आर्द्रा *f.* the sixth lunar mansion.

आवृत *past part. pass* of *with* filled, covered.

आसन्नमरण *m. n. f.* (आसन्न *m. n. f.* near, and मरण *n.* death) one whose death is near, about to die.

आहुति *f.* sarificial oblation.

इतिकर्तव्यता *f.* method or the way of doing enything.

करणीय *pot. part.* what is to be doen.

गृहदेवता *f.* family deity.

तिमिर *n.* darkness.

धमनी *f.* a pipe.

नित्यकर्मन् *n.* daily religious performance.

पर्जन्य *m.* rain.

* प्रशाम्यतमित्यादिशत्

प्रदीप्त *past part.* of दीप् to shine *with* प्र, shining brightly.
भाग *m.* division.
रिक्थ *n.* property, wealth.
रुचिकर *m. n. f.* palatable.
वन्दितव्य *pot. part.* of वन्द्, fit to be bowed to.
वृष् *1st conj. Parasm.* to rain.
वेणु *m.* a bamboo.
संपादन *n.* accomplishing.
समान *m. n. f.* equal.
सावित्री *f.* the holy mantra or verse of the Rigveda, generally called Gâyatrî, and repeated by all the Brâhmaṇas every day.
सो *4th conj. Parasm.* to end; *with* परि and अव, to end in to result in.

Act the traitor द्रुह् *4th conj. Parasm.*
Bitterly प्रमुक्तकण्ठम्, *used as an adv.*
Chandraketu *m.* name of the son of Lakshmaṇa, brother of Râma.
Evil अनर्थ *m.* पीडा *f.* संकट *n.*
Frangrant सुरभि *m. n. f.*
Law धर्मशास्त्र *n.*
March against गम् with अभि.
Medicine (as a science) वैद्यक *n.* आयुर्वेद *m.*
More mournful दुःखतर *m. n. f.*

VOCABULARY XXIII.

Part I.

AORIST—*contd.*

Fourth and Fifth Varieties.

1. The most general varieties of the Aorist are the fourth and the fifth. Any root that does not belong to any of the preceding ones takes one or other of these In the some manner a root that takes one or the others optionally, or in the Parasmaipada only, has its other or Âtmanepada forms made up in either of these ways.

2. (*a*) The fifth differs from the fourth in prefixing the augment to the terminations and consequently it is the Aorist of *Set* roots and the fourth that of *Anit* roots. (*b*) स्तु and सु when *Parasm.* belong to the fifth variety, though *Anit;* and (*c*) वृ and roots ending in ऋ preceded by a conjunct consonant or in long ॠ, when Âtmanepadi, and (*d*) such as are optionally *Set* to either. (*e*) धू when *Parasm.* and अञ्ज् take the fifth only.

3. स्तु and क्रम् do not admit इ when they take the Âtmanepda terminations.

4. *a*. The forms of the Imperfect of अस् 'to be' with the initial आ dropped, are appended to the roots as terminations. *b*. The third person plural has instead of सन्. *c*.When in the fifth variety इ is prefixed, the स् of the second and third person singular is dropped. *d*. The rule about the change of ध्वे to ढ्वे given in 4, p. 79, hold good in the case of ध्वम् in this tense. ध्वम् is changed to ढ्वम् when preceded by र् also.

I. स् preceded and follwed by any consonant except a nasal or a semi-vowel is dropped; as अभिद् + स्ता = अभित्त; अभैद् + स्ताम् =अभैत्ताम्.

Fourth Variety.			Fifth Variety.		
parasm.			*Parasm.*		
Sing.	*Dual*	*Plur.*	*Sing.*	*Dual*	*Plur.*
सम्	स्व	स्म	इषम्	इष्व	इष्म
सीः	स्तम्	स्त	ईः	इष्टम्	इष्ट
सीत्	स्ताम्	सुः	ईत्	इष्टाम्	इषुः
Âtm.			*Âtm.*		
सि	स्वहि	स्महि	इषि	इष्वहि	इष्महि
स्थाः	साथाम्	ध्वम्	इष्ठाः	इषाथाम्	इध्वम्
स्त	साताम्	सत	इष्ट	इषाताम्	इषत

PARASMAIPDA.

Fourth Variety.

5. In the Parasmaipada forms of the fourth variety the vowel of a root takes its Vṛiddhi substitute; as भिद् = अभैत्सीत्.

Fifth Variety.

6. In the Parasmaipada fifth, (*a*) the ending इ, उ, ऋ, and ऌ shot or long, and (*b*) the penultimate अ of roots ending in र् or ल् and (*c*.) that of वद् and व्रज् take Vriddhi necessarily; as लू- अलो+इषम्-अलाविषम्, चर्-अचारिषम्, फल्-अफालिषम्.

7. The अ if not prosodially long, of roots having an initial consonant and ending in any consonant except र् and ल् takes Vriddhi optionally; as गद्-अगदीत् or अगादीत्.

8. Exceptions.—Roots ending in ह्, म्, य्, and the roots क्षण्, श्वस्, जागृ, कद्, लग्, हस्, श्वि and some others, do not take Vriddhi; as क्रम्-अक्रमीत्.

9. The penultimate short इ, उ, ऋ, लृ and the final vowels of जागृ andश्वि take their Guna in the fifth form; as सिध्-असेधीत्, शुच-अशोचीत्, कृत्-अकर्तीत्.

ATMANEPADA.

Fourth Variety.

10. In the Âtmanepada fourth variety, (*a.*) the ending इ or उ, short or long, takes Guna while (*b.*) the endingऋ and the penultimate vowel remain unchanged; as नी-अनेष्ट, सु-असोष्ट, भृ-अभृषत 3rd pers. plur., भिद्-अभित्त. Ending ॠ (long) is treated as in 9, p. 2; as स्तॄ-अस्तीर्ष्ट, वॄ-अवूर्ष्ट.

11. After a short vowel the स् of स्त and is dropped; as हृ-अहृत.

12. In the Âtmanepada, दा, धा, and such roots as assume those forms in the non-conjugational tenses, and स्था substitute इ for the final आ, and this इ does not take Guna; as अदित, अदिषाताम्.

Fifth Variety.

13. The ending vowel or the penultimate short takes its Guna sustitute in the fifth variety; as लू-अलविष्ट, मुद्-अमोदिष्ट.

---

14. In the Âtmanepada fourth Aorist, हन् drops its nasal necessarily; and गम्, and यम् when it means 'to marry', optionaly. वध् is used instead of हन् in the Parasmipada and optionally in the Âtmanepada वध् does not take Vṛiddhi.

हन्. with आ Âtm.-आ+अ+हन्+स्त—ह+त by 11 above–अहत-आहत; *dual* आहसाताम्–plur. आहसत. Another form is आवधिष्ट, &c. यम् with उप Âtm.-उपायत, उपायसाताम्, &c. or उपायंस्त उपायंसाताम्, &c. गम् with सम् Âtm.–समगत or समगंस्त, &c.

15. The third person singular of the Aorist of पद् is अपादि, *i. e.*, it is made up by using the termination इ instead of स्त, दीप्, जन्, बुध् *4th conj.* पूर्, ताय्, and प्याय् substitute this इ for स्त (or इष्ट) optionally.

16. *a.* As in the case of other non-conjugational tenses the passive of the Aorist is made up simply by appending

Âtmanepada terminations to the prepared base. (See also Art. 3, p. 103). *b.* The first, second, third and sixth Aorists are active, wherefore the roots belonging to them take the Âtm. fourth, fifth or seventh in the passive. *c.* In the passive of the Aorist all roots take for the third person singular instead of (or) or

17. Before this the ending vowel and the penul. timate take Vṛiddhi and any other penultimate short takes Guṇa. The of and the *Seṭ* roots ending in (except with and) is not changed.

18. Final takes the augment before the

19. The of is changed to when the vowel undergoes Vṛiddhi (See 7, p. 150).

भृ *Parasm.*

	Sing.	*Dual*	*Plur.*
1st pers.	अभार्षम्	अभार्ष्व	अभार्ष्म
2nd "	अभार्षीः	अभार्ष्टम्	अभार्ष्ट
3rd "	अभार्षीत्	अभार्ष्टाम्	अभार्षुः

अ+भृ+सीत्—भार् by 5, p. 168—अभार्षीत् (note ‡ p. 97, F. B.)

Âtm.

1st pers.	अभृषि	अभृष्वहि	अभृष्महि
2nd "	अभृथाः	अभृषाथाम्	अभृढ्वम्
3rd "	अभृत	अभृषाताम्	अभृषत

अ+भृ+स्त—the vowel remaining unchanged by 10 (*b*), p. 169—the स् is dropped by 11, p. 169—अभृत.

लू *Parasm.*

	Sing.	*Dual*	*Plur.*
1st pers.	अलाविषम्	अलाविष्व	अलाविष्म
2nd "	अलावीः	अलाविष्टम्	अलाविष्ट
3rd "	अलावीत्	अलाविष्टाम्	अलाविषुः

अ+लू+ईत्—लौ+ईत् by 6' (*a.*), p. 168—अलावीत्.

Âtm.

	Sing.	*Dual*	*Plur.*
1st pers.	अलविषि	अलविष्वहि	अलविष्महि
2nd "	अलविष्टाः	अलविषाथाम्	अलविध्वम्ढ्वम्
3rd "	अलविष्ट	अलविषाताम्	अलविषत

अ+लू+इष्ट-लू-लो by 13, p. 169—अलविष्ट.

1. प्रछ् being Anit belongs to the 4th variety; अ+प्रछ्+सीत् प्राछ् by 5, 168—प्राष् by IX. p. 52—प्राक् by IV., p. 49—प्राक्+षीत् by note‡ p. 97, F. B.—अप्राक्षीत्. *Dud,* अ+प्रछ्+स्ताम्-प्राछ् + ताम् by I.

and 5, p. 168–प्राष्+ताम्-प्राष्टाम् by note* p. 21, F. B.—अप्राष्टाम्; *plur.* अप्राक्षुः. *2nd pers.* अप्राक्षीः—अप्राष्टम्—अप्राष्ट. *1st pers.* अप्राक्षम्-अप्राक्ष्व-अप्राक्ष्म.

2. तृप्-one from is अतृपत् by 4 *b.*, p 157. The root takes इ optionally by 6, p. 79; hence it takes both the 4th and 5th varieties. अ + तृप् + सीत्-त्रप् optionally by 19, p. 82–त्राप् by 5, p. 168—अत्राप्सीत्; तृप्-तार्प् 5, p. 168—अतार्प्सीत्; *duals*, अत्राप्ताम् and अतार्प्ताम्, स् being dropped by I., p. 168. The fifth is, अतर्पीत्, Guna by 9, p. 169; *dual*, अतर्पिष्टाम्, &c. So this root has four forms. दृप् is similar.

3. त्यज्—अ + दह + सीत्-त्याज् by 5, p. 168—त्याक् bynote‡ p. 97, F. B.- त्याक् + षीत् note ‡ . p. 97, F. B—अत्याक्षीत्; *dual*, अत्याक्ताम्, स् being dropped by I., p. 168.

4. दह्—अ + दह + सीत्-दाह by 5, p. 168—दाघ् by V., p. 50—धाघ् by VII., p. 51—धाक् by note‡ p. 5, F. B.—अधाक्षीत्; *dual*, अ + दह् + स्ताम्-अ + दाह् + स्ताम्. First of all स् is dropped; then we have अ + दाह् + ताम्-दाघ् + ताम् by V., p. 50—दाघ् + धाम् by II., p. 49—अदाग्धाम् by VI., pp. 50-51; *plur.* अधाक्षुः .

5. वस्-अ + वस् + सीत्-वास्-वात् by I., p. 97*– अवात्सीत्. *Dual*, अ + वास् + स्ताम्. Here the स् of वस् must be changed to त् before dropping the स् of स्ताम् by I., p. 168. So अ + वात + स्ताम्-अवात्ताम्.

6. वह्-अ + वह + सीत्-वाह्-वाढ् by I. p. 49-वाक् by IV., p. 49-वाक् + षीत्-अवाक्षीत्, *dual*. अ + वह् + स्ताम्-वाह् + ताम्-वाढ् + ताम्-वाढ् + धाम् by II. p. 49–वाढ् + ढाम्-वाढाम् by III., p. 49-अवोढाम् by II., p. 88. Similar changes take place before तम्, त, and *Âtm.* त, थास् and ध्वम्.

7. रुध् is both *Parasm.* and *Âtm.* By 4 *b.*, p. 157 one form of its Aorist is अरुधत्. As to the other, we have first अ + रुध् + सीत्-रौध्- by 5, p. 168-रौत् by note† p 5, F. B—अरौत्सीत्; *dual*, रौध् + स्ताम्-रौध् + ताम्, स् being dropped-रौध् + धाम् by II., p. 49-रौद्धाम् by VI. pp. 50-51—अरौद्धाम्; *plur.* अरौत्सुः. *Âtm.* अरुध् + स्त-रुध् + त by dropping स, then रुद्ध as above-अरुद्ध, *dual* अरुत्साताम्, *plur.* अरुत्सत.

8. लभ् *Âtm.*—अलभ् + स्त-लभ् + त-लभ् + ध-लब्ध-अलब्ध; *dual* अ + लभ् + साताम्-अलप्साताम् by note† p. 5., F. B.

9. स्खल-अस्खालीत् by 6 (*b.*), p. 168; नद्-अनदीत् or अनादीत् by 7, p. 168; नन्द-अनन्दीत्.

10. सृज् being Aniṭ belongs to the 4th variety. अ + सृज् + सीत्-स्रज् by 18, p. 82—स्राज् by 5, p. 168-स्राष् by IX., p. 52-स्राक् by IV., p. 49-स्राक् + षीत् by note‡ p. 97, F. B.—अस्राक्षीत्

---

*The initial स् of the termination is, of course, a sign of the Aor., and therefore non-personal.

11. वृ *Parasm.* and Âtm. being Seṭ belongs to the 5th variety; Parasm. अवारीत्. In the Âtm. it takes both the 4th and 5th varieties by 2 (c.), p. 167. अ + वृ + स्त—अ + वृ + त by 11, p. 169—अवरिष्ट;—वर् + ईष्ट optionally by 3, p. 96–अवरीष्ट.

12. इ with अधि being Anit belongs to the 4th variety; अधि + आ + इ + स्त—अधि + आ + ए + स्त-अधि + ऐ + स्त-अध्यैष्ट; or अधि + अ + गा + स्त-गी + स्त सुज् by 2, p. 98—अध्यगीष्ट.

दुष्टाञ् शब्दान्मा प्रयुक्ष्महि म्लेच्छाश्च मा भूमेत्यध्येयं व्याकरणम्।

ओदानं शाकांश्च सूदा अपाक्षुरतोऽधुना सर्वान्ब्राह्मणान्भोजय।

कनिष्ठं पुत्रमहमब्रवं पुत्रक कुसुमपुरं गत्वा तत्रैकस्मिन्गृहे मया निक्षिप्तं धनमास्ते तद्गृहाण। सोऽगच्छत्। निवृत्य च मामब्रवीत्तात भ्रातरो मे तत्रागत्यास्मभ्यमेतद्धनं पितादादिति वदन्तः सर्वमेव तदादिषत।

यत्त्वं सत्यमवादीस्तत्तुभ्यमहमेतद्गवां शतं ददामि।

त्वमात्मनः पूर्वभार्यामत्याक्षीरन्यां च पर्यणैषीरिति यदश्रौषं तत्किं सत्यम्।

मुग्धाकृतिरतीव प्रियश्चावयोः शिशुरमृतेति शोकविकलोऽहं भार्या च मे। परं तु किं वृथाशोकेन सत्यमेव तद्यत्कविराह।

कस्यैकान्तं सुखमुपगतो दुःखमेकान्ततो वा।

नीचैर्गच्छत्युपरि च दशा चक्रनेमिक्रमेण॥

ऋषयो वै सरस्वत्यां सत्रमासत। ते कवषमैलूषं सोमादनयन्दास्याः पुत्रः कितवोऽब्राह्मणः कथं नो मध्येऽदीक्षिष्टेति।

साचिव्ये मामेवान्यान्सर्वाननादृत्य राजाऽयौक्षीदतोऽभियुक्तेन मनसा मया कार्यमनुष्ठेयम्॥

अस्मिन्क्षेत्रे विपुलं धान्यमवाप्सम्।

अङ्गीकृतं महत्कार्यं पारयितुमक्षमा वयमुदस्राक्ष्म।

अखिला मनोरथा मेऽफलिषुरतोऽहं सुखमस्वाप्सं न किंचिदवेदिषम्।

किं नाद्याप्यग्निरथमद्राष्ट प्रत्यहं त्रिरनेन मार्गेण स नीयते।

मुक्तकेशीं मां दृष्ट्वा दुर्योधनस्य भार्या भानुमत्यहसीत्तन्मे दहति देहमित्यब्रवीद्भीमं द्रौपदी।

असमर्थोऽयमर्जुनो धार्तराष्ट्रैः सह योद्धुमतः सङ्ग्रामान्न्यवर्तिष्टेति जना ब्रूयुः॥

भार्या मे पुत्रमसविष्ट। अतो जातकर्मादिसंस्काराणां संभारान्करोमि।

अधुनैव सोऽत्रागत्यायं पुरुषः सुविनीतोऽयं दुर्विनीत इति बहु प्रालपीत्। मैवं पुनः प्रलपीदित्येकदा तं भृशं ताडय।

अस्माभिराज्ञसः पौराणिकः पुराणकथाः कथयितुमारब्ध तदेहि श्रोतुम्।

परिचारकं मे दन्दशूकोऽदाङ्क्षीत्तत्त्वरस्व भिषजं गत्वौषधमानय।

इयन्तं कालमुद्यमं कुर्वन्नपि सुखं नालप्सि तस्मान्नियतिर्बलीयसी।

महता प्रयत्नेन तेन संचितं धनमहृथास्तस्मात्पापोऽसि गर्हणीयचरितोऽसि।

तेऽभ्यगुर्भवनं तस्य सुप्तं चैक्षिषताथ तम्॥

अवोचत्कुम्भकर्णस्तं वयं मन्त्रेऽभ्यधाम यत्।
न त्वं सर्वं तदश्रौषीः फलं तस्येदमागमत्॥

प्राज्ञवाक्यान्यवामंस्था मूर्खवाक्येष्ववास्थिथाः।
अध्यगीष्ठाश्च शास्त्राणि प्रत्यपत्था हितं न च॥

मूर्खास्तवामवञ्चन्त ये विग्रहमचीकरन्।
अभाणीन्माल्यवान्युक्तमक्षंस्थास्त्वं न तन्मदात्॥

ततोऽक्रन्दीद्दशग्रीवस्तमाशिश्वसदिन्द्रजित्।
निरयासीच्च संक्रुद्धः प्राचिंचच्च स्वयंभुवम्॥

सोऽलब्ध ब्रह्मणः शस्त्रं स्यन्दनं च जयावहम्॥

प्रोदपाति नभस्तेन स च प्रापि महागिरिः।
यस्मिन्नज्वालिषू रात्रौ महौषध्यः सहस्रशः॥

एतं ह वा ऐन्द्रं महाभिषेकं वासिष्ठः सात्यहव्योऽत्यरातये जानंतपये प्रोवाच। तस्माद्धत्यरातिर्जानंतपिरराजा* सन्विद्यया समन्तं सर्वतः पृथिवीं जयन्परीयाय। स होवाच वासिष्ठः सात्यहव्योऽजैषीर्वै समन्तं सर्वतः पृथिवीं महन्मा‡ गमयेति स होवाचात्यरातिर्जानंतपिर्यदा ब्राह्मणोत्तरकुरूञ्जयेयमथ त्वमु हैव पृथिव्यै‡ राजा स्याः सेनापतिरेव तेऽहं स्यामिति। स होवाच वासिष्ठः सात्यहव्यो देवक्षेत्रं वै तन्न वै तन्मर्त्यो जेतुमर्हत्यद्रुक्षो§ वै म आऽत इदं दद इति। ततो हात्यरातिं जानंतपिमात्तवीर्यं निःशुक्रममित्रतपनः शुष्मिणः शैब्यो राजा जघान।

The enemise have burned [दह्] twenty villages, and are now marching against the capital.

The birds confined in the cage have all flown [डी Âtm. with उद्] away.

The firends, whom I expected so long, are come [गम् or इ, with आ], and have just alighted [तॄ with अव] from their carriages.

We have lopped off [लू or छिद्] the branches of the trees in the garden.

They have dug [खन्] many canals communicating with the river Sindhu, for agricultural purposes.

When he said [वच्] he could be Sanskrit Paṇḍita in ten days, I smiled [स्मि].

Yajñadatta has recently performed [कृ, धा with वि, or स्था with अनु] his son's Upanayana ceremony. He gave [दा] much Dakshiṇa on that occasion.

It was but just now that they remember [स्मृ] they had sent a man to call Govinda for aid.

---

*The canges of the final, which some words undergo at the end of compounds, do not take place in the case of Tatpurusha compounds with अ or अन्.

† Acc. *sing.* of अस्मद्.

‡ Dative used in the sense of the Genitive

§ द्रुह् here takes the seventh form, as it should by the general rules, and its द् is not changed to घ्.

Do not be afraid [भी with मा], it is not a cobra that you see before you, but a rope.

The-English have killed [वध्] the ring-leaders and reconquered [जि with पुनर्] the country.

From his constantly sitting at home and not doing anything, have resulted [जन्, or पद् with निस्] poverty, and many painful diseases.

Have you made [कृ] the ornaments that I told you to make? Show them to me if you have.

The king's surveyors have not yet measured [मा] the whole land.

We have torn [दॄ] all those papers, now that they are of no use.

He has pounded [क्षुद्] the mdicine, emptied [रिच्] the vessel, put [क्षिप् with नि] that powder into it, poured* water and placed it on fire.

Govinda's wishes are gratified [तृप्] and he is now happy.

He has abandoned [त्यज् with परि] all worldly affairs and has now become a recluse [व्रज् with परि].

We have not yet accepted [ग्रह् with परि] the money they gave us yesterday.

They have served [सेव्] their king faithfully.

The traders have bought [क्री with परि] all the cotton in the market, and sent [हि with प्र] it off of England.

The monkeys have broken [भञ्ज्] the roof of the house.

The brothers have divided [भज् with वि] the ancestral property.

I have endured [सह्] all the taunts of the people calmly and borne [वह्] the responsibility of goerning uninterruptedly.

The two kings have equipped [नह् with सम्] their armies for a battle.

---

* पॄ with जलेन or सिच् with नि. सिच् becomes षिच् after नि.

VOCABULARY XXIV.

अक्षम *m. n. f.* unable.

अग्निरथ *m.* fire-carriage, railway carriage [triya-

अत्यराति *m.* name of a Ksha-

अनुष्ठेय *pot. part.* of स्था *with* अनु what is to be exeuted.

अभियुक्त *past part. of* युज् *with* अभि, assiduous.

अमित्र *m.* an enemy. [manded.

आज्ञप्त *past part pass.* com-

आत्त *m. n. f.* from अ and दत्त *past part. pas.* of दा to give, taken away.

आस् *with* सत्र to hold a sacrificial session, to perform a succession of sacrifices.

उत्तरकुरवः *m. plur.* name of a country beyond the Himalayas (probably the original seat of the Aryas).

उपरि *adv.* above.

एकान्त *m. n. f.* invariably.

एकान्ततः *adv.* invariably.

ऐलूष *m.* son of Ilûshâ.

औषध *n.* a medicine.

कवष *m.* name of a person.

कितव *m.* a rogue, a dishonest person, a swindler.

कुसुमपुर *n.* name of a town.

जयावह *m. n. f.* that which brings victory.

जातकर्मन् *n.* birth-ceremony.

जानंतपि *m.* son of Janaṁtapa.

तपन *m.* an oppressor.

तृप् *4th conj. Parasm.* to be gratified or satisfied.

दंश् *1st conj. Parasm.* to bite.

दन्दशूक *m.* a snake.

दशा *f.* state, condition.

दह् *f. conj. Parasm.* to burn.

दीक्ष् *1st conj. Âtm.* to consecrate and thus fit oneself for performing a sacrifice.

दुर्विनीत *m. n. f.* rude.

दृ *6th conj. Âtm with* आ, to pay respect to, to regard.

देवक्षेत्र *n.* the land of the gods.

नियति *f.* destiny,

निःशुक्र *m. n f.* powerless.

नीचैः *adv.* down, below.

नेमि *f.* teh cricumference of a wheel. [into.

पत् *with* प्र and उद्, to fly, to fly.

पद् *with* प्रति, to know or understand, to accept, to do, to practise.

पौराणिक *m.* one who reads and explains the Purâṇas.

फल् *1st conj. Parasm.* and *Âtm.* with वि, to divide.

भज् *1st conj. Parasm.* and *Âtm. with* वि, to divide.

भानुमती *f*. wife of Duryodhana, the eldest son of Dhṛitarâshṭra.

मन् *with* अव, to disregard.

महत् *n.* lustre, greatness.

महत्त्व *n.* greatness, power.

माल्यवत् *m.* name of a giant, the maternal grandfather of Râvaṇa.

मुक्तकेशी *f.* having the hair disordered or dishevelled.

मुग्धाकृति *m. n. f.* a lovely form or shape.

म्लेच्छ *m.* a barbarian.
लप् *1st conj. Parasm. with* प्र, to speak, to prattle.
वञ्च् *10th conj. Âtm.* to deceive.
वासिष्ठ *m.* a descendant of Vasishtha.
शाक *m.* vegebale.
शुष्मिण *m. n. f.* powerful.
शैब्य *m.* name of a king.
शोकविकल *m. n. f.* overcome with sorrow.
सत्र *n.* a sacrificial session.
सरस्वती *f.* name of a river.
साचिव्य *n.* counsellorship.
सात्यहव्य *m.* name of a priest.
सुविनीत *m. n. f.* modest.

Agricultural purposes, for, कृषिहेतोः, कृषिकर्मणे.
Ancestral पितृपैतामह *m. n. f.*
Cage पञ्जर *m.*
Canal कुल्या *f.*
Capital राजधानी *f.*
Cobra फणिन् *m.* नाग *m.*
Communicating संगत *Past part.* or संगच्छमान *pres, part.*
Confined नियन्त्रित *past part. pass* निबद्ध *past part. pass.*
Cotton तूल *m.* पिचु *m.*
Disease व्याधि *m.*
Faithfully भक्त्या, निष्ठया.
Market पण्यवीथिका *f.* आपण *m.*
Medicine औषध *n.* ओषधि *f.* a medicinal herb. genger an herb.
Painful व्यथाकर *m. n. f.* पीडाकर *m. n. f.*
Paper पत्रक *n.*
Poverty दारिद्र्य *n.* दुर्गति *f.*
Powder क्षोद *m.* चूर्ण *n*
Property रिक्थ *n.* वित्त *n.*
Responsibility of governing राज्यधुरा *f.*
Ringleader प्रधानराजद्रोहिन् *m.*
Roof छदिस् *n.* पटल *n.*
Surveyor भूमापक *m.*
Taunt उपालम्भ *m.*
Trader वणिज् *m.*
Uninterruptedly अविरतम् *adv.*
Yajñadatta यज्ञदत्त *m.* a proper name.

Part II.

BENEDICTIVE MOOD.

1. The Parasmaipada terminations of this mood are made up by adding यास् to those of the Imperfect. The 3rd pers. plur. is यासु and the स् of यास् is dropped before the त् and स् of the 3rd and 2nd pers. sing.

2. To the terminations of the Âtmanepada Potential and to the त् and थ् occurring in them prefix स्. These will be the terminations of the Âtmanepada pendictive. षीध्वम् becomes षीढ्वम in the circumstances mentioned in 4 *d.*, p. 168.

3. The Parasmaipada terminations are weak, and the Âtmanepada strong.

Rules regarding the Parasmaipada forms.

4. Arts 2 *a, b, c, e, f* and *g,* in Lesson XV. Pt. II hold good here also,

The roots anumerated in Art, *2 d.* on page 102 change their final vowel to ए.

6. Other roots ending in आ (whether originally or in virtue of Art. 14, p. 82.) preceded by a conjunct consonant change their आ to ए optionally; as ग्लेयात्-ग्लायात्, ग्लेयास्ताम्-ग्लायास्ताम् &c. from ग्लै.

Âtmanepada forms.

7. The terminations take इ after Se roots and optionally after those that are optinoally *Seṭ.*

8. Roots ending in ॠ (long), and in ऋ (short) preceded by a conjunct consonant, and वृ, admit of इ optionally; as वरिषिष्ट, वृषीष्ट (see below) from वृ, स्तरिषीष्ट, स्तृषीष्ट, from स्तृ.

9. The final ॠ or ऋ and the penultimate vowel do not undergo their Guna substitute when the terminations do not take इ; as ह्वषीष्ट from ह्व, स्तरिषीष्ट, स्तीर्षीष्ट, from स्तॄ, मुक्षीष्ट from मुच्.

10. In addition to the general rule for forming the passive of non-conjugational tenses and moods by appending the Âtmanepada terminations to the prepared base, Art. 3. p. 103, also holds good in the case of this mood.

कृ

Parasm.

	Sing.	*Dual*	*Plur.*
1st pers.	क्रियासम्	क्रियास्व	क्रियास्म
2nd "	क्रियाः	क्रियास्तम्	क्रियास्त
3rd "	क्रियात्	क्रियास्ताम्	क्रियासुः

Âtm.

1st pers.	कृषीय	कृषीवहि	कृषीमहि
2nd "	कृषीष्ठाः	कृषीयास्थाम्	कृषीढ्वम्
3rd "	कृषीष्ट	कृषीयास्ताम्	कृषीरन्

a. Explain the following forms, referring to the several rules applicable in each case:–

दिश्यात्, दिक्षीष्ट, रुध्यात्, रुत्सीष्ट, उध्यात्, स्मर्यात्, स्तर्यात्, नीयात्, नेषीष्ट, देयात्, दासीष्ट, घाक्षीष्ट, गाहिषीष्ट, घ्रेयात्, घ्रायात्, तीर्यात्, पूर्यात्, उह्यात्, वक्षीष्ट, मोदिषीष्ट, धुक्षीष्ट, दुह्यात्.

b. Give the Benedictive forms of the following roots:–

ह, ह्व, वप्, यज्, सह्, नह्, रुह्, लिह्, बन्ध्, ग्लै, हा, भिद्, भृ वृत्, रुच्, दु, लू, सो, स्तु, रु, शाम्.

LESSON XXV.
DESIDERATIVES.

1. a. The termination स् is appended to the root; and then the root reduplicated according to the general rules given in Lesson XI, and Art. 3, pp. 158-9. In the conjugational tenses is added to स्.

b. The अ in the reduplicative syallable is changed to इ.

2, To this स् the augment इ is to be prefixed or not according as te root is *Set* or *Ant*; subject to the following exceptions:- -

a. ग्रह्, गुह्, and roots ending in उ or ऊ do not amit of इ; as जिघृक्षति, बुभूषति.

b. ऋ *Âtm.*, धृ *Âtm.*, कॄ, गॄ, all of the 6th conj. स्मि, पू Âtm., अञ्ज्, प्रच्छ्, ऋ, and अश् admit of इ; as पिपृच्छिषति, दिधरिषते, &c.

c. Roots ending in (long) ॠ and इव्, and the roots धृ, दम्भ्, श्रि, यु, भृ, and ज्ञप् take इ optionally; as *दुद्यूषति, or दिदेविषति from दिव्, शिश्रीषति or शिश्रयिषति from श्रि, &c.

3. The general rule† as to Guṇa should be applied, subject to the following exceptions:—

a. Roots ending in इ, उ, and ऋ (all of them short or long), or having these vowels for their penultimates do not admit of Guṇa, when the स् to be appended to them does not take the augment इ; as बुभूषति, निनीषति.

b. रुद्, विद्, and मुष् do not take Guṇa. Other roots having उ or इ short for their penultimate, and beginning with any consonant and ending with any except य् and व् admit of Guṇa optionally, when the स् takes the augment इ; as रुरुदिषति, मुमुदिषते or मुमोदिषते, &c.

4. Roots ending in a vowel lengthen it when the स् is unaugmented; as जिगीषति from जि 'to conquer.' हन् also lengthens its अ.

5. *a.* ग्रह्, स्वप्, and प्रच्छ् change the र् and व् to ऋ and उ; as सुषुप्सति; (see 6, p. 87).

b. The य् of द्युत् is changed to in the reduplicative syllable.

---

*See note, p. 185.

† See Art. 6, p. 12.

c. The vowel of the following roots is changed to इ and the roots are not reduplicated:–

मि, मी, मा, दा, धा, and other roots assuming the forms of दा and धा, रभ्, लभ्, शक्, पत्, पद् Of these, those ending in a vowel add a त्.

(*d*) आप् has ईप्सति, and ज्ञप्, ज्ञीप्सति and जिज्ञपयिषति.

e. दम्भ् has three forms, धिप्सति, धीप्सति, दिदम्भिषति. तन्* has तितांसति, तितंसति, तितनिषति; and पत्, पित्सति, पिपतिषति.

f. पू Âtm. has पिपविषते and यु, when it takes इ, यियविषति.

g. ऋ has अरिरिषति and इ with प्रति, when it means 'to be connvinced,' प्रतीषिषति, इ in the sense of 'to go' substituting गम्.

h. The ज् of जि is changed to ग् after the reduplicative syllable, the ह of हि and हन् to घ्, and the च् of चि optionally to क्.

6, Desideratives may to formed from the causal base, or roots of the tenth conjugation, according to the general rules.

7. Art, 4, p 159, is applicable to the Desideratives of the Causal and of roots fo the 10th conjugation.

8. *a.* A root in its desiderative form takes the same terminations (Parasmaipada, Âtmanepada, or both) that it does in the primitive.

b. The desideratives of ज्ञा, श्रु, स्मृ and दृश् are Âtmanepadi.

कृ + स्-कॄ † by 4, स् not taking इ by 2-कीर् by 9, p. 2, ऋ not taking Guna by 3 *a.*-चिकीर् by 1 *a.*- चिकीर्षति, स् being changed ot ष् and अ appended to it by 1; *Parasm.* by 8 *a.* मृ + स् = मूर्-मुमूर्-मुमूर्षति.

भू + स्-बुभू by 1 *a* -बुभूषति, स् not taking इ by 2 *a.* and ऊ not being changed to Guna by 3 *a.*

ग्रह् + स्-जग्रह् + स, स् not taking इ by 2 *a.*-जिगृह् by 5. *a.* = जिगृह्-जिघृह्-जिघृक्-जिघृक् + सति-जिघृक्षति.

द्युत् + स्-दिद्युत् by 5. *b.* ‡- दिद्योत् or दिद्युत् by 3 *b*, स् taking इ by 2- दिद्योतिषते or दिद्युतिषते: Âtm. by 8 a.

भिद् + स-बिभिद् by 1 a.; no Guṇa by 3 *a.*- बिभित्सति.

9. *a.* By affixing to the desiderative form, nouns sig-

---

* तन् and पत् are optionally Set in the case of theis स्.

† Before an unaugmented स् the prescribed vowel changes are made first and then the root is reduplicated.

‡ See note*, p. 88.

nifying the wisher' are formed. These nouns governan accusative, as चिकीर्षुः कटम्.

b. By affixing abstract nouns are fomed; as जिज्ञासा 'desire of knowledge', curiosity.

प्रारिप्सितस्य ग्रन्थस्याविघ्नपरिसमाप्तय इष्टदेवतां स्तौति।

स्वयंवरकाले सीतां लिप्सवो रावणादयो बहवो राजानो विदेहाञ्जग्मुः। किं तु रुद्रधनुर्नमयितुमशक्ताः सर्वे भग्नाशा बभूवुः।

अभितापसंपदमथोष्णरुचिर्निजतेजसामसहमान इव।

पयसि प्रपित्सुरपराम्बुनिधेरधिरोढुमस्तगिरिमभ्यपतत्॥

ब्रह्मतत्त्वं जिज्ञासमानः कश्चिदाचार्यमुपेत्याध्यापय भो ब्रह्मेत्युवाच।

तस्यां सभायामेव दुर्योधनं गदाघातेन जिघांसुर्भीमसेनो युधिष्ठिरेण निवारितः।

यियक्षमाणेनाहूतः पार्थेनाथ द्विषन्मुरम्।

अभिचैद्यं प्रतिष्ठासुरासीत्कार्यद्वयाकुलः॥

प्रासादतलमारुरुक्षुः सोपानपङ्क्तिषु पदं निधत्ते।

यूरोपीयवैभवं दिदृक्षमाणाः प्रतिसंवत्सरं कतिचिद्भरतखण्डीया अङ्ग्लभूम्यादिदेशानग्निनौकाभिर्गच्छन्ति।

ब्राह्मणो बुभूषू राजर्षिर्विश्वामित्र उग्रं तपश्चक्रे।

प्रभूतवर्षणादस्या नद्याः कूलं पिपातिषति। तदस्मिन्मा पदं निधेहि।

सूर्यवंशसंभवानां राज्ञां यशो जिगासुः कालिदास आह।

क्व सूर्यप्रभवो वंशः क्व चाल्पविषया मतिः।

तितीर्षुर्दुस्तरं मोहादुडुपेनास्मि सागरम्॥

भूरि धनमादित्सुना बलेनानुगम्यमानः शरदारम्भे दिगन्ताञ्जिगीषू रघुरयोध्यायाः प्रतस्थे।

बटुमुपनिनीषुराचार्यः स्वाधिकारसिद्धये कृच्छ्रत्रयं कुर्यात्।

राजगृहं प्रविविक्षुर्ऋषिकुमारको हठान्निसारितो दुर्विनीतैर्द्वारपालैः।

आत्मनः कौशलं दिदर्शयिषन्त्यङ्गना महान्तं कालमनृत्यत्।

अर्थयन्ते द्विजन्मानो तस्मादर्थं यियक्षवः।

अर्थापयत्यसौ सम्यग् दुर्बुद्धं वैदिकं वचः॥

The dog is about to die* [मृ]; do not disturb him.

Wishing to bend [caus. of नम्] the branch of the tree he raised his hand.

A very violent storm arose, the sun was invisible, and it appeared as if the wind was *going to tear up* [मूल. with उद्] all trees by the roots, and *to destroy* [भञ्ज्] all houses.

Viś vâmitra practised austerities for a thousand years, till his whole frame, instinct with the subtle principle of Brahman, became refulgent, and he appeared to be *about to burn* [दह्] the whole universe by his extraordinary splendour.

Having sen his own kinsmen *prepared to fight* [युध्] with him, his face became pale.

This child is *inclined to sleep* [स्वप्]; put him into the cradle, and rock him to sleep.

There is a man waiting at the door who wants to speak [वच्] to you on matters of great importance.

He who *wishes to be free* [मुच्] from the trammels of the world (life) should go to a philosopher, become acquainted with the Brahman, and meditate on it.

Those who *wish to introduce* [caus. of वृत् with प्र] the system of widow-marriages should proceed at once to the task; the time for discussion is gone.

In that battle there was a soldier, who, being wounded, was afficted with a raging *thirst* (*desire to drink* [पा]).

Dhṛshṭaketu was *about to strike* [हृ with प्र] a Rishi with his sword, mistaking him for his enemy when I caught hold of his hand.

I went to Kâśî *intending to bathe* [स्ना] in the holy waiars of the Ganges, and to live [वस् with नि] there for two years to study the Sâṁkhya philosophy.

The two girls went into the garden intending to gather [चि with अव] flowers.

The self-existent God, *desirous to create* [सृज्] the world, appeared on the surface of the waters, which covered the whole space.

---

* Use desiderative forms for the expressions printed Italics.

The parrot that was confined in the cage this morning is *about to fly away* [डी, or पत् with उद्].

VOCABULARY XXV.

अधिकार *m.* fitness to perform any ceremony.

अपराम्बुनिधि *m.* (other, *i. e.*, western, and ocean) the western ocean.

अभिचैद्यम् *adv.* (from चैद्य *m.* the king of Chedi, who was Kṛishṇa's enemy) towards chaidya.

अभिताप *m.* violent heat.

अर्थ् *10th conj. Âtm.* to beg.

अर्थापय *denom. Parasm.* and Âtm to explain.

अल्पविषया *f.* not comprehensive, whose range is small.

अविघ्न *m. n. f.* without obstacles.

अस्तगिरि *m.* the western mountain, on which the sun, the moon, and the stars are suposed to set.

आचार्य *m.* a religious teacher who invests the student with the sacred thread, and instructs him in the Vedas.

आशा *f.* hope.

इष्टदेवता *f.* tutelar (desired) deity.

उग्र *m. n. f.* raging, severe.

उडुप *m. n.* a raft, a canoe.

उष्णरुचि *m.* the sun.

कतिचित् *pron.* several.

कार्यद्वयाकुल *m. n. f.* distracted by having two things to do at one time.

कूल *n.* a bank.

कृच्छ्रत्रय *n.* (कृच्छ्र *n.* a penance, and त्रय three) three penances.

ग्रह् *with* सम्, to store.

दिगन्त *m.* the end to the quarters, countries in all directions.

दुर्बोध *m. n. f.* difficult to be understood, obsure.

द्वारपाल *m.* a porter; a doorkeepre.

नी *with* उप, to perform the ceremony of the investiture with the sacred thread.

पङ्क्ति *f.* a line, a row.

पत् *with* अभि, to jump towards.

परिसमाप्ति *f.* end, accomplishment.

प्रचण्ड *m. n. f.* voilent.

बल *n.* an army.

भग्न *past part. pass.* of भञ्ज् to destroy, blown up, destroyed.

भूरि *m. n. f.* much.

मुर *m.* name of an enemy of Vishnu or Kṛishṇa.

यूरोपीय *m. n. f.* pertaining to the continent of Europe

रुह् *with* अधि, to ascend.

वर्षण *n.* rain-fall, raining.

वृ *10th conj.* with नि, to oppose, to dissuade from.

वैदिक *m. n. f.* belonging ot a Veda.

संभव *m.* birth.

सांख्य *n.* name of a system of philosophy.

सृ (caus.) with निर्, to drive away, to expel.

सिद्धि *f.* accomplishment.

Afflicted आर्त *past part.* अर्दित *past part. pass.*
Cage पञ्जर *m.*
Cardle प्रेङ्खा *f.*
Discussion वादविवाद *m.*
Disturb क्षुद्
Extraordinary अद्भुत *m. n. f.*
Importance गुरुत्व *n.* महत्त्व n.; a matter of importance गुरुकार्य *n.*
Instinct उत्तेजित *past part. pass.* उद्दीपित *past part. pass.*
Invisible अदृश्य *m. n. f.*

सूर्यवंश *m.* the family fo the sun, the solar race.

सोपान *n.* stairs, steps.

हठात् *adv.* by violence.

Kinsman ज्ञातिबन्धु *m.*
Pale पाण्डु *m. n. f.* विवर्ण *m. n. f.*
Philosopher तत्त्वविद् *m.*
Raging प्रबल *m. n. f.* बलीयस् *m. n. f.*
Raise गम् *caus. with* उद्.
Refulgent देदीप्यमान *pres. part.* विभ्राजमान *pres. part.*
Rock दोलय *den.* or आन्दोलय *den.*
Subtle principle तन्मात्र *n.*
System विधि *m.* पद्धति *f.*
Trammel बन्धन *n.* निगड *m. n.*
Violent प्रचण्ड *m. n. f.*

LESSON XXVI.

VERBAL DERIVATIVES.

1. After Set roots the augment इ is to be prefixed to the तुम् of the infinitive of purpose, and not after *Anit* ones, and optionally after those that are both *Set* and *Anit*.

2. a. The त of the past participle is to be considered as a weak* termination.

Therefore the Guna change (6., p. 12) does not take place; and such rules as 4, p. 87, and 9, p. 2, are applicable; कृ-कृत वद्-उदित.

b. The general rule about the augment इ (1, above) should be attended to. There are, however, many exceptions.

c. The following roots do not admit इ :—

(1) Those ending in उ, ऊ and ऋ; श्रु-श्रुत, भू-भूत, कॄ-कीर्ण.

* By this expression is meant such a termination as does not occasion a Guna or Vriddhi change in the preceding.

(2) Such as take इ optionally before any termination whatever.

इष्-इष्ट (2, p. 96), दम्भ्-दब्ध (2*c.*, p. 179), सिव्-स्यूत* (2*c.*, p. 179), मुह्-मुग्ध or मूढ (6, p. 79 and I a., p. 88), क्रम्-क्रान्त (6 *a.*, p. 186 and *h.* below).

And there are several more.

d. After a final द् and र् the त becomes and the preceding द् is also changed to न्; as भिन्न from भिद्, शीर्ण from शॄ.

e. It is also changed to न after roots ending in आ and begining with a conjunct consonant containing य, व्, र्, or ल्, and also after several other roots.

Excepions—नुद्, विद् 7th conj., वै, घ्रा, and ह्री change the त to न optionally; and ध्यै, ख्या, and मद्, do not.

f. The vowels of शी, स्विद् 1st conj., मिद्, क्ष्विद्, and धृष् undergo Guna substitutes when they admit of इ.

g. The nasals of यम्, रम्, नम्, हन्, मन्, तन्, क्षण्, क्षिण्, ऋण्, and वन् are dropped; as गत from गम्, तत from तन्.

h. Other roots ending in अम् and अन् lengthen their vowel when they do not take इ; as शम्-शान्त, क्षम्-क्षान्त, दम्-दान्त (6 a., p. 186 and 6, p. 79).

i. The penultimate nasal is dropped when त does not take इ; as रञ्ज्-रक्त, अञ्ज्-अक्त.

3. a. The active past participle is formed by affixing वत् to the passive; as कृतवान् from कृ, लब्धवान् from लभ्.

b. The feminine of this is formed by adding ई; as कृतवती.

4. *a.* The active participle of the Perfect is formed by adding वस् Parasm. and आन Âtm. to that form of the root which it assumes before the weak terminations of the Perfect, such as that of the third person plural.

b. When this form is monosyllabic *i. e.*, contains one vowel only, or when the root ends in आ, इ should be prefixed to वस्; घस् also admits of इ; as ददिवस् from दा, पेतिवस् from पत्; but चकृवस्-चक्राण from कृ, जहृवस्-जह्राण from हृ. *c.* After गम्, हन् विद् 6th

---

* Final व् is changed to ऊ before a weak termination begining with any consonant except a nasal or a semi-vowel. This ऊ forms Vṛiddhi with the preceding अ or आ.

conj., विश्, and दृश्, वस् takes इ optionally; as जग्मिवस् or* जगन्वस् from गम्,

d. Before वस् and आन, some roots such as बन्ध्, अञ्ज् &c., drop the nasal and roots in long ॠ do not take Guna; as आजिवस्, तितीर्वस्. The first change, however, does not take place in the Perfect and the last does.

e. The form of the 3rd pers. plural of the Perfect should be taken as the base of the participle before the vowel terminations of the cases beginning with the accusative plural and before the ई of the feminine and of the dual nom, voc. and ac. of he neuter: as चिक्रीवस्-चिक्रियुषा Instr. Sing., चिक्रियुषी f.; जगन्वस् or जग्मिवस्-जग्मुषा Instr. Sing., जग्मुषी f.

The form, however, should be modified according to *d.* in the particular cases.

5. The participle of the Second Future is formed by adding अत् Parasm. and मान Âtm. ot a form of that tense divested of its personal termination. The preceding अ is to be dropped before अत्; as करिष्यत् 'being about to do, करिष्यमाण (active) 'being about to do', (passive) 'being about to be done;' द्रक्ष्यत् 'being about to see,' द्रक्ष्यमाण 'being about to be seen.'

The feminine of स्यत् is स्यन्ती or स्यती.

6. *a.* The त्वा of the indeclinable past participle takes इ in the case of *Seṭ* roots, and optionally in the case of ordinary *Seṭ* roots ending in अम् or अन्.

b. It is a weak termination; but in some cases when it takes इ the vowel takes its Guna substitute.

c. 2. g. and *h.* above are applicable when त्वा does not take इ. तन्-तत्वा or तनित्वा by 6 *a.* and this, मन्-मत्वा, शम्-शान्त्वा or शमित्वा, &c.

d. यम्, रम्, गम्, and नम् drop their final nasal optionally before the of the indeclinable past participle, and the remaining roots out of those given in 2 g. above drop it necessarily.

* See Note † p. 79

7. *a.* The terminations of the potential* passive participle are तव्य, अनीय, and य.

b. Before तव्य and अनीय, the ending vowel and the penultimate short take their Guṇa.

c. तव्य admits of इ in the case of *Seṭ* roots, &c.

d. (1) Before य the final and the penultimate इ and उ take their Guṇa, the final ओ becoming अव्; as कु-को-काव्य, नी-नेय्.

(2) The ending आ is changed to ए; as देय from दा.

(3) Roots ending in ऋ change it to its Vṛiddhi; as कार्य from कृ.

(4) इ, स्तु, वृ *Parasm and Âtm.*, ह, जुष्, and roots having a penultimate short ऋ do not change their vowel before य.

After a short vowel त् is prefixed to य; as स्तुत्य.

There are some exceptions to these rules, which are too various to be mentioned.

8. *a.* The affixes तृ and अक form nouns denoting the doer of the action expressed by the root. *b.* Before the former the ending vowel and the penultimate short take their Guna substitute; and *c.* before the latter, the ending vowel and the penultimate अ (except that of *Seṭ* roots ending in म्) take Vriddhi. and any other penultimate short, Guṇa; as नेतृ, नायक from नी; वक्तृ, वाचक from वच्; बोद्धृ, बोधक from बुध्; शमक from शम्; चम् with आ forms आचामक.

d. Roots ending in आ have य added on to them before this अक: as स्थायक, दायक from स्था and दा.

e. The न् of हन् is changed to त् before a derivative suffix which effects a Vṛiddhi change in the vowel; as घातक (see 19, p. 170).

f. The feminine of तृ is त्री and of अक, इका and some times अका.

9. *a.* अन, अ, and ति form abstract nouns from roots

b. ति is weak termination. Before it, the roots undergo nearly the same changes as before the termination of the past participle; as वच्-उक्ति, मुच्-मुक्ति

* This is passive when the verb is transitive, and imper sonal when the verb isintransitive.

c. Before अ some roots take Guṇa and some Vṛiddhi; and before अन the ending vowel and the penultimate short take Guṇa; as भू-भाव-भवन, जि-जिय, हन्-घात-हनन, बुध्-बोध-बोधन.

d. The final च् or ज् is changed to क् or ग् before this अ; as पच्-पाक, युज्-योग.

e. Nouns ending in ति are feminine and those ending in अ are masculine, while those ending in अन are neuter, as a general rule.

तस्मादेवं विदुषे ब्राह्मणायैवं चकुषे न क्षत्रियो द्रुह्यात्।

राजा यक्ष्यमाणो ब्राह्मणं पुरोदधीत।

छन्दांसि वै देवेभ्यो हव्यमूढ्वा* श्रान्तानि जघनार्धे यज्ञस्य तिष्ठन्ति यथाश्वो वाश्वतरो वोहिवांस्तिष्ठेदेवम्।

असुरैः सह योत्स्यमान इन्द्रो वरुणस्य साहाय्यं ययाचे।

वरुणसाहाय्यं लब्धवतस्तस्मात्सर्वेऽसुरा अबिभयुः।

व्यर्थं मे जन्म न मया कृतं कर्तव्यं न भुक्तं भोक्तव्यं न दृष्टं द्रष्टव्यं न श्रुतं श्रोतव्यम्।

निषेदुषीं राज्ञीं दृष्ट्वा दास्योऽपि सपत्नीवृत्तं कथयिष्यन्त्योऽधस्तस्थुः।

ब्राह्मणेभ्यो दत्तसर्वस्वो रघुः प्रत्यग्रागतायार्थिने धनं दित्सुः कुबेरात्तभिन्नश्च्कष्टुं चकमे। कुबेरस्तु तेनाभियास्यमानमात्मानं प्रेक्ष्य स्वयमेव तस्य कोशे धनवृष्टिं पातयामास। तत्सर्वं धनमात्मने ददिवांसं रघुं वक्ष्यमाणामाशिषं सोऽर्थ्युवाच।

आशास्यमन्यत्पुनरुक्तभूतं श्रेयांसि सर्वाण्यधिजग्मुषस्ते।

पुत्रं लभस्वात्मगुणानुरूपं भवन्तमीड्यं भवतः पितेव॥

ततो रघुः पुत्रं प्रापाजं नाम। तं कतिभिः संवत्सरैर्विवाहयोग्यदशं ज्ञात्वा ससैन्यमिन्दुमतीस्वयंवराय विदर्भान्प्रस्थापितवान्।

मार्गे नर्मदारोधस्येकरात्रमुषितवतस्तस्य सेनानिवेशो वन्यगजत्वमृषिशापात्समापेदानेन केनचिद्गन्धर्वेण तुमुलश्चक्रे।

---

* The metres of the verses repeated at a sacrifice are supposed to carry the offerings to the gods.

तमापतन्तं नृपतेरवध्यो वन्यः करीति श्रुतवान्कुमारः ।
निवर्तयिष्यन्विशिखेन कुम्भे जघान नात्यायतकृष्टचापः ॥

स विद्धमात्रः स्वीयं दिव्यं रूपं प्राप। ततः प्रजहुषेऽप्यात्मन उपचकुषेऽजाय संमोहनाख्यमस्त्रं ददौ।

एवं तयोरध्वनि दैवयोगादासेदुषोः सख्यमचिन्त्यहेतु ।
एको ययौ चैत्ररथप्रदेशान्सौराज्यरम्यानपरो विदर्भान् ॥

तं नगरोपकण्ठे तस्थिवांसं तदागमनहृष्टो विदर्भनाथः प्रत्युज्जगाम नगरं चानीय सर्वां सत्क्रियां चकार।

त्रैलोक्यदीपके देवे लोकान्तरमुपेयुषि ।
तमस्तान्तमभूद्विश्वं कः सुखी महदापदि ॥

Vâlmîki cursed the Nishâda, who had killed † [] one of a pair of Krauñcha birds.

The Rishi blessed the prince, *who had promised* [श्रु with प्रति] to give him a hundred cows.

Vidura gave the Pândavas some adivce when *they were about to go* [गम् or इ] to Vâranâvatî.

Before he burnt [] the town, the General removed all the women and children from it.

Before ordering [with] that the money should be restored to him, the judge counselled him to conduct himself properly.

Before Yajñadatta *was permitted* [with] to go away from Kâśî, Devadatta told him to perform penances for the sins he had committed.

When she was about to be sent [or with] to her husband's house, Kanva told Sakuntalâ to go round the fire, and counselled her not to be proud of her greatness.

The garments *which are to be given* [] to Vishnu are very good and costly,

---

* The termination मात्र, as applied to nouns, means "only, simply"; विद्धमात्र, "simply or only hit."

† The student should use verbal derivatives for the words and expressions printed in Italics.

That tree *is to be cut down* [छिद्].

What is *to be understood* [बुध्] from the curious message he has sent?

Jarâsaṁdha, *who had conquered* [जि] all kings and *imprisoned* them, was killed by Krishna and Bhîma.

His words is not *trustworthy* [श्वस् with वि] and his deeds are *censurable* [निन्द्],

That is not an *eatable* [भक्ष् or ह with and अव] nor *drinkable* [पा] thing; why should we seek it?

He, having shown some signs of wisdom, is no more *to be regarded* [मन्] as a fool.

VOCABULARY XXVI.

अज m. name of Raghu's son.

अत्यायत *adv.* or *m. n. f.* very far, very long.

अधस् *adv.* down.

अनुरूप *m. n. f.* in accordance with

अश्वतर *m.* amute.

आख्या *f.* name.

इन्दुमती *f.* the name of a lady.

उपकण्ठ *n.* s[ace mear a town or village, or its boundary.

कुम्भ *m.* the frontal globe on the upper part of the forehead of an elephant.

कृ *with* उप, to dog.

गम् *with* प्रति and उद्, to advance towards.

चैत्ररथ *m.* the country orregion of the Gandharvas.

छन्दस् *n.* a metre.

जघनार्ध (जघन *n.* the hip, the ninder part of any thing, and अर्ध half) the latter or hinder part.

तप् *4th conj. Parasm.* to be distressed.

दीपक *m. n. f.* that which lights up.

धा *with* पुरस्, to make one a family priest.

नर्मदा *f.* name of a river.

पुनरुक्तभूत *m. n. f.* (पुनरुक्त repeated or a repetition, and भूत become) like a repetition.

प्रत्यग्र *m. n. f.* or *adv.* recent, fresh. *m.* a region.

रोधस् *n.* bank.

लोकान्तरम् *n.* (अन्यो लोकः लोकान्तरम्) another world.

वच् with आशिषम्, to give a blessing.

वन्य *m. n. f.* produced or existing in a forest.

वरुण *m.* God of the sea.

विदर्भ *m.* (*in the plur.*) the name of a country, the moderu Berars.

विशिख *m.* an arrow.
वृष्टि *f.* rain.
शाप *m.* curse.
शास् *with* आ *2nd conj. Âtm.* to wish, to bless.
संमोहन *n.* name of a miraculous weapon.
सत्क्रिया *f.* hospitality.
सर्वस्व *n.* (सर्व all and स्व *n.*) all wealth or possession.
सेनानिवेश *m.* the camp of an army.
सौराज्य *n.* good government.
हव्य *n.* an offering.

Conduct oneself properly सदाचारं प्रतिपद्, सदाचारेण वृत्.
Costly महार्ह *m. n. f.*
Curious विलक्षण *m. n. f.*
Go round प्रदक्षिणीकृ.
Imprison कारागृहे निक्षिप्.
Jarâsaṁdha जरासंध *m.* name of a king of Magadha.
Krauñcha क्रौञ्च *m.* a species of birds.
Nishâda निषाद *m.* name of a wild tribe or an individual of it.
Proud उत्सिक्त *past part.* उत्सेकिन् (—नी *f.*)
Restore दा *with* प्रति
Sign चिह्न *n.*
Vâranâvati वारणावती *f.* name of a place.
Vidur विदुर *m.* a proper name.

SELECTIONS FOR EXERCISE.

1. (*From the* AITAREYA BRAHMANA-PANCHIKÂ 7).

हरिश्चन्द्रो ह वैधस ऐक्ष्वाको राजाऽपुत्र *आस। तस्य ह शतं जाया बभूवः। तासु पुत्रं न लेभे। तस्य ह पर्वतनारदौ गृह ऊषतुः। स ह नारदं पप्रच्छ।

यन्निवमं पुत्रमिच्छन्ति ये विजानन्ति ये च न।
किंस्वित्पुत्रेण विन्दते तन्म आचक्ष्व नारद॥ इति।
स एकया † पृष्टो दशाभिः ‡ प्रत्युवाच।
ऋणमस्मिन्त्संनयत्यमृतत्वं च गच्छति।
पिता पुत्रस्य जातस्य पश्येच्चेज्जीवतो मुखम्॥
यावन्तः पृथिव्यां भोगा यावन्तो जातवेदसि।
यावन्तो अप्सु प्राणिनां भूयान्पुत्रे पितुस्ततः॥
शश्वत्पुत्रेण पितरोऽत्यायन्बहुलं तमः॥

* Perfect of अस्, to be.' In classical Sanskrit it is used only as an auxiliary to form the Periphrastic Perfect.

† Understand after this the corresponding case of गाथा a verse.'

‡ Of these only two and a half are given here.

* त् is optionally inserted between a final न् and स्.

अथैनमुवाच वरुणं राजानमुपधाव पुत्रोमे जायतां तेनत्वा यज्ञा इति। तथेति। स वरुणं राजानमुपससार पुत्रो मे जायतां तेन त्वा यजा इति। तथेति। तस्य ह पुत्रो जज्ञे रोहितो नाम। तं होवाचाजनि ते वै पुत्रो यजस्व मानेनेति। स होवाच यदा वै पशुर्निर्दशो भवत्यथ स मेध्यो भवति निर्दशो न्वस्त्वथ त्वा यजा इति। तथेति। स ह निर्दश आस। तं होवाच निर्दशो न्वभूद्यजस्व मानेनेति। स होवाच यदा वै पशोर्दन्ता जायन्तेऽथ स मेध्यो भवति दन्ता न्वस्य जायन्तामथ त्वा यजा इति। तथेति। तस्य ह दन्ता जज्ञिरे। तं होवाचाज्ञत वा अस्य दन्ता यजस्व माननेति। स होवाच यदा वै पशोर्दन्ताः पद्यन्तेऽथ स मेध्यो भवति दन्ता न्वस्य पद्यन्तामथ त्वा यजा इति। तथेपि। तस्य ह दन्ताः पेदिरे। तं होवाचापत्सत वा अस्य दन्ता यजस्व मानेनेति। स होवाच यदा वै पशोर्दन्ताः पुनर्जायन्तेऽथ स मेध्यो भवति दन्ता न्वस्य पुनर्जायन्तामथ त्वा यजा इति। तथेति। तस्य ह दन्ताः पुनर्जज्ञिरे। तं होवाचाज्ञत वा अस्य पुनर्दन्ता यजसव मानेनेति। स होवाच यदा वै क्षत्रियः सांनाहुको भवत्यथ स मेध्यो भवति संनाहं नु प्राप्नोत्वथ त्वा यजा इति। तथोति। स ह संनाहं प्रापत्तं होवाच संनाहं नु प्राप्नोद्यजस्व मानेनेति। स तथेत्युक्त्वा पुत्रमामन्त्रयाम्बास ततायं वै मह्यं त्वामददाद्धन्त त्वयाहमिमं यजा इति। स ह नेत्युक्त्वा धनुरादायारण्यमपातस्थौ। स संवत्सरमरण्ये चचार।

अथ हैक्ष्वाकं वरुणो जग्राह। तस्य होदरं जज्ञे। तदु ह रोहितः शुश्राव। सोऽरण्यद्ग्राममेयाय तमिन्द्रः पुरुषरूपेण पर्येत्योवाच।

नानाश्रान्ताय श्रीरस्तीति रोहित शुश्रुम।
पापो नृषद्वरो जन इन्द्र इच्चरतः सखा॥

चरैवेति। चरैवेति वै मा ब्राह्मणोऽवोचदिति ह द्वितीयं संवत्सरमरण्ये चचार। सोऽरण्याद्ग्राममेयाय। तमिन्द्रः पुरुषरूपेण पर्येत्योवाच।

3rd pers. plur. Aorist of जन् (*Vedic*).

पुष्पिण्यौ चरतो जङ्घे भूष्णुरात्मा फलग्रहिः।
*शेरेऽस्य सर्वे पाप्मानः श्रमेण प्रपथे हताः॥

चरैवेति। चरैवेति वै मा ब्राह्मणोऽवोचदिति ह तृतीयं संवत्सरमरण्ये चचार। सोऽरण्याद्ग्राममेयाय। तमिन्द्रः पुरुषरूपेण पर्येत्योवाच।

आस्ते भग आसीनस्योर्ध्वस्तिष्ठति तिष्ठतः।
शेते निपद्यमानस्य चराति चरतो भगः॥

चरैवेति। चरैवेति वै मा ब्राह्मणोऽवोचदिति ह चतुर्थं संवत्सरमरण्ये चचार। सोऽरण्याद्ग्राममेयाय। तमिन्द्रः पुरुषरूपेण पर्येत्योवाच।

कलिः शयानो भवति संजिहानस्तु द्वापरः।
उत्तिष्ठंस्त्रेता भवति कृतं संपद्यते चरन्॥

चरैवेति। चरैवेति वै मा ब्राह्मणोऽवोचदिति ह पञ्चमं संवत्सरमरण्ये चचार। सोऽरण्याद्ग्राममेयाय। तमिन्द्रः पुरुषरूपेण पर्येत्योवाच।

चरन्वै मधु विन्दति चरन्स्वादुमुदुम्बरम्।
सूर्यस्य पश्य श्रेमाणं यो न तन्द्रयते चरन्॥

चरैवेति। चरैवेति वै मा ब्राह्मणोऽवोचदिति ह षष्ठं संवत्सरमरण्ये चचार। सोऽजीगर्तं सौयवसिमृषिमशनया परीतमरण्य उपेयाय। तस्य ह त्रयः पुत्रा आसुः शुनःपुच्छः शुनःशेपः शुनोलाङ्गूल इति। तं होवाच ऋषेऽहं ते शतं ददाम्यहमेषामेकेनात्मानं निष्क्रीणा इति। स ज्येष्ठं पुत्रं निगृह्णान उवाच न न्विममिति नो ऐवममिति कनिष्ठं माता। तौ ह मध्यमे संपादयांचक्र तुः शुनः शेपे। तस्य ह शतं दत्त्वा स तमादाय सोऽरण्याद्ग्राममेयाय। स पितरमेत्योवाच तत हन्ताहमनेनात्मानं निष्क्रीणा इति। स वरुणं राजानमुपससारानेन त्वा यजा इति। तथेपि भूयान्वै ब्राह्मणः क्षत्रियादिति

---

* 3rd pers. plu. of शी pres. tense *(Vedic)*,

वरुण उवाच। तस्मा एतं राजसूयं यज्ञक्रतुं प्रोवाच। तमेतमभिषेचनीये पुरुषं पशुमालेभे।

तस्य ह विश्वामित्रो होतासीज्जमदग्निरध्वर्युर्वसिष्ठो ब्रह्मायास्य उद्गाता। तस्मा उपाकृताय नियोक्तारं न विविदुः। स होवाचाजीगर्तः सौयवसिर्मह्यमपरं शतं दत्ताहमेनं नियोक्ष्यामीति। तस्मा अपरं शतं ददुस्तं स निनियोज। तस्मा उपाकृताया नियुक्तायाप्रीताय पर्यग्निकृताय विशसितारं न विविदुः। स होवाचाजीगर्तः सौयवसिर्मह्यमपरं शतं दत्ताहमेनं विशसिष्यामीति। तस्मा अपरं शतं ददुः। सोऽसिं निःशान एयाय। अथ ह शुनः-शेप ईक्षांचक्रेऽमानुषमिव वै मा विशसिष्यन्ति हन्ताहं देवता उपधावामीति। स प्रजापतिमेव प्रथमं देवतानामुपससार। तं प्रजापतिरुवाचाग्निर्वै देवानां नेदिष्ठस्तमेवोपधावेति। सोऽग्निमुपससार। तमग्निरुवाच सविता वै प्रसवानामीशे तमेवोपधावेति। स सवितारमुपससार। तं सवितोवाच वरुणाय वै राज्ञे नियुक्तोऽसीति तमेवोपधावेति। स वरुणं राजानमुपससार। तं वरुण उवाचाग्निर्वै देवानां मुखं सुहृदयतमस्तं नु स्तुह्यथ त्वोत्स्रक्ष्याम इति। सोऽग्निं तुष्टाव। तमग्निरुवाच विश्वान्देवान्स्तुह्यथ त्वोत्स्रक्ष्याम इति। स विश्वान्देवांस्तुष्टाव। तं विश्वेदेवा ऊचुरिन्द्रो वै देवानामोजिष्ठो बलिष्ठः सहिष्ठः सत्तमः पारयिष्णुतमस्तं नु स्तुह्यथ त्वोत्स्रक्ष्याम इति। स इन्द्रं तुष्टाव। तस्मा इन्द्रः स्तूयमानः प्रीतो मनसा हिरण्यरथं ददौ। तमिन्द्र उवाचाश्विनौ नु स्तुह्यथ त्वोत्स्रक्ष्याम इति। सोऽश्विनौ तुष्टाव। तमश्विना ऊचतुरुषसं नु स्तुह्यथ त्वोत्स्रक्ष्याम इति। स उषसं तुष्टाव तस्य ह स्मर्च्यृच्युक्तायां विपाशो मुमुचे। कनीय ऐक्ष्वाकस्योदरं भवति। उत्तमस्यामेवर्च्युक्तायां विपाशो मुमुचे। अगद ऐक्ष्वाक आस।

* Instead of the first syllable of the root, the preposition seems to be reduplicated here.

† 3rd pers. sing. pres. *Ved.*; regularly it ought to be ईष्टे.

‡ This stands for the hymn sung by Śunaḥsepa in praise of Ushas or the Dawn.

II. त्रयाणां धूर्तानाम्।

कस्मिंश्चिदधिष्ठाने मित्रशर्मा नाम ब्राह्मणः प्रतिवसति स्म। स कदाचिन्माघमासे पशुप्रार्थनाय ग्रामान्तरं गतः। तत्र तेन कश्चिद्यजमानो याचितः। भो यजमान आगागमिन्याममावास्यायां यक्ष्यामि यज्ञं तद्देहि मे पशुमेकम्। अथ तेन तस्य शास्त्रोक्तः पीवरतनुः पशुः प्रदत्तः। सोऽपि तं समर्थमितश्चेतश्च गच्छन्तमवलोक्य स्कन्धे कृत्वा सत्वरं स्वपुराभिमुखः प्रतस्थे।

अथ तस्य गच्छतो मार्गे त्रयो धूर्ताः संमुखा बभूवुः। तैश्च तादृशं पीवरतनुं पशुं स्कन्धमारूढमवलोक्य मिथोऽभिहितम्। अहो अस्य पशोर्भक्षणादद्यतनो हिमपातो व्यर्थतां नीयते। तदेनं वञ्चयित्वा पशुमादाय शीतत्राणं कुर्मः।

अथ तेषामेकतमो वेषपरिवर्तन विधाय संमुखो भूत्वा तमूचे। भो भोः किमेवं जनविरुद्धं हास्यकार्यमनुष्ठीयते यदेष सारमेयोऽपवित्रः स्कन्धारूढो नीयते। ततश्च तेन कोपाभिभूतेनाभिहितमहो किमन्धो भवान्यपशुं सारमेयं प्रतिपादयसि। सोऽब्रवीच्छ्रह्मान् कोपस्त्वया न कार्यो यथेच्छं गम्यतामिति।

अथ यावत्किंचिदध्वान्तरं गच्छति तावद्द्वितीयो धूर्तः संमुखः समुपेत्य तमुवाच। भो ब्रह्मन् कष्टं कष्टं यद्यपि वल्लभोऽयं ते सारमेयस्तथापि स्कन्धमारोपयितुं न युज्यते। अथासौ सकोपमिदमाह। भोः किमन्धो भवान्यत्पशुं सारमेयं वदसि। सोऽब्रवीद्भगवन् मा कोपं कुर्वज्ञानान्मयाभिहितम्। त्वमात्मरुचितं समाचरेति।

अथ यावत्स्तोकं वर्त्मान्तरं गच्छति तावत्तृतीयोऽन्यवेषधारी धूर्तः संमुखः समुपेत्य तमुवाच। भो अयुक्तमेतद्यत्त्वं सारमेयं स्कन्धाधिरूढं नयसि तत्त्यज्यतामेष यावदन्यः कश्चिन्न पश्यति। अथासौ बहु विमृश्य तं पशुं सारमेयमेव मन्यमानो भयाद्भूमौ प्रक्षिप्य स्वगृहमुद्दिश्य पलायितः। ततस्ते त्रयो मिलित्वा तं पशुमादाय प्रतिस्थिरे।

ब्राह्मणभुजंगमयोः।

अस्ति कस्मिंश्चिदधिष्ठाने हरिदत्तो नाम ब्राह्मणः। तस्य च कृषिं कुर्वतः सदैव निष्फलः कालोऽतिवर्तते। अथैकस्मिन्दिवसे स ब्राह्मणे धर्मार्तः स्वक्षेत्रमध्ये वृक्षच्छायायां प्रसुप्तः। अनतिदूरे वाल्मीकोपरि प्रसारितं भीषणं भुजंगमं दृष्ट्वासौ चिन्तयामास। नूनमेषा क्षेत्रदेवता कदाचिदापि न पूजिता तेनेदं मे कृषिकर्म विफलीभवति तदहमस्याः पूजामद्य करिष्यामि। इत्यवधार्य कुतोऽपि क्षीरं याचित्वा शरावे निक्षिप्य वल्मीकान्तिकमुपगम्योवाच। भोः क्षेत्रपाल मयैतावन्तं कालं न ज्ञातं यत्त्वमत्र वससि तेन पूजा न कृता तत्सांप्रतं क्षमस्वेति। एवमुक्त्वा दुग्धं निवेद्य गृहाभिमुखं प्रायात्।

अथ प्रातर्यावदागत्य पश्यति तावद्दीनारमेकं शरावे दृष्टवान्। एवं च प्रतिदिनमेकाकी समागत्य तस्मै क्षीरं ददात्येकैकं च दीनारं गृह्णाति।

अथैकस्मिन्दिवसे वल्मीके क्षीरनयनाय पुत्रं नियुज्य ब्राह्मणो ग्रामं जगाम। पुत्रोऽपि क्षीरं तत्र नीत्वा संस्थाप्य च पुनर्गृहं समायातः। दिनान्तरे तत्र गत्वा स दीनारमेकं दृष्टवा गृहीत्वा च चिन्तितवान्। नूनं सौवर्णदीनारपूर्णोऽयं वल्मीकस्तदेनं भुजंगं हत्वा सर्वमेकवारं ग्रहीष्यामि। एवं संप्रधार्यान्येद्युः क्षीरं ददता ब्राह्मणपुत्रेण सर्पो लगुडेन शिरसि ताडितः। स च दैववशादमुक्तजीवितो रोषात्तं ब्राह्मणकुमारं तीव्रविषैर्दशनैस्तथादशद्यथा स सद्यः पञ्चत्वमुपागतः।

अथ पुनरपि ब्राह्मणः प्रत्यूषे क्षीरं गृहीत्वा तत्र गत्वा तारस्वरेण सर्पमस्तौत्। तदा सर्पो वाल्मीकान्तर्लीन एव ब्राह्मणं प्रत्युवाच। त्वं लोभादत्रागतः पुत्रशोकमपि विहाय। इतः परं तव मम च प्रीतिर्नोचिता। तव पुत्रेण यौवनोन्मत्तेनाहं ताडितो मया च स दष्टः। कथं मया लगुडप्रहारो विस्मर्तव्यस्त्वया च पुत्रशोकदुःखं कथं विस्मर्तव्यम्। इत्युक्त्वा बहुमूल्यं हीरकमणिं तस्मै दत्वा पुनस्त्वया नागन्तव्यमिति कथयित्वा विवरं प्रविष्टः। ब्राह्मणोऽपि मणिं गृहीत्वा पुत्रबुद्धिं निन्दन्स्वगृहमागतः।

अज्ञः सुखमाराध्यः सुखतरमाराध्यते विशेषज्ञः।
ज्ञानलवदुर्विदग्धं ब्रह्मापि नरं न रञ्जयति॥ १॥

लभेत सिकतासु तैलमपि यत्नतः पीडय—
न्पिबेच्च मृगतृष्णिकासु सलिलं पिपासार्दितः।
कदाचिदपि पर्यटञ्शशविषाणमासादये—
न्न तु प्रतिनिविष्टमूर्खजनचित्तमाराधयेत्॥ १॥

व्यालं बालमृणालतन्तुभिरसौ रोद्धुं समुज्जृम्भते
छेत्तुं वज्रमणीञ्छिरीषकुसुमप्रान्तेन संनह्यते।
माधुर्यं मधुबिन्दुना रचयितुं क्षाराम्बुधेरीहते
नेतुं वाञ्छति यः खलान्पथि सतां सूक्तैः सुधास्यन्दिभिः॥ ३॥

स्वायत्तमेकान्तगुणं विधात्रा विनिर्मितं छादनमज्ञतायाः।
विशेषतः सर्वविदां समाजे विभूषणं मौनमपण्डितानाम्॥ ४॥

साहित्यसंगीतकलाविहीनः साक्षात्पशुः पुच्छविषाणहीनः।
तृणं न खादन्नपि जीवमानस्तद्भागधेयं परमं पशूनाम्॥ ५॥

येषां न विद्या न तपो न दानं ज्ञानं न शीलं न गुणो न धर्मः।
ते मृत्युलोके भुवि भारभूता मनुष्यरूपेण मृगाश्चरन्ति॥ ६॥

वरं गहनदुर्गेषु भ्रान्तं वनचरैः सह।
न मूर्खजनसंपर्कः सुरेन्द्रभवनेष्वपि॥ ७॥

हर्तुर्याति न गोचरं किमपि शं पुष्णाति यत्सर्वदा—
प्यर्थिभ्यः प्रतिपाद्यमानमनिशं प्राप्नोति वृद्धिं पराम्।
कल्पान्तेष्वपि न प्रयाति निधनं विद्याख्यमन्तर्धनं
येषां तान्प्रति मानमुज्झत नृपाः कस्तैः सह स्पर्धते॥ ८॥

अम्भोजिनीवननिवासविलासमेव
हंसस्य हन्ति नितरां कुपितो विधाता।
न त्वस्य दुग्धजलभेदविधौ प्रसिद्धां
वैदग्ध्यकीर्तिमपहर्तुमसौ समर्थः॥ ९॥

केयूरा न विभूषयन्ति पुरुषं हारा न चन्द्रोज्ज्वला
न स्नानं न विलेपनं न कुसुमं नालंकृता मूर्धजाः।
वाण्येका समलंकरोति पुरुषं या संस्कृता धार्यते
क्षीयन्ते खलु भूषणानि सततं वाग्भूषणं भूषणम्॥ १०॥
विद्या नाम नरस्य रूपमधिकं प्रच्छन्नगुप्तं धनं
विद्या भोगकारी यशः सुखकरी विद्या गुरूणां गुरुः।
विद्या बन्धुजनो विदेशगमने विद्या परा देवता
विद्या राजसु पूजिता न तु धनं विद्याविहीनः पशुः॥ ११॥
सूनुः सच्चरितः सती प्रियतमा स्वामी प्रसादोन्मुखः
स्निग्धं मित्रमवञ्चकः परिजनो निष्क्लेशलेशं मनः।
आकारो रुचिरः स्थिरश्च विभवो विद्यावदातं मुखं
तुष्टे विष्टापहारिणीष्टदहरौ संप्राप्यते देहिना॥ १२॥
प्राणाघातान्निवृत्तिः परधनहरणे संयमः सत्यवाक्यं
काले शक्त्या प्रदानं युवतिजनकथामूकभावः परेषाम्।
तृष्णास्रोतोविभङ्गो गुरुषु च विनयः सर्वभूतानुकम्पा
सामान्यः सर्वशास्त्रेष्वनुपहतविधिः श्रेयसामेष पन्थाः॥ १३॥
प्रारभ्यते न खलु विघ्नभयेन नीचैः
प्रारभ्य विघ्नविहता विरमन्ति मध्याः।
विघ्नैः पुनः पुनरपि प्रतिहन्यमानाः
प्रारब्धमुत्तमजना न परित्यजन्ति॥ १४॥
प्रिया न्याय्या वृत्तिर्मलिनमसुभङ्गेऽप्यसुकर-
मसन्तो नाभ्यर्थ्याः सुहृदपि न याच्यः कृशधनः।
विपद्युच्चैः स्थेयं पदमनुविधेयं च महतां
सतां केनोद्दिष्टं विषममसिधाराव्रतमिदम्॥ १५॥
स्वल्पं स्नायुवसावशेषमलिनं निर्मांसमप्यस्थिकं
श्वा लब्ध्वा परितोषमेति न तु तत्तस्य क्षुधाशान्तये।
सिंहो जम्बुकमङ्कमागतमपि त्यक्त्वा निहन्ति द्विपं
सर्वः कृच्छ्गतोऽपि वाञ्छति जनः सत्वानुरूपं फलम्॥ १६॥

लाङ्गूलचालनमधश्चरणावपातं
भूमौ निपत्य वदनोदरदर्शनं च।
श्वा पिण्डदस्य कुरुते गजपुंगवस्तु
धीरं विलोकयति चाटुशतैश्च भुङ्क्ते ॥ १७॥

परिवर्तिनि संसारे मृतः को वा न जायते।
स जातो येन जातेन याति वंशः समुन्नतिम्॥ १८॥

कुसुमस्तबकस्येव द्वयी वृत्तिर्मनस्विनः।
मूर्ध्नि वा सर्वलोकस्य विशीर्यंत वनेऽथवा॥ १९॥

तानीन्द्रियाणि सकलानि तदेव कर्म
सा बुद्धिरप्रतिहता वचनं तदेव।
अर्थोष्मणा विरहितः पुरुषः स एव
अन्यः क्षणेन भवतीति विचित्रमेतत्॥ २०॥

दौर्मन्त्र्यान्नृपतिर्विनश्यति यतिः सङ्गात्सुतो लालना-
द्विप्रोऽनध्ययनात्कुलं कुतनयाच्छीलं खलोपासनात्।
ह्रीर्मद्यादनवेक्षणादपि कृषिः स्नेहः प्रवासाश्रया-
न्मैत्री चाप्रणयात्समृद्धिरनयात्त्यागात्प्रमादाद्धनम्॥ २१॥

दानं भोगो नाशस्तिस्रो गतयो भवन्ति वित्तस्य।
यो न ददापि न भुङ्क्ते तस्य तृतीया गतिर्भवति॥ २२॥

रे रे चातक सावधानमनसा मित्र क्षणं श्रूयता-
मम्भोदा बहवो वसन्ति गगने सर्वेऽपि नैतादृशाः।
केचिद्वृष्टिभिरार्द्रयन्ति धरणीं गर्जन्ति केचिद्वृथा
यं यं पश्यसि तस्य तस्य पुरतो मा ब्रूहि दीनं वचः॥ २३॥

जाड्यं ह्रीमति गण्यते व्रतरुचौ दम्भः शुचौ कैतवं
शूरे निर्घृणता ऋजौ विमतिता दैन्यं प्रियालापिनी।
तेजस्विन्यवलिप्तता मुखरता वक्तर्यशक्तिः स्थिरे
तत्को नाम गुणो भवेत्सुगुणिनां यो दुर्जनैर्नाङ्कितः॥ २४॥

लोभश्चेदगुणेन किं पिशुनता यद्यस्ति किं पातकैः
सत्यं चेत्तपसा च किं शुचि मनो यद्यस्ति तीर्थेन किम्।

सौजन्यं यदि किं निजैः सुमहिमा यद्यस्ति किं मण्डनैः
सद्विद्या यदि किं धनैरपयशो यद्यस्ति किं मृत्युना ॥ २५ ॥

न कश्चिच्चण्डकोपानामात्मीयो नाम भूभुजाम्।
होतारमपि जुह्वानं स्पृष्टो दहति पावकः ॥ २६ ॥

आरम्भगुर्वी क्षयिणी क्रमेण लघ्वी पुरा वृद्धिमती च पश्चात्।
दिनस्य पूर्वार्धपरार्धभिन्ना छायेव मैत्री खलसज्जनानाम् ॥ २७ ॥

मृगमीनसज्जनानां तृणजलसंतोषविहितवृत्तीनाम्।
लुब्धकधीवरपिशुना निष्कारणवैरिणो जगति ॥ २८ ॥

वाञ्छा सज्जनसंगमे परगुणे प्रीतिर्गुरौ नम्रता
विद्यायां व्यसनं स्वयोषिति रतिर्लोकापवादाद्भयम्।
भक्तिः शूलिनि शक्तिरात्मदमने संसर्गमुक्तिः खले-
ष्वेते येषु वसन्ति निर्मलगुणास्तेभ्यो नरेभ्यो नमः ॥ २९ ॥

प्रदानं प्रच्छन्नं गृहमुपगते संभ्रमविधिः
प्रियं कृत्वा मौनं सदसि कथनं नाप्युपकृतेः।
अनुत्सेको लक्ष्म्यां निरभिभवसाराः परकथाः
सतां केनोद्दिष्टं विषममसिधाराव्रतमिदम् ॥ ३० ॥

संपत्सु महतां चित्तं भवत्युत्पलकोमलम्।
आपत्सु च महाशैलशिलासंघातकर्कशम् ॥ ३१ ॥

संतप्तायसि संस्थितस्य पयसो नामापि न ज्ञायते
मुक्ताकारतया तदेव नलिनीपत्रस्थितं राजते।
स्वात्यां सागरशुक्तिमध्यपतितं सन्मौक्तिकं जायते
प्रायेणाधममध्यमोत्तमगुणः संवासतो जायते ॥ ३२ ॥

नम्रत्वेनोन्नमन्तः परगुणकथनैः स्वान्गुणान्ख्यापयन्तः
स्वार्थान्संपादयन्तो विततबहुतरारम्भयत्नाः परार्थे।
क्षान्त्यैवाक्षेपरूक्षाक्षरमुखरमुखान्दुर्मुखान्दूषयन्तः
सन्तः साश्चर्यचर्या जगति बहुमताः कस्य नाभ्यर्चनीयाः ॥ ३३ ॥

भवन्ति नम्रास्तरवः फलोद्गमैर्नवाम्बुभिर्भूरिविलम्बिनो घनाः।
अनुद्धताःसत्पुरुषाः समृद्धिभिः स्वभाव एवैष परोपकारिणाम् ॥ ३४ ॥

श्रोत्रं श्रुतेनैव न कुण्डलेन दानेन पाणिर्न तु कङ्कणेन।
विभाति कायः करुणापराणां परोपकारैर्न तु चन्दनेन॥३५॥

पापान्निवारयति योजयते हिताय
गुह्यं च गूहति गुणान्प्रकटीकरोति।
आपद्गतं न च जहाति ददाति काले
सन्मित्रलक्षणमिदं प्रवदन्ति सन्तः॥३६॥

एते सत्पुरुषः परार्थघटकाः स्वार्थान्परित्यज्य ये
सामान्यास्तु परार्थमुद्यमभृतः स्वार्थाविरोधेन ये।
तेऽमी मानवराक्षसाः परहितं स्वार्थाय निघ्नन्ति ये
ये तु घ्नन्ति निरर्थकं परहितं ते के न जानीमहे॥३७॥

इतः स्वपिति केशवः कुलमितस्तदीयद्विषा—
मितश्च शरणार्थिनः शिखरिणां गणाः शेरते।
इतोऽपि वडवानलः सह समस्तसंवर्तकै—
रहो विततमूर्जितं भरसहं च सिन्धोर्वपुः॥३८॥

तृष्णां छिन्धि भज क्षमां जहि मदं पापे रतिं मा कृथाः
सत्यं ब्रूह्यनुयाहि साधुपदवीं सेवस्व विद्वज्जनान्।
मान्यान्मानय विद्विषोऽप्यनुनय प्रच्छादय स्वान्गुणा—
न्कीर्तिं पालय दुःखिते कुरु दयामेतत्सतां लक्षणम्॥३९॥

मनसि वचसि काये पुण्यपीयूषपूर्णा—
स्त्रिभुवनमुपकारश्रेणिभिः प्रीणयन्तः।
परगुणपरमाणून्पर्वतीकृत्य नित्यं
निजहृदि विकसन्तः सन्ति सन्तः कियन्तः॥४०॥

रत्नैर्महार्हैस्तुतुषुर्न देवा न भेजिरे भीमविषेण भीतिम्।
सुधां विना न प्रययुर्विरामं न निश्चितार्थाद्विरमन्ति धीराः॥४१॥

ऐश्वर्यस्य विभूषणं सुजनता शौर्यस्य वाक्संयमो
ज्ञानस्योपशमः श्रुतस्य विनयो वित्तस्य पात्रे व्ययः।
अक्रोधस्तपसः क्षमा प्रभवितुर्धर्मस्य निर्व्याजता
सर्वेषामपि सर्वकारणमिदं शीलं परं भूषणम्॥४२॥

*देवि किमत्र क्रियतां दैवयात्ते वस्तुनि। अलं रुदितेन। न वयमनुग्राह्याः प्रायो देवतानाम्। आत्मजपरिष्वङ्गामृतास्वादसुखस्य नूनमभाजनमस्माकं हृदयम्। अन्यस्मिञ्जन्मनि न कृतम-वदातं कर्म। जन्मान्तरविहितं हि कर्म फलमुपनयति पुरुषस्येह जन्मनि। न हि शक्यं दैवमन्यथा कर्तुमभियुक्तेनापि7 यावत्तुमानुष्यके शक्यमुपपादयितुं तावत्सर्वमुपपाद्यताम्। अधिकां कुरु देवि गुरुषु भक्तिम्। द्विगुणामुपपादय देवतासु पूजाम्। ऋषिजनपरिचर्यासु दर्शितादरा भव। परं हि दैवतमृषयो यत्नेनाराधिता यथासमीहितफलानामतिदुलपराक्रमं दातारों भवन्ति। श्रूयते हि पुरा चण्डकौशिकप्रसादान्मगधेषु बृहद्रथो नाम राजा जनार्दनस्य जेतारमतुलबलपराक्रमं जरासंधं नाम तनयं लेभे। दशरथश्च राजा परिणतवया अपि विभाण्डकमहामुनिसुतसयर्ष्यश्रृङ्गसय प्रसादान्नारायणभुजानिवाप्रति-हतानुदधीनिवाक्षोभ्यानवाप चतुरः पुत्रान्। अन्ये च राजर्षयस्तपोधनानाराध्य पुत्रदर्शनामृतस्वादसुखभाजो बभूवुः। अमोघफला हि महामुनिजनसेवा। अहमपि खलु कदा समुपारूढगर्भभरालसामापाण्डुरमुखीमासन्नचन्द्रोदयामिव पौर्णमासीनिशां देवीं द्रक्ष्यामि! कदा मे तनयजन्ममहोत्सवानन्दनिर्भरी हरिष्यति पूर्णपात्रं परिजनः। कदा हारिद्रवसनधारिणी सतुसनाथोत्सङ्गा द्यौरिवोदितरविमण्डला सबालातपा मामानन्दयिष्यति देवी। कदा सर्वौषधिपिजरजटिलकेशो गोरोचनाचित्रितकण्ठसूत्रग्रन्थिरुत्तानशयो दशनशून्यस्मिताननः पुत्रको जनयिष्यति मे हृदयाह्लादम्। कदा गोरोचनाकपिलद्युतिरन्तःपुरिकाकरतलपरंपरासंचार्यमाणमूर्तिरशेषजनाभिनन्दितो मङ्गलप्रदीप इव में शोकान्धकारमुन्मूलयिष्यति चक्षुषोः। कदा च क्षितितलरेणुधूसरो मण्डयिष्यति मम हृदयेन दृष्टया च सह परिभ्रमन्भवनाङ्गनम्। कदा केसरिकिशोरक इव संजातजानुचङ्क्रमणारम्भः संचरिष्यतीतस्ततः स्फटिकमणिमय भित्त्यन्तरितान्भवनमृगशावका-नाजिघृक्षुः। कदान्तःपुरिकानूपुरनिनादसंगतान्गृहकलहंसकाननुसरन्कक्षान्तर

---

* This is a speech addressed by a king to his queen who was deeply grieved on account of her being childless.

प्रधावितः कनकमेखलाघण्टिकारवानुसारिणीमायासयिष्यति धात्रीम्। कदा मातुश्चरणरागोपयुक्तशेषेण पिण्डालक्तकरसेन कञ्चुकिनां विडम्बयिष्यति मुखानि। कदा कुतूहललोललोचनो मणिकुट्टिमेष्वधोदत्तदृष्टिरनुसरिष्यति स्खलद्गतिरात्मनः प्रतिबिम्बानि। कदा नरेन्द्रसहस्रप्रसारितभुजयुगलाभिनन्द्यमानागमनो भूषणमणिमयूखलेखाकुलीक्रियमाणलोलदृष्टिरास्थानस्थितस्य मम पुरः पर्यटिष्यति सभान्तरेषु। इत्येतानि चान्यानि मनोरथशतानि चिन्तयतोऽन्तःसंतप्यमानस्ययान्ति रजन्यः। मामपि दहत्येवायमहर्निशमनल इवानपत्यतासमुद्भवः शोकः। शून्यमिव मे प्रतिभाति जगत्। अफलमिवाखिलंपश्यामि जीवितं राज्यं च। अप्रतिविधेये तु विधातरि किं करोमि। तन्मुच्यतां देवि शोकानुबन्धः। आधीयतां धैर्यं धर्मे च धीः। धर्मपरायणानां हि सदा समीपसंचारिण्यः कल्याणसंपदो भवन्ति। एवमभिधाय सलिलमादाय स्वयं करतलेनाभिनवपल्लवेनेव विकचकमलतुल्यमाननमस्याः साश्रुलेखं ममार्ज।

---

1. GENERAL GLOSSARY OF SANSKRIT WORDS OCCURRING IN THE BOOK.

अ

अकरुण *m.n.f.* (अ not, and करुणा *f.* compassion) ruthless, one who has no compassion.

अकिंचन *m.n.f.* (अ not and किंचन *n* something) he who has nothing, poor.

अक्ष *m.* dice used in gambling.

अक्षज्ञ *m.n.f* destitute of क्षत्रिय.

अक्षनैपुण *m.n.f* one who is possessed of skill in playing at dice.

अक्षम *m.n.f.* unable.

अक्षमाला *f.* (अक्ष *m.* name of a plant or its seed, and माला *f.* wreath or a string) a rosary of अक्ष.

अक्षरशः *adv.* literally.

अक्षहृदय *n.* the secret of managing dice.

अक्षि *n.* the eye.

अक्षोभ्य *m. n. f.* not to be ruffled, not to be frightened, immoveable. [healthy.]

अगद *m. n. f.* without disease,

अगस्त्य *m.* the name of a sage.

अगार *n.* house.

अग्नितप्त *m.n.f* (अग्नि and तप्त heated) heated by fire.

अग्निरथ *m.* fire-carriage, railway carriage.

अग्निष्टोम *m.* a kind of sacrifice.

अग्निहोत्र *n.* sacrifice to Fire.

अङ्क *m.* the lap.

अङ्गन *n.* a courtyard, a place.

अङ्गार *m.n.* burning charcoal.

अचिन्त्य *m.n.f* inconceivable, unimaginable.

अज *m.* name of Raghu's son *m.n.f* unborn.

अजस्र *m.n.f.* continnous, frequent.

अजा *f.* a she-goat.

अजीगर्त *m.* name of a Brâhmaṇa.

अञ्ज् *7th conj. Parasm.* to anoint; with वि, to make manifest, or lay open.

अञ्जन *n.* a black pigment, lamp-black.

अञ्जलि *m.* the cavity formed by joining the hands.

अण् *4th conj. Âtm* to breathe, to live.

अणु *m.n.f.* (अति very, very much) very horrible or wicked.

अतिघोर *m.n.f* (अति very, very much) very horrible or wicked.

अतिनिष्करुण *m.n.f.* very pitiless or cruel.

अतिनिष्फल *m.n.f.* very fruitless.

अतिप्रमाद *m.* a great error, great carelessness.

अतुल *m.n.f.* incomparable.

अत्यर्थम् *adv.* exceedingly, greatly, very long.

अत्यराति *m.* name of a Kshatriya.

अत्यायत *adv.* or *m.n.f.* very far, very long.

अद्भुत *m.n.f.* vonderful.

अद्यतन *m.n.f.* of to-day, belonging to this day.

अद्यप्रभृति *adv.* (**अद्य** to-day, and **प्रभृति** from) from to-day, or henceforward.

अधम *m.n.f.* low.

अधर *m.n.f. pron.* lower, low.

अधस् *ind.* below, down.

अधिकार *m.* post, power, office, fitness to perform any ceremony.

अधिज्यधन्वन् *m.* one whose bow is strung.

अधिष्ठान *n.* a place.

अधीर *m.n.f.* not of a sound or grave mind, little-minded, inpatient.

अध्वन् *m.* road.

अध्वर्यु *m.* asacrificial priest whose duty it is to prepare and throw the oblations into the fire.

अन् *2nd. conj. parasm.* to breathe; *with* **प्र**, to breathe, to live.

अनडुह् *m.* an ox.

अननुष्ठान *n.* (**अनुष्ठान** n. doing, execution) not doing, omission to do.

अनपत्यता *f.* (**अपत्य** n. a child) childlessness.

अनपराधिन् *m.n.f.* guiltless.

अनय *m.* want of prudence.

अनर्ह *m.n.f.* not deserving.

अनल *m.* fire.

अनवेक्षण *n.* not taking care.

अनागस् *m.n.f.* innocent, not guilty.

अनाथ *m.n.f.* helpless.

अनाद्यनन्त *m.n.f.* (**अनादि** without beginning, and **अनन्त** without end) having neither beginning.

अनारम्भ *m.* not beginning.

अनार्जवोपेत *m.n.f.* (**अन्** not, **आर्जव** *n.* straightness, straighforwardness, **उपेत** *past. part. pass.* of **इ** with **उप** accompanied) not possessed of straightforwardness, one who is without straight for wardness.

अनिग्रह *m.* (**निग्रह** *m.* restraint) not restraining, want of restraint.

अनिल *m.* wind.

अनिशम् *adv.* frequently, constantly, continuously.

अनिषण्ण *m.n.f.* not sitting.

अनीक *n.* an army.

अनीकस्थ *m.n.f.* (**अनीक** *n.*, **स्था** to stand) one in the army, a soldier.

अनुकम्पिन् *m.n.f.* compassionate.

अनुचर *m.* an attendent, a servant.

अनुत्सेक *m.* humility.

अनुपहत *m.n.f.* uninterrupted.

अनुबन्ध *m.* continuance.

अनुमरण *n.* following in death, or dying after, as in the case of widows burning themselves with the dead bodies of their husbands.

अनुराग *m.* love, liking.

अनुरूप *m.n.f.* in accordingly.

अनुलेपन *n.* an ointment.

अनुविधेय *m.n.f.* to be followed, to be done accordingiy.

अनुषक्त (अनु and सक्त *past pass. part. of* सञ्ज्) accoumpanied.

अनुष्ठान *n.* doing, excuting.

अनुष्ठेय *pot. part.* of स्था *with* अनु, what is to be executed.

अन्त *m.* end, destruction.

अन्तःपुरिका *f.* an inmate of the seraglio, a woman.

अन्तक *m.* the god of death.

अन्तगमन *n.* going to the end.

अन्ततः *adv.* at last.

अन्तर *n.* difference.

अन्येद्युः *adv.* on another day.

अन्वाह (आह with अनु,) he recites, repeats.

अन्वित *past. part. pass.* of इ *with* अनु, followed, accompanied *with,* rull of.

अन्विष्यत् (*pass. part.* of इष् *4th conj. Parasm. with* अनु) searching.

अप् *f.* water (*used in the plur).*

अपचिति *f.* worship.

अपथ्य *n.* any unwholesome or wrong thing.

अपयशस् *n.* infamy.

अपर *m.n.f. pron.* other, another.

अपराधसहस्र *n.* (सहस्र *n* a thousand) a thousand of faults.

अपराम्बुनिधि *m.* (अपर other, *i.e.*, western, and अम्बुनिधि ocean) the western ocean.

अपवित्र *m.n.f.* unsacred, sinful.

अपेक्षित *n. (past. part. pass.* of ईक्ष् *with* अप*)* what is desired.

अप्रणय *m.* want of tenderness.

अप्रतिविधेय *m.n.f.* irremediable, uncontrollable.

अप्रतिहत *m.n.f.* unchecked, irremediable.

अप्रमत्त *m.n.f.* (अ and प्रमत्त careless) not careless, careful.

अब्ज *n.* a lotus.

अभाजन *n.* not a receptacle, something not destined for a particular parpose.

अभिगीत *past. part.* of गै *1st conj. Parasm. with* अभि, sung.

अभिचैद्यम् *adv.* (चैद्य *m.* the king of Chedi, who was Krsihpa's enemy) towards Chaidya.

अभिताप *m.* violent heat.

अभिनव *m.n.f.* new. freash, tender.

अभिमन्यु *m.* name of the son of Arjuna.

अभिमुख *m.n.f.* facing.

अभियुक्त *m.n.f.* assiduous, of great merit or desert.

अभिषेचनीय *m.* a particular ceremony performed in the Râjasûya sacrifice, or the day on which it is performed.

अभिसंधा *f.* promise, determination.

अभिहित *past. part. pass.* of धा *with* अभि, spoken to.

अभ्यागत *past.part.* of गम् *with* अभि and आ, come, arrived; *m.* a (male) guest.

अम् *1st conj. Parasm.* to move.

अमावास्या *f.* the thirtieth day of the month, the day of the new moon.

अमित्र *m.* an enemy.

अमुत्र *adv.* in the next world.

अमृत *n.* the beverage of the gods, nectar.

अमोघ *m.n.f.* fruitful, real.

अम्भस् *n.* water.

अम्भोजिनी *f.* lotus, plant. [rise. अय् *1st cònj. Âtm. with* उद्, to अयस् n.iron.

अरण्यवास *m.* (अरण्य *n.* forest, and वास *m.* dwelling) forest residence.

अरिस्त्री *f.* the wife of an enemy.

अरुण *m.* the charioteer of the sun.

अरुस् *m.n.* a sore or wound.

अर्घ्यसत्कार *m.* (सत्कार *m.* hospitality) hospitality done by means of अर्घ्य, *i.e.* the materials for worshipping or honouring a guest.

अर्ज् *1st conj. Parasm* and *10th conj.* to acquire, to obtain, to earn.

अर्थ् *10th conj. Âtm.* to beg; *with* प्र, to request.

अर्थ *m.* meaning, true sense, object of desire.

अर्थसंशय *m.* (संशय *m.* doubt, danger) danger to wealth.

अर्थापय *denom. Parasm.* and *Âtm.* to explain.

अर्थिन् *m.* a suppliant, a beggar; *m.n.f.*

अर्द् *1st* and *10th conj. Parasm.* and *Âtm.* to afflict, tc torment.

अर्धकोटी *f.* (अर्ध *n.* half; कोटी *f.* ten millions) five millions.

अर्यमन् *m.* name of a deity, one of the dead forefathers.

अर्वन् *m.* a horse.

अर्ह् *1st conj. Parasm.* and *10th conj.* to deserve.

अलक्ष्मी *f.* bad luck, poverty.

अलस *m.n.f.* dull, heavy, slow.

अलाभ *m.* loss.

अलोभ *m.* comtentument, absence of greed.

अल्प *m.n.f.* little, few; अनल्प *m.n.f.* many, much.

अल्पविषय *m.n.f.* whose range is small, not comprehensive.

अवज्ञात *past. part. pass.* of ज्ञा *with* अव, despised, disregarded, disobeyed.

अवदात *m.n.f.* beautiful, white, pure, meritorious, virtuous.

अवर *m.n.f. porn.* hinder, posterior, inferior.

अवलम्बमान *Pres. Part. act.* of **लम्ब्** with **अव**, hanging.

अवलेप *m.* pride.

अवश *m.n.f.* being in the power of another, dependent, helpless.

अवश्यम् *adv.* certainly, inevitably, necessarily.

अवस्थान *n.* residence.

अवहित (*past part.* of **धा** *with* **अव**) attentive.

अवाच् *m.n.f.* southern.

अविघ्न *m.n.f.* without obstacle.

अविनाशिन् *m.n.f.* imperishable, undergoing no transformation.

अविलम्बितम् *adv.* without delay.

अव्यय *m.n.f.* immutable.

अश् *9th conj. Parasm.* to eat.

अशक्त *m.n.f.* weak, unable.

अशन *n.* eating.

अशना *f.* hunger.

अशोक *m.* name of a kind of tree.

अश्वतर *m.* a mule.

अश्वहृदय *n.* the secret of managing house.

अश्विन् *m.* (used in the dual) the twin celestial physicians so called.

अष्टावक्र *m.* name of a person.

अस् *4th conj. Parasm. with* **निर्**, to repeal, to abolish.

अस् *2nd conj. Parasm.* to be.

असंशयम् *adv.* undoubtedly.

असत्पुरुषसेवा *f.* (**सत्** *m.n.f.* good **सेवा** *f.* service) service of a person who is not good, service done to a bad or wicked person.

असन् *n.* blood.

असह्य *m.n.f.* (*pot. part.* of **सह्** with **अ**) insufferable.

असार *m.n.f.* (**सार** *m.* essence) unsubstantial, unprofitable, useless.

असिधारा *f.* (**धारा** *f.* edge) the edge of a sword.

असिधाराव्रत *n.* a vow as severe as that of lying on the edge of a sword.

असु *m.* vital breath; life (in this sense it is used in the plural, the vital breathes being five in number).

असुभङ्ग *m.* destruction of life, death.

असूयय *denom.* to wish ill to, to bear malice to.

असृज् *n.* blood.

अस्त *m.* sunset.

अस्तगिरि *m.* the western mountain, on which the sun, the moon and the stars are supposed to set.

अस्थि *n.* a bone.

अहन् *n.* a day.

अहरहः *ind.* every day.

अहर्निशम् *adv.* day and night; *n. coll. dvandva*, day and night.

अहि *m.* a snake.

अहोरात्र *m.* day and night.

अह्नाय *ind. adv.* instantly, soon, speedily.

आ

आ a particle showing *up to.*

आकार *m.* form.

आकाशवायु *m.* the wind in the sky.

आक्षेप *m.* reproach, slander.

आख्या *f.* name.

आगामिन् *m.n.f.* coming.

आङ्गिरस *m.* a descendant of अङ्गिरस्

आचरित *m.n.f.* followed, practised; n. parctice, act.

आचार्य *m.* a religious teacher who invests the student with the sacred thread, and instructs him in the Vedas.

आजि *m.f.* a fight, a battle.

आज्ञप्त *past. part. pass.* commanded.

आत्त *m.n.f.* (form आ and दत्त *past. part. pass.* of दा to give) taken away.

आत्मघातक *m.n.* (आत्मन् self and घातक destroyer) self-destroyer, one who ruine himself.

आत्मघातिन् *m.n.f.* one who commits suicide.

आत्मदमन *n.* self-restr int.

आत्मभाज् *m.* one possessed of a soul, a man.

आत्मरुचित *m.n.f.* liked by oneself.

आत्महित *n.* (आत्मन् self, and हित good)one's own good. [own.

आत्मीय *m.n.f.* intimate, one's

आदर *m.* attention, regard.

आदिहेतु *m.* the first cause.

आनन *n.* the mouth.

आनीत *past. part. pass.* of नी *with* आ, brought.

आन्तर *m.n.f.* internal.

आप् *5th conj. Parasm.* to obtain; *with* अव, to attain.

आपराह्णिक *m.n.f.* belonging to the latter part of the day.

आपाण्डुर *m.n.f.* slightly pale.

आप्त *m.* a friend, a well-wisher.

आप्रित *m.n.f.* consecrated by repeating certain verses called Âprî.

आमिष *m.n.* flesh, bait.

आमोद *m.* fragrant smell, perfume.

आयत्त *m.n.f.* dependent on, in the power of.

आयास्य *m.* the name of a Ṛishi

आयुष्काम *m.* one wishing to live a long life.

आयुस् *n.* life.

आराधना *f.* worship.

आराधित *m.n.f.* pleased, propitiated.

आरूढ *past. part. of* रुह् *with* आ, ascended.

आर्त *m.n.f.* troubled, distressed.

आर्द्र *m.n.f.* wet.

आर्द्रा *f.* the sixth lunar mansion.

आलवाल *n.* basin for water round the root of a tree.

आलाप *m.* a talk.

आली *f.* a line or row.

आविक्षित *m.* the son of अविक्षित्.

आवृत *past. part. pass.* of वृ *with* आ, filled, covered.

आशा *f.* hope.

आशिस् *f.* blessing.

आशीविष *m.* a snake.

आस् *2nd conj. Âtm.* to sit; *with* **अधि**, to sit; *with* **उप**, to adore, to worship; *with* **सत्र** to hold a sacrificial session, to perform a succession of sacrifices.

आसन् *n.* the mouth.

आसन्नमरण *m.n.f.* (**आसन्न** *m.n.f.* near and **मरण** *n.* death) one whose death is near, about to die.

आसाद्य *m.n.f.* obtainable.

आसीन *m.n.f.* sitting (*pres. part.* of **आस्**).

आस्थान् *n.* a hall of audience, an assembly room.

आस्य *n.* mouth.

आस्वाद *m.* taste, tasting.

आहव *m.* battle.

आहुति *f.* sacrificial oblation.

इ

इ *2nd conj. Parasm.* to go; *with* **अभि**, to go towards; *with* **अव**, to know; *with* **आ**, to come; *with* **उद्**, to rise, to flourish; *with* **निर्** to set out; *with* **परि**, to transform oneself, to circumambulate; *with* **वि** and **अप**, to separate; *with* **शरणम्** and **उप**, to submit; *with* **सम्**, to unite, to come together.

इ *Ist conj. Parasm. with* **उद्**, to rise.

इ *with* **अधि** *2nd conj. Âtm.* to [study.

इक्ष्वाकु *m.* the progenitor of the solar race of kings.

इच्छु *m.n.f.* wishing, wisher.

इतस्ततः *adv.* to and fro.

इतिकर्तव्यता *f.* method or the way

इतस्ततः *adv.* to and fro.

इतिकर्तव्यता *f.* method or the way fo doing anything.

इन्द्रादि (**इन्द्र** and **आदि** begining. Indra at the head) Indra and others.

इन्द्रिय *n.* vigour (to limbs).

इन्द्रियसौष्ठव *n.* (**इन्द्रिय** *n.* limb or sense, and **सौष्ठव** *n.* beauty, goodness) handsome make, healthy or sound frame.

इन्द्रियार्थोपसेवन *n.* (**अर्थ** *m.* object, **उपसेवन** *n.* resorting to, enjoyment) enjoyment of the objects of the senses, sensual enjoyment.

इन्दुमती *f.* the name of a lady.

इन्ध् *7th conj. Âtm.* to kindle.

इष्टद *m.n.f.* giving what is desired.

इष्टदेवता *f.* tutelar (desired) deity.

ई

ई *4th conj. Âtm. with* **उद्**, to rise, to rise up.

ईक्ष् *with* **प्रति**, to see, to care.

ईड् *2nd conj. Âtm.* and *10th conj. with* to praise.

ईदृश *m.n.f.* such.

ईर् *Ist conj. Parasm.* and *10th conj. with* **उद्**, to utter, to speak. [of, to rule.

ईश् *2nd conj. Âtm.* to be master

ईश्वर *m.* ruler. [to aim.

ईह् *Ist conj. Âtm.* to endeavour,

उ

उ a particle.

उख् *Ist conj. Parasm.* to go.

उग्र *m.n.f.* raging, severe.

उग्रम् *adv.* mightily, powerfully, formidably.

उच्चैः *ind. adv.* loudly, aloud.

उज्झ् *6th conj. parasm.* to throw.

उडुप *m.n.* a raft, a canoe.

उत्तम *m.n.f.* last.

उत्तमफलक *m.n.f.* (उत्तम *m.n.f.* good, excellent, फल *n* furit, and क suj.) of good fruit or result.

उत्तर *m.n.f. pron.* over, upper, after, subsequent.

उत्तरकुरवः *m. plur.* name of a country beyound the Himâlayas (Probably the original seat fo the Aryas).

उत्तरा *f.* daughter of a king named Virâṭa.

उत्तरीय *n.* an upper garment.

उत्तान *m.n.f.* with the back downwards, lying on the back.

उत्पथास्थित *m.n.f.* (उत्पथ *m.* a wrong path, आस्थित *past part.* of स्था *with* आ) one who has taken to a wrong path.

उत्पन्न *past. part.* of पद् *with* उद् born.

उत्पल *n.* a lotus flower.

उत्सङ्ग *m.* lap.

उत्सृष्ट *past. part. pass.* of सृज् *with* उद्, let go, discharged.

उदच् *m.n.f.* northern.

उदन् *n.* water.

उदर *n.* dropay, stomach.

उदरंभरि *m.n.f.* (उदर and भृ to fill) one who fills his belly or stomach, selfishly greedly.

उदार *m.n.f.* noble, generous.

उदुम्बर *m.* name of a tree; *n.* its fruit.

उद्गम *m.* source, springing up.

उद्गातृ *m.* a sacrificial priest whose duty it is to sing Sâma-Veda.

उद्दामवृत्ति *m.n.t.* of a wild disposition. inordinate, excessive.

उद्दालक *m.* name of a person.

उद्धत *m.n.f.* (*past. part.* of हन् *with* उद्) haug

उद्धतम् *adv.* carelessly, tumultuously.

उद्भूतविस्मय *m.n.f.* (उद्भूत *past part.* of भू *with* उद् to rise, to be produced) one in whom wonder or amazement has been born.

उद्यमभृत् *m.n.f.* one who is industrious.

उन्नति *f.* loftiness, magnanimity.

उन्माद *m.* joy, bloom.

उपकण्ठ *n.* the space near a town or village, or its boundary.

उपकार *m.* a banevolent action, doing good to another.

उपकारिन् *m.n.f.* benevolent.

उपकृति *f.* dong good to others.

उपचित *past. part. pass.* of चि *with* उप, collected.

उपजनित *past. part. pass.* of the *causal* of जन् *with* उप, produced.

उपनयन *n.* the ceremony of the उपनायन investiture with the sacred thread.

उपभोग *m.* enjoyment.
उपयुक्त *m.n.f.* used.
उपरत *past part.* of रम् *with* उप, deat, deceased, ceased.
उपरि *adv.* above.
उपरितन *m.n.f.* what is above.
उपशम *m.* satisfaction.
उपाकृत *m.n.f* brought.
उपायन *n.* present.
उपालभ्य *m.n.f.* blameable, deserving reproach.
उपेत *past. pass. part.* of इ *with* उप, united with, possessing.
उभ *pron.* both.
उभय *pron. m.n.f.* belonging to both sides.
उर्वी *f.* the earth.
उलूपी *f.* the name of a serpent damsel, for some time a wife of Arijuna.
उशनस् *m.* name of the preceptor of the *Asuras.*
उष् *1st conj. Parasm.* to burn.
उषस् *f.* the dawn, the goddess of dawn.
उष्णम् *adv.* hotly.
उष्णरुचि *m.* the sun.
उष्मन् *m.* warmth, heat.

ऊ

ऊर्जित *m.n.f.* lofty, excellent, fat, stout.
ऊर्ध्व *m.n.f.* exect, upper.

ऋ

ऋ *1st conj. Parasm.* to go.
ऋज् *1st conj. Âtm.* to acquire, to obtain.
ऋजु *m.n.f.* simple, straight, plain.
ऋण *n.* debt.
ऋत्विज् *m.* a sacrificial priest.
ऋभुक्षिन् *m.* a name of Indra.

ए

एकदा *adv.* once.
एकमनस् *m.n.f.* of one mind.
एकरात्र *n.* one night.
एकाकिन् *m.n.f.* alone, solitary.
एकान्त *m.n.f.* invariable.
एकान्तगुण *m.n.f.* one whose property is certain, of an unvarying virtue or efficacy.
एकान्ततः *adv.* invariably.
एकैक *pron. m.n.f.* one by one, each one.
एतादृश *m.n.f.* of this kind.
एनस् *n.* sin.

ऐ

ऐक्ष्वाक *m.* a descendant of Ikshvâku.
ऐन्द्र *m.n.f.* belonging to Indra.
ऐलूष *m.* son of liûshâ.

औ

औषध *n.* medicine.

क

कक्षा *f.* a room, an apartment.
कङ्कण *n.* a bracelet.
कच *m.* the hair.
कट *m.* a mat.
कण्व *m.* the name of a Ṛishi.
कतिचित् *pron.* several.
कनक *n.* gold.
कन्यका *f.* a daughter, a girl.
कपाल *m.n.f.* head, skull.
कपिल *m.n.f.* yellowish brown.
कम् *10th conj. Âtm.* to love.
करणीय *n.* what is to be done, work to be got through, a duty.
करिन् *m.* an elephant.
करुण *m.n.f.* doleful, lamentable.

करुणापर *m.n.f.* merciful.

कर्कोटक *m.* name of a serpent.

कर्ण *m.* proper name.

कर्मपथ *m.* (कर्मन् action, and पथिन् a way) way of action, *i.e.* the performane of religious ceremonies, &c., as a way to eternal bliss.

कलत्र *n.* wife.

कलह *m.* quarrel

कलहंसक *m.* a kind of a duck or [goose.

कला *f.* an art.

कलाप *m.* a bundle, a collection.

कलि *m.* the Kali age. *i.e.* the age in which the world at present is, being the last and most sinful of the four ages; the principle of evil.

कलिङ्ग *m.* name of a country (*in the plur*).

कल्पान्त *m.* (कल्प *m.* duration of the world and अन्त *m.* the end)the end of the duration of the world.

कल्पित *past. part. pass.* of the causal of क्लृप्, planned, invented.

कवच *m.* name of a person.

कविता *f.* learning, poetry.

कष्ट *m.n.f.* distressed.

कष्टं कष्टम् *adv.* woe!

कस् *with* वि *1st conj. Parasm.* to blow out as a flower; to open.

काकुत्स्थ *m.* a male descendant of Kakutstha, Râma.

कात्यायन *m.* name of a great Grammarian.

कादम्बरी *f.* name of a damsel.

कानन *n.* a forest, a grove.

काम *m.* desire.

कामदुह् *m.n.f.* one fulfilling any wish.

कामप्ति *m.* one whose desires are fulfilled.

काय *m.* body.

कारय *caus.* of कृ, to cuase anything to be done.

कार्तिकैकादशी *f.* (कार्तिकी *f.* belonging to hte month of Kârtika, and एकादशी *f.* eleventh) the eleventh day of Kârtika.

कार्पण्य *n.* meanness.

कार्मुक *n* a bow; *with* अधिज्य *m.n.f.* one who has his bow strung.

कार्य *m.n.f.* deserving or fit to be done, business, work.

कार्यकर *m.n.f.* one who does some business (for another).

कार्यद्वयाकुल *m.n.f.* distracted by having two things to do at one time.

कालेय *m.* name of certain giants.

काव्य *n.* a poem.

काश *m.n.* a kind of white flower.

काष्ठलोष्टसम *m.n.f.* (काष्ठ *n.* wood लोष्ठ *m.* and *n.* a lump of earth, and सम like) like wood and a lump of earth.

काहल *m.* a sound.

किंनर *m.* a certain class of demigods.

किंस्वित् what sort of a thing?

कितव *m.* a rogue, a dishonest person, a swindler.

कियत् *m.n.f.* how much.

किरण *m.* a ray of light.
किर्मीर *m.* name of a giant.
किशोरक *m.* a cub (as of a lion).
कीर्ति *f.* fame.
कु (as prefixed to nouns) bad, censurable.
कुक्कुर *m.* a dog.
कुञ्जर *m.* an elephant.
कुटुम्बक *n.* family.
कुट्टिम *m.n.*paved floor, a pavement;
मणिकुट्टिम a pavement of crystals.
कुडवक *m.* a measure of corn.
कुण्डल *n.* a kind of ear-ornament.
कुण्डिनपुर *n.* name of a city, the capital of the Vidarbhas or Berars.
कुतूहल *n.* wonder, curiousity.
कुमारक *m.* a young boy.
कुमुद *n.* a night lotus.
कुम्भ *m.* the frontal globe on the upper part of the forehead of an elephant.
कुम्भकर्ण *m.* name of a brother of Râvaṇa.
कुरुक्षेत्र *n.* name of a place where the Kurus fought.
कुल *n.* a family.
कुलज *m.n.f.* (**कुल** and **ज** form **जन्** to be produced) born in a family, of the race of.
कुश *m.* and **लव** *m.* sons of Râma.
कुसुमपुर *n.* name of a town.
कूल *n.* a bank.
कृ *8th conj. Parasm.* and *Âtm.* to do; *with* **अङ्गी**, to betake oneself to, to accept; *with* **अधि**, to aim at; **अधिकृत्य** having aimed at. *i.e.* referring to; *with* **अप** and **आ**, to remove; *with* **अलम्**, to adorn; *with* **आविस्**, to lay bare, to open; *with* **उप**, to do good; *with* **तिरस्** to despise; *with* **नमस्** to bow to; *with* **नि**, to injure, to wrong; *with* **निस्** and **आ**, to repudiate, to give up, to forsake; *with* **प्रति**, to retaliate, to resist; *with* **वशी**, to conquer.
कृ *5th conj. Parasm.* and Âtm. to kill.
कृच्छ्रत्रय *n.* (**कृच्छ्र** *n.* a penance, and **त्रय** three) three penances.
कृत् *6th Parasm* to cut.
कृत *n.* the first and best or the golden
कृतयुग age of the world.
कृतिका *f.* adopted (daughter).
कृतिन् *m.n.f.* one who has accomplished his purposes, good, virtuous.
कृते *ind.* for, on account of.
कृत्स्न *m.n.f.* whole.
कृपण *m.n.f.* mean, miserly, little-minded.
कृपानिधि *m.* (**कृपा** *f.* mercy and **निधि** *m.* store) store of mercy, one very merciful.
कृपालु *m.n.f.* kind.
कृश *m.n.f.* weak, thin.
कृष् *1st conj. Parasm.* to draw; *with* **वि** and **प्र**, to make worse, to reduce.
कृषि *f.* husbandry.

कृष्ण *m.* the eighth incarnation of Vishṇu.

कृष्णपक्ष *m.* the dark half of the lunar month.

[son.

कृष्णसाहाय्य *n.* help of Kṛishṇa.

कृ *9th conj. Parasm.* to strew; *with* वि, to scatter.

कृ *9th conj. Parasm.* and *Âtm.* to kill, to destroy.

कृत् *10th conj.* celebrate to praise, to glorify.

केयूर *m.* a kind of ornament worn above the elbow.

केश *m.* a hair.

केसरिन् *m.* a lion.

कैतव *n.* fraud, deceit

कोटि-टी *f.* a crore.

कोप *m.* anger, resentment.

कोशगार *n.* a store house, a treasure-house.

कौमारक *n.* boyhood. [Kurus.

कौरव *m.* a descendant of the क्रन्दित (*past. part. pass used as a substantive*) *n.* a cry.

क्रम् *1st conj. Parasm.* and *4th conj. Parasm.* to walk, to step, Âtm to operate, to have effect; *with* अति, to step or go beyond, to part from, to cross over, to transgress; *with* आ, to approach, to step or tread upon, to rise, rise up.

क्री *9th conj. Parasm.* and *Âtm* to buy; *with* निस् ; to by off, to redeem, to ransom; *with* वि, *Âtm.* to sell.

क्रीडाशैल *m.* (क्रीडा *f.* amusement, diversion, शैल *m.* a mountain) a pleasure mountain or embankment.

क्रुध् *4th conj. Parasm.* to be enraged, *with* अभि and सम् to be angry with. [to cry, cut.

क्रुश् *1st conj. Parasm. with* वि,

1st and *4th conj. Parasm.* to be or become fatigued, to be exhausted, to be depressed.

क्लम् *1st* and *4th conj. Parasm.* to be or become fatigued, to be exhausted, to be depressed.

क्लान्त *past part.* of क्लम् fatigued, exhansted, languishing.

क्लिद् *4th conj. parasm.* to be or become wet or damp.

क्लन्द् *1st conj. Parasm.* to lament.

क्लिश् *9th conj. Parasm.* to torture, to give pain to.

क्लीब *m.n.* neuter, impotent.

क्वथ् *1st conj. Parasm. with* उद्, to boil. [wound.

क्षण्, क्षिण् *8th conj. Parasm.* to torture, to give pain to.

क्षणध्वंसिन् *m.n.f.* (क्षण *m.* a moment, ध्वंसिन् perishing) Perishing in a moment.

क्षणिकत्व *n.* momentariness.

क्षत *past. part. pass.* of क्षण्, wounded.

क्षम् *4th conj. Parasm.*to for give.

क्षमिन् *m.n.f.* patient, forbearing.

[crease.

क्षय *m.* destruction, ruin, de-

क्षिति *f.* the earth, the ground.

क्षितीश *m.* (क्षिति *f.* the earth) lord of the earth, a king.

क्षीर *n.* milk.

क्षुद् *7th conj. Parasm.* and *Âtm.* to pound, to reduce to powder or dust.

क्षुद्र *m.n.f.* small, mean.

क्षुभ् *9th conj. Parasm.* to agitate.

क्षेत्रदेवता *f.* (क्षेत्र *n.* a field, देवता *f.* a deity) the deity of a field.

क्षै *1st conj. Parasm.* to pine or waste away.

ख

ख *n.* cavity of the human body, as mouth, nose, &c.

खड्गकृष्ट *m.n.f.* (खड्ग *m.* a sword) one who has drawn out his sword.

खलभुजङ्ग *m.* (खल *m.* a villain, भुजङ्ग *m.* a serpent) a serpent in the form of a villain.

खलु *ind.* verily.

खादिर *m.n.f.* of a tree named खदिर.

खिद् *7th conj. Âtm, 4th conj. Âtm.* and *6th conj. Parasm.* to be distressed, to be displeased or offended.

ख्या *2nd conj. Parasm.* to tell.

ग

गगनमध्य *m.n.* (गगन *n.* the sky, मध्य *m.n.f.* the middle) the middle of the sky.

गजघटाशत *n.* (घटा *f.* an army, a host, शत *n.* a hundred) a hundred arrays or hosts of elephants.

गजपुंगव *m.* the best of elephants.

गण्डकी *f.* name of a river; कण्डकीतीर *n.* a bank of the Gaṇḍakî.

गण्डस्थल *n.* temples of an elephant.

गतजीवित *m.n.f.* dead.

गति *f.* walk, gait, resousce, refuge.

गद् *1st conj. Parasm.* to speak

गदा *f.* a mace.

गन्तुकाम *m.n.f.* desirous to go.

गन्धर्वकन्या *f.* the daughter of a Gandharva.

गभीर *m.n.f.* deep, grave.

गम् *with* अभि, to attack; *with* प्रति and उद्, to advance towards.

गरुड *m.* an eagle, the bird of that species used by Vishṇu as his car.

गरुडाज्ञा *f.* order or command of Garuda, the enemy of the serpent-race.

गर्भ *m.* foetus, embryo

गर्भाष्टम *m n.f.* (गर्भ *m.* conception, and अष्टम eighth) eighth from conception.

गर्ह् *1st conj. Parasm.* and *10th conj.* to think meanly of. to [spurn.

गल *m.* the throat.

गलित *past part* of गल् dropped.

गहन *m.n.f.* unpassable, impregnable; *n.* a wood, thicket.

गाण्डीव *n.* the name of Arjuna's bow.

गात्र *n.* limb, body.

गाधोदक *n.* (गाध *m.n.f.* shallow and उदक *n.* water) shallow water.

गान्धर्व *m.* a particular form of marriage in which the only thing essential is the mutual consent of the bridegroom and the bride.

गार्हपत्य *m.* a sacred fire kept perpetually by a house holder, household duties.

गिर् *f.* speech.

गुण *m.* efficacy, advantage.

गुप् *1st conj. parasm.* to protect.

गुप्ति *f.* secrecy, protection.

गुर्वी *f.* greatness, grandeur, majesty.

गुल्मपाल *m.* (गुल्म *m.* a fort) protector or kesper of a fort.

गुह् *1st conj. parasm.* and *Âtm.* to conceal.

गृध् *4th conj. Parasm.* to be greedy for, to covet.

गृह् *1st conj. Âtm* to think meanly of, to spurn.

गृहदेवता *f.* family deity.

गृहमेधिन् *m.* tue householder who performs domestic rites.

गृ *6th conj. Parasm.* to swallow; *with* सम् *Âtm.* to promise.

गृ *9th conj. Parasm. with* सम्, to speack.

गो *m.* bull; *f.* a cow, speech, the earth.

गोचर *m.* reach, scope.

गोमती *f.* name of a river.

गोरोचना *f.* a bright yellow pigment.

ग्रन्थ् *9th conj. Parasm.* to put together.

ग्रन्थि *m.* a knot.

ग्रह् (गृह्) *9th conj. Parasm.* and *Âtm.* to take; *with* अनु, to receive in a friendly manner, to favour, *with* नि, to curb; *with* वि, to be at war with; *with* सम्, store.

ग्रामणी *m.* the leader or headman of a village.

ग्रावन् *m.* a stone.

ग्लै *1st conj. Parasm.* to become exhausted.

ग्लौ *m.* the moon.

घ

घण्टिका *f.* a small bell.

घर्म *m.* heat.

घर्मज *m.n.f.* produced or caused by heat.

घस् *1st conj. Parasm.* to eat.

घोर *m.n.f.* horrible.

घ्रा *1st conj. Parasm. with* उप, to smell.

च

चकास् *2nd conj. parsam.* to shine.

चक्रवद्वृत्ति *m.n.f.* (चक्रवत् like a wheel) one whose movement is like that of a wheel, everrevolving.

चक्ष् *2nd conj. Âtm.* to speak; *with* आ, to tell; *with* वि and आ, to explain.

चङ्क्रमण *n.* moving.

चण्डकौशिक *m.* name of a sage.

चत्वार: *numer. nom. plur.* four.

चन्दन *m.n.* sandal wood.

चन्दनमञ्जरी *f.* (चन्दन *m.* a sandal tree, मञ्जरी *f.* a blossom, a flower-stalk, a sprout)a blossom, &c., of the sandal tree.

चन्द्रगुप्त *m.* name of a king.

चन्द्रापीड *m.* name of a prince.

चम् *1st conj. Parasm.* to lick up, to drink; *with* आ, to take in a little water into the mouth and drink it as a religious ceremony, to lick up, to drink.

चम्पकपुष्परेणु *m.* (**चम्पक** *m.* a kind of tree with fragrant flowers, **रेणु** *m.* pollen) the pollen in the flowers of *champakas.*

चम्पकवन *n.* a collection or grove of *champaka* trees.

चर् *1st conj. Parasm.* to go, to stalk abroad.

चरणराग *m.* dyeing the feet, the dye of the fest.

चरम *m.n.f.* last.

चरित *past. part. pass.* of **चर्**, practised or done.

चर्चित *past. part. pass.* of **चर्च्**, besmeared.

चर्मचक्षुस् *n.* (**चर्मन्** *n.* hide, skin, and **चक्षुस्** *n.* the eye) the physical eye.

चल् *with* **प्र** and **वि**, to remove, move aside.

चाटु *m.n.* a pleasing discourse.

चाणक्य *m.* name of person

चाण्डाल *m.* name of person.

चारणस्तुत *m.n.f.* (**चारण** *m.* a bard.) praised by bards.

चारुदत्त *m.* name of a person.

चारुसर्वाङ्गी *f.* (**चारु** beautiful, **सर्वाङ्ग** all limbs) having all limbs beautiful.

चार्वङ्गी *f.* a beautiful woman, a *belle.*

चि *5th conj. Parasm.* and *Âtm.* to collect; *with* **उप**, to grow fat; *with* **निस्**, to determine, to conclude; *with* **वि**, to search, to seek, to look for; with **सम्** to hoard.

चित् *10th conj. Âtm.* to have life or motion.

चित्रवन *n.* name of forest.

चित्रालाप *m.* (**चित्र** *m.n.f.* diversified, and **आलाप** *m.* conversation) conversation on diverse subjects.

चित्रित *m.n.f.* variegated, adorned.

चिरप्रवृत्त *m.n.f.* having long been in practice.

चिराद् *adv.* after a long time.

चूत *m.* a mango tree; *n.* its flower.

चूर्ण *m.n.* dust, powder; **चूर्णवत्** like dust, to dust.

चेत् *ind.* if.

चेतस् *n.* the heart, intellect. [mind

चैत्र *m.* the first month of the Hindu year.

चैत्ररथ *m.* the country or region of the Gandharvas.

छ

छद् *10 conj. with* **प्र**, to conceal anything.

छन्दस् *n.* a metre.

छल *n.* fraud.

छादन *n.* covering.

छिद् *10th conj.* and *7th conj. parasm.* and *Âtm.* to cut, to cut off, to divide.

ज

जक्ष् *2nd conj. parasm.* to eat.

जगदात्मन् *m.* (**जगत्** the world, the universe, and **आत्मन्** *m.* soul) Soul of the world.

जगन्नाथ *m.* (**जगत्** and **नाथ** *m.* lord) the Lord of the universe.

जगन्नायक *m.* (जगत् and नायक *m.* the lord) the Lord of the universe.

जघनार्ध *n.* (जघन *n.* the hip, the hinder part of anything, and अर्ध half) the latter or hinder part.

जङ्घा *f.* the thigh.

जटा *f.* matted hair.

जटिल *m.n.f.* besmeared with, mixed with.

जड *m.n.f.* inanimate.

जन् *with* सम् to be bron, to flourish.

जनमेजय *m.* the name of the son of Parikshit, grandson of Arjuna.

जनय *causal* of जन् to cause, to bring about; जनयितुम् *inf.*

जनार्दन *m.* a name of Kṛishna

जन्तु *m.* a creature.

जन्मभाज् *m.n.f.* one who is bron; *m.* a man.

जन्मान्तर *n.* (अन्यजन्म जन्मान्तरम्)another birth.

जप् *1st conj. parasm.* to pronounce in a low voice, to mutter (as prayers).

जम्बुमालिन् *m.* name of a Rākshasa.

जय *m.* victory, trrumph.

जयावह *m.n.f.* that which brings victory.

जागृ *2nd conj. Parasm.* to be awake.

जाड्य *n.* dullness.

जात *n.* a collection.

जातकर्मन् *n.* birth ceremony.

जातवेदस् *m.* fire.

जानंतपि *m.* son of Janamtapa.

जानु *n.* the knee.

जाया *f.* wife, women.

जाह्नवी *f.* the Ganges.

जीवन *n.* livelihood.

जीवनाशा *f.* (जीवन living, life, आशा *f.* hope, desire)desire for living.

जीवलोक *m.* the world of living beings, this world.

जीवित *n.* life.

जीवितलघूकृत *m.n.f.* disgraced or degraded by life or by continuing to live.

जृम्भ् *with* सम् and उद् *1st conj Ātm.* to endeavour, to attempt, to accomplish.

जॄ *1st, 4th* and *9th conj. Parasm* and *10th conj.* to grow old, to waste away, to wear out-

जैन *m.* follower of Jina, a person belonging to the Jain sect.

ज्ञा (जा) *9th conj. Parasm.* and *Ātm.* to know; *with* अनु, to permit; *with* अभि, to recognize.

ज्ञानमार्ग *m.* (ज्ञान *n.* knowledge, मार्ग *m.* a way) the knowledge of God as way to eternal bliss.

ज्वल् *1st conj. Parasm.* to blaze, to brun, to be ardent, to glow.

त

तक्ष् *1st conj. Parasm.* to parc to chop; *with* सम् to cut to pieces, to wound, to hurt by words.

तट *m.n.f.* bank, margin.

तत *m.* a fond name for any relative.

तत्त्ववेदिन् *m.n.f.* one who knows the truth or real philosophy.

तदीय *m.n.f.* belonging to him.

तद्वत् *adv.* like that, in the same manner.

तद्विषयक *m.n.f.* concerning him.

तन् *8th conj. Parasm.* and *Âtm* to stretch; to spread, as a sacrifice, *i.e.,* to perform it; *with* **प्र**, to spread.

तनय *m.* a son.

तनु-तनू *f.* body.

तन्तु *m.* a thread.

तन्त्री *f.* a musical instrument, lute.

तन्द्रय *den.* or *nom. verb* (from **तन्द्रा** *f.* laziness or stupor) to be lazy.

तन्मध्ये (**तद्** and **मध्ये**) in the midst of it.

तप् *4th conj. Âtm. with* **सम्**, to be pained or afflicted.

तपन *m.* an oppressor.

तपोधन *m.* one whose penitential virtues are his riches, an ascetic.

तम् *4th conj. Parasm.* to be distressed.

तरी *f.* a boat.

तर्ज् *1st conj. Parasm.* and *10th conj. Âtm.* to threaten, to menace, to reprove.

तादृश् *m.n.f.* like that, in that manner.

ताप *m.* heat.

ताय् *1st conj. Âtm.* to spread.

तार *n.* a shrill sound; *m.n.f.* shrill.

तावत्कालम् *adv.* for so long a time.

तावद् *adv.* during that time, in the meanwhile.

तिग्म *m.n.f.* austere, severe.

तिथि *f.* a day of the month.

तिमिर *m.n.* darkness, dark.

तिर्यञ्च् *m.* a lower animal; *m.n.f.* horizontal, sideways.

तीर्थोदक *n.* (**तीर्थ** *n.* holy thing such as a river, and **उदक** *n.* water) holy water.

तुमुल *m.n.f.* violent, tumultuous.

तुरग *m.* a horse.

तुरासाह् *m* a name of Indra.

तूर्णम् *adv.* quickly.

तृणराजफल *n.* (**तृणराज** *m.* a plamtree) a fruit of the palm-tree.

तृप् *4th conj. Parasm.* to be gratified or satisfied.

तृष् *4th conj. Parasm.* to feel thirsty.

तृष्णा *f.* thirst, greed, convetousness.

तृह् *7th conj. Parasm.* to kill, to destroy.

तेजस्विन् *m.n.f.* brilliant, splendid, bright, spirited.

तोय *n.* water.

त्याग *m.* giving alms, charity.

त्रय *n.* a collection of three.

त्रस् *1st* and *4th conj. Parasm.* to tremble, to be afraid; *with* **सम्** to be afraid.

त्राण *n.* protection.

त्रिः *adv.* thrice.

त्रिवर्ग *m.* collection of three, viz., *Dharma* or religious merit, *Artha* or wealth, and Kâma, *i.e.* desires, or fulfilment of desires.

त्रिविष्टपास्थान *n.* (त्रिविष्टप *n.* heaven, आस्थान *n.* assembly) the heavenly assembly, the assembly of the gods.

त्रुट् *4th conj. 6th conj. Parasm.* to break, of snap.

त्रेता *f.* the second or silver age of the world.

त्रैलोक्य *n.* the three worlds.

त्र्यम्बक *m.* an epithet of Rudra, Siva.

त्विष् *f.* light, splendour, brightness.

द

दंश् *1st conj. Parasm.* and *10th conj. Âtm.* to bite, to sting.

दंष्ट्रा *f.* a jaw, a fang.

दंष्ट्रिन *m.* an animal having sharp teeth, a snake.

दक्षिण *m.n.f. pron.* southern.

दक्षिणीय *m.n.f.* deserving of *Dakshiṇá.*

दत् *m.* a tooth.

दत्त्वा (*absol.* of दा 'to give',) having given.

दद् *1st conj. Âtm.* to give.

ददत् *pres. Part.* of दा to give.

दधि *n.* curdled milk.

दन्त *m.* a tooth.

दन्दशूक *m.* a snake.

दमयन्ती *f.* name of a woman, the wife of Nala.

दम्पती *m.du.* wife and husband.

दम्भ *m.* hypocrisy.

दय् *1st conj. Âtm.* to have compassion.

दयालुत्व *n.* kindness.

दरिद्र *m.n.f.* poor.

दरिद्रा *2nd conj. Parasm.* to be poor.

दर्प *m.* pride. [to tear.

दल् *1st conj. Parasm.* to burst,

दशन *m.* a tooth.

दशम *m.n.f.* tenth.

दशा *f.* states, condition.

दह् *1st conj. parasm.* to burn.

दा *3rd conj. Parasm.* and *Âtm.* to give.

दा *2nd conj. Parasm.* to cut.

दानव *m.* a demon.

दारक *m.* a male child, son.

दाव *m.* a forest conflagration, a forest.

दाशरथि *m.* son of Daśaratha.

दिगन्त *m.* the end of the quarters, countries in all directions.

दिग्विजय *m.* (दिश् *f.* quarter, विजय *m.* conquest) conquest of the quarters, or of all regions.

दिदृक्षु *m.n.f.* disirous of seeing.

दिनेदिने *adv.* every day, day by day.

दिव् *f.* a day heaven.

दिवा *ind. adv.* by day.

दिव्य *m.n.f.* clestial, beautiful.

दिव्याश्रमपद *n.* (दिव्य, आश्रमपद *n.* hermitage) beautiful hermitage.

दिश् *f.* direction, quarter.

दिह् *2nd conj. Parasm.* and *Âtm.* to besmear.

दीक्ष् *1st conj. Âtm.* to consecrate and thus fit oneself for performing a sacrifice.

दीन *m.n.f.* poor, needy, afficted, helpless.

दीनबन्धु *m.* (दीन, बन्धु *m.* brother) brother of those that are poor.

दीनार *m.* a particular coin (Roman).

दीप् *4th conj. Âtm.* to shine.

दीपक *m.n.f.* that which lights up.

दीप्ति *f.* splendour.

दीर्घम् *adv.* for a long time, long, deeply.

दु *5th conj. Parasm.* to give pain to, to tease, to afflict.

दुःखपीडित *m.n.f.* afflicted with pain.

दुःखभाज् *m n.f.* one who suffers pain, unhappy.

दुःखसंताप *m.* (दुःख, संताप *m.* heat) heat of pain, sorrow affiction.

दुःखित *m.n.f.* afficted.

दुग्ध *n.* milk.

दुरन्त *m.n.f.* whose end is difficult to be reached, infinite.

दुराप *m.n.f.* difficult to obtain.

दुरुक्त *n.* improper words, words not well spoken.

दुर्ग *n.* a place beset with difficulties and inaccessible.

दुर्गत *m.n.f.* distressed, miserable.

दुर्दम *m.n.f.* difficult to be controlled or put down.

दुर्धर्ष *m.n.f.* inaccessible, unapproachable.

दुर्नीत *n.* an evil or imprudent act.

दुर्बुद्ध *m.n.f.* difficult to be understood, obscure.

दुर्मुख *m.n.f.* one who has a bad mouth, one who speaks evil.

दुर्योधनभीमसेनौ *m. dual* दुर्योधन and भीमसेन (comp.)

दुर्विदग्ध *m.n.f.* vainly proud of one's learning.

दुष्कृत *n.* a wicked deed, wicked ness.

दुष्ट *m.n.f.* wicked.

दुस्तर *m.n.f.* difficult to be surmounted insurmountable.

दुह् *2nd conj. Parasm.* and *Âtm* to milk.

दू *4th conj. Âtm.* to be pained

दृ *6th conj. Âtm. with* आ, to pay respect to, to regard.

दृढ *m.n.f.* firm, strong.

दृप् *4th conj. Parasm.* to be pround.

दृश् *f.* sight, an eye.

दॄ *9th conj. Parasm.* to tear.

देव *m.n.f.* shining.

देवकी *f.* mother of Krishṇa.

देवक्षेत्र *n.* the land of the gods.

देवता *f.* a deity.

देवशुनी *f.* the bitch of the gods.

देवेज् *m.n.f.* worshipper of gods.

देश *m.* country.

देहिन् *m.* he who has a body, man; *m.n.f.* embodied, having a body.

दै *1st conj. Parasm. with* अव, to purify, to cleanse.

दो *4th conj. Parasm. with* अव, to cut, to cut off.

दोष *m.* censure or calumny.

दोषन् *m.n.* an arm.

दोहनकाल *m.* (दोहन *n.* milking, काल *m.* time) time of milking.

दौर्बल्य *n.* weakness.

दौर्मन्त्र्य *n.* bad or evil counsel.

द्युति *f.* complexion.

द्युम्न *n.* wealth.

द्यो *f.* heaven.

द्रविण *n.* wealth, money.

द्रव्य *n.* a thing.

द्रु *1st conj. Parasm.* to run.

द्रोण *m.* a proper name.

द्वय *n.* collection of two.

द्वयी *f.* two-fold.

द्वाःस्थ *m.n.f.* door-keeper.

द्वापर *m.* the third age of the world.

द्वार *n.* door.

द्वारपाल *m.* a porter, a doorkeeper.

द्विगुण *m.n.f.* two-fold.

द्विजन्मन् *m.* (द्वि two, जन्मन् *n.* birth) one who has two births, one belonging to any of the first three castes, a Brâhmaṇa.

द्विजिह्व *m.* (जिह्वा tongue) one who has two tongues, a serpent.

द्विजोत्तम *m.* one who is best among Brâhmanas.

द्विष् *2nd conj. Parasm.* and *Âtm.* to hate.

द्विष् *m.* an enemy.

ध

धनाशा *f.* desire for wealth.

धनुर्ज्या *f.* (ज्या. *f.* the string [of a bow]) the string of a bow.

धमनी *f.* a pipe.

धराधिप *m.* (धरा *f.* the earth, अधिप *m.* a lord) lord of the earth, a king.

धरित्री *f.* the earth.

धर्मदूषण *m.n.f.* one who contaminates or violates what is right.

धर्मषष्ठांशभाग *m.* one-sixth part of religious merit as a share.

धर्मसूत्रकार *m.* (धर्म *m.* law, सूत्र *n.* an aphorism) one who composes aphorisms on law, a writer on law.

धा *3th conj. Parasm.* and *Âtm.* to hold, to put; *with* अन्तर्, to hide or conceal; *with* अपि or पि, to shut; *with* उप and सम्, to join, to cause to attain; *with* नि, to place, to keep, *with* परि, to wear; *with* पुरस्, to make one a family priest; *with* वि, to execute, to do, to command (as in religious works); *with* सम् to make peace, to put or lay on, to fix on.

धात्री *f.* a nurse.

धामन् *n.* lustre, glory.

धारा *f.* continuous flow as of water, edge.

धि *6th conj. Parasm. with* सम्, to make peace with.

धिक् *ind.* fie upon!

धी *f.* intellect.

धीवर *m.* a fisherman.

धु or धू *5th conj. Parasm.* and *Âtm.* to shake.

धुर् *f.* a yoke.

धू *1st* and *9th conj. Parasm.* and *Âtm.* and *6th conj. Parasm.* to shake, to set in motion, to agitate.

धू [धूञ्] *10th conj. with* वि, to shake.

धूप् *1st conj. Parasm.* to heat.

धूर्त *m.* a rogue.

धूसर *m.n.f.* dirty, dust coloured.

पञ्च *numer. nom.* and *acc. plur.* five. [to read.

पठ् *1st conj. Parasm.* to repeat,

पठ्यमान (*pres. part. pass.* of **पठ्** to recite or read) what is being recited.

पण् *1st conj.* to praise, to bet or stake at play, to gamble.

पत् *with* **अधि**, to jump towards; *with* **प्र** and **उद्** to fly, to fly into.

पतङ्गवत् *adv.* like moths.

पतञ्जलि *m.* name of the author of a great grammatical work called the Mahâbhâshya.

पतन *n.* falling, falling from virtue, depravation, ruin.

पति *m.* master, husband.

पतित *m.n.f.* sinful, apostate.

पथः (*ablativs sing.* of **पथिन्** *m.* road) from the way.

पथिन् *m.* path, a way.

पथ्य *n.* what is wholesome or salutary.

पद् *4th conj. Atm.* to drop, to be dislocated, to fall; *with* **प्रति**, to know or understand, to accept, to do, to practise, to attain; *with* **सम्** to become, to amout to; *causal* with **प्रति**, to think, to consider, to set forth, to prove, to make over, to give; *causal with* **सम्** to strike a bargain.

पद् *m.* the foot.

पद *n.* a footstep.

पदवी *f.* a road, a way.

पदार्थ *m.* a thing, an object.

पद्धति *f.* a way, a mode.

पद्म *n.* a lotus that blooms by day.

पन् *1st conj.* to praise.

पपी *m.* the sun, a protector.

पर *pron.m.n.f.* other, belonging to another or the other party.

पर *m.n.* the highest thing, God.

परंपरा *f.* a line, a row, a succession.

परम् *conj.* but.

परमेश्वर *m.* the supreme Ruler of the Universe, God.

परमेष्ठिन् *m.* the god Brahmâ.

परायण *n.* object of attention or devotion.

परार्थघटक *m.n.f.* one who brings about the good of others.

परासु *m.n.f.* dead.

परिकीर्तित *past. part. pass.* of **कृत्** *with* **परि**, enumerated.

परिक्षित् *m.* son of **अभिमन्यु** and grandson of **अर्जुन**.

परिचर्या *f.* service, attendance on, worship.

परिचारिक *m* attendant.

परिजन *m.* attendant, a servant.

परिणत *m.n.f.* old, advanced.

परित्यक्त *past. part. pass.* of **त्यज्** *with* **परि** abandoned.

परित्याज्य *m.n.f.* (*pot. part.* of **त्यज्** *with* **परि**) deserving to be abandoned.

परिपन्थिन् *m.n.f.* one who stands in the way or obstructs; **तत्परिपन्थिनी** *f.* standing in its way.

परिपाक *m.* becoming mature, maturity.

परिप्लुष्ट *past. part.* of **प्लुष्** *with* **परि**, scorched, burnt.

परिभ्रष्ट *past. part.* of भ्रंश् *with* परि, deprived of, fallen, depraved.
परिवर्तन *n.* change.
परिवर्तिन् *m.n.f.* turning, changing.
परिवार *m.* retinue.
परिवृढ *m.* a master, owner.
परिवेष्टृ *m.* one who distributes food at the table.
परिव्राज् *m.* a recluse.
परिष्वङ्ग *m.* embrace.
परिसमाप्ति *f.* end, accomplishment.
परिताप *m.* pain, affliction.
परोपकार *m.* a benevolent deed.
पर्जन्य *m.* rain.
पर्यग्निकृत *m.n.f.* one round whom fire has been carried. Fire is carried round the victim before it is slaughtered.
पर्याप्तम् *adv.* fully, to one's heart's content.
पर्वत *m.* the name of a sage.
पलायमान (*pres. part.* of अय् *1st conj. Âtm.* to go, *with* परा, the र being changed to ल) running.
पलाश *m.* a kind of tree.
पल्लव *m.n.* a tender leaf.
पा *2nd conj. Parasm.* to protect.
पात *m.* falling, fall.
पातित (*past part. pass.* of the *causal* of पत्) thrown.
पात्र *n.* a fit object (of charity).
पान्थ *m.* a traveller.
पापकृत् *m.n.f.* (पाप *n.* sin, and कृ to do) one who has committed sin.
पापहर *m.n.f.* one who takes away sin.
पारयिष्णुतम *m.n.f.* able in the highest degree to accomplish anything.
पारिक्षित *m.* son of Parikshit.
पार्थ *m.* son of पृथा, name of the Pâṇḍavas.
पावक *m.* fire.
पावन *m.n.f.* purifying, pure, holy.
पाश *m.* a net, a snare.
पिञ्जर *m.n.* a yellow-red powder.
पिण्डद *m.n.f.* one who gives a morsel of food.
पिण्डालक्तक *m.* a red dye.
पिनाकिन् *m.* name of Śiva.
पिशुन *m.n.f.* malicious.
पिशुनता *f.* malice.
पिष् *7th conj. Parasm.* to grind.
पीडाकर *m.n.f.* that which gives pain.
पीयूष *n.* nectar.
पुंस् *m.* a man.
पुण्डरीक *m.* a proper name; a lotus flower.
पुण्यकृत् *m.n.f.* (पुण्य *n.* merit and कृ to do) mertorious.
पुण्य पुरुष *m.* a holy or virtuous man.
पुनरुक्तभूत *m.n.f.* (पुनरुक्त repeated or repetition, and भूत become) like a repetition.
पुनर्भू *f.* a widow remarried.
पुर् *f.* a town.
पुरंधि *m.* name of a deity.
पुरद्वार *n.* the gate of a city.
पुरस् *ind.* in fornt, to the fornt.
पुरस्तात् *adv.* before in front.
पुरोधस् *m.* a family priest.
पुरोहित *m.* a family priest, a chaplain.

पुष् *9th conj. Parasm.* to nourish.

पुष्कर *m.* a proper name.

पुष्टि *f.* nourishment.

पुष्पमित्र *m.* name of a king.

पुष्पस्रज् *f.* (**पुष्प** *n.* and **स्रज्** *f.* a garland) a garland of flowers.

पुष्पिणी *f.* having flowers, fruitful.

पू *9th conj. Parasm.* and *Âtm.* to purify.

पूर्ण *past. part. pass.* of **पृ**, filled, full.

पूर्णपात्र *n.* a present given to servants and others on joyful occasions.

पूर्व *m.n.f. pron.* previous, eastern.

पूर्वरात्र *m.* (**पूर्व** prior, **रात्रि** *f.* the night) the prior or first part of night.

पूर्वाह्ण *m.* the first part of the [day.

पृ or **पृ** *3rd conj. Parasm.* to full.

पृच् *1st* and *7th conj. Parasm.*, *2nd conj. Âtm* and *10th conj. with* **सम्**, to come in contact, to associae.

पृत् *f.* an army.

पृथग्जन *m.* a low person, a mean fellow.

पृथु *m.n.f.* large, great.

पृ *3rd* and *9th conj. Parasm.* to fill.

पौराणिक *m.* one who reads and explains the pnrâṇas.

पौरुष *n.* manliness.

पौर्णमासी *f.* the day of the full moon.

प्रकृति *f.* dispastition; *plur* subjects, people, ministerial efficers.

प्रकृष्ट *m.n.f.* magnificent, great.

प्रचण्ड *m.n.f.* hot, fierce, violent.

प्रचार *m.* progress, prevalence.

प्रच्युत *past. part.* of **च्यु** to fall *with* **प्र**.

प्रजापति *m.* the god Brahmâ.

प्रजापशुकाम (**प्रजा** *f.* progeny, **पशु** *m.* cattle, and **काम** *m.* wish), one wishing for progeny and cattle.

प्रजापीडनज *m.n.f.* (**प्रजा** *f.* subjects, **पीडन** *n* oppression and **ज** from **जन्** arising) arising from the oppression of the subjects.

प्रणिहित *past. part. pass.* of **धा** *with* **प्र** and **नि**, placed; **सम्यक्प्रणिहित** well-disposed, wellcontrolled.

प्रतापनिधि *m.* (**प्रताप** *m.* heat) store of heat.

प्रतिकार *m.* help against an evil, a **प्रतीकार** remedy.

प्रतिनिविष्ट *m.n.f.* inveterate, irremediable, self-willed, obstinate perverse.

प्रतिपक्ष *m.* an enemy.

प्रतिबिम्ब *n.* an image reflected as in a mirror.

प्रतिषिद्ध *past. part. pass* of **सिध्** *with* **प्रति**, forbidden, prohibited.

प्रतिहारी *f.* a female door-keeper

प्रत्यग्र *m.n.f.* or *adv.* recent, freash.

प्रत्यच् *m.n.f.* western.

प्रत्यहम् *ind.* (**प्रति** every, **अहन्** *n.* day every day.)

प्रत्युज्जीवन *n.* restoring to life again, revival.

प्रत्युत्पन्नमति *m.n.f.* (प्रत्युत्पन्न *past. part.* of पद् *with* प्रति and उद्) ready-witted, quick, sharp.

प्रत्यूष *m.* dawn, day-break.

प्रदीप्त *past. part.* of दीप् to shine *with* प्र, shining brightly.

प्रदेश *m.* a region.

प्रद्युम्न *m.* the god of love.

प्रधी *m.n.f.* keen, acute, talented.

प्रपन्न *m.n.f.* (*past. part.* of पद् *with* प्र) one who has subruitted or surrendered himself.

प्रभविष्णु *m.* a great lord.

प्रभात *m.n.f.* (*past. part.* of भा *with* प्र) disappeared (as darkness) and appeared (as light); *n.* daybreak.

प्रभाव *m.* prowess, greatness

प्रमति *m.* name of a man.

प्रमद्वरा *f.* name of a woman.

प्रमाण *n.* measure, extent.

प्रमाद *m.* name of a man.

प्रयाण *n.* starting, march. [प्र, used.

प्रयुक्त *past. part. pass.* of युज् *with*

प्रवासिन् *m.* a traveller.

प्रवृत्त्युपलब्धि *f.* (प्रवृत्ति *f.* intelligence, and उपलब्धि *f.* getting) getting intelligence.

प्रव्रजित *past. part.* of व्रज् *with* प्र, exiled or turned a recluse.

प्रसन्न *past. part.* of सद् *with* प्र, pleased, propitious.

प्रागल्भ्य *n.* blodness.

प्राच् *m.n.f.* eastern.

प्राण *m.* (*plural*) life.

प्राणाघात *m.* destruction of life.

प्रादुस् *adv.* or *prep.* (used with *verbs*) visible, manifest.

प्रान्त *m.* border.

प्रापितवत् *past. part. act.* of the *caus.* of आप् *with* प्र, having made to get, having given.

प्राप्तकाल *m.n.f.* (प्राप्त *past. part.* of आप् *with* प्र, having made to get, having given.)

प्रायस् *ind.* mostly, in most cases, generally.

प्रार्थना *f.* seeking.

प्रियदर्शन *m.n.f.* one with a pleasing look.

प्रियशर्मन् *m.* name of a Brâhmaṇa.

प्रियसंवास *m.* (संवास *m.* dwelling together) dwelling together of beloved persons, the company of beloved persons.

प्री *9th conj.* Parasm. and *Âtm.* to love, to please.

प्रीत *past. part. pass.* of प्री, pleased.

प्लवंगम *m.* a monkey.

प्लुष् *1st* and *9th conj. Parasm.* to burn. [devour.

प्सा *2nd conj. Parasm.* to

फ

फण् *1st conj. Parasm.* to go.

फल् *1st conj. Parasm.* to be crowned with success, to bear fruit.

फलग्राहि *m.n.f.* one who gathers the fruit of, or is benefited by, a certain course.

फलमूलादि *m.n.f.* (**मूल** root fruits, roots and others.)

फूत्कार *m.* sobbing.

ब

बटु *m.* a boy.

बत *ind. particle* implying surprise, sorrow, &c.

बन्ध् *9th conj. Parasm.* to tie, to fasten.

बन्धन *n.* restraint, imprisonment.

बल *n.* an army.

बहिरुपाधि *m.* (**उपाधि** *m.* an attribute, a peculiarity, environment) outward attributes, peculiarities, or environment.

बहिस् *adv.* out.

बहु *adv.* highly, much.

बहुविध *m.n.f.* of various sorts.

बाणजाल *n.* (**जाल** *n.* a collection) a number or multitude of arrows.

बाणपथ *m.* (**पथिन्** *m.* a way) the way or range of an arrow.

बाणवृष्टि *f.* (**वृष्टि** *f.* shower) shower of arrows.

बालातप *m.* morning sun-shine.

बालिका *f.* a girl.

बाष्प *m.n.* a tear.

बाहुक *m.* the name of Nala disguised as a charioteer.

बिभीषण *m.* a name of a brother of Râvaṇa and ally of Rama.

बुद्धिलक्षण *n.* (**बुद्धि** *f.* talent **लक्षण** *n.* a sign) a sign of talent.

बुभुक्षित *m.n.f.* hungry.

बृहद्रथ *m.* name of a king of Magadha, father of Jarâsamdha.

बोध *m.* awaking.

ब्रह्मन् *n.* the Divine Cause and Essence of the Universe;m a sacrificial priest whose duty it is to exercise a general superintendence over the performance.

ब्रह्मवर्चसिन् *m.n.f.* illumined by the Vedas, possessing the splendour conferred by the practice of the Vedic rites.

ब्रह्मादि *m.* (**ब्रह्मन्** *m.* and **आदि** beginning) the god Brahmâ and others.

ब्राह्म *m.* a particular form of marriage in use among Brâhmaṇas.

ब्रू *2nd conj. Parasm.* and *Âtm.* to speak.

भ

भक्तिमार्ग *m.* (**भक्ति** *f.* love, devotion and **मार्ग** *m.* a way) devotion to or love of. God as a way to eternal bliss.

भग *m.* name of a deity, lick, prosperity.

भग्न *past. part. pass.* of **भञ्ज्** destroyed, broken down, run away (from the field).

भज् *1st conj. Parasm* and *Âtm.* to take. to resort to; with **वि**, to divide; *with* **सम्** and **वि**, to admit to a share, to bestow upon.

भञ्ज् *7th conj. Parasm.* to destroy, to break.

भट *m.* a solder.

भण् *1st conj. Parasm.* to speak

भयाक्रान्त *m.n.f.* (आक्रान्त *past. part. pass. of* क्रम् with आ, overtaken, overcome) overcome by fear.

भव *m.* the world, worldly existence.

भवन *n.* a house.

भवितव्यता *f.* fate, destiny.

भा *2nd conj. Parasm.* to seem, to appear, to shine.

भाग *m.* division.

भागधेय *n.* lot.

भाग्ययोग *m.* (भाग्य *n.* luck, good fortune, योग *m.* accession) the accession of good luck or fortune.

भाज् *10th conj. with* सम् and वि, to admit to a snare, to bestow upon.

भानु *m.* the sun.

भानुमती *f.* wife of Duryadhana, she eldest son of Dhṛitarâshtra.

भार्गव *m.* name of a Rishi.

भाव *m.* a thing.

भाष् *1st conj. Âtm. with* प्रति, to answer.

भाष्यकृत् *m.* the writer of a Bhâshya or explanatory discourse, a commentator.

भास्कर *m.* the sun.

भित्ति *f.* a wail.

भिद् *7th conj. Parasm.* and *Âtm. to* split.

भिन्न *m.n.f.* different.

भी *3rd conj. Parasm.* to fear.

भीषण *m.n.f.* dreadful.

भुक्ति *f.* pessession, enjoyment.

भुज् *7th conj. Parasm.* to enjoy; *Âtm.* to dine, to eat.

भुजङ्गम-भुजग *m.* a cobra, a serpent.

भू *f.* the earth.

भू *with* अभि, to overcome; *with* परि, to despise, to treat contemptuously.

भूतसमागम *m.* coming together or union of animals or beings.

भूरि *m.n.f.* much.

भूष्णु *m.n.f.* about to become.

भृ *3rd conj. Parasm.* and *Âtm.* to support, to bear.

भृश *m.n.f.* much, mighty.

भेक *m.* a frog.

भोगकर *m.n.f.* producing enjoyment (री *f.*)

भोगतृष्णा *f.* (भोग *m.* wordly enjoyment, तृष्णा *f.* thirst) thirst for worldly enjoyment.

भ्रंश् *1st conj. Âtm.* and *4th conj. Parasm.* to fall.

भ्रम् *1st* and *conj. Parasm.* to wander, to revolve.

भ्रस्ज् *6th conj. Parasm.* and *Âtm.* and *Âtm.* to oake, to search.

भ्राज् *1st conj. Âtm.* to shine.

भ्राश् *1st conj. Âtm.* to shine.

भ्रू *f.* an eyebrow.

भ्लाश् *1st conj. Âtm.* to shine.

म

मघवन् *m.* a name of Indra.

मङ्गल *n.* welfare, prosperity, what is holy, anything fortunate or auspicious.

मङ्गलकाल *m.* (मङ्गल *n.* and काल time) an anupicious occasion.

मङ्गलप्रदीप *m.* an auspicious lamp.

मञ्जु *m.n.f.* agreeable, sweet.

मण्डन *n.* decoration or ornament.

मण्डप *m.* a temporary hall erected on festive occasions, a shed, an enclosure.

मण्डल *n.* an orb, a circle.

मत *n.* opinion, advice, counsel.

मत्त *past. Part.* of मद् intoxicated.

मथिन् *m.* a churning handle.

मदर्थं *adv.* for me.

मद्य *n.* spirituous liquor.

मधुपर्क *m.* an offering of honey, curdled milk, etc., to a guest on his arrival.

मधुरम् *adv.* sweetly.

मधुलिह् *m.* a black bee.

मध्यम *m.n.f.* middle;*n.* waist.

मध्याह्न *m.* (मध्य middle, and अहन् *n.* day) midday, noon.

मन् *with* अव, to disregard.

मनस्विन् *m.n.f.* intelligent.

मनुज *m.* a man.

मनुजन्मन् *m.* (मनु *m.* one of the progenitors of men) one born of Manu, a human being, a man.

मनोरथ *m.* wish, desire.

मन्त्र् *10th conj. Âtm.* to hold a consultation, to consult.

मन्त्राक्षर *n.* a syllable of a holy of Vidic verse.

मन्थ् *9th conj. Parasm.* to churn.

मन्दता *f.* dullness, withered condition.

मन्दभाग्यता *f.* (मन्द dull, भाग्य fortune, मन्दभाग्य one who is unfortunate) misfortane.

मय *m.* name of an architect.

मयूख *m.* a ray.

मराली *f.* a female swan.

मरुत् *m.* a god.

मरुत्त *m.* name of a king.

मरुत्सुत *m.* the son of the Wind, Mâruti, a monkey soldier devoted to Râma.

मर्यादा *f.* bound, limit.

मस्ज् *6th conj. Parasm.* to sink, to be immersed.

मस्तक *m.n.* the head

महत् *n.* lustre, greatness.

महत्त्व *n.* greatness, power.

महाज (महत् and अज) *m.* a great goat.

महाजव *m.n.f.* (महत् and अभिषेक *m.* sprinkling water as on the head of a king when he is crowned) great coronation.

महानुभाव *m n.f.* of great nobility, noble.

महाभिषेक *m.* (महत् and अभिषेक *m.* speed) very swift.

महाराज *m.* lord, a great king.

महार्ह *m.n.f.* of great virtue or value.

महार्हशयनोचित *m n.f.* (महार्ह, शयन *n.* a bed, उचित *m.n.f.* used to) accustomed or used to costly or rich beds.

महाश्वेता *f.* name of the daughter of a Gandharva.

महोक्ष *m.* (उक्षन् *m.* a bull) a great bull.

महोदधि *m.* the great ocean.

महोपकारित *m.n.f.* very benevolent.

मा *3rd conj. Âtm.* to measure.

मान *m.* respect, self-respect, pride, arrogance.

मानव *m.* man.

मानवराक्षस *m.* an evil spirit in the form of a man.

मानुष्यक *n.* the whole race of men, mankind.

मानोन्नति *f.* (**मान** *m.* respect) loftiness of respect, great selfrespect.

मामक *m.n.f.* mine.

माया *f.* jugglery, deceitful tricks.

मारुत *m.* wind.

मारुतात्मज *m.* the son of the god of wind, Mâruti.

मालाकार *m.* a gardener.

मालिन्य *n.* darkness, dirtiness.

माल्यवत् *m.* name of a giant, the maternal grandfather of Râvaṇa.

मांस् (**मान्स्**) *n.* flesh.

मांस

मास् *m.* a month.

मिथः *adv.* mutually, with each other, together.

मिथुन *n.* a couple, a pair.

मिथ्या *ind. adv.* falssly.

मी *9th conj. Parasm.* and *Âtm.* to destory.

मुकुटज्योत्स्नाजल *n.* (**मुकुट** *n.* a crown) the water [in the form] of the light or lustre of crowns.

मुक्तकेशी *f.* having the hair disordered or dishevelled.

मुक्ता *f.* a pearl.

मौक्तिक *n.*

मुखरता *f.* garrulity.

मुखोच्छ्वासगन्ध *m.* (**उच्छ्वास** *m.* breathing **गन्ध** *n.* perfume, smell) the fragrance of the mouth.

मुग्धाकृति *m.n.f.* of a lovely form or shape.

मुर *m.* the name of an enemy of Vishṇu or Kṛishṇa.

मुष्टि *m.f.* a fiṣt.

मुष् *9th conj. Parasm.* to steal

मुह् *with* **प्र**, to faint.

मूकभाव *m.* dumbness.

मूर्च्छ् *1st conj. Parasm.* to faint

मूर्धन् *m.* head.

मूल *n.* a root, basis.

मूषक *m.* a mouse; **मूषकराज** *m.* a king of mice.

मृग् *10th conj. Âtm.* to look for to search.

मृगतृष्णिका *f.* mirage.

मृगया *f.* chase, hunting.

मृगानुसारिन् *m.n.f.* following or pursuing an antelope.

मृज् *2nd conj. Parasm.* and *10th conj.* to wipe, to wipe off, to clear; *with* **प्र**, to wipe off; *with* **सम्**, sweep.

मृणाल *m.n.* the stalk of the lotus plant.

मृद् *9th conj. Parasm.* to pound, to reduce to atoms.

मेखला *f.* a girdle round the waist.

मेध्य *m.n.f.* fit or destined to be sacrificed.

मेनका *f.* name of a celestial damsel.

मैथिली *f.* princess of Mithilâ, Sitâ.

मोह *m.* follishness, infatuation.

मौन *n.* silence.

मौर्ख्य *n.* folly.

म्ना *1st conj. Parasm.* to repect over in the mind, to repeat; *with* सम् and आ, to repeat, to repeat by tradition, to prescribe, to rule.

म्लेच्छ *m.* a barbarian.

म्लै *1st conj. Parasm.* to grow weary, to become faint or languid.

य

यजमान *m.* a sacrificer.

यज्ञ *m.* a sacrifice.

यज्ञक्रतु *m.* a protion of a sacrificial ceremony.

यज्ञमण्डप *m.* an enclosure prepared for a sacrifice.

यज्ञवर्मन् *m.* a proper name.

यज्ञिय *m.n.f.* pertaining to sacrifices.

यत् *with* सम्, to struggle.

यत्कृते *ind.* for whose (*relative*) sake, for whom.

यत्नतः *adv.* with efforts.

यथाविधि *adv.* according to the rules laid down in ceremonial works, according to the sacred precepts.

यथेष्टम् *adv.* according to fancy, to one's heart's content, as one choose.

यम् *1st conj. Parsm.* to restrain.

यम *m.* the god of death, the deity presiding over death.

यमुना *f.* a name of a river.

यवी *m.* a way.

यस् *4th conj. Parasm.* to strive, to endeavour, *with* प्र.

या *2nd conj. Parasm.* to go; *with* वि and निस्, to go away, to pass away.

यावज्जीवेन *adv.* as long as life endures.

यावत् *adv.* for which while, while, as long as.

यु *2nd conj. Parasm.* to join.

युग *n.* a pair, a couple. **वासोयुग** *n.* pair of clothes.

युग *m.n.* a yoke.

युगान्तर *n.* (युग age. period, अन्तर another) another age or period.

युज् *1st conj. Parasm.* and *10th conj.* to unite; *with* नि, to appoint.

युज् *7st conj. Parasm.* and *Átm.* to join; *with* अनु, to put a question to; with उद्, to endeavour, to exert; *with* नि, to appoint.

युज् *4th conj. Átm.* to curb one's mind.

युज् *with* वि, *in the pass.* to be separated from.

युध् *f.* a battle.

युवति *f.* a young lady or woman.

युवन् *m.* a youth, a young man.

यूप *m.* a sacrificial post to which the animal is tied.

यूरोपीय *m.n.f.* pertaining to the continent of Europe.

योजितवत् *past. part. act.* of the *caus.* of युज् having joined.

योधसमाज *m.* (योध *m.* a warrior, समाज *m.* a multitude) a multitude of warriors, an army.

यौवन *n.* youth.

र

रक्त *n.* blood.

रङ्ग *m.* the place where any great thing is done, stage.

रङ्गागत *m.n.f.* come to the stage.

रच् *with* **वि**, *to* arrange, to effect, to perform.

रज्जु *f.* a rope.

रण *m.n.* a battle, a battlefield.

रणधुरा *f.* (**रण** and **धुर्** *f.* yoke) the brunt of battle.

रति *f.* love.

रध् *4th conj. Parasm.* to hunt.

रभस *m.* hastiness, rashness.

रम् *with* **उप**, *1st conj. Parasm.* to die; *with* **वि**, to stop.

रम्य *m.n.f.* pleasant. [sun.

रश्मिवत् *m.* (**रश्मि** *m.* a ray) the

रस् *1st conj. Parasm.* to scream.

रह् *10th conj.* to quit.

रहस् *n.* secrecy, solitariness, a secret; *adv.* secretly. solitarily.

रहित *m.n.f.* deprived of, bereft of.

रा *2nd conj. Parasm.* to give.

राघव *m.* a descendant of Raghu.

राज् *1st conj. Parasm.* and *Âtm. with* **वि**, to shine.

राज् *m.* a king; *m.n.f.* shining.

राजक *n.* a multiude of kings, all the kings.

राजकुल *n.* (**राजन्** *m.* and **कुल** *n.* a house, a palace) a royal palace.

राजसूय *m.* a sacrifice performed by kings.

राध् *with* **आ**, *caus.* to propitiate.

रामभार्या *f.* the wife of Râma.

रामादि *m.* (**राम** proper name and **आदि** beginning) Râma and others.

राष्ट्र *n.* a kingdom, a nation.

रिक्थ *n.* property, wealth.

रिच् *7th conj. Parasm. & Âtm.* to evacuate.

रु *2nd conj. Parasm.* to make noise, to cry aloud.

रुक्ष *m.n.f.* harsh.

रुचिकर *m.n.f.* palatable.

रुचिर *m.n.f.* agreeable, handsome.

रुद् *2nd conj. Parasm.* to weep. to bewail, to lament for.

रुद्र *m.* the god Śiva.

रुध् *7th conj. Parasm.* and *Âtm.* to obstruct, to prevent, to besiege.

रुरु *m.* the name of a man.

रुष् *f.* anger.

रुह् *with* **अधि**, to ascend.

रूप *n.* form.

रेणु *m.* dust.

रै *m.* wealth.

रोग *m.* disease, sickness.

रोदसी *n.* daul. heaven and earth.

रोधस् *n.* a bank.

रोहित *m.* name of the son of Harischandra.

ल

लक्ष्मी *f.* the goddess of wealth and beauty; splendour, glory.

लगुड *m.* a stick, a staff.

लघु *m.n.f.* small.

लघुत्व *n.* littleness, dishonour.

लघुलघु *adv.* early.

लङ्घ् *1st* and *10th conj. Parasm.* and *Âtm.* to go; *with* **उद्**, to violate, to transgress.

लप् *1st conj. Parasm. with* **प्र**, to

speak, to prattle; *with* वि, to lament.

लभ् *with* आ, to get or design a certain animal as a victim to be sacrificed.

लम्ब् *with* अव, *1st conj. Âtm.* to depent on.

लष् *1st* and *4th conj. Parasm.* to desire; *with* अभि to desire, to covet, to crave.

ला *2nd. conj. Parasm.* to give or take.

लाभ *m.* acquistion, gain.

लालन *n.* indulgence, indulging.

लावण्य *n.* beauty, loveliness.

लिप् *6th conj. Parasm.* and *Âtm.* to smear, to anoint.

लिह् *2nd conj. Parasm.* and *Âtm.*to lick.

ली *4th conj. Âtm.* to cling or press closely, to be absorbed. to be dissolved.

ली *9th conj. Parasm.* to melt, to be dissolved, to be absorbed; *with* वि, to melt.

लीन *past. part.* of ली, concealed, hidden.

लुट् *1st conj. Âtm.* to roll on the ground.

लुप् *4th conj. Parasm.*to be destroyed, to disappear or vanish.

लुप् *6th conj. Parasm.* and *Âtm.* to take away, to rob, to plunder, to deprive of.

लुब्धक *m.* a hunter, a fowler.

लू *9th conj. Parasm.* and *Âtm.* to cut, to lop off.

लेखा *f.* a line.

लोक् *with* अव *1st conj. Âtm.* and *10th conj.* to look at, to see.

लोकत्रयपति *m.* (त्रय *n.* a collection of three, पति *m.* lord) the lord of the three worlds, *viz.* Heaven, the Earth and the lower regions.

लोकवाद *m.* censure of people.

लोकान्तरम् *n.* (अन्यो लोका लोकान्तरम्) *n.* another world.

लोकापवाद *n.* censure by people, ill repute.

लोचन *n.* the eye.

लोमन् *n.* a hair.

लोमश *m.* the name of a Rishi.

लोल *m.n.f.* moving, unsteady.

लोहबन्ध *m.* (लोह *m.n.*iron, बन्ध *m.* a bond, a fetter) a fetter of iron.

व

वङ्गाः *m. plural,* the name of a people or their country.

वच् *with* आशिषम् to give a blessing.

वच् *with* प्रति, to answer.

वज्र *m.n.* adamant.

वञ्च् *10th conj. Âtm.* to deceive.

वटवृक्ष *m.* a banian tree.

वडवानल *m.* the firesupposed to exist at the bottom of the sea.

वणिग्जन *m.* (वणिज् *m.* a merchant) merchants.

वत्सतरी *f.* a heifer.

वत्सा *f.* dear, a female child.

वधक्रम *m.* the process or manner of killing.

वधस्तम्भ *m.* (वध *m.* killing, and स्तम्भ *m.* a post) gallows.

वन् *8th. conj. Âtm.* to beg.

वन्दितव्य *pot. part.* of वन्द् fit to be bowed to.

वन्य *m.n.f.* produced or existing in a forest.

वप् *1st conj. Parasm.* and *Âtm.* to shear, to cut, to sow; *with* निर् to offer sacrificial food, to present.

वपुस् *n.* the body.

वम् *1st conj. Parasm.* to vomit.

वर् *10th conj.* to choose.

वरुण *m.* the god of water or the sea.

वर्मन् *n.* armour.

वर्षण *n.* rain-fall, raining.

वर्षाभू *m.* a frog.

वल् *1st conj. Âtm.* to cover.

वल्मीक *m.n.* an anthill.

वश् *2nd conj. Parasm.* to wish.

वषट्कार *m.* the cry वौषट् at the time of throwing an oblation into the fire; this is considered a deity.

वस् *2nd conj. Âtm.* to dress; *caus. with* नि, to put on a garment, to dress.

वसन *n.* cloth, a garment.

वसन्तसेनाघातक *m.* (वसन्तसेना *f.* name of a woman and घातक *m.* destroyer) murderor of वसन्तसेना.

वसा *f.* fat, marrow.

वसुधा *f.* the earth.

वस्तुजात *n.* (वस्तु and जात *n.* a collection) a collection of things.

वह् *1st conj. Parasm.* and *Âtm. with* आ to bring.

वह्नि *m.* fire.

वा *2nd conj. Parasm.* to blow.

वाच्यता *f.* censurableness, liability to censure.

वापय *caus.* of वा, *with* निर् to extinguish.

वारंवारम् *adv.* often.

वारिद *m.* a cloud.

वालिपुत्र *m.* the son of Vâli, a monkey chief.

वाल्मीकि *m.* name of a sage.

वासर *m.n.* a day.

वासव *m.* the god Indra.

वासिष्ठ *m.* a descendent of Vasishha.

विकच *m.n.f* blown out, opened.

विक्रान्त *m.n.f.* courageous, possessing prowess.

विचार्यमाण (*pres. part.* of *the pass.* of the *caus* of चर् to go, *with* वि) being thought or considered.

विचित्र *m.n.f.* wonderful, curious.

विच्छ् *1st conj. Parasm.* to go, to approach.

विज् *1st conj. Âtm.* and *7th conj. Parasm. with* उद्, to tremble, to fear, to be disgusted.

विज् *3rd conj. Parasm.* and *Âtm.* to separate, to distingish; *with* वि.

विडम्ब् *10th conj.* to distort, to make ridiculous, to mock.

वित्तवत् *m.n.f.* wealthy.

वितृष्ण *m.n.f.* (**वि** devoid of, and **तृष्णा** *f.* desire) free from any desire.

विद् *2nd conj. Parasm.* to know.

विद् *7th conj. Âtm.* to reason upon, to discuss.

विदर्भ *m.* (*in the plur.*) the name of a country, the modern Berars.

विदेशगमन *n.* (**विदेश** *m.* a foreign country) going to a foreign country.

विदेह *m.* name of a country (*in* [*the plural*).

विद्ध *past. part. pass.* of **व्यध्** pierced, struck, wounded.

विद्या *f.* learning, lore.

विद्वस् *pres. part.* of **विद्** to know, knowing.

विद्विष् *m.* an enemy.

विधातृ *m.* the creator, fate.

विनष्ट *past. part.* of **नश्** *with* **वि**, destroyed.

विपाश *m.* bondage, tie.

विपिन *n.* a forest.

विप्र *m.* a Brâhmaṇa.

विबुध *m.* a god.

विभङ्ग *m.* destruction.

विभाण्डक *m.* name of a sage.

विभूति *f.* wealth, prosperity, power or greatness.

विमतिता *f.* want of intelligence.

विमुख *m.n.f.* with the face turned away from.

विरहित *m.n.f.* separated.

विरोध *m.* opposition; **अविरोध** *m.* harmony.

विलसित *n.* a wanton pastime.

विलुप्त *past. part.* of **लुप्** *with* **वि**, destroyed.

विवाहविधि *m.* (**विवाह** *m.* marriage and **विधि** *m.* a ceremony) the ceremony of marriage.

विविध *m.n.f.* of several kinds.

विश् *with* **सम्** and **आ**, to enter in, come in.

विश् *m.* the third order or caste among the Hindus; *f. pl.* subjects, people.

विशसितृ *m.* a slaughterer.

विशिख *m.* an arrow. [sons).

विशिष्ट *m.n.f.* respectable (per.

विश्रुत *m.n.f.* (*past part. pass.* of **श्रु** *with* **वि**) famous, famed as.

विश्वतः *adv.* in all directions.

विश्वनाथ *m.* Lord of the Uniyerse, God.

विश्वपा *m.* the Protector of all, God.

विश्ववाह् *m.* the protector Supporter of the Universe.

विश्वसनीयता *f.* capecity to inspire, confidence.

विश्वसृज् *m.* the creator, Brahmâ.

विश्वावसु *m.* the name of a Gandhrva.

विश्वेदेवाः *m.plur.* all the gods.

विष् *3rd conj. parasmand Âtm.* to surround.

विषय *m.* an object giving sensual pleasure.

विषाण *m.n.* a horn.

विष्टपहारिन् *m.* he who pleases heaventl̄y beings, Vishun.

विष्णुशर्मन् *n.* a proper name.

विस्तरतः *adv.* in detail.

विस्तार *m.* extent.

विस्मय *m.* admiration, amazement.

विस्मित *past. part.* of स्मि *with* वि, surprised.

विहत *m.n.f.* interrupted.

विहाय (*abso.* of हा to abandon *with* वि) having abandoned.

विहित *past. part.* of धा *with* वि, prescribed by the scriptures.

विहीन *m.n.f.* destitute of.

विह्वल *m. n. f.* overwhelmed, efflicted.

वीररस *m.* warlike feeling, one of the nine poetic sentiments.

वीरवरूथिनी *f.* (वरूथिनी *f.* and army) an army of warriors or heroes.

वुवूर्षु *m.n.f.* desirous of choosing.

वृ *5th conj. Parasm.* and *Âtm.* to cover; *with* आ, and आ, to open; *with* वि, to expound, to express; *with* सम्, to shut.

वृ *10th conj. with* नि, to oppese, to dissuade from.

वृक्षमूल *n.* (वृक्ष *m.* tree and मूल *n.* root) the root of a tree.

वृज् *1st* and *7th conj. Parasm., 2nd conj. Âtm.* and *10th conj.* to avoid, to shun.

वृजिन *m.* a wicked person.

वृत् *with* अति, to pass away; *with* आ, to trun round, to trun back.

वृत् *with* प्र, (*in the causal*) to introduce, to bring into pracnce.

वृत्त *n.* what has taken place. [an event.

वृत्तान्त *m.* account, occurrence.

वृत्तान्तश्रवण *n.* (वृत्तान्त, श्रवण *n.* hearing) hearing of history or account.

वृत्ति *f.* livelihood, maintenance.

वृत्रहन् *m.* killer of वृत्र, Indra.

वृथा *adv.* in vain, uselessly.

वृद्ध *m.n.f.* old

वृद्धि *f.* prosperity.

वृश्चिक *m.* a scorpion.

वृष् *1st conj. Parasm.* to rain, to shower down, t[illegible] ur down.

वृषल *m.* a Śudra, [illegible]inner, a reprobate.

वृष्टि *f.* rain.

वृ *9th conj. Parasm.* and *Âtm.* to choose.

वेग *m.* speed, velocity.

वेणि-वेणी *f.* braided hair.

वेणु *m.* a bamboo.

वेदना *f.* agony.

वेश *m.* dress.

वेष

वै *ind.* an expletive.

वैक्लव्य *n.* agony, affiction.

वैदग्ध्य *n.* skill.

वैदिक *m.n.f.* belonging to a Veda.

वैधस *m.* son of Vedhas.

वैयाकरण *m.* a grammarian.

वैषम्य *n.* difficulty, calamity.

व्यक्त *Past. part. pass.* of अञ्ज् *with* वि, plain, manifest.

व्यतिरेक *m.* exclusion or absence.

व्यथित *past. part.* of व्यथ्, afflicted.

व्यध् *4th conj. Parasm.* to pierce, to wound.

व्यय *m.* expenditure.

व्याकरण *n.* grammar.

व्याधित *m.n.f.* sick.

व्याल *m.* a mad elephant.

व्यास *m.* the reputed author of the Mahábhárata, a Ṛishi.

व्रतरुचि *m.n.f.* one who has a for fasts and other derotional vows.

व्रश्च् *6th conj. Parasm.* to cut, to mow, to tear.

व्रीडा *f.* shame.

श

शंस् *with* आ, *1st conj. Âtm.* to hope.

शक् *5th conj. Parasm.* to be able.

शकट *m.n.* a cart.

शकन् *n.* animal-dung.

शकुन्तला *f.* name of a lady, wife of a king named Dushyanta.

शक्य *m.n.f.* possible.

शक्र *m.* a name of Indra.

शक्रजित् *m.* the conqueror of Śakra or Indra, the son of Râvana.

शङ्खध्मा *m.* a conch-blower.

शठ् *10th conj.* to deceive, to defraud.

शचीपति *m.* the husband of शची, Indra.

शतायुष् *m.n.f.* living for a hundred years.

शत्रुतस् *adv.* from an enemy.

शद् *1st conj.* to perish, to decay.

शनैः *adv.* gradually, slowly.

शप् *1st conj. Parasm.* and *Âtm.* to curse; शप्त्वा *ind. past. part.*

शब्द *m.* voice, a word.

शम् *ind.* happiness, welfare.

शरणार्थिन् *m.n.f.* one seeking refuge.

शरमण्डप *m.n.* a bower or shed made of arrows.

शराव *m.* a kind of pot.

शरीरिन् *m.n.f.* one having a body; *m.* a human being, a man.

शर्वरीश *m.* (शर्वरी *f.* the night) the lord of the night, the moon.

शश *m.* a rabbit, a hare.

शशाङ्क *m.* the moon

शश्वत् *adv.* perpetually.

शस् *1st conj. parasm. with* वि, to kill, to destory.

शस्त्रसंपात, *m.* (शस्त्र and विद्या) art or knowledge of war.

शस्त्रविद्या *f.* (शस्त्र, संपात *m.* falling on) a stroke of a weapon.

शस्त्रास्त्र *n.* weapons of all kinds.

शाक *m.* a vegetable.

शाप *m.* a curse.

शावक *m.* the young of beasts.

शाश्वत *m.n.f.* eternal, everlasting.

शास् *2nd conj. Parasm.* to govern, the regulate, to discipline.

शास् *2nd conj. Âtm. with* आ, to wish, to desire, to bless.

शास्त्रप्रतिषेध *m.* (शास्त्र *n.* scripture and प्रतिषेध *m.* prohibition) scriptural prohibition.

शिखिन् *m.* a peacock.

शिरस् *n.* the head.

शिरीष *n.* a kind of flower.

शिलासंघात *m.* a collection of stones.

शिष् *7th conj. Parasm.* to distinguish; *with* वि to partionlarise.

शी *2nd conj. Âtm.* to lie down, to sleep; *with* अति, to surpass.

शीत *m.n.f.* cold.

शीतत्राण *n.* protection from cold.

शीतल *m.n.f.* cool.

शील *n.* good disposition.

शुक्ति *f.* an oyster-shell

शुचि *m.n.f.* pure.

शुनःपुच्छ *m.* a proper name.

शुनोलाङ्गूल *m.* a proper name.

शुल्क *m.n* the money given to the parents of a bride, originally as a purchase price.

शुश्रूषा *f.* service, attendance on.

शुष्मिण *m.n.f.* powerful.

शून्य *m.n.f.* vacant, empty.

शून्यमुखी *f.* having to liveliness on the face, pale-faced, of a dejected countenance.

शूलिन् *m.* a name of Śiva.

शृङ्ग *n.* a horn.

शॄ *with* वि, to fade (as *pass*).

शेष *m.n.* remainder, all others.

शैब्य *m.* a name of a king.

शोकविकल *m.n.f.* overcome with sorrow.

श्याम *m.n.f.* dark green.

श्रम *m.* fatigue.

श्रा *2nd conj. Parasm.* to cook.

श्रान्त *past. part.* of श्रम्, fatigued.

श्रावण *m.* the fifth month of the Hindu year.

श्रि *1st conj. Parasm.* and *Âtm. with* आ, to cling to, to go to, to resort to; *with* सम् to resort to to rest on, to depend upon.

श्री *9th conj. Parasm.* and *Âtm.* to cook.

श्री *f.* wealth, goddness of wealth. beauty.

श्रीहरि *m.* the name of the god Vishṇu.

श्रु *5th conj. Parasm.* to hear.

श्रुतिमनोहर *m.n.f.* (श्रुति *f.* ear and मनोहर *m.n.f.* charming) charming to the ear.

श्रेणि-णी *f.* a line.

श्रेमन् *m.* splendour.

श्रोत्र *n.* ear.

श्रोत्रद्वय *n.* a pair of ears.

श्वकार्य *n.* to-morrow's duty or [work.

श्वस् *2nd conj. Parasm.* to breath; *with* नि, to respire; *with* वि, to believe, to confide; *with* सम् and आ, to calm one-self, to take courage.

श्वापद *m.* a beast of prey, a beast.

स

संख्यातीत *m.n.f.* (संख्या *f.* number, अतीत *m.n.f.* gone beyoud) innumerable.

संगत *past. part.* of गम् with सम् united.

संग्राम *m.* a battle.

संजय *m.* a proper name.

संतुष्ट *past. part.* of तुष् with सम्, pleassed satishied, gratified.

संदेह *m.* battle.

संध्या *f.* twilight [at the morning and evening twilights and in the noon prayers are offered by Brâhmaṇas].

संनाह *m.* armour.

संपर्क *m.* contact.

संपादन *n.* accomplishing.

संप्रदाय *m.* cuntom, a traditional observance.

संभव *m.* possibility, probability, birth, source.

संभावित *past. part. pass.* of the *caus.* of भू with सम् thought of, thought possible.

संभ्रमविधि *m.* bustle (on account of the arrival of a guest), hospitality

संमोहन *n.* name of a miraculous weapon.

संयम *m.* restraint.

संयमिन् *m.*a sage who has curbed his passions, an ascetic.

संवत्सर *m.* a year

संवर्त *m.* the name of a priest.

संवर्तक *m.* a species of submarine fire.

संवास *m.* company, living together with.

संसर्गमुक्ति *f.* the abandoning of connection.

संसार *m.* the world.

संसारसुख *n.* (संसार *m.* worldly existence, सुख *n.* happiness, enjoyment) enjoyment of a worldly existence.

संसृतिगर्ता *f.* (संसृति *f.* this world, worldly existence.

संस्मर्तव्य *m.n.f.* to be remembered.

सकल *m.n.f.* entire, whole, all.

सकाश *m.* nearness, proximity.

सक्रोध *m n.f.* angry.

सखि *m.* a friend, a companion.

सङ्ग *m.* attactment to worldly things, contact.

सच्चरणव्रत *n.* (व्रत *n.* a vow) the vow of good or virtuous conduct.

सञ्ज् *1st conj. Parasm.* to cling, to adhere to; *with* वि and अति [व्यतिषङ्ग], to join together; *with* सम् and आ, to become atached.

सत्कृति *f.* a meritorious deed, a good action

सत्क्रिया *f.* hospitality.

सत्तम *m.n.f.* best.

सत्त्व *n.* power, greatness

सत्त्वानुरूप *m.n.f.* worthy of one's power or greatness.

सत्पुरुष *m.* a good man.

सत्र *n.* a sacrificial session; सत्रभूमि *f.* the place of sacrifice.

सत्संगति *f.* company of the virtuous.

सद् *1st conj.* Parasm. to sit; *with* आ, to approach, to come to; *with* प्र, to be gracious or pleased; *with* सम् and आ, to find.

सद् *with* प्र (in the causal) to please, to propitiate.

सदसत् *m.n.f.* good and bad.

सदाचार *m.* (सत् *m n.f.* good and आचार *m.* conduct) good conduct; *m.n.f.* one whose conduct is good.

सद्यः *adv.* instantly, at present.

सनाथ *m.n.f.* occupied, filled with, protected.

सपत्नी *f.* fellow-wife.
सभासद् *m.* a member of an assembly or court.
समक्रिय *m.n.f.* (सम equal, and क्रिया *f.* doing) equally, evenhanded.
समन्तम् *adv.* round about.
समन्तात् *adv.* round about.
समन्त्रकम् *adv.* by mantras, *i.e.* by repeating mantras.
समस्त *m.n.f.* all.
समाकुल *m.n.f.* occupied with, full of.
समाकुल *m.n.f.* occupied with, full of.
समागम *m.* company, association.
समान *m.n.f.* equal.
समारोपित *past. part. pass.* of the *caus.* of रुह् *with* सम् and आ, placed.
समाहृत *past. part. pass.* of हृ *with* सम and आ, collected.
समिध् *f.* small sticks of a sacred tree, such as udumbara, to be thrown into the sacrificial fire.
समीहित *m.n.f.* what is desired; *n.* a desired object.
समुद्यम *m.* exertion.
समुपारूढ *m.n.f.* grown, increased.
समुपाहृत (*past part. pass* of हृ *with* सम्, उप and आ) coloected.
सम्यक् *adv.* correctly, well.
सम्यच् *m.n.f.* good. [peror.
सम्राज् *m.* a great king, an em-
सरणि-णी *f.* path, disposition or arrangement of things.
सरमा *f.* name of the bitch of the gods.
सरस्वती *f.* name of a river.
सर्वतः *adv.* in every direction.
सर्वभूतानि *n. Nom & Acc. plur.* all existing things.
सर्वस्व *n.* (सर्व and स्व *n.*) all wealth or possessions.
सर्वाभिप्रेतहेतु *m.* (अभिप्रेत *past part. pass.* of इ *with* अभि and प्र, desired, aimed at) the cause of [the attainment of] all desired objects.
सलिल *n.* water.
सवितृ *m.* the sun.
सविस्मय *m.n.f.* with wonder, wondering.
सशोक *m.n.f.* (स with शोक *m.* sorrow) afflicted with sorrow.
ससैनिक *m.n.f.* accompanied by soldiers.
सस्ज् *6th conj. Parasm.* to be or become ready.
सह् *with* उद्, to be able, to be adequated, to be up to, to feel equal to.
सहस्र *n.* a thousand. [parts.
सहस्रधा *adv.* into a thousand
सहस्रशः *adv.* by thousands.
सहाय *m.* a helper, companion.
सहिष्ठ *m.n.f.* mightiest.
सांख्य *n.* name of a system of philosophy.
सांनाहुक *m.n.f.* one wearing an armour.
साक्षात् *adv.* in the presence of, in sight of.
सागर *m.* the ocean.
साचिव्य *n.* counsellorship.

सात्यहव्य *m.* name of priest.
साध् *5th conj. parasm.* to accomplish.
साधारण *m.n.f.* ordiuary.
साधु *adv.* well.
साधुवृत्त *m.n.f.* (साधु *m.n.f.* good and वृत्त *n.* conduct) well-conducted.
सामान्य *m.n.f.* ordinary, common to one with others.
सामिधेनी *f.* a verse repeated at the time of kindling the sacred fire.
सायम् *ind.* in the evening.
सार *m.* power, pith.
सारमेय *m.* the son of Saramâ, a [dog.
सार्धम् *ind.* with (used with the *instrumental).*
सार्वभौम *m.n.f.* universal (sovereign).
सावधान *m.n.f.* (स and अवधान *n.*)attentive.
सावित्री *f.* the holy mantra or verse of the the Ṛigveda, generally called Gâyatrî, and repeated by all Brâhmanas every day.
साश्चर्यचर्य *m.n.f.* (*Bah. comp.*) of wonderful conduct.
साहाय्य *n.* friendship, help.
साहित्य *n.* literature, composition.
सिकता *f.* sand.
सिद्धि *f.* accomplishment.
सिध् *1st conj. Parasm.* to regulate, to turn out well or auspiciously.
सिव् *4th conj. parasm.* to sew together.
सु *5th conj. Parasm.* and *Âtm.* to extract Soma juice.
सु *1st conj. Parasm.* and *2nd conj. Parasm. with* प्र, to produce.
सु (*as prefixed to words*) good, well.
सुग्रीव *m.* name of a monkey chief and ally of of Râma.
सुत्यादिन *n.* the day on which Soma juice is drunk in the Soma sacrifice.
सुधास्यन्दिन् *m.n.f.* (सुधा *f.* nectar) dropping nectar.
सुभद्रा *f.* a wife of Arjuna.
सुभिक्ष *n.* abundance of food.
सुरभि *m.n.f.* fragrant.
सुरालय *m.* (सुर *m.* a god, आलय *m.* a place of abode) the abode of the gods, heaven.
सुवर्णशत *n.* (सुवर्ण *m.* a golden coin, and शत *n.* a hundred) a hundred coins of gold.
सुविनीत *m.n.f.* modest.
सुहृदयतम *m.n.f.* intimate, dearest.
सू *2nd conj. Âtm.* to give birth to; with प्र, to produce.
सू *4th conj. Âtm. with* प्र, to produce.
सू *6th conj. Parasm.* to impel, to push forward.
सूक्ति *f.* (सु and उक्ति speech) good words or speech, correct exposition.
सूच् *10th conj.* to indicate.
सूत *m.* charioteer.
सूनृत *m.n.f.* agreeable, pleasent.
सूर्यवंश *m.* the family of the sun, the solar race.

सृ *1st conj. Parasm.* to run.

सृ (*caus*). *with* निर् to drive away, to expel.

सृज् *with* सम् to bring in contact with, to unite with; *with* उद्, to abandon.

सेनानिवेश *m.* the camp of an army.

सेन्द्र *m.n.f.* with Indra.

सेवन *n.* serving, resorting to, pructising.

सेवा *f.* service.

सो *4th conj. Parasm.* to bring to an end, to finish, to destroy; *with* परि and अव, to end in, to result in; *with* वि and अव, to determine, to resolve, to endeavour, to strive.

सोच्छ्वास *m.n.f.* having breath.

सोपान *n.* stairs, steps.

सोमवंशविभूषण *m.n.f.* (सोम *m.* the moon) one who adorns the lunar race, an ornament of the lunar race (of kings).

सौम्य *m.n.f.* gentle.

सौयवसि *m.* son of Suyavasa.

सौराज्य *n.* good government.

सौवर्ण *m.n.f.* goldren.

स्खलित *pres. part.* tumbling, tripping.

स्खलत् *n.* a slip, a mistake.

स्तन् *1st conj. Parasm.* to cry, to thunder.

स्तन *m.* the female breast, the nipple.

स्तबक *m.* a bunch.

स्तम्भ् *1st conj. Âtm.* and *5th conj. parasm.* to become fixed or rigid, to become haughty.

स्तम्भ् *9th conj. Parasm.* to stop, to become stiff or rigid, to become haughty.

स्तम्भ *m.* a past a column.

स्तु *2nd conj. Parasm.* and *Âtm.* to praisa; *with* अभि, to praise.

स्तृ *5th conj. Parasm.* and *Âtm.* to cover; to spread, to strew; *with* सम्

स्तॄ *9th conj. Parasm.*and *Âtm.* to cover; *with* आ, to cover, to spread.

स्त्री *f.* woman, wife.

स्था *with* अव, to stay, to abide; *with* उप, to go to.

स्थावरजङ्गम *m.n.f.* (स्थावर *m.n.f.* immoveable and जङ्गम *m.n.f.* moveable) immoveable an dmoveable.

स्थित *past, part.* of स्था, abiding, being, existing.

स्थूलकेश *m.* the name of a sage.

स्ना *2nd conj. Parasm.* to bathe.

स्नायु *f.* a muscle.

स्निह् *4th conj. Parasm.* to bear affection to.

स्नु *2nd conj. Parasm.* to flow, to drop, to ooze.

स्नु *m.n.* summit.

स्पृहा *f.* wish, desire.

स्फुट् *6th conj. Parasm.* to break, to split asunder.

स्फुटितातिमुक्त *n.* an opened *atimukta* flower.

स्मित *n.* smile.

स्मृ *with* वि, to forget; विस्मृत forgotten.

स्यन्दन *m.* a chariot.

स्वकर्तव्य *n.* one's duty.
स्वकीय *m.n.f.* one's own.
स्वजनवियोग *m.* separation from one's own men or relations.
स्वन *m.* noise, roar.
स्वप् *2nd conj. Parasm.* to sleep.
स्वप्न *m.* a dream.
स्वप्नाय *denom. Âtm.* to be in a dream. to speak in a dream.
स्वयंभू *m.n.f.* self-existent.
स्वयंवरकाल *m.* (**स्वयंवर** *m.* choice of a husband by a woman herself, and **काल** *m.* time) time of choosing a husband.
स्वयम् *ing.* in person, of himself.
स्वर *m.* a sound.
स्वर्गकाम *m.n.f.* one longing after heaven.
स्वहित *n.* one's own good.
स्वाति *f.* a lunar mansion, name of a constellation.
स्वाद *m.* taste, tasting.
स्वादु *m.n.f.* sweet, palatable.
स्वामिन् *m.* owner.
स्वायत्त *m.n.f.* dependent on oneself.
स्वृ *1st conj. Parasm.* to sound.
स्वेद *m.* sweat, perspiration.
स्वेदलव *m.* a particle or drop of perspiration.

ह

ह an expletive used in narrations.
हठात् *adv.* by violence.
हत *past. part. pass.* of **हन्**, struck.
हन् *2nd conj. Parasm,* to kill; with **अभि** or **आ**, to strike; *with* **नि**, to kill, to destroy, to ruin.
हनुमत् *m.* name of a monkey devotee of Râma.
हन्त *ind. interj.* experssing wonder or sorrow.
हन्तृ *m.n.f.* a killer.
हय *m.* a horse.
हर *m.* the god Śiva.
हरिदत्त *m.* name of a Brâhmaṇa.
हरिद्वार *n.* name of a holy place at the foot of the Himâlayas.
हरिश्चन्द्र *m.* name of a king.
हव्य *n.* an offering.
हा *3rd conj. Parasm.* to abandon.
हा *3rd conj. Âtm.* to go; *with* **उद्** to go upwards, to ascend; *with* **उद्** to go upwards, to ascend; *with* **सम्** to be sitting.
हारिद्र *m.n.f.* dyed yellow with turmeric.
हास्य *n.* smile, laughter.
हास्यकार्य *n.* a ludicrous act.
हि *5th conj. Parasm.* to go; *with* **प्र**, to send.
हिंस् *1st* and *7th conj. Parasm.* and *10th conj.* to kill, to destroy.
हिंस्र *m.n.f.* murderous, carnivorous.
हिमपात *m.* frost, snow cold weather.
हिमाचल *m.* the Himâlayas.
हिरण्यक *m.* name of a mouse.
हीन *m.n.f.* destitute of.
हीरकमणि *m.* a diamond.
हु *3rd conj. Parasm.* to sacrifice.
हृ *with* **उप** and **अव** *1st conj. Parasm.* and *Âtm.* to take down.
हृदयमर्मच्छिद् *m.n.f.* (**हृदय** *n.* the heart,

मर्मन् *n.* the vital parts and भिद् to cut) piercing the vital parts of the heart.

हे *interja* a vocative particle, O !

हेतु *m.* a cause.

होतृ *m.* a sacrificial priest whose duty it is to repeat the mantras.

ह्नु *2nd conj. Âtm.* to conceal; *with* अप or *with* नि.

ह्रस्व *m.n.f.* short.

ह्री *3rd conj. Parasm.* to blush, to be ashamed.

II. GENERAL GLOSSARY OF ENGLISH WORDS OCCURRING IN THE BOOK.

A

Abode आस्पद *n.* आवास *m.*

Absurd अयुक्त *past. part.* अनुपपन्न *past part.*

Accordingly तथा च, तथा, इत्थम्.

Acquire अर्ज् *1st conj. parasm.* and *10th conj. with* उप.

Act the traitor द्रुह् *4th conj. Parsm.*

Adjoining संभिहित *past part.* अर्दित *past part.pass.*

Agricultural purpose for, कृषिहेतोः, कृषिकर्मणे.

Aja अज *m.* name of a person.

Alive जीवन्ती *f. pres. part. act.* of जीव्, सजीवा *f.* (जीव *m.* life, and स for सह *ind.* with).

Alliance संधि *m.* सख्य *n.*

Aloud उच्चैः *ind.*

Ancestral पितृपैतामह *m.n.f.*

Angada अङ्गद *m.* a kind of ornament.

Angas अङ्गा *plur.* name of a people or their country.

Aphorism सूत्र *n.*

Assistance साहाय्य *n.*

Astray उत्पथम् *adv.*

Âśvina आश्विन *m.* name of a month.

Atimukta creeper अतिमुक्तलता

Attracted विलोभित *past. part pass.* of the *caus* of लुभ् *with*

Axe परशु *m.* [वि

B

Babhruvâhana बभ्रुवाहन *m.* son of Arjuna, the Pâṇḍava.

Bad (adverse) प्रतिकूल *m.n.f.*

Battle-field रणभूमि *f.*

Because यतः *ind.* हि *ind.*

Bee भ्रमर *m.*

Beginning अग्र *n.* आदि *m.*

Belief नामित *past. part. pass.* of *the causal* of नम्; रामेण धनुषि नामिते 'Rama having bent the bow.'

Bhṛigu भृगु *m.* the name of a Ṛishi.

Bid दिश् *6th conj. with* आ

Bitterly (wept) प्रमुक्तकण्ठम् *used as an adv.*

Blessing आशिस् *f.*

Blind अन्ध *m.n.f.*

Blood शोणित *n.*

Bodily form तनु *f.* वपुस् *n.* आकृति *f.*

Brâhmaṇa-murder ब्राह्मणराज *m.*

Brâhmaṇa-murder ब्रह्महत्या *f.*

Branch शाखा *f.*

Breast वक्षस् *n.*

Bright half (of the lunar month) शुक्लपक्ष *m.*

Bring up वर्धय, *causal* of वृध् *with* सम्, पोषणं or भरणं कृ.

Broad विशाल *m.n.f.*

Brute पशु *m.* [निर्

Build मा *3rd conj. Âtm. with* By hundreds शतशः *ind.*

C

Cage पञ्जर *m.*

Calf वत्स *m.* [ed.

Call धा *with* अभि; अभिहित call-

Calling अभिदधान *pres. part.* of धा *with* अभि.

Caual कुल्या *f.*

Canto सर्ग *m.*

Capital गृहीत *past. part. pass.* of ग्रह्.

Captured कुथ *m.*

Carpet damsel अप्सरस् *f.* सुराङ्गना *f.*

Chandrketu चन्द्रकेतु *m.* name of the son of Lakshmaṇa brother of Râma.

Chest वक्षस् *n.*

Churning handle मन्थानदण्ड *m.* (मन्थान *n.* churning and दण्ड *m.* handle), मन्थान *m.*

Cobra फणिन् *m.* नाग *m.*

Column स्तम्भ *n.*

Commander चमूपति *m.* सेनापति *m.*

Commentator टीकाकार *m.* टीकाकृत्

Common साधारण *m.n.f.* सामान्य *m.n.f.*

Communicating (with the river) संगत *past part.* or संगच्छमान *pres. part.*

Conceited अवलिप्त *past. part.*

Conclave समाज *m.* परिषद् *f.* सभा *f.*

Conduct oneself properly सदाचार प्रतिपद्, सदाचारेण वृत्.

Confined नियन्त्रित *past part. pass.* निबद्ध *past. part. pass.*

Conqueror विजिगीषु *m.*

Constantly अनिशम् *adv.*

Construct मा *with* निर्.

Convince इ with प्रति *caus* प्रतीतिं कृ.

Cooking utensil स्थाली *f.*

Costly महार्ह *m.n.f.*

Cotton तूल *m.* पिचु *m.*

Counsellor मन्त्रिन् *m.* धीसचीव *m.*

Cradle प्रेङ्खा *f.*

Croak रट् *1st conj. Parasm. with* आ.

Cruel नृशंस *m.n.f.*

Cry रु *2nd conj. Parasm.* क्रन्द् *1st conj. Parasm.*

Curious विलक्षण *m.n.f.*

Cutting छेद *m.*

D

Dark श्याम *m.n.f.*

Death वध *m.*

Deceive धा *with* अति and सम्, लभ् *with* वि and प्र, वञ्च् *10th conj. Âtm.*

Deposit न्यास *m.* निक्षेप *m.*

Deprive of ह *1st conj. with* अप.

Descendant वंश्य *m.n.f.* कुलज *m.n.f.*

Desire कांक्षा *f.* काम *m.*

Desperatey प्रसह्य *ind. adv.* आत्मनिरपेक्षम् *adv.* साहसेन *instr.* used as an *adv.*

Destroy छिद् *7th conj. with* उद्, सूद् *10th conj. with* नि; उच्छेत्तुम् *ind.* निषूदयितुम् *ind.*

Destroyed ध्वस्त *past. part.* of ध्वंस्, उच्छिन्न *past part. pass.* of छिद् with उद्.

Destruction ध्वंस *n.* नाश *m.* अवसाद *m.* [भिद्

Different भिन्न *past part. pass.* of

Different (various) विविध *m.n.f.*

Diffculty असौकर्य *n.* कष्ट n.

Dirghatamas दीर्घतमस् *m.* name of a Ṛishi.

Discussion वादविवाद *m.*

Disease व्याधि *m.*

Dishonest gambling कपटद्यूत *n.* (कपट *n.* fraud, and द्यूत *n.* gambling).

Disturb तुद्.

Doctor भिषज् *m.* वैद्य *m.*

Dramatic play नाटक *n.*

Drive नुद् *10th conj. with* प्र.

Duty धर्म *m.*

E

Earn अर्ज् *1st conj. parasm.*

Ease सौकर्य *n.*

Eastern पूर्व *m.n.f. pron.* प्राच्य *m.n.f.*

Education विद्या *f.* अध्ययन *n.* विनयन *n*; of good aducation कृतविद्य *m.n.f.* संस्कृतचित्त *m.n.f.* सुविनीत *m.n.f.*

End कार्य *n.* फल *n*; फलावाप्तये *dat.* for the attainment of the fruit or end.

End उदर्क *m.* अवसान *n.* परिणाम *m.*; उदर्के &c. in the end.

Enraged क्रुद्ध *past part.* of क्रुध्.

Enumerated परिकीर्तित *past. part. pass.* परिगणित *past. part. pass.*

Eternal शाश्वत *m.n.f.*

Every प्रति *prep.*

Every year प्रतिसंवत्सरम् *adv. ind.*

Evil अनर्थ *m.* पीडा *f.* संकट *n.*

Excavate खन् *with* उद्; उत्खनितुम् *inf.*

Except ऋते *ind.*

Existence भाव *m.* अद्भुतचरित *n.*

Exploit पराक्रम *m.* अद्भुचरित *n.*

Exterminate मूल् *10th conj. with* उद्; उन्मूलयितुम् *inf.*

Extraordinary अद्भुत *m.n.f.*

F

Faithfully भक्त्या, निष्ठया.

Family कुल *n.*

Fastened नियुक्त *past. part. pass;* धुरि नियुक्त: fastened to the yoke.

Fasting-day उपवासदिन *n.* (उपवास *m.* a fast, दिन *n.* a day).

Father-in-law श्वशुर *m.*

Felicity सुख *n.*

Fellow कापुरुष *m.*

Field of battle रणभूमि *f.*

Fight, to युद्धाय, युद्धे, योद्धुम्.

Fix बन्धू *9th conj. Parasm.*

First *adv.* प्रथमम् *adv.* आदौ *loc. sing.* of आदि.

Flame शिखा *f.*

Flee अय् *1st conj. Âtm. with* परा changed to पला.

Fleet of ships नौसाधन *n.*

Floor भूमि *f.*

Food अन्न *n.*

Fortress दुर्ग *m.*

Found उपलब्ध *past. part. pass.* समधिगत *past. part. pass.*

Fragrant सुरभि *m.n.f.*

Fraudulent scheme कपटप्रबन्ध *m.* अ

Free मुक्त *past. part. pass.* of मुच् (मुक्ता *f.*); to be free मुच् *Pass.*
Furniture गृहोपस्कर *m.*

G

Gâdhi गाधि *m.* the name of a king.
Gamble दिव् *4th conj. Parasm.*
Gate द्वार *n.*
Gently मन्दम् *adv.*
Ghost प्रेत *m.* वेताल *m.* पिशाच *m.*
Go round प्रदक्षिणीकृ. [*m.n.f.*
Good समीचीन *m.n.f.* निपुण
Gourd कमण्डलु *m.*
Grain धान्य *n.*
Greed शोक *m.*
Guardian of a quarter दिक्पाल *m.*

H

Harmless अनपकारिन् *m.n.f*
Harsh परुष *m.n.f.*., (words) परुषाक्षर *m.n.f.*
Haste, in, ससंभ्रमम् *adv.*
Haughty उद्धत *past. part.*
Held (as a meeting) मिलित *past. part.*
Helpless अनाथ *m.n.f.*
Hemangada हेमाङ्गद *m.* the name of a king.
Hermit वानप्रस्थ *m.* यति *m.*
High उच्च *m.n.f.*
How many times कतिकृत्वः *ind.*

I

Ikshâkus, the, इक्ष्वाकु *m.* (*used in the plural*) name of the line of kings to which Râma belonged.
Ill रुग्ण *m.n.f.*
Immortal अमृत *past. part.* of मृ *with* अ, अमर *m.n.f.*
Importance गुरुत्व *n.* महत्त्व *n,;* a matter of importance गुरुकार्य *n.*
Imprison कारागृहे निक्षिप्
In person स्वयम् *ind.*
Indiscretion व्यभिचार *m.*
Indrajit इन्द्रजित् *m.* the son of Ravaṇa.
Inexpressible अनिर्वचनीय *m.n.f.* अनिर्वर्णनीय *m.n.f.* किम् *m.n.f. with* अपि added.
Ingratitude कृतघ्नता *f.*
Inhuman मानवानर्ह *m.n.f.* निरनुकोशं (कर्म)
Instinct उत्तेजित *past. part. pass.* उद्दीपित *past. part. pass.*
Instructor अध्यापक *m.n.f.*
Invade हृ *1st conj. Parasm. with* अभि.
Invisible अदृश्य *m.n.f.*

J

Jamadagni जमदग्नि *m.* name of a Ṛishi.
Jarâsamdha जरासंध *m.* name of a king of Magadha.
Juice रस *m.*
Justly धर्मेण, न्यायेन.

K

Kaikeyi कैकेयी *f.* name of one of the wives of Dasaratha.
Kalingas कलिङ्ग *plur.* name of a people or of their country.
Kârtavîrya कार्तवीर्य *m.* the name of a king killed by Parasurâma.

Kansalyâ कौसल्या *f.* name of one of the wives of Dasaratha.

Keep contented रञ् *caus. with* अनु

Keeping contented अनुरञ्जन *n.* (as applied to the subjects of a king).

Kick लता *f.* ; लत्तया प्रहरति gives a kick.

Killed हत *past. part. pass.*

Kinsman ज्ञाति *m.* बन्धु *m.*

Krauñcha क्रौञ्च *m.* a species of birds.

Kumârasambhava कुमारसंभव *m.* name of a poem by Kâlidâsa.

L

Last चरम *m.n.f.*

Last night गता रात्रि *f.*

Law धर्मशास्त्र *n.*

Lazy अलस *m.n.f.* तन्द्रिल *m.n.f.*

Length आयाम *m.*

Line व्यूह *m.* column of an army.

Littleness लघुता *f.*

Locust शलभ *m.*

Lord नाथ *m.*

Lore विद्या *f.*

Lost नष्ट *past part.*

Love, to, स्निह् *4th conj. Parasm.*; he is loved तस्मिन्स्निह्यति.

Love अनुराग *m.*

M

Magadha मगधाः *m.* (*used in the plural*) name of a country or its people.

Mahâbhârata महाभारत *n.* name of an epic poem celebrating the quarrels and wars between the sons of Pâṇdu and Dhṛitarâshṭra.

Mahendra महेन्द्र *m.* name of a mountain and the adjacent country.

March against गम् *with* अधि.

Market पण्यवीथिका *f.* आपण *m.*

Mathurâ मथुरा *f.* name of a place.

Maurya मौर्य *m.* name of a dynasty, an individual of it.

Means उपाय *m.* अभ्युपाय *m.*

Medicinal drug ओषधि *f.*

Medicine औषध *n.* औषधि *f.* a medicine herb, *gener.* an herb.

Medicine (as a science) वैद्यक *n.* आयुर्वेद *m.*

Might प्रभाव *m.*

Miser कदर्य *m.*

Moist आर्द्र *m.n.f.*

Moment क्षण *m*

More mournful. दुःखतर *m.n.f.*

Moth पतङ्ग *m.*

Movement व्यापार *m.*

N

Naked नग्न *m.n.f.*

Nala नल *m.* name of a king.

Named नाम *ind.* नाम्ना *instr sing.* of नामन्

Nature निसर्ग *m.*

Necklace हार *m.*

Net जाल *n.*

Never न कदा *ind.* नैव *ind.* न कर्हिचित् *ind.*

Nishâda निषाद *m.* name of a wild tribe or an individual of it.

Now-a-days संप्रति *adv. ind.*

Number संख्या *f.*

O

Object प्रयोजन *n.* उद्देश *m.* [शात्.

Occasionally कालेकाले, प्रसङ्ग-

Ocean अर्णव *m.*

Office अधिकार *m.*

Office of the king राजपुरुष *m.*

Originally अग्रे *loc. sing.* of अग्र, आदौ *loc. sing.* of आदि.

Overcome अभिभूत *past. part. pass.* of भू *with* अभि, पर्याकुल *m.n.f.* आकुल *m.n.f.*

Own स्वीय *m.n.f.*

P

Paid back प्रत्यर्पित *past. part. pass.* of the *caus.* of ऋ *with* प्रति.

Painful व्यथाकर *m.n.f.* पीडाकर *m.n.f.*

Pale पाण्डु *m.n.f.*

Pâñchâlî पाञ्चाली *f.* princess of the country of the Pañchâlas.

Paper पत्रक *n.*

Paramtapa परंतप *m.* name of a king.

Parṇâda पर्णाद *m.* a proper name.

Parvan पर्वन् *n.* a section, a canto.

Passage original, मूलग्रन्थ *m.*

Passion मनोधर्म *m.* इन्द्रियवृत्ति *f.* इन्द्रिय *n.*

Pâtâla पाताल *n.* the nether region.

Pâṭaliputra पाटलिपुत्र *n.* name of a city in Magadha.

Person शरीर *n.* देह *m.*

Philosopher तत्त्वविद् *m.*

Piety भक्ति *f.* देवनिष्ठा *f.*

Pilgrimage यात्रा *f.*

Pity दया *f.* दयार्द्र *m.n.f.* melted with pity.

Place of refuge आश्रयस्थान *n.*

Plunder लोप्त्र *n.* लुण्ठन *n.*

Polities नीतिशास्त्र *n.*

Post पद *n.*

Pot कुम्भ *n.*

Poverty दारिद्र्य *n.* दुर्गति *f.*

Powder क्षोद *m.* चूर्ण *n.*

Power प्रभाव *m.*

Prasravaṇa प्रस्रवण *m.* name of a mountain.

Prepard उद्यत *past. part.* of यम् *with* उद्.

Presence, in one's, समक्षम् *adv.* प्रत्यक्षम् *adv.*

Pressing against each other परस्परसंघट्टन *n.*

Principle तत्त्व *n.* नय *m.*

Proper युक्त *past part.* of युज्, उचित *m.n.f.*

Property रिक्थ *n.* वित्त *n.*

Pround उत्सिक्त *past. part.* उत्सेकिन् *m.n.f.* (नी *f.*)

Prowess प्रताप *m.* पराक्रम *m.*

Prudent दूरदर्शिन् *m.n.f.* चतुर *m.n.f.*

Punishment दण्ड *m.*

Purâṇa पुराण *n.* name of a class of works containing legendary accounts of many things and of a religious and ritualistic character.

Pure विशुद्धशील *m.n.f.*

Purpose प्रयोजन *n* कार्य *n.*

Pushed afar दूरोत्सारित; उत्सारित *past. part. pass.* of the *caus.* of सृ with उद्.

Q

Quarter (तृतीयो भागः) (of the day or night); याम *m.*

R

Raghuvaṁśa रघुवंशः *m.* name of a poem by Kâlidâsa.

Raging प्रबल *m.n.f.* बलीयस् *m.n.f.*

Rains वर्षा *plur.*

Raise नम् *caus. Parasm.*

Râjagriha राजगृह *n.* name of a city in Magadha.

Read पठ् *1st conj. Parasm.*

Recovery (regaining) प्रत्यागम *m.*

Refulgent देदीप्यमान *pres. part.* विभ्राजमान *pres. part.*

Region between अन्तर *n.* अन्तराल *n.*

Relation बन्धु *m.* बन्धुजन *m.* ज्ञाति *n.*

Released मुक्त *past part. pass.* of मुच्

Religious austerities तपांसि *plur.*

Religious book धर्मग्रन्थ *m.*

Remarriage पुनरुद्वाह *m.*

Reṇuka रेणुका *f.* wife of Jamadagni and mother of Parasuâma.

Repeat पठ् *1st conj. Parasm.*

Reprove भर्त्स्, *10th conj. Âtm. with* निर्, दिश् *6th conj. with* प्रति and आ.

Reputed अभिमत *past part. pass.* प्रसिद्ध *past. part.* कर्तृत्वेनाभिमतौ reputed as authors (two).

Respectable विशिष्ट *m.n.f.*; of a respectable family अभिजन वत् *m.n.f.* कुलीन *m.n.f.*

Responsibility of governing राज्यधुरा *f.*

Restore दा *with* प्रति.

Return वृत् *1st conj. Âtm. with* नि.

Revive *intr.* जीव् *with* पुनर्.

Ṛichâka ऋचीक *m.* name of a Ṛishi.

Rigveda ऋग्वेद *m.* name of a [Veda.

Ring-leader प्रधानराजद्रोहिन् *m.* Rock दोलय *den.* or आन्दोलय *den.*

Root मूल *n.*

Rudeness अविनय *m.*

Rukmiṇi रुक्मिणी *f.* wife of Kṛishna.

Running विद्रवण *n.*

Ruthless निर्घृण *m.n.f.*

S

Sagara सगर *m.* name of a king.

Sâketa साकेत *n.* name of a town.

Sâmaveda सामवेद *m.* name of a Veda.

Samdhyâ-adoration सध्यावन्दन *n.*

Śami शमी *f* a kind of tree.

Sarayû सरयू *f.* a river near Ayodhyâ

Satyabhâmâ सत्यभामा *f.* name of one of the wives of Kṛishna.

Saushadmana सौषद्मन *m.* name of a king.

Saying वचन *n.* उक्ति *f.*

Self-respect स्वाभिमान *m.*

Sense अर्थ *m*

Sign चिह्न *n.*

Simple ऋतु *m.n.f.* आर्जवयुक्त *m.n.f.* सरल *m.n.f.*